WOMEN IN DIVORCE

H. deB. Hachlas, Ph.D.

BY WILLIAM J. GOODE

COLUMBIA UNIVERSITY

H. deB. Hachlas, Ph.D.

THE FREE PRESS, *New York*

COLLIER-MACMILLAN LIMITED, *London*

For information, address:

THE FREE PRESS

A DIVISION OF THE MACMILLAN COMPANY

The Crowell-Collier Publishing Company

60 Fifth Avenue, New York, N.Y. 10011

Collier-Macmillan Canada, Ltd., Toronto, Ontario

DESIGNED BY SIDNEY SOLOMON

Library of Congress Catalog Card Number: 55-10992

FIRST FREE PRESS PAPERBACK EDITION 1965

PREFACE
TO THE PAPERBACK EDITION

WOMEN IN DIVORCE, originally published as *After Divorce,* was intended as a contribution to sociological theory, as nearly all my writings on the family have been. It analyzes the processes by which mothers in an ambiguous social situation, in which the social structure does not specify their role obligations or their rights, are gradually moved by their role network into a new position. This is structurally like their situation prior to divorce, in which they can more easily discharge their role obligations, and in their self-conceptions they no longer view their status of "ex-wife of Y—" as primary. It is an analysis of status sequences, of phases in role interaction.

Nevertheless, and in spite of my obvious attempt to model my inquiry after Emile Durkheim's *Suicide,* which tried to use a type of "deviance" to explore differences in social structures, the study had no such grandiose beginnings. Its conception took place in an undergraduate class in research methods, when I assigned two budding librarians to summarize all the research on post divorce adjustment. I greeted with scepticism their report that no such body of work existed, other than Willard Waller's *The Old Love and the New,* and sent them back to the library. After a new confirmation, I set the class to designing and executing a pilot study of this adjustment process. As I note in Appendix I, I did not learn as much from my blunders at this stage as I should have, since one unexpected finding (the *negative* correlation between class ranking and the divorce rate) convinced me (erroneously) that my sample was wildly askew.

Yet neither this simple accidental origin, nor even the next expanded phase, when I dragooned into my research group all who did not actively resist, presaged the final more complex outcome. We sociologists complain about the great length of time between field work and publication, but perhaps this work suggests that not all delay need be unproductive. For in my effort to interpret the data, I was again and again driven to seek out other relevant research. As a result, the book integrates the data from one field project with the materials from numerous other studies. Thereby, the inquiry avoided somewhat the inherent narrowness of a survey.

Sociological theory *did* precede the actual analysis of the data (as our

(iii)

textbooks say it should) in the very strict sense that I wrote hundreds of pages *before* I knew in detail what the data reported, and many before having any data at all. I can state with wry amusement that most of these pages had to be discarded, though the failure was instructive. For I learned, as I had in the sociology of religion, and was to learn again in the sociology of the professions, that our general theory is not precise or rigorous enough to predict the specific relations in any given area of concrete social action: we have to *discover* these specific relations. And the effort to theorize *without* the data did sharpen and enrich the questions that the data finally were able to answer.

Fully committed to the necessity of remaining on one theoretical level, the sociological, and not applying other theoretical schemata, such as the psychological or the economic, until the sociological variables have been exhausted, I was startled to see that in fact I frequently violated my own rule: I *have* used psychological variables to interpret social relations. Granted, the analysis does not *rest* on them, but their intrusion does suggest an important problem to the sociologist: As long as we persist in dividing the "fields" of sociology into *concrete* areas of action (e.g., formal organization, family, religion, stratification, small groups) and do not define our problems by purely sociological variables, we shall not be able to obtain the maximum power from any theoretical system. To the extent that we define the problem concretely, we need to use *any* variables, from the biological and physical to the psychological, to explain the data. Yet such descriptions are least likely to yield generalizations of wide validity in different times and cultures.

A major failure in the research design, the use of a *time cross-section* instead of a true panel—i.e., not following a cohort of mothers over the observation period, and interviewing them repeatedly—was caused by simple impatience and lack of money. It is also highly unlikely that all these women would have permitted a *series* of interviews, and thus the losses might have been great. Perhaps as in other panels, the continuing interviewing relation might also have changed their behavior. Asking retrospective questions as I did will in part remedy the gaps which a panel easily bridges, the comparison of an individual with himself at different times, but it is not an adequate substitute.

The study would also have been enriched if I had obtained social structural data, not merely from the wife-mother, but also from the husband, kin, ex-in-laws, and friends. This is especially true since the data show clearly that the divorcee, by virtue of the conflict itself, often does not know the facts about the opinions of such people. Granted, the focus *was* the social reality as the divorced mother herself experienced it. However, such networks of relationships, we know, shape the actions and emotions of all human beings. At present, the costs in energy, money, and losses of respondents are very great if we try to obtain such *sets* of social structures. How to reduce those costs is a major technical problem to be solved in the decade to come.

Such data would have enlightened us especially in the area of role analysis. As is obvious, a guiding conception in this study was the social role—the primacy of the mother role, the role bargaining between husband and wife or ex-husband and ex-wife, the gradual emergence of a new role in which "ex-wife of X—" is not a prominent element, the new role conceptions that arise from dating, etc.—but information from the other people in these mother's role networks would have yielded a much better understanding of *which* kinds of action from others created *which* kinds of new role behaviors and conceptions.

The social science reader may respond, as I did, in contrary ways to one characteristic of this book, its bulging contents: literally dozens of relations are explored and tested. Not only is a given link between two variables brought to our attention (e.g., the effect of the ex-husband's attitude on her adjustmental pattern) but this link is further tested by eliminating or introducing other possible factors that might be thought to play a part. Only the dedicated reader can hold his attention firmly to the task through such complexities, however interesting each may be.

On the other hand, the serious reader is thereby permitted an inside look at the complexity of relations in this domestic drama, instead of being given merely a general view. He can then either study selectively those phases that interest him more, or he can use these data as raw materials for still further analyses of his own.

Moreover, and more fundamentally, two facts justify this presentation of detailed relations. The progress of science is hampered more by incorrect observation, as Darwin observed, than by poor theory. These data are specific enough to be used in other theoretical work, and to be tested further. Second, theory is a *structure* of empirical propositions, of *sets* of relations. Consequently, we evaluate the theoretical contribution of a study not only by its general or specific truths, but also by how well-linked propositions emerge from it. A full presentation of these interrelations among many variables is thus more useful in theoretical inquiry.

Finally, and still more broadly, this is a study of how a boundary maintaining unit, a small group known as the family, dissolves and then re-forms. Much research has been expended on the factors that are associated with marital happiness, but this is not sociologically so important, nor is its predictability likely to be so high, as marital dissolution, which would include separation, divorce, and internal dissolution (the "empty shell" family). We do not have even a good theory to explain why some societies, such as Tokugawa and Meiji Japan or Arabic Islam, have had high divorce rates and others have not—though Africanists have made some good steps in this direction, and Paul Bohannon is making a serious study of the problem.

It is striking that although much of our sociological rhetoric has centered on the maintenance of the social group, in fact we have developed neither macrostructural nor microstructural theory to explain it. No adequate theory exists to explain the dissolution of the total society, partly for lack of cases to analyze. The so-called "functional requisites for the continued existence of a society" are, obviously, merely one *definition* of a society. Perhaps we might focus more fruitfully on some of the conspicuous types of group dissolution in our society, such as the failure of business corporations or voluntary associations. If we seriously aim at an understanding of how groups form, maintain themselves, and dissolve, then the study of family dissolution can also profit the theorist.

Usefulness in Personal Guidance. After it is published, a book and its audience find one another by processes that are shaped little by author or publisher. This study was heralded and accompanied by articles in national magazines, and hundreds of book reviews, newspaper columns, and radio programs over the nation. Yet it did not become popular. Its *intended* audience was the sociologist, and its real audience became the sociologist of the family or the social worker.

Nevertheless, parallel to its social science readership was another, those who sought practical guidance.

This is not entirely surprising. After all, there is no inherent contradiction between utility and good theory. I have long asserted the potential *theoretical* importance of "practical" social research or social engineering, as well as the *practicality* of theoretical research. However, my personal taste has always run to the theoretic. Given the choice, I have preferred to make a theoretical contribution. Yet valid scientific findings *are* likely to be useful, too, if only because they give us a correct map of social reality. Thereby, we can at least go in the direction we choose, whether or not someone else approves our route.

Owing to the publicity this work received, I received many personal letters in response, asking for guidance and sometimes even offering to pay for help. Not being a marital counsellor, of course I could only direct these people to the appropriate family service agencies. On the other hand, on innumerable occasions, new acquaintances have told me that they had found the book itself helpful—thus perhaps paying a tribute to the prescience of the *New York Times,* which listed *After Divorce* under "How to do it" books.

How could such a book, containing only scientific results, be helpful to a man or woman who goes through the often painful adjustment to a divorce?

The prime utility is that most people are comforted to learn that what they live through as a unique personal trouble is in fact shared by hundreds of thousands of others each year. The husband who cringes at the charges hurled at him by an angry wife, or who feels guilty because he was not always a model spouse, learns that though he has failed, other reasonable men have done so, too. The lonesome ex-wife learns that her problems are part of the human condition of our time.

Almost as important is the assurance, derived from research, that though the individual may despair in his or her lonesomeness, longing, or hurt, or perhaps worry about the effect of the divorce on the children, in nearly all instances a second husband or wife will enter their lives (not without effort, to be sure); and though their ultimate chances of a happy second marriage are less than those of people who marry only once, still their chances of a happy marriage *are* higher than in the first.

And though their children would certainly be more likely to avoid juvenile delinquency, divorce, or personality problems if they had been able to create a secure and warm family atmosphere, merely *willing* it will not create it; and, as to the real area of choice, the data show that families in turmoil and conflict are even more likely to produce children with problems than are divorced couples.

Laymen have not studied each specific relationship explored in this book —such as whether mothers with more children remarry as fast as those with fewer children, or whether mothers who have discipline problems with their children want their husbands to visit more or less often. Thus the book is a more useful guide, and sometimes solace, than even a wise layman (or that oracle cited so frequently by the popular press, the "family doctor"), simply because thereby the divorcee can better predict the outcome of a given course of action. The work can, to that degree, be used as a "reference" book, rather than as a narrative to be read at one sitting. Knowing what to expect, the divorced person can act with somewhat greater rationality, perhaps even to avoid some of the difficulties analyzed here.

Doubtless, too, this applies to the kin and friends of the divorcee, who may give better advice, or may help more sympathetically, because they understand better what is taking place. The social situation of the divorcee is an ambiguous one, but it exhibits many regularities. Knowing normal social processes described here will be of more help than the badly timed intervention of kin or friends.

If I may close on a personal note, it is that the scientist, of whatever discipline, is likely to regard certain of his research experiences as periods of high excitement, an alternation of catastrophes and little victories, so that the final report embodies much more for him than the many findings its presents. For me, this study was one of those periods, and if in re-living it I remember far more of the pleasure than the despair, it is not only because finally I was pleased with the book itself (with all its imperfections) but also because for those who throw themselves wholeheartedly into sociological inquiry as a process, there is indeed joy in work.

W. J. G.

January 1965

PREFACE

THIS EXPLORATION of an increasingly common experience in our time, adjustment to divorce, seeks to understand divorce within the larger framework of our kinship system. In our analysis, we have been led to develop and amend existing theory, and to correct many commonly held notions about divorce. Though not technically impeccable, the research procedures seem good enough to allow confidence in the final results; and our results are in agreement with the facts which can be tested by previous studies. Thus, it seems likely that there is also some basis for confidence where our conclusions go beyond previous studies.

Our aim is to find out what *is*, not what *ought* to be, though of course knowing what is often leads to some reasonable conclusions about corrective policy. The morality of divorce is not called into question here. Our society has in fact a high divorce rate, and this study attempts to find out how people make their adjustment to this sometimes tragic experience. We take note of moral data, of course, since in a deep sense these are the main focus of sociology; but our aim is analysis of them, not preachment about them.

Good research procedures prevent any personal bias of the researcher from "making the data conform to one's prejudices." Since, nevertheless, the subject is emotionally loaded, it may be useful to the reader if the author gives what may be his own most pertinent layman's prejudice, relative to divorce.

It is as follows. If marital stability, divorce, and postdivorce adjustment were a matter of rational planning, like consulting a chef before attempting a bouillabaisse, there would be little life importance in it. Failure would be a function of knowledge, facilities, and materials. However, even with the best of will and intelligence we cannot always make a happy home. Our value-standards, and those of our partner, get in the way. We are asked "to adjust," but it is an ethical question of great import whether we *ought* to adjust to all things. Adjustment to certain types of marriages, or marriage and living demands, may destroy all we hold dear: our goals, our friends, our esthetic rights, our personality needs. Then, even if we *could* adjust, given our backgrounds, our goals, our personalities, it is not morally clear that we *ought* to do so. The traditional morality demands that we stay in marriage. A more modern and less powerful morality states that we "ought to adjust to reality."

But, aside from whether in fact we are able to do either of these, an equally defensible morality of personal rights and dignity insists that under certain circumstances we ought *not* to do so.

With reference to the study itself, in the divorce situation there are many alternatives, but unsure moral guides in our time. In consequence, most who go through it are likely to have an emotionally upsetting experience. Here, we are investigating that experience.

The history of this study is long and at times anguished. It was interrupted again and again by lack of money and time. There seems little reason now to outline the difficulties of carrying out a large-scale project without a permanent staff. I do wish, however, to record my thanks to the many people and organizations that have facilitated its final appearance.

The initial field work expenses were met by the Curtis Publishing Company. The original willingness of Ben Hibbs and Robert Fuoss to risk this money made possible the gathering of the data. Perhaps central among their goals were business aims, but they never asked more from me than that the study be carried out well. I am grateful for their original help.

It will be clear to the social scientist, at least, that no adequate list of divorces could be obtained without working with the County Records. I wish to thank Edgar M. Branigin, Wayne County Clerk, for his cooperation, on our promise never to divulge any information about any individual in those records. Without his help the study would have been impossible, and we on our part have kept that promise. Hazen E. Kunz, Chief Assistant of the Friend of the Court, also gave us considerable help, as well as encouragement, and we record our thanks here.

To my many colleagues and students (both undergraduate and graduate) at Wayne University I also owe thanks for advice, help, and encouragement. It was in our classes on the Family that we first wrestled with this structurally interesting aspect of kinship theory. Moreover, at that time the University had no research budget at all, and many of these friends among both colleagues and students gave time and energy to the study, from theoretical discussions to time at the tabulating machines after midnight (to which we had no legitimate access). Theirs was a grand spirit, and amid the joshing such support as researchers do not often obtain.

These colleagues include in particular Dean Victor A. Rapport, Don Hecock, and various members of the Sociology Department: Henry Baker, my close friend and office mate; H. Warren Dunham; Frank E. Hartung; Norman D. Humphrey; Donald C. Marsh; Edgar A. Schuler; and Harold Sheppard. My students are too many to list, but some of them must be mentioned: Arnold S. Feldman (now Field Director at the University of Puerto Rico); Dr. Irving Rosow (now carrying out a community mental health study in England); Nancy Berr; Pauline Wilson; Mildred Perlis (now a marital counselor in Detroit); Raymond Zweig (now an attorney in Detroit); Richard Marks (now Research Director of the Detroit Interracial Commission); and Mabel Dee Rhodes.

I had gambled that once the field data were in my hands the study could be completed without much money. In this I was naive. However, the Social Science Research Council made a grant-in-aid available, so that first analyses could be made. Later, the American Philosophical Society gave a larger grant-in-aid, and thanks are hereby tendered to both these organizations.

The facilities of Columbia University finally made possible the completion of this report. The Columbia Council for Research in the Social Sciences has helped generously, and I am glad to record my gratefulness to this agency. Moreover, I have often received aid from the Bureau of Applied Social Research, from Dean Louis M. Hacker, and from my colleagues in the Sociology Department, in the form of encouragement, counsel, and even help in small but essential matters such as typing, tabulation, tabulation machines, and graduate assistance.

I am particularly grateful to Terence K. Hopkins, one of my graduate assistants (now teaching at Upsala College), who not only performed uncomplainingly the ordinary tasks of helping me in my courses, but devoted hundreds of voluntary hours to this study. His persistent inquiry into many puzzling relationships has often aided me in understanding these phenomena. In addition, he carried out (with the guidance and help of Arnold Simmel) the several latent attribute analyses which we used in our work. I have also been aided by Robert Somers, who helped eliminate many inconsistencies and errors from the tabulations and manuscript.

Among my colleagues at Columbia University, I owe particular thanks to Kingsley Davis, whose theoretical inquiries into family institutions have often given me clues toward understanding especially the kinship institutions of divorce.

Finally, my friend Melvin Tumin of Princeton University has helped me greatly by a careful reading of the final manuscript. Unfortunately, it was not in my power to achieve in the further revision all he demanded, but his many suggestions improved the end result immensely.

Piermont, N. Y.
Spring, 1955

CONTENTS

CHAPTER I

THE AIMS OF THIS STUDY

THE PRESENT report focuses on the process of adjustment after divorce. It is an account of the first field survey of postdivorce adjustment problems carried out in this country. It does not give advice on how to avoid divorce, or even how to avoid the problems that are caused by divorce. It does describe those problems, as well as how the divorcee met them. Since some divorcees may only slowly assimilate that experience, the study tries to locate some of the characteristics which are associated with a slow or rapid adjustment.

Since no previous field study has blocked out the basic facts in any detail, it can be taken for granted that much of the present report is exploratory. Many of the survey problems were not met in the best possible manner, and later research can benefit from these failures.

The present chapter is concerned with the place of divorce and postdivorce adjustment in the American kinship system: the widespread interest in divorce, how divorce has been interpreted, and its importance for understanding the workings of the family system.

Widespread Interest in Divorce. Divorce research has occupied the energies of many social scientists during the past several decades. If one includes marital conflict, the number would be increased. Its fascination is just as great among the American population as among social scientists. Investigations into divorce have been carried out not only by social scientists, but by lawyers, judges, social workers, psychiatrists, physicians, and others. Divorce is one of the predominant themes of modern literature.[1] Specific divorces are considered newsworthy. There are many "how to do it" books whose aim is to show the popular reading public how to avoid this problem.

Most of these analyses focus on two main themes: (1) Divorce as an index of social disorganization or pathology; and (2) Paths to marital happiness. Let us look at each of these.

The Classical Family of Western Nostalgia, and Social Disorganization. Divorce has been viewed by many as an *index* of "social disorganization," or of the anomie of modern urban life. It has particularly been so viewed by those sociologists who are nostalgic for the rural "harmony" which they so eagerly left as youngsters. We are all guilty of loosely contrasting an undefined urban,

---

1. See J. H. Barnett, *Divorce and The American Divorce Novel 1858-1937* (Ph.D. dissertation, Philadelphia: University of Pennsylvania, 1939); and Donald N. Koster, *The Theme of Divorce in American Drama, 1871-1939* (Ph.D. dissertation, Philadelphia: University of Pennsylvania, 1942).

supposedly pathological family life, with a rural, idyllic family pattern of some generations ago: the classical family of Western nostalgia is cited and praised in practically every public speech on the breakdown of the modern family and modern society. Idealizing the past and the distant, some have failed to do justice to the complexities of both rural and urban family patterns. Many analysts see in the "rising tide of divorce" abundant evidence that the country may be approaching moral disintegration. It is not alone the clergy and the professional moralists who have taken this position.

This view need not be criticized here. If divorce is seen as a mere index of social pathology, then as a consequence there is not much stimulus to analyze what happens to an individual *after* he has had this experience. The question that appears to loom as of far greater significance, is how to return to an older societal form, in which the "classical family" can flourish, rather than to chart what happens to those who become involved in a modern divorce.

Marital Happiness and Romantic Love. When research in divorce and marital conflict concentrates on marital happiness, what happens after divorce is likely to be ignored. There are several factors that lead to this result.

If happiness is the focus, then divorce is an end point, a finality. If the emphasis is mainly on how to avoid or resolve marital conflict (and thereby prevent divorce), then postdivorce adjustment will not usually receive much attention.

Interestingly enough, even those social analysts who assert that the romantic complex of our courtship system is an unstable basis for marriage, usually continue to view divorce against the backdrop of an ideal love relationship. But divorce is an official recognition of unhappiness, and it denies one basic premise of the romantic complex, that a couple marries because both are deeply in love and the love will, of course, continue.[2] If the love was "real," then the divorce could not have happened—or, in the words of the more hopeful, the love *must* have been real and therefore there is still hope for maintaining the marriage. In any event, if we view divorce in such terms we are likely to think of divorce as such a finality that we do not peer beyond this final veil.

Indeed, the shaping of research by these notions may be seen quite clearly in the characteristic parallel drawn between bereavement and postdivorce adjustment.[3]

---

2. We are not here assuming that the romantic love complex is indeed as widely distributed as many marital counselors seem to believe it to be. There is good reason for suggesting serious research into its meaning for and impact upon those who contemplate marriage. It is undoubtedly true that love is considered almost a *sine qua non* in our culture, but it also seems likely that very few couples marry without much calculation on both sides about the relative advantages to be gained from marriage with alternative suitors. Anyone who contemplates marriage obtains much free advice from his peer groups, relatives, etc. It is just possible that we have romanticized the romantic love complex. A more accurate charge against our courtship patterns might be that the areas of shared experience between fiances are so *narrow:* We have little opportunity to discover all the major facets of the potential spouse's behavior under different circumstances. If it does not seem too cynical, the author would like to suggest that, while love is undoubtedly important, lovers themselves like to romanticize publicly their irrationality, while mentally counting pennies; and that the display of irrationality is utilized as a challenge to parental authority, even to the extent of the young couple utilizing this display for exploiting the anxieties of parents. Some relevant data are found in E. W. Burgess and Paul W. Wallin, *Engagement and Marriage* (New York: Lippincott, 1953).

3. This notion is expounded in Willard Waller, *The Old Love and the New* (New York: Liveright, 1930). It has, of course, been developed by others, notably Howard Becker. See

The consequences of this focus on happiness go further. They help to shape some of the assumptions and contentions which, though not actually tested by analysts, have been repeated in the standard literature on divorce. Many of these notions are to be found in Waller's pioneer work, in which he insightfully analyzed some 33 selected cases. One such contention has been that the divorcee is of a different breed than ordinary people, that he is likely to be a neurotic who carries within himself the seeds of his own marital destruction, and will destroy a second marriage and a third, if he embarks on them. He cannot be happy in marriage.

Moreover, if happiness is viewed as the central problem, then the failure to be happy is tied to the violation of our official monogamic ideals, and we should remedy the latter problem by solving the former.

Indeed, our society typically views failure as remediable. Failure is due to lack of ability, knowledge, or hard work, and we can compensate for one of these by a greater quantity of the other. It hardly needs to be said that these are not the only themes expressed, but these are of importance in the usual analyses of marital happiness and how to achieve it.

When failure does occur, it is the general assumption that the postdivorce processes are mostly destructive. Doubtless this assumption rests in part on moral bases. A postdivorce "trauma" or personal disorganization is expected, because the failure *ought* to be punished. The person who has violated our faith in the romantic love complex and the monogamic ideal ought to suffer.

Measuring Marital Happiness. Because happiness seems so important, various instruments have been developed, which attempt to measure the chances of marital "success" (i.e., happiness) or failure, for those contemplating marriage. Most of these studies were done under the leadership of Ernest W. Burgess, whose first major report on this topic appeared in 1939.[4]

This work will continue and will ultimately furnish instruments of great utility for marital counsellors. At the present time, these tools contain many weaknesses. These, of course, are known to the men whose energies have been turned in that direction. We are not here concerned with these weaknesses or the ultimate usefulness of such researches for counseling and especially for the prevention of potentially unstable marriages. Rather, we emphasize that certain assumptions and values regarding marriage and divorce have diverted research attention away from what happens *after* divorce.

Happiness Not a Strategic Sociological Variable. But it is not at all clear that happiness and unhappiness are the most strategic variables to be used in studying marital institutions. Sociologically, the most important justification for the study of divorce is not that we thereby deal with unhappiness, but that we thereby locate and analyze *points of strain,* personal and social. Strain

---

Reuben Hill's revision of Willard Waller, *The Family* (New York: Dryden, 1951), esp. Chapter 22; Becker, *A Social-Psychological Study of Bereavement* (unpublished M.A. thesis, Northwestern University, 1926); Thomas D. Eliot, "Bereavement Inevitable But Not Insurmountable," in Howard Becker and Reuben Hill, *Family, Marriage and Parenthood* (Boston: Heath, 1942), esp. pp. 665-667.

4. Ernest W. Burgess and Leonard S. Cottrell, Jr., *Predicting Success or Failure in Marriage* (New York: Prentice-Hall, 1939). A previous study at the University of Chicago was done as a Master's thesis by Richard Otto Lange. "A Study of the Degree of Happiness or Unhappiness in Marriage, as Rated by Acquaintances of the Married Couples." (M.A. thesis, University of Chicago, June, 1932.) Terman's work was begun later, though published earlier, than Burgess' report.

points seem to be strategic for beginning an analysis of social structures. In the same fashion, it is possible that personality strain is important for understanding the somewhat narrower field of personality phenomena.

(1) We can, at such strain points, most effectively *observe* (a) the conflicts of values, and (b) the antagonisms and inconsistencies among the various roles played by an individual, or among statuses occupied by the same or different individuals. (2) How people decide between such strains tell us in part the direction of future social *change*. (3) The *distribution* of such strains suggests the extent to which different values are actually believed in (if they are not believed in, they cannot create strain. (4) The punishments and rewards meted out to individuals who decide one way rather than another tell us of the intensity with which given values are held by the society. (5) Finally, it is at such strain points that we can locate the most important variables in the decision-making process.

A study of postdivorce adjustment, then, deals with one such strain point, the decision to divorce; and with the sequel to that resolution. Divorce is a strain point within a kinship system that values marital stability highly.

But the points of strain in a society cannot be defined in merely literary terms, and they are not identifiable with merely personal tragedy, or even with what is known as "social problems." Pain, sadness, or even public indignation are not adequate criteria for either social strain or personal disorganization, although they may all be correlated somewhat with one another. For example, there is pain in a ritual ordeal such as sub-incision or scarification, but these are prepared for by anticipatory socialization of the individual, and by the immediate preparations of the group for the ritual. Predesignated groups carry out anxiety-reducing activities which lower the personal threat, or even the possible group threat, implicit in these situations. Similarly, there is sadness in bereavement, but this is not a strain point for the social structure.

It is, rather, sociologically crucial that such points are where values, norms, and role obligations come into conflict with one another. Put another way, strain points are where we have moral options or choices as, for example, between being a good father or a good employee, a good friend or a loyal citizen.

Consequently, marital unhappiness can not be taken as an index of strain on the kinship structure. There is no problem of moral choice between unhappiness and happiness. Leaving aside the neurotic, we do not feel ashamed if we are happy, or morally triumphant if we are unhappy. There is no competition between unhappiness and happiness, and only under the most deviant circumstances will anyone advocate either on moral grounds.

The assertion that happiness is not of prime significance sociologically is not common, and deserves further comment. Social action is the resultant of choice, and the basis of the choice is one or more norms: rationality, beauty, self-expression, monogamy. We sometimes fail to see this fact, because we habitually *phrase* the choice as one between (a) a given norm, and (b) happiness. But this is loose phrasing. The choice in this type of situation—shall I be tempted by tobacco, rich food, or a pretty girl?—can be analyzed properly as only two kinds of choice, both of them being viewed in normative terms: (1) Conformity with or violation of a given norm (e.g., monogamy); or (2)

A choice between conflicting norms (monogamy, vs. "self-expression," "spontaneity," "experience," or bon-vivant-Casanova-masculinity).

Viewed in rigorous sociological terms, these are not choices between "conformity and happiness." Such a phrasing reflects our self-dramatizing, literary inclinations, rather than fact. In point of fact—both commonsense, and sociological—there is some happiness in conforming to values which we hold. For particular circumstances and individuals, this pleasure may not be so great as would result from violating the norm, but then the choice is strictly speaking between adhering to the norm, or violating it. The consequences must also be chosen: one measure or type of pleasure or contentment, against another; or one set of undesired results, against another.

Thus, if we are married, we may indeed be "tempted," but our choice is between conformity to the norm of monogamy, or violation of it. In our generation, other relevant norms also play a role, such as "being free." And the choice of consequences is not, once again, "happiness vs. conformity." We have a moral objection to "being unfaithful," and succumbing to temptation would violate that norm, and to some degree make us unhappy. Indeed, the society would not survive at all if the choice were between conformity and happiness. Conformity could never win. One can formulate a sort of hedonistic theory in which the members of the society are viewed as choosing among various kinds of happiness—the happiness of fatherhood, motherhood, philanthropy, devotion to the church, hard work, movies, sports, etc. Or, one can translate all choices into choices of a normative character, structured by a system of rewards and punishments in the society. But it is a false view of social action to think of norms as isolated from "happiness," and thus offered as a choice, or option, contrasted with happiness.

Consequently, the attempts to predict marital happiness are not likely to be strategic sociologically. Moreover, the concrete attempts to predict marital happiness have usually failed precisely where a general theory of social organization has not been used. In particular, a marriage is a boundary-maintaining system whose stability results from many factors in interaction, and the "happiness" of its members also results from those same factors. It is more important to study that stability than the much more variable item of happiness. If we analyze the breakdown of that system, we must locate the strain points, i.e., the situations or structural loci at which normative choices are made. If we do this, then there is no sociological need to measure *in addition* that emotional conglomerate we call happiness.

The Norms of Marital Stability and Expression of Conflict. We insist, then, that happiness is not, and can not be, built into any family system as either a statistical average, or as a moral norm. As members of the society, we can *not* be morally required to be happy or unhappy. Family *stability,* on the other hand, can be the focus of major value complexes, and often is. Just as marital happiness can not be a moral prescription in any society, so can marital unhappiness or conflict not be morally proscribed. Social or physical inevitabilities are rarely, if ever, prohibited.

Of course, such matters are not left socially unstructured. Hostility or conflict can not be allowed to develop without check, for any such lack of harmony may become overt and thus disrupt existing and approved role relations. There are moral and ethical norms to prohibit many kinds of behavior which might tend to excite or intensify hostility and conflict. (Thus, it is wrong for me to sneer often at my wife.) We are also socialized to accept many *common* values so that *grounds* for conflict are lessened. (E.g., both my wife and I have been socialized to believe that we ought to live together, that we shall have sexual access to one another, etc.) Moreover, we are taught to regard many differences and difficulties as *unimportant,* so that we can over-look, or live comfortably with, potential sources of conflict. This is reinforced by values which state that we are "immature," "petty," etc., if we base our conflict on such differences. (Thus, I may not base my conflict with my wife on her failure to butter my toast properly.)

We need not outline these types of patterns systematically. We merely illustrate the fact that values and norms *do* proscribe conflict *indirectly,* by defining as improper various kinds of actions that might *lead* to conflict and hostility.

Correspondingly, the moral structure will not prohibit falling in love with someone who is not one's spouse, but it can and does define as improper those activities of married people which have a good chance of leading to outside love relationships: dating, courtship, being alone with the outsider, especially in situations culturally defined as romantic, and so on.

We therefore assert that some marital conflict is inevitable in any society so long as husband and wife are two different people, and their actions are important to one another.

Correspondingly one may surmise it to be an uncorrectable error in historical reconstruction and nostalgia to believe that our Victorian (or any other) ancestors lived in marital placidity. Doubtless they were stable, but their *stability* is no reliable index of happiness or of absence of conflict, and we have no objective data for exploring that traditional reconstruction adequately. We can accept neither the sketches of avant-garde literary men who for many reasons concentrated upon deviations, nor the preachments of latter-day moralists and rootless urbanites who seek a calm in the past which can be no part of their present lives.

Variation in Conflict Intensity, Acceptance of Conflict and Solutions for It. This is not to say (1) that cultures do not vary in the *degree* of such marital conflict. Undoubtedly, for example, in periods of great change in the role definitions of the sexes there is (a) far *more* disagreement and conflict between spouses, and (b) certainly more expression of this conflict in *overt behavior.* We are merely asserting the inevitability of family conflict and personal unhappiness in all cultures, and the impossibility of there being meaningful, *direct* moral proscriptions against them.

Moreover, (2) what the culture defines as a *bearable* level or degree of conflict will also doubtless vary from one epoch or society to another; and (3) what the society or culture defines as an *appropriate solution* for conflict also varies. The first of these three propositions is borne out by general observations and some theory, although intensity of marital conflict has not been measured in any culture. With reference to the second, there are beginnings of systematic theory in the structural-functional hypotheses of the past decade, specifically those dealing with mechanisms for alleviating and preventing conflict.[5] Here, let us simply note, once more, the possibility of analyzing various elements in any kinship system by reference to their effect upon the *stability* of marriage. The universal nuclear family[6] is to be viewed as one type of boundary-maintaining social unit, under various internal and external pressures toward boundary dissolution and maintenance. Marital unhappiness is only a resultant of various factors that predispose toward marital instability. Among these factors, there are also various mechanisms which (1) *prevent* the building of tensions or external forces; (2) alleviate or deflect such forces; (3) define various difficulties as bearable; (4) and offer various solutions for changing the structure or direction of these forces, or even for removing them.

Within such a view, divorce is to be seen as one kind of mechanism for dealing with the pressures and problems inevitably caused by marriage. Divorce is in a basic sense "caused" by marriage.

A typical set of preventive mechanisms was found in pre-revolutionary China.[7] According to traditional descriptions of this "classical" family, the roles of husband and wife were *clearly* defined. Respect and not romantic love was demanded between husband and wife. There was an extended family system, so that intimate emotional interaction between husband and wife was less continuous or intense than in our own system. Extended deviations from proper marital patterns were prevented in part by the continuous supervision by other, older relatives. If the wife built up any large reservoir of hatred and fear, it was more likely to be aimed at the mother-in-law, rather than at the husband, who was only rarely the most powerful member of the family in the first decade of a marriage.

When conflict *does* reach high limits, there are different solutions in different cultures. One rare solution is that of Dobu, where overt conflict is viewed as standard. There are, however, many outlets for aggression. There is an alternation of family residence each year, from the village of wife's family to that of husband's family. Thus, each of the two spouses may look forward to a period in which great freedom of unchecked, mostly unilinear aggression is permitted.[8]

Perhaps the most common solution is that of divorce, the extended families of each spouse offering at times the necessary help. *Divorce is, then, an institutionalized element of certain kinship systems.* It is not always a kind of excrescence, a sort of pathology or unpredictable deviation. This does not ignore or minimize the difficulties that individuals experience in divorce, or the devastation that may occur in their private lives when a divorce conflict occurs. Rather, we are noting that *all* family systems have *some* kinds of escape mechanisms built into them, to permit individuals to survive the pressures of the system, and one of these is divorce.

Nor is this solution confined to industrial societies. As Murdock has shown,

---

5. Note, for example, the analysis model or paradigm in Robert K. Merton, "Manifest and Latent Functions," in *Social Theory and Social Structure* (Glencoe, Ill.: The Free Press, 1949), pp. 73 ff. Merton has gone far beyond these illustrative beginnings in his unpublished work on functional theory. See also Talcott Parsons, *The Social System* (Glencoe, Ill.: The Free Press, 1951), pp. 283 ff.

6. See George P. Murdock, *Social Structure* (New York: Macmillan, 1949), Ch. I.

7. For a modern sociological analysis of that family type, see Marion J. Levy, Jr., *The Family Revolution in Modern China* (Cambridge: Harvard University Press, 1949).

8. Reo Fortune, *The Sorcerers of Dobu* (London: Routledge, 1932).

and as Hobhouse began to show earlier, divorce is very common in many pre-literate societies. Even without a complete set of data, it is clear that the rate of divorce is often higher than in our own, or than in the other few nations that have at various times had still higher rates than the U. S.[9]

It is then an error to think that, because primitive societies are mostly "rural," they are therefore to be identified with the classical family of Western nostalgia, an idealized picture of the rural family in America at some unspecified period prior to the 1900's.

Theoretical Importance of Divorce. We do not have, unfortunately, any adequate analysis of the values relating to divorce in these societies. We know that in our own, divorce has been a possible, but disapproved, solution for marital conflict. That is, it seems that divorce is not as yet fully *institutionalized* in our own cultural structure. Certainly among some groups of our society it is still disapproved strongly. It is equally certain that this attitude is *changing*. Thus, although a rise in our divorce rate can not be viewed as a simple index of social pathology or even of personal disorganization, it is without question an index of social change.

In the light of these hypotheses, divorce as a phenomenon and as an experience is theoretically very interesting. It is closely tied to several sets of strong value patterns relating to the family and to marital conflict. It is an index of interpersonal strain, and within our own society it is also an index of strain in the social structure, in that (a) there are many strong, if gradually weaker, moral proscriptions against it; but (b) in spite of these proscriptions, the divorces continue to occur and the rate of divorce continues to rise as a mass phenomenon. Moreover, (c) since marital stability in our society is morally approved, since the roots of this attitude are to be found in the three major sects of the Judeo-Christian religious tradition, and since divorce is also judged to be an act of self-seeking or of moral failure, it is likely that few couples divorce in our culture without a guilt component on both sides with specific reference to the divorce (aside from guilts with other sources). Thus, on both the psychodynamic and the socio-structural levels there are interesting ramifications.

Furthermore, (d) divorce as a large-scale solution for marital conflict is a relatively recent reappearance in the cultural history of Western society (for Rome in its "decline," as for Athens, the rate must have been high), yet it has been an always *potentially* institutionalized element in the social structure because of its many Semitic religious antecedents (both Arab and Hebrew, of course). Since these potentialities did not become actual, divorce as a social deviation is in certain respects not like crime or juvenile delinquency, treason or sacrilege.

These latter and other violations are like divorce in that they can be predicted to some extent on the basis of individual characteristics, and to a very great extent on a mass basis. However, they are very different in that prescribed modes of official and unofficial behavior exist for dealing with such deviations. We are socialized to react against these deviations with a fairly

---

9. George P. Murdock, "Family Stability in Non-European Cultures," *Annals,* 272 (1950) 195-201; also J. L. Hobhouse *et al., The Material Culture and Social Institutions of Primitive Peoples* (London: Chapman and Hall, 1930), pp. 159 ff.

specific behavioral and emotional set, and we are even told to some extent how they ought to be punished.

This is not the case for divorce. Neither the participants nor their close friends and relatives have been taught to react in a culturally approved fashion with respect to divorce. We are all taught how to grieve at the death of a relative. We are not taught how we should behave as a divorcee. We are given many culturally approved rationalizations for failing to achieve high status in our occupation, but we are not taught how to solve or to adjust to the failure of our marriage. The general preferences in our culture for rationalistic approaches to problems fail us in this area of great emotionality. Consequently, we should expect to find a set of social phenomena of considerable interest for understanding the family patterns in our culture. Finally, since divorce is a personal and often familial crisis, study of it should add to our knowledge about how individuals adjust to crises.

Numerical Importance of Divorce. A rather substantial segment of the population has, at one time or another, been involved in the divorce process. We do not have an exact figure for the segment composing all who have ever divorced. However, even allowing a substantial amount of cohort mortality, this group must number nearly ten million. Kingsley Davis has estimated that 150,000 to 200,000 children are affected by divorce each year in this country, and calculates further that for the year 1940 the total number of children, then under the age of 18 years, whose parents had ever been divorced, numbered 1,533,000.[10] The figure has certainly not declined. In addition, although the divorce rate fluctuates somewhat from one year to the next, it is clear that the secular trend of divorce is still upward. It seems a conservative estimate to assert that the experience of divorce is likely to occur to one-fifth to one-sixth of the men and women in this country who live out an average life span.[11]

On the other hand, as we have noted before, several countries have exhibited a *higher* rate of divorce than even the United States. Burgess and Locke have assembled these rates for several countries, and show that under the old family system in Japan, there were approximately 367 divorces per 1,000 marriages for the years 1884-1888.[12] Russia, Palestine, and Egypt had higher rates than the United States for the period in or about 1938. As we also noted previously, many primitive societies have relatively high divorce rates. At any given time, approximately 2% of the adult population of the United States is in the marital status "still divorced."[13] Finally, we must remember that death still dissolves more marriages than does divorce.[14]

10. "Children of Divorced Parents: A Sociological and Statistical Analysis," *Law and Contemporary Problems*, Summer, 1944, p. 713.

11. Such an estimate rests on two rough but reasonable assumptions: that 80% to 90% of the population living out an average life span will marry, and that the ratio of marriages to divorces over this period would be from one in four, to one in five. Kingsley Davis suggests that the rate will level off. (*Annals*, [272, 1950], pp. 9-22).

12. Ernest W. Burgess and Harvey J. Locke, *The Family* (New York: American Book Co., 1945), pp. 627-8.

13. *Current Population Reports, Population Characteristics*, "Marital Status and Household Characteristics, March 1950," Series P-20, No. 33 (Washington, D. C.: Bureau of the Census, February 12, 1951), pp. 10-11.

14. Paul H. Jacobson, "Total Marital Dissolutions in the United States: Relative Importance of Mortality and Divorce," in *Studies in Population*, ed. George Mair (Princeton: Princeton University Press, 1949), p. 7; and *Statistical Bulletin*, 30, No. 11 (New York: Metropolitan Life Insurance Company, 1949), pp. 1-3.

The Structural Importance of Divorce. Whether or not we judge this segment of the population or this rate to be large, it seems at least likely that in our society the group impact of divorce is much greater than in most others. We have elsewhere noted some of the behavioral indices of this concern. They may be summarized as follows: (1) A widespread condemnation of the extent of divorce and of its increase; (2) the emotional difficulties suffered by the individuals in the divorce; (3) the number of panaceas offered as general solutions for the problem; (4) its frequency as an object of clinical research; and (5) the development of organizations and experts whose aim is to ameliorate this distress.[15]

The kinship structure fails to define clearly an acceptable behavior pattern for this experience in the life history of a substantial segment of the population. The kinship system fails to furnish unambiguous arrangements for the following kinds of problems.

1. There are no ethical imperatives for relatives or friends that would make them feel constrained to furnish material support during the crisis and afterwards to the divorcees *as* divorcees. This is a period of dissolution of certain household arrangements. Most often, the two spouses separate from one another, and at least one of them must set up a new abode. There are new problems of purchasing food and housing, and, of course, there are various legal fees. These costs cannot usually come out of existing income. There is no room for such added expenses. In addition, of course, one or both spouses may lose their jobs, and there is only rarely enough money for both to continue their usual activities without need for added funds.

2. Similarly, there are no ethical imperatives for friends and relatives to furnish *emotional* support during this period. There is a general ethical imperative to furnish support to close friends during any kind of crisis, and to some extent this is applicable to the divorce situation. It is not comparable, however, to the kind of crisis created by an emergency operation or sudden illness, death, loss of job, etc. In the event of divorce, the friend must make an adjustment among several other imperatives, such as whether he *should* support the break-up of a family, whether he approves his friend's conduct, or how friendly he is to the other spouse. What we are distinguishing here is the difference between a crisis situation in which the imperatives are clear and one in which they are not clear. As we shall show later, friends and relatives actually do help in this situation, but this is not the crucial point at issue. Whether a given individual gives such support is the resultant of many factors, but he cannot, in our society, base his action upon a simple rule of the kinship or friendship structure. The most striking contrast, of course, is with death of the spouse, for in this case the relative or friend who is unwilling to provide economic or emotional support is viewed with disapproval by all within the group.

3. A further point of ambiguity centers around the *readmission* of participants into their former kinship structure or into a new one. The importance of this ambiguity is not to be underestimated, and it is indeed the base on

---

15. For a series of reports on various aspects of this "social problem," see the November, 1950 issue of the *Annals*, 272, especially William J. Goode, "Social Engineering and the Divorce Problem," pp. 86-94.

which other ambiguities rest. By contrast, among the Zuñi, for example, the kinship is matrilineal, divorce is relatively common, and it is accompanied by little public concern and attention. This is the case generally, as it happens, for merely private matters of marital conflict and even marriage. In this society the property in land is owned by the woman's side of the family and descends through her line. In one sense, divorce means that the man is "dismissed." We are not, however, concerned with the personal impact of this situation, but with the fact that in the case of a divorce, all the parties concerned know what they are supposed to do. The man returns to his mother's household, where there is a known place for him. He is part of her family line, and marriage has not changed that fact. He does not carry away the corn he has raised, and there is no argument about the ownership of real property, for that remains in the possession of his wife's lineage. There can be no argument about the children, since the children belong to his wife's line. Whether she herself rears the children or they are given to one of her male relatives to rear, the children are nevertheless part of her family, and it is the right of her family to make decisions about the children's welfare. There is no alimony and no child support, since both sides are simply reabsorbed into an existing and usually extended familial network. These provisions exist whether or not either family approves the behavior of either spouse. There may, of course, be some deviations from these rough rules laid down here, for in no society does everyone live up to the ideal. Nevertheless, these are the general moral imperatives, and the individual or family who failed to live by them would be criticized.

In our own society, by contrast, we are not at all clear as to where the members of the divorcing family ought to go. Indeed, in our society the emphasis is so much on the single family unit, the nuclear family, with only rather tenuous and increasingly vague connections with the older generation or with collateral relatives, that often there is almost no other family cell to which the members of the divorced family *can* go. This is a somewhat exaggerated statement, but it does describe the *norms*. The husband's original family has no moral imperative to take him back. He has made a claim to adulthood and independence, having founded his new family. He has left the family nest. There is no room for him, not alone spatially as is so often the situation in our time, but in kinship terms. It is assumed that if he divorces he will continue to work and support himself, together with perhaps his divorced spouse and children, but this is not a necessary concern of the family from which he originally came. Again, we must emphasize that, concretely, his original family may help him and be friendly to him, but there is no moral injunction that *as divorcee* he has such rights.

The wife is in an even more ambiguous position. Our own society is patrilineal, and patriarchal to a degree. By the Judeo-Christian traditions of the Western world, the wife leaves her original family and becomes a member of the husband's family. Actually, because of the pattern of small nuclear families in our generation, husband and wife simply form a new family unit. In any event, she is considered to be part of that new unit, and no longer part of her family of orientation. This is emphasized by the fact that she takes her husband's name and, if she has children, usually keeps her husband's name even after the divorce. The children also have her husband's name, so that even if she returns with her children to her own family's home, her name and kinship designation lie with the family of her husband. To this degree, then, the divorce asserts a legal cleavage which is only partially carried out in institutional fact.

In any event, for all the family members involved in the divorce, there is some ambiguity about the family status and role to which each must *return* when a divorce is made final. Neither of the two families of orientation is given clear definitions of the approved kinship status to be reassumed by the two married children.

4. As an almost necessary consequence of these ambiguities, the kinship structure does not point out avenues for the *formation of new families*. In some strata, after what is considered an appropriate period of emotional recovery, the divorced wife gradually forms new male friendships. In others, this behavior is considered vaguely or definitely improper. What is certain, however, is that the family's obligation to help her form a new family is not clear. This is in contrast with the moral imperatives families feel for helping the younger generation find a first husband or wife. Daughters are admonished by both parents that they must look for the right kind of husband, and parents usually make at least token gestures toward helping in this process.[16] Even the most protective mother gives at least lip service to the notion that she must help her son find a wife. The push toward marriage is strong in our culture, and it affects both generations. The family has, however, discharged its obligations when the child is married. The unhappiness and disorganization of the divorced spouse may lead in time to the parent family offering help in moving toward a second marriage. However, this is a result of the personal affection of family members for one another and the distress caused by the other's suffering, and is not so much due to a socially recognized obligation to offer this type of aid to a divorced child.

5. Correlative with these gaps is a further ambiguity concerning the proper behavior and emotional attitudes of the spouses most directly concerned. We have just noted the failure to specify the proper behavior for various activities which might be carried out by relatives or even friends. However, the other side of all such sets of definitions is a specification of the appropriate role behavior of the two spouses. There is no clear definition as to whether they should be grieved or relieved. They are in some sense now "single," but the role behavior of the never married is much more definitely specified. Having *once* been defined as adult and married, a status which is in turn defined as being chronologically *later* than the status of "never married," neither the spouses nor their families have a simple definition of an in-between state: they are neither old nor young, adult nor child, married nor single. Lacking such a specification, the divorced spouse is subject to criticism by some, no matter what she or he does. Behavior and emotion may seem inappropriate to some members of the family or to some friends. In particular, the proper relationship *between the divorced spouses* is not clearly defined.

These ambiguities do not necessarily create great emotional distress and,

---

16. Of course, due to various emotional involvements one or both parents may also sabotage their own child's efforts by destructive criticism and similar behavior.

as we shall see later on, many women may adjust to divorce with relatively little anguish. However, social behavior is simplified in all societies by role definitions, accepted and known to almost all participants, and morally approved. When these definitions are lacking, the necessary decisions must be made on a more individual basis, and the people concerned can not count on general social approval, whether or not their previous behavior has been proper.

Divorce and Adjustment to Divorce: Hypotheses. It is in these terms that divorce is a point of strain in the social structure. In general, such strains are reflected in the personal distress of the individual. This distress has, of course, many other roots, notably the guilt at a moral, religious or personal failure, and the difficult and complex problems of previous emotional attachments.

The crisis of divorce is, then, one which requires a considerable amount of adjustment for the participants. The kinds of adjustment which must take place in each case will vary somewhat. The general patterns of kinship in our society, however, impose a considerable number of adjustments which are common to almost all of these cases.

Waller's work pioneered in this area. Some of the reasons for the failure of social analysts to test Waller's hypotheses, with more adequate research techniques, have been noted. There are no more than perhaps four or five serious attempts at research in this field since Waller's time. There has probably been no attempt by anyone to make a field survey of a random sample of those undergoing adjustment to divorce. The problems of such a research are many, of course, and they will be discussed later on.

Despite the lack of systematic research, the attention given to this phase of the family cycle has yielded a substantial number of hypotheses. The present report, then, explores and describes the process of adjustment to divorce, with some concentration upon major hypotheses and assumptions made by previous investigators. Some of these are the following, not all of which can be adequately answered by the present research.

1. One general hypothesis concerning the adjustment process is that this period is a traumatic one, with considerable personal disorganization.

2. An assumption generally made, though not often made explicitly, has been that divorce is in the main a phenomenon of the middle class and particularly of the upper middle class. Thus, Terman: "It is well known that more divorces occur in the higher classes . . . but this is thought to be because it is too expensive for others."[17] It is also an assumption or a hypothesis that the divorce rate is much higher for whites than Negroes.[18]

3. It has been hypothesized or assumed that those who divorce are likely

---

17. Lewis M. Terman, *Psychological Factors in Marital Happiness* (New York: McGraw-Hill, 1938), p. 167.

18. Some of these assumptions or hypotheses represent an interesting problem for the sociology of knowledge. As I have noted earlier (William J. Goode, "Economic Factors and Marital Stability," *American Sociological Review*, 16 [1951], 802-812), there were several previous studies which seemed to suggest or even demonstrate that the divorce rate is higher as one descends the economic strata, and that the Negro divorce rate is higher than that of the white, for the United States as a whole, and sharply so for Northern urban situations. Nevertheless it can be shown by a study of the standard textbooks in the field that these facts have not been assimilated or utilized although their relevance for many related facts, such as suicide, disease, and crime among the divorcees is apparent. It is an interesting problem as to why these important facts were not assimilated, accepted and used.

to be neurotics who are doomed to a series of unhappy marriages, each ending in divorce. This notion is not often stated with such explicitness, and it frequently takes the form of couching much of the analysis of divorce in terms of "immature personalities," or "personality conflict." The present research did not contain any of the standard measures of personality problems used in psychology. This study does contribute some information as to the apparent patterns of adjustment in the second marriages. Future research may demonstrate that the proportion of successful marriages among second marriages is not greatly lower than the proportion of successful marriages among first marriages. In any event, this general hypothesis as to the inferior caliber of divorcees needs to be questioned.

4. A further hypothesis is often to be found, again sometimes expressed as an assumption, and, of course, sometimes judged to be applicable to only part of the divorcees: This assumption is that divorce is essentially an act of "irrationality," that is, it is usually decided upon for essentially trivial reasons, or even whimsy, and spouses who were serious, mature, "rational" people would not get divorces. The emphasis on rationality is particularly important, as hinted earlier. It is a broad assumption throughout our culture that one *should* be rational, and that adequate knowledge and a rational attitude would solve most problems of morals. The activities of marital counsellors and of marriage "experts" generally emphasize these aspects and frequently fail to query the extent to which the problems of marital conflict and of divorce can be solved on such a basis.[18a]

5. It follows from the above hypotheses that adjustment in any ordinary sense might be an unusual phenomenon. As Waller comments, a real adjustment after divorce "is quite rare."[19] Granted the difficulty of defining the term without introducing value biases, the question must be raised as to whether adjustment is indeed so infrequent. In any event, this research asks how adjustment proceeds in its various facets, and even how rapidly it proceeds.

6. It is also a hypothesis, or a statement generally made and easily accepted, that the divorcee is rejected by society. The proposition is made particularly about female divorcees, but it is frequently extended even to the *children* involved in the divorce. Undoubtedly, to some extent this extension is correct, but we need to know its *extent,* and to some degree the *meaning* of this rejection. We need also to know how much the attitudes of the society have *changed* with respect to divorce. It is possible that much of the rejection is on a relatively abstract and ideal level. That is to say, society disapproves of divorce and even of the divorcee in general, but does not object greatly in a concrete situation to the presence of the divorcee or to social interaction with him or her. Here we would also need considerable further research on the differences among various strata and groups of the population. In any event, we can ask the divorcee what his or her experiences have been in this regard.

7. As a consequence of the previous "facts" about divorce, it is generally hypothesized that the divorcee "drifts" to other areas, especially low-class, transitional and other areas (such as boarding house neighborhoods, commercial districts, slums, etc.), to escape from the problems created by the new

---

18a. Goode, "Social Engineering and the Divorce Problem," *Annals,* 272 (1950), 86-94.
19. *Op. cit.,* p. 290.

social status and to start new lives. The fact of mobility for the divorcee can hardly be questioned, although we do not know how much greater it is than that of the larger urban population. Yet it must be kept in mind that *some* mobility is created by the breaking up of the household. This mobility can not be defined as an "escape to anonymity" without considerably greater probing. In any event, we can investigate what kinds of lives these divorcees are building for themselves after divorce, and thus shed some light on the kind of mobility their movement has exhibited.

8. Among the more sophisticated students of the family and divorce, a further problem has been raised with respect to the place of *economic* factors in marital stability. It is a commonsense assumption that economic factors are of considerable importance. In attempting to assess this point, however, students of the family, notably those who have worked with Burgess, have cast doubt upon this commonsense formulation, at least to the extent of suggesting that when economic factors seem to influence the family toward divorce, they are the facts of occupation rather than income *per se*. In this report we shall take a further step with respect to this matter, by suggesting some of the social dimensions of economic factors. It is clear that economic factors do influence adjustment, but we know enough about the society to understand that they rarely do so directly: we do not ordinarily calculate economic advantage in such close terms. It is rather the social *meaning* of any economic factor which is most crucial.

9. Most students of the family have pointed out the evil effects of divorce upon children, and indeed many have used this as the main charge against divorce. It is known that the rate of juvenile delinquency is higher among children of divorced parents, and it is generally assumed that these children are unhappy.

However, the further question must be asked, whether the strains in the child's role adjustment, which are due to divorce, are greater than those which would result from remaining within a disrupted household. Perhaps it is the happiness and adjustment between the child and his parent or parents which are most crucial; and when this relationship is a warm one, divorce itself does not have such a destructive effect on the child. Moreover, if divorce is to a great extent a lower-class phenomenon, and juvenile delinquency is also, then we would expect these two to be associated, even though not causally related.

As is true of any research, none of these rather large questions can be answered fully in this volume. However, our facts will shed light upon these hypotheses, and point out various gaps which still exist.

Definition of the Term "Adjustment." A research that purports to deal with "postdivorce adjustment" must also attempt to define the term. Often used by social analysts, the term will be difficult to define with precision. Even if the term were defined exactly, the linguistic habits of readers from various fields might nevertheless prevail, and their own definitions would be read into the use of the term here.

The general usage of the term is value-laden, and this appears especially in the professional attitudes of counselors and therapists, who strongly approve "adjustment" and condemn "escapism." The term often means "adjustment to reality," with a tone of deprecating any behavior which seems to be wishful thinking or fantasy. Sometimes the term is almost equal to "being mature," and we are expected in some way to come to terms with our own destiny, accepting it at one or many levels. Consequently the term often contains the further meaning of "happiness." The individual who is well-adjusted is said to be content, or to enjoy life. It is held that if we can only adjust, then we will also be happy.

In addition, the term has roots in biological and psychological theory, and there refers to the process of solving a problem. Thus plants or animals may change their habits in some fashion, so as to survive in a new or threatening environment. Although this sense does not necessarily contain value implications, our heritage gives approval to problem-solving, and this usage may often have a tone of approval. It is difficult to avoid the historical burden of complex meaning to be found in such a common term.

Now, in most cases of divorce, the two spouses do undergo a rather powerful experience. Whether it is the legal action of the divorce which has the greatest emotional effect, or the prior experience of long conflict, misunderstandings, bitterness, boredom, embarrassment, or guilt, the total experience is a difficult one for most individuals. The difficulties may be experienced as severe or of moderate intensity, and may extend over years or weeks.

All this suggests that there is *something to which adjustment* has been made or must be made. It is indeed a rare case in which both parties, with no guilt or bitterness, separate and divorce in a cool fashion, with no regrets, and with simple solutions of their practical problems. To the extent that the individuals ever committed themselves to the relationship, and most do in our culture at some time or another, some emotional and practical problems must be faced.

Adjustment, however, cannot mean conformity to the customs or "mores." Our culture does not furnish a standardized and morally approved pattern of behavior for the divorcee. We do not have mores for divorce adjustment. Furthermore, the couple has already violated the mores by getting into the difficulty in the first place.

Now "adjustment" cannot mean, either, that the individual then *reverts* to the pattern of growth he had before he married. He cannot truly go home again. He does not possess the potentialities for becoming the person he was or would have been, had there been no marriage or divorce. On the other hand, (1) there are problems which the individual does face: new friends, dating and sexual adjustment, remarriage, finances and jobs, the children, the exspouse, or the attitudes of family, and we can ask about them. We can also (2) ask whether the individual is gradually assimilating his difficulties into some new pattern of life. Of course, the individual does not act as though the divorce had never been. But to what extent does the individual take up the broken or raveled threads (as he or she sees them), and attempt to weave a new pattern?

The definition, then, does not include but doubtless points to attitudes and actions associated with greater or less satisfaction. To the extent that the divorcee does begin to solve her problems, as she sees them, and with reference to the opportunities that exist, to that extent is she also likely to express some attitude of contentment or pleasure. We view this, however, as a *consequence* of attempting to solve or actually solving the problems. It is, then, a *derivative* datum, not a primary one. We ask, then, (a) what kinds of problems the individual does have, and (b) what has she done about them. These are *descriptive* matters, not value-judgmental ones. In our culture the individual who attempts to solve his problems with energy and dispatch is approved, and particularly if he or she solves them in approved ways. However, that approval is largely irrelevant to our usage of the term. The focus of our problem is how these divorced mothers attempted over a period of time to solve the problems which they experienced.

The postdivorce adjustmental process, then, is one by which *a disruption of role sets and patterns, and of existing social relations, is incorporated into the individual's life pattern, such that the roles accepted and assigned do not take the prior divorce into account as the primary point of reference:* In more commonsense terms, the woman is no longer "ex-wife," or "divorcee" primarily, but first of all "co-worker," "date," or "bride."

Defining the term for psychodynamic analysis is equally difficult, but that is not our concern here. It is clear that the process of restructuring emotional tensions and energies, and rechannelling them to other areas and interests, takes place at the same time, and to somewhat the same degree, as the solution of problems of social relations.

Summary. In the present chapter, we have outlined some of the reasons for considering postdivorce adjustment as a serious intellectual problem. With reference to its theoretical importance, its numerical importance, and its emotional impact, it is worth analysis. We have noted several factors that have prevented this problem from being the focus of field research. In addition, we have shown in what ways a divorce disrupts the role patterns that are established in a marriage, and how the family structure fails to provide clear directives for the participants after the divorce. Relevant to these structural factors, and growing from previous analysis of family patterns, a series of general questions have been raised about divorce, and these are to be investigated in this study. Finally, we have tried to offer a simple definition of postdivorce adjustment, for the purpose of guiding our analysis.

In the next chapter, we turn to a description of the study itself.

CHAPTER II

DESCRIPTION OF THE STUDY

PROBLEMS OF SAMPLING. The present report is taken from the answers which were given to interviewers in a study conducted in metropolitan Detroit, in the early winter of 1948.[1] Those who were interviewed were all divorced urban mothers, aged 20 to 38 years at the time of the divorce.[1a] The 425 respondents were divided into four Time Groups: Group I—divorced approximately two months at the time of the interview; Group II—divorced eight months; Group III—divorced fourteen months; and Group IV—divorced 26 months. The cases were drawn from the complete county records of Wayne County, Michigan. For each group a time point was selected such that half of the cases fell on one side of this point and half on the other. Thus, for the group divorced two months at the time of interviewing, one-half of the cases were drawn from the period *prior* to two months, and one-half were drawn from the period *after* two months. Because of the volume of cases in such a large metropolitan area, it was possible to narrow this range to about one month for Group I, and a similarly narrow range was used for each of the other three groups. Within that time range *every* case was chosen which fitted our requirements: (a) original address in metropolitan Detroit; (b) mother, (c) aged 20 to 38 years at the time of the divorce.

A major criticism against American family research has been that only rarely have random samples been used.[2] Thus a frequent criticism of the pioneer work of Burgess and Cottrell, and of Terman, is that their samples were mainly white collar respondents who were interested in bettering themselves in various ways.

The reports by Popenoe and other marital counselors have been similarly criticized because their respondents were *self-chosen*. That is, the fact that they initiated contact with the counsellor suggests that they differed in other respects from the average person in the married population. It is likely, for example, that they had more education and had a greater sophistication about and willingness to discuss problems of sex adjustment.

---

1. See William J. Goode, "Problems in Postdivorce Adjustment," *American Sociological Review*, XIV (1949), 394-401.

1a. Later checks indicated that five respondents were younger than 20 years of age at the time of the divorce. We have however not excluded them from the study, since all runs had been made by the time we learned this.

2. Leonard S. Cottrell and Nelson N. Foote, *New Directions of Research on the American Family* (mimeographed, no date), Ch. V.

However, it is difficult to obtain a random sample. The clinician is engaged in counseling and has little time for other than self-chosen cases. The few researches which have attempted a strictly random sample have, for the most part, tried to utilize the data already contained in the courthouse records.[3] Some national sample data on marital characteristics exist because of the work done by the Special Surveys group in the Census Bureau. The nearest approach to a *field* survey of a random sample of the divorced population is that of Harvey J. Locke.[4] Locke drew his original list of divorcees from county courthouse records, but also located a few additional divorcees through the people on his first list. The happily married couples were selected by the divorced couples originally drawn, and Locke tried to "match" the divorcees with the happily married. Since, however, the divorced and the married couples are different in many characteristics, such an attempt to *balance* actually succeeds in *biasing* the resulting total sample. However, Locke's work undoubtedly approaches more closely to a random sample for a field survey of the divorced than any previous attempts.

The only complete list of the divorced population is to be found in County Courthouse records. A sample drawn from this list can be considered random, if it follows a defensible sampling plan. In the case of our own sample, one bias might be found in the fact that we are essentially using a time sample. That is, we are selecting *all* the cases from four particular periods of time in an attempt to see the process of adjustment. We have checked the possible bias, and at the present time we see none from this source. The respondent has little or no control over *when* the divorce is to be granted, and there appears to be no bias as to when it would be filed. In the State of Michigan, sixty days are required between the filing of the divorce suit and the granting of the decree.[5] However, many delays are possible. The case may be shifted from one docket to another. A given divorce case may drag out for a long period of time, delaying those which follow, and, of course, the press of divorce suits in the Chancery Courts means some delay under any circumstances. Finally, although the curve of divorces granted does drop during the summer, it is because of the fact that judges simply do not decide as many cases then, and frequently take their vacations at that time. Consequently, if there were ethnic, religious or class differentials in time of filing the divorce, they would for the most part be evened out by the time the divorces were actually granted. There seems, then, to be no source of bias in the time sampling.

We were able to avoid one possible source of bias: self-selection of cases. It is the general experience of social research that when a research instrument, such as a questionnaire, is to be filled out on the initiative of the respondent, or even filled out by the respondent, there is likely to be a substantial bias.

3. An example is Clarence W. Schroeder, *Divorce in a City of 100,000 Population* (Peoria: Bradley Polytechnic Institute, 1939). A more recent project is that of William M. Kephart, "Divorce—A Philadelphia Project," paper read at meeting of the Eastern Sociological Society, New Haven, March 31, 1951.

4. Harvey J. Locke, *Predicting Happiness or Divorce in Marriage* (New York: Holt, 1951).

5. Shortly before the research began, a new law instituted a mandatory period of six months before possible remarriage, when there were children. However, the couple was not required to appear again and the divorce became final automatically. This period caused some confusion in the minds of divorcees as to whether they were "completely" divorced.

For example, the returns from white collar groups will be much greater. Consequently, the mailed or self-administered questionnaire has been most useful for population segments in the upper economic and educational brackets who have a strong interest in giving the information.[6]

Consequently, we could not leave to the respondent the choice of answering or not answering our interview schedule. The schedule itself, as is seen in Appendix II, was a 26-page document containing many questions, some of which required unstructured comments or discussion. We therefore decided that it would be necessary to approach each respondent without asking her permission. For most cases, the approach was made not only without the respondent's permission, but even without the respondent's previous knowledge that such a survey was being conducted. We thus ran the risk of a high rate of refusals. However, it seems likely that an even higher rate of refusal would have resulted from asking the respondent's permission. Although most respondents exhibited considerable gratefulness at the rather lengthy discussions, and even confessions, which they took part in, it seems unlikely that many of them would have admitted beforehand that they wanted to talk to a complete stranger about these matters.

As was to be expected, a considerable amount of emotional display occurred, and some refusals resulted from the presence of male fiancés, relatives, or new husbands. It seemed nevertheless a correct judgment, then and now, to make such a "cold" approach to the respondent. Only in this way could we keep as close as possible to a defensible sampling plan. Both the plan and its results are analyzed in Appendix I; clearly, the sample results *are* generally representative.

We wanted to keep as sharp as possible the *time* distinctions in our research design. We wished to be certain that, on the average, Time Group I (divorced one and one-half to two and one-half months) actually had about six months less for adjustment than Group II (seven and one-half to eight and one-half months after divorce). Obviously, if we allowed interviewing to continue indefinitely until every case originally drawn had refused or accepted, we might extend interviewing over a period of eight or ten months. Consequently, the time distinctions would be somewhat blurred. Therefore we made an arbitrary time cut-off, ending the period of interviewing before these time distinctions were lost. Interviewing thus extended over a period of perhaps one and a half months. We thus had a substantial group of respondents whom we had *not yet contacted* but who *had been drawn* in our original sample. We cannot ignore these, since we had already begun to trace them. A criticism might therefore be made that the people whom we did not attempt to interview, but whom we did draw, were actually different in some important way from those we did interview, and the difference is suggested by the fact that they were not immediately found. Actually, this group does not represent those who were nontraceable, but represents those who had not gone through our rather elaborate tracing process. We used eight different techniques for tracing our cases. We began by assigning a block of names to an interviewer. No name could be dropped by an interviewer merely

---

6. For a simple analysis of this point, see William J. Goode and Paul K. Hatt, *Methods in Social Research* (New York: McGraw-Hill, 1952), Chapter 12.

because the respondent was difficult to locate. No new names were assigned until the old were *finished:* that is, listed as refusals, nontraceable, completed, or out of reach. Therefore, it was not possible to interview only the easily found respondents. Consequently, the "unfinished" were not much different from those whom we did contact.

Nevertheless, we must answer the question as to whether the characteristics of this group are different from those from whom we did obtain interviews. Luckily, we do have information on those we did not interview. In general, we can now say that the various types differ little, but in Appendix I this question is answered in more detail.

Moreover, throughout this study, our results will be compared whenever possible with those from other research. Where the two differ, we shall evaluate that difference. The conclusion from both kinds of comparison is that our sample is representative of urban divorced mothers in this age group.

Telling the Truth. Sampling, however, is only one of the problems of probing into such an emotional area. Were these women telling the truth? There is an important related question: the usefulness of the former husband's testimony in getting "the" truth.

The experience of social research has been that for a wide range of subject matters, good questions and good interviewing will elicit the truth from respondents. It is generally understood that the function of an interviewer is not alone to insist upon an answer, but also to question further, to "probe," when the respondent's answer seems insufficient or ambiguous. A third fundamental function exists, however, for questions of great emotionality. This is the *emotional support* given by the interviewer, during this period of reawakening the hurts and anxieties of the past. The reports of our interviewers show without question that for many respondents the interview served as a cathartic experience, allowing them a release of emotion and the opportunity of discussing matters which had long been troubling them, but which they could not ordinarily discuss even with relatives or close friends.

However, the questions themselves do attempt to get at rather intimate experiences, and many respondents might be *unwilling* or emotionally *unable* to tell the truth. For this there can be no ultimate guarantee except the repetition of these questions in future research studies. The experience of research in the past is that, over a long period of interviewing—and these interviews lasted from one and a half to several hours—very few respondents deliberately and consistently lie about themselves. Once an atmosphere of emotional protection and understanding has been created and the respondent has developed a "set" toward dealing with these rather delicate matters, we can in general count on continued cooperation. It almost never happens, for example, that a respondent breaks off an interview once it is really under way. In two cases the respondents did break off the interview in the first few minutes, but in both the respondents had tried to avoid the interview altogether, prior to that point. In general, it seems reasonable to suppose that the respondents were *trying* to tell the truth.

However, the much more fundamental question is whether the respondent *knows* the truth well enough to be able to tell it. In most public opinion polling this problem is not serious. Of course, an interviewee may not be able to answer questions about political issues simply because he has no attitude toward those issues. It is rare, however, that the respondent in a political research is *unable* to tell the *truth* simply because he or she does not know his or her own situation. However, a major element in the adjustment process, for any type of emotional crisis, may be the restructuring of reality into a new form that is more acceptable to the new life pattern the individual is working out. Some divorcees, for example, male and female, manage to convince themselves after a period of time that their spouse "was no good anyway," and thus both justify their own behavior and make understandable the fact that they were rejected by that spouse. Thus, they may be able to *face* the truth, but do not *know* it.

We must take a fairly radical position with respect to this point. We are trying here to investigate the *adjustment which the spouse made to the reality as she saw it and sees it.* It is this reality to which she must make her adjustment.

This limitation is potentially dangerous, though it can be defended. It should nevertheless be defined closely. We have just commented on several aspects of her ability and willingness to tell the truth. We further emphasize that we are mainly interested in the problems as *she* experienced them; we have only interviewed her, and not her husband.

We thus pose two questions: (1) Do we have to pay any attention to any "objective reality," except hers? (2) What kinds of distortions or gaps are possible, if we have not interviewed the husband?

The answer to the first is clear. We *are* interested in the reality; otherwise we report only psychodynamic structures and patterns of emotional and mental processes. The divorcee is in the real world, and must adjust to that real world. Her recognition of it is even important for her postdivorce adjustment. For example, if she did not understand that in her own circle or stratum to receive as much as $70 weekly from her semi-skilled husband was exceptionally good in 1948 (she may have complained that he did not bring in enough money) then she may also fail to adjust to the economics of a second marriage in that same stratum. If she believes that the children "have no problems at all" after the divorce, when they actually do feel resentments toward her, and have deep feelings of divided loyalty, she may later be unable to cope with the behavioral problems they exhibit.

The answer to the second question, what we miss when we fail to interview the ex-husband, is more complex. For most questions, there should be no more distortion or error than in any survey. That is, most data we seek (1) could have been answered reasonably correctly by *either* husband or wife: e.g., age and sex of the children, duration of marriage, type of custody, division of accumulated property, whether either or both spouses agreed to this division, or how much child support the husband was supposed to pay.

For this first category, we would expect some differences in the answers of husband and wife, but in any good sized sample the average difference should not be great.

A second, and most important, category of data (2) could have been answered *only* by the wife: e.g., her dating after the divorce, the help she got from family and friends, how much total income she received after the divorce, whether she thinks the second marriage is better, or how she feels toward the ex-husband. These are crucial for understanding the postdivorce adjustment process, and her answers seem to be reasonably adequate.

There are a few questions (3) which could have been answered best by the ex-husband: e.g., whether *his* family approved the marriage or the divorce, or how he felt toward his ex-wife after the divorce, or perhaps whether he was really in love with another woman prior to the divorce.

This gap contains many complexities. First, (a) the information would of course be useful. Second, (b) the wife *did* have some basis for the answers she gave to us. For example, she may not have known definitely how her husband felt, but she would have a rather good judgment from his behavior, as to whether he was in love prior to the divorce. She might know less exactly than he just how his family and friends felt toward the marriage or divorce, but she did have ordinarily some opportunity to evaluate their attitudes and behavior in these respects.

Third, (c) she may have misjudged the feelings of others, but in part because they wanted her to do so. For example, she may believe that her ex-husband was still very fond of her after the divorce, while if we questioned *him* we would learn that in reality he was indifferent toward her. However, we suspect from our analysis of divorce strategy between husband and wife that in many cases he *allows* her to believe after the divorce that he still loves her or is fond of her. She errs, then, in her report to us, but for us as social analysts "the" reality is not his indifference alone, but also the factors that lead him to deceive her.

Fourth, (d) in most of these items for which the ex-husband would be the best respondent, we can guess fairly accurately what the reality was, by cross-tabulating various answers. For example, many women claim they did not know whether their husbands were in love with another woman prior to the divorce. We could get the reality from the ex-husband. But we can also guess from the ex-wife's answers to questions about who first suggested the divorce, the degree of postdivorce trauma, or contact with the ex-husband, that these husbands *were* at least following the behavioral patterns of husbands who were in love with another. Similarly, it is clear from the low proportion of definite approvals or disapprovals of the divorce by *his* circle of friends and kin, that she often does not have enough contact with them, as the conflict develops, to know their attitudes. Thus, from the ex-husband we could get a more definite profile of approval-disapproval, but she has not distorted the social reality for us. She has moved away from them (or they have moved from her) to such a social distance that their influence on her or their expectations of her response to them are socially equivalent to a true indifference.

So far, the distortions or gaps created by interviewing only the wife are not extensive or many. A fourth category of data is more complex, and brings up a basic problem in research method. There are data (4) whose best source *is not the interview but observation*. That is, interviewing the ex-husband would give us added insights and questions, and a richer view of the reality, but would not be necessarily more *valid* than interviewing the ex-wife, or relatives, friends, and neighbors. We would need all these, but in addition some observation by trained observers, in order to get "the" reality.

For this category, then, confining our interview to the ex-wife is unfortunate, but it is not the lack of the ex-husband that is damaging, but the lack of genuine observation.

Here we cannot explore this interesting problem in research method, but it is necessary to state a methodological position that can be discussed elsewhere: it is not the failure to include historical data in our research that makes much of sociological analysis two-dimensional; it is the failure to integrate observation with interview materials. We have ample data now, particularly after Hyman's study, to show that interviewing is highly effective.[7] We can probe rather deeply into the respondent's life, and obtain both "objective reality" and "emotional reality" through the interview. However, interviewing is not enough for many data, even though observation may be formidably difficult to carry out.

Let us look at two cases. Almost every adult has tried to find out the "reality" of a fight between two young children, with no witnesses. Lengthy questioning often fails to establish what those facts were. The personal interpretation put on deed and word, gesture and intonation, do remain, and they can be put on paper by the interviewer. He is often helpless, however, in his attempt to grasp the reality. In some senses, the only such reality is the emotional structure which develops in and from the experience. Detailed observation by an unseen, objective, trained observer would add a further dimension, and would yield a more valid reality, than the interview.

A second case is the complexity of conflict and complaint in divorce. For much of the relationship between spouses in conflict, there is usually a deep emotional involvement between the two. For much of this interaction, there are *no* witnesses. For much of the rest, there are only partial, biased, or untrained witnesses. We are not referring to the bias whose roots lie in the possibly neurotic and internal conflicts of the individuals, but to the simple types of distortion or partial perception induced by ego needs in a situation of great strain.

A simple and relatively uninvolved example is "steadiness of work," and "steadiness of child support payments." The wife may report that the husband was not very steady in either, while he claims that he was. It is possible in this case to obtain employment and payment records to prove one assertion or the other. Here, we need only a minor type of outside "observation," or record of it.

Somewhat more complex, however, would be her claim that he nagged and bullied her a great deal. His view may be that she was a slovenly housekeeper, neglectful of the children, a poor manager of household funds, and a not particularly loving wife. Do we have, in his report, "the" truth? Or, rather, do we now need an unseen observer who has observed that marital conflict? If we had the report of his family, or of hers, could we get at the truth? Doubtless, if we had *all* these reports, we could obtain a closer approxi-

---

7. Herbert Hyman *et al.*, *Interviewing in Social Research*, (Chicago: University of Chicago Press, 1954).

mation to validity. Certainly, we could begin to extract the *standards* that were being followed by each circle. In most cases, we would probably begin to get consensus, or some areas of agreement among various respondents. In those cases, interviewing would be successful, but might be inefficient because of (a) the possible losses (i.e., we need the same key people, e.g., father, mother, for each marriage, and many would refuse, crippling the total design); and (b) the time consumption for each divorce case.

For still other cases, the conflicting reports would yield confusion, and we would once more need real observation. The details of living together are so innumerable, their meaning so complex, the corroboration and interpretation so difficult, that even *with* observation one sometimes sighs for a wire recording, plus narcohypnosis of the husband and wife, in order to understand what really happened.

In any event, it seems clear that the lack of observation does prevent a fully adequate evaluation of the reality, but that for most aspects of the data we can rely upon our respondents. For a few, we would like to have the ex-husband's testimony, but this is not a crucial gap. For the conflict in their testimony, if we had that conflict recorded, we need a much less biased witness than the ex-husband.

A Period of "Normalcy." The field work in this study was carried out in the early winter of 1948, and the reader will recognize that this was also part of the postwar adjustment period. Because of the ages of the women involved (20 to 38 years at the time of divorce), the husbands were relatively young, and 46% of them were veterans. About half of these marriages were contracted prior to 1940. The question can be raised, then, as to whether these marriages were not simply "war" marriages, and therefore not to be compared with ordinary ones during a calmer period. Indeed, in an effort to avoid some of the fly-by-night war marriages, we selected only those families in which there were children.

However, for the purposes of family analysis, there has been no period in the last thirty years which was *not* an "unusual" one. There was a first World War, with its strong influences upon marital statistics. There was an important aftermath period, in which family patterns seem to have changed substantially. This occurred both during the post-World War I recession and the succeeding speculative boom. The latter was ended by an intense and prolonged depression, which ended in turn with the boom and war period of the late 1930's and early 1940's. The past years have been a period of war, postwar, and war again. If we wait until there is a so-called stable period, we may have to drop the study of the American family entirely. We have to study divorces and marriages as they occur. If we assert that the *period* in which the study occurred might change the results, we must specify exactly how the adjustment to divorce would be different than in any supposedly stable period. It is, of course, quite possible such a period affects the rate of divorce, because it affects the composition of the marriages contracted at that time. Whether these same factors would affect the pattern of adjustment to divorce must be left for that future halcyon period in which "things are back to normal once more."

"Fly-by-Night" Marriages. The study concentrated upon the adjustment of the divorced *mother* for several reasons. As we noted a moment ago, we wished to avoid as much as possible the transient marriages of the war and postwar period, and it seems at least a fairly safe assumption that most parents once thought their marriages were possibly stable ones. Even if we indulge in some cynicism regarding the motives for having children, it seems safe to suppose that most couples had at some time wanted to continue the marriage, if they were willing to have children.

Why Study Young Mothers? Since we were interested in studying the adjustment to crisis, it seemed useful to concentrate upon the person who feels that crisis most severely. The status of the wife in our generation requires her to bear a series of burdens, when she is divorced, that seem greater than those of the divorced husband.

It is the tradition of American law that custody be given to the wife; in some 95% of our cases custody was granted to the wife, and this proportion is not much lower in other states. This means that she must care for the child and be ultimately responsible for his physical well-being and his expenses. The husband, of course, must pay for the child's support, but in some cases this is her sole support, and the arrangement does not take account of the different emergencies for which she alone must be responsible. The crises when the husband, in an ongoing family, would locate additional sources of money for these expenses will now occur without that added help.

In our society, husband and wife must share the burdens of children, illness, and even (to some degree) of housekeeping. When divorce occurs it will usually be the mother who bears these burdens unremittingly.

The reader will have noted also the age range of these mothers. They are all in the marriageable ages. Indeed, as has been demonstrated by considerable research, the female divorcee in these ages has a far greater chance of ultimate marriage, age for age, than does the single woman. Presumably, the comparison would not be so striking for divorced *mothers,* but we shall show that even mothers are not likely to remain unremarried. In any event, all of them are marriageable, and most of them will ultimately remarry. For female divorcees as a group, this age cohort has some 68 to 95 chances in 100 of ultimate remarriage.[8] Consequently, these women face a double problem of adjustment, readjusting their lives to the dissolution of a marriage, and to the formation of a new one. There are many difficulties and ambiguities in these roles, and we must say that this segment, then, experiences the divorce crisis to a much greater degree than other divorcees, male or female.

Being mothers, these women would have been married longer than the average divorcee in the same age group, and their ties with ex-spouses might be stronger. They would have greater financial problems than the husband, since for any given occupational level the woman usually receives a smaller salary than the man.

---

8. "The Chances of Remarriage for the Widowed and Divorced," *Statistical Bulletin,* 26, No. 5 (New York: Metropolitan Life Insurance Company, 1945), pp. 1-3. These calculations are based on the marriage records for 22 states and Washington, D. C., the remarriage records for New England, and particularly Massachusetts; and the mortality rates, by marital status, of the State of New York, excluding New York City. Glick reports (Paul C. Glick, "First Marriages and Remarriages," *Am. Soc. Rev.,* 14 [1949], p. 730) on the basis of data from the National Office of Vital Statistics, that within 5 years, 75 per cent of *all* divorcees of *all* ages have remarried.

For these reasons, then, we have concentrated on the group which might be expected to face the greatest problems in postdivorce adjustment. We should thereby be able to explore the general problem more adequately, and to pose sharper hypotheses about other divorce segments whose crisis is a lesser one.

The Happily Married and the Conflict Process. Because we are attempting to study the process of *adjustment to* divorce, it would not be useful to create a "control group" of those whose marriages are happy. Since we are trying to learn what happens after the divorce, we have included material on the process of conflict prior to divorce, so as to find out how these factors change the adjustment process. That is, our proper comparison is among different patterns of divorce conflict and divorce adjustment. Finally, we have made many references to research on the nondivorced, so as to identify better the characteristics of the divorced.

Urban Sample and Negro Divorcees. Because the sample was urban, it was possible to contact all of these respondents within a relatively short period of time, and with a minimum expense. However, an equally important justification for using such a population is simply that our nation is becoming more and more urban, and that divorce rates are higher in urban areas.[9] We thus approximate more closely a description of the typical divorce adjustment pattern in this country. Moreover, we guess that the urban divorcee can count on less help from relatives than can the rural divorcee. Thus the adjustment problems would be greater.

Since, further, this is a sample of *all* the divorcees in this category, both Negro and White divorcees are included. This seems not to be true for previous work in the field. The gap is of some importance, since all of the major urban areas have increasingly large concentrations of Negro populations, and because our data on the family pattern of this, as of other ethnic groups, are insufficient.

Moreover, the Negro divorce rate is *higher* than that of the White. We cannot fully analyze this fact now, and it would be particularly difficult to do so since it is our private conviction that a full analysis of this and related facts (such as the extremely low reproduction rate of Negroes in cities, the apparently indigenous development of neighboring and similar practices in urban areas, the urbanization of rural patterns, etc.) suggest a major revision of some of our theorizing about rural-urban patterns.

It does seem clear, however, that the Negro group has so assimilated the usual patterns of family interaction, attitudes, norms, etc., of White society, that they go to the divorce court to solve their difficulties. Just to that extent would we expect the pattern of postdivorce adjustment to be similar to, or the same as, that of Whites. Corroborating evidence will be presented on this point.

Naturally, the economic position of Negro families is different, but we must separate the differences due to economic position from those due to the social patterns of the races. Moreover, the focus is not Negro-White marital

---

9. In 1950, 59% of the U. S. population lived in places of 2,500 inhabitants or more, 29% in cities of 100,000 or more. Table 56, *The Seventeenth Census of the United States: 1950, Population, Volume I,* United States Summary, p. 1-6.

adjustment patterns, but the adjustment of the ex-spouse to her new post-marital situation. As can be seen in the standard literature on the subject, the position of the divorced Negro urban mother in her own social structure may be entirely parallel to that of the White urban divorced mother. In any event, we are calling to the reader's attention the fact that the Negroes do constitute a segment of the divorced population, and that as a consequence they are part of our sample.

Marital Adjustment in Different States. An objection may be raised as to whether the process of adjustment to divorce is different in different states, since the permissible grounds for divorce do vary from one state to another.[10] It does seem reasonable that in states with strict divorce laws the marital conflict between spouses would have to become more intense before a divorce would be attempted. There might then be somewhat more bitterness on both sides, and perhaps a greater crisis. In states with much easier divorce laws the opposite might be the case. This remains, of course, only a hunch until the problem is investigated further. We can at least suggest that Michigan belongs to what may be called the "liberal" group of states, with respect to divorce, near the center of the range between South Carolina and Nevada. It is relatively easy to get a divorce in Michigan, if one is a resident and can assert grounds of adultery, cruelty, desertion, alcoholism, impotency, long separation, or imprisonment for three years. Actually, of course, most divorces are granted upon grounds of cruelty and, as it happens in states with such grounds, cruelty is defined rather liberally. Even in states where *physical* cruelty is the main basis for a divorce suit, judges are usually willing to accept the assertion that the behavior of one spouse affects the health of the other, by inducing psychosomatic illnesses, nervous breakdowns, asthma, etc. Consequently, divorce laws themselves are more stringent than the actual behavior of the divorce court. Spouses from other states will not see any advantage in going to Michigan for divorce. On the other hand, divorce is easy enough in Michigan so that no one need go to another state for divorce, except to avoid publicity.

Summary. In this chapter, we have tried to describe the study upon which the present report is based. We have essentially taken four time groups, which we will compare with one another so as to ascertain how the female divorcee with children meets the problems she sees. We have approximated a random sample, and in Appendix I we analyze our procedure and results in more detail. We seem to have achieved a representative sample of the urban, divorced mothers in the ages 20-38 years at the time of the divorce, resident in the metropolitan area of Detroit. The present chapter has also concerned itself with the apparent gap created by the lack of the ex-husband's testimony, and with the problem of interviewing as a means of finding out about divorce and adjustment. Finally, we have shown why the study selected this segment of the divorced, rather than another; why we were willing to study divorcees in a

---

10. For a brief resumé of the grounds for divorce, as of January 1, 1945, see Meyer F. Nimkoff, *Marriage and the Family* (New York: Houghton Mifflin, 1947), pp. 652-653. However, it omits cruelty as grounds in Michigan. Nearly 80% of Michigan divorces were granted on grounds of cruelty in 1939. See Mabel A. Elliott, "The Scope and Meaning of Divorce," in Howard Becker and Reuben Hill, eds., *Family, Marriage and Parenthood* (New York: Heath, 1948), p. 695.

period of "social change"; why we have also included Negroes; why we have not made a "control group" of the happily married; and have raised the question of differential adjustment in different states.

In the succeeding chapter, we present some of the backgrounds of these divorcees. What kinds of people entered these marriages?

CHAPTER III

SOCIAL BACKGROUNDS
OF THE COUPLE

IN THE SUCCEEDING CHAPTERS we present the social and economic characteristics of both the couple and the marriage, before the divorce occurred. Thereby, we corroborate the findings of previous studies of the American family system, and thus increase their reliability. Reciprocally, we may then place more reliance upon the further conclusions of the present work, which go beyond previous research. Third, we thus obtain a clearer picture of the divorcee in our society and time. Finally, these background characteristics not only structure marital patterns somewhat, but will be later shown to affect postdivorce adjustment as well.

In the present chapter, then, we look at the origins and backgrounds of the couple: rural-urban background, religion, race, education, and age at marriage.

Rural-Urban Backgrounds. Because the largest proportion of our respondents grew up in the city, we would not expect to find much of the "cultural marginality" that might result from the rural person's poor adjustment to city ways. Since the analyses of American sociologists a generation ago, we have not had any new analyses of this supposed impact in our time. Moreover, we would not be prepared to apply it to the problem of *postdivorce* adjustment. We would expect it to be most relevant, if anywhere, for the process of decision to divorce.

A slightly greater percentage of husbands than of wives came from nonurban backgrounds:

RURAL-URBAN BACKGROUND OF HUSBAND AND OF WIFE

	Husband	Wife
Urban	62%	70%
Small Town	26%	22%
Rural	11%	8%
Total	99%	100%

Of course, when we consider wives and husbands as *couples* and group "urban" and "small town" together, the proportion of urban cases increases somewhat:

RURAL-URBAN BACKGROUND OF COUPLE*

	Percent
Both urban	84
One urban	13
Neither urban	3
Total	100

*"Urban" here means both large city and small town.

Ethnic Groups. Like all large American cities, Detroit contains many ethnic groups, and members of these groups are in our sample. On the other hand, the age segment which we have selected does reduce considerably any effect from the conflict which is supposed to be characteristic of recent immigrants, and which might add to the personal disorganization of the divorced respondent. The immigration restrictions of 1922 and 1924 mean that almost any "immigrants" would have had to be immigrants at a very early age in order to appear in our sample. Again, as in the case of our comment on the rural-urban distribution, although American sociology has dealt at great length with immigration and assimilation, we do not have any hypotheses on the impact of these processes on the postdivorce lives of the immigrants. To the extent that we can utilize existing theory, we can only guess that the process of assimilation would lead to some marital disorganization, or might predispose in certain ways to divorce. It gives us no clues to understanding the postdivorce adjustment process.

We do not have systematic data on ethnic distribution in Detroit, but the effect of the "Little Hungary" or other ethnic settlements seems to be much more limited in Detroit than in, say, the New York of a generation ago. There are concentrations of ethnic groups, but these concentrations did not in the 1940's usually exhibit a clear-cut community life. An exception might be made for the Armenians and the Greeks, and, with less assurance, for the Jews. The patterns of ecological distribution show up mainly in food habits. Furthermore, we must remember that by far the largest immigrant group in Detroit is made up of Canadians.

It might be asserted, on the other hand, that in the *second* generation there would be greater evidence of "cultural marginality," with its concomitant disorganization. Again, we have no way of knowing to what extent this would affect the process of postdivorce adjustment, and we have not attempted to isolate it as an independent variable.

Religion. In any large segment of the American population it seems likely that Protestants would appear in the divorce court in a greater proportion than they appear in the general population.[1] If Catholics oppose divorce more strongly, perhaps the postdivorce adjustment of Protestants is different from that of Catholics. We therefore obtained information as to the religious preferences of the divorced wives. The answers are distributed as follows:

---

1. Monahan and Kephart report from their Philadelphia sample that "Catholics account for one-half to two-thirds the number of divorces which one might expect from their proportion in the population." Thomas P. Monahan and William M. Kephart, "Divorce and Desertion by Religious and Mixed Religious Groups," *Am. J. Soc.*, 59 (1954), p. 460. On the other hand (p. 463), Catholics contribute *more* than their share of desertion cases.

RELIGIOUS PREFERENCES OF WIFE

Religion	Percent	Cases
Protestant	58	247
Catholic	32	135
Eastern Orthodox	1	6
Jewish	3	12
Other or Not known	6	25
Totals	100	425

The caseworkers for the Friend of the Court recorded corresponding data from their interviews, and these are incorporated in the divorce court records. The only important discrepancies with our results appear to be a reflection of the differing goals of the respondents in the two interview situations. Of the entire sample, 3.8% admitted "No preference" to us, but gave "Protestant" as their preference to the Friend of the Court investigator; 1.7% of our total sample claimed "No preference" but gave "Catholic" as their preference to the Friend of the Court. The court records were made by investigators who were assigned to judge (among other things) whether or not the home surroundings were proper for the rearing of children, in case the divorce were granted. Consequently, we would expect most respondents to claim *some* church preference. Since our own interviews had no such official consequence, we would expect some respondents to shift, as they did, to the category of "No preference."

We do not recalculate our table in terms of some "Index of Proneness to Divorce by Religion," because there are no adequate figures for religious affiliation in Detroit or in this country. There has never been a U.S. Census question as to religious preference. The sporadic U.S. Census of Religious Bodies uses only the report of the various churches, with no checks on their claims. The last published data for such a Census refer to the year 1936. Consequently, we question the wisdom of calculating a numerical index, with its specious precision.

The Detroit Council of Churches gave this admittedly crude estimate in 1948: Catholics, 40%; Protestants, 55%; Jews, 2.5%. Representatives of the Jewish community claim that the figure for Jews is an underestimate. If these estimates are close to accuracy, we see that Protestants contribute more than their share to the divorce courts, with the Jews contributing almost exactly their share.[2] The Catholics show the least proneness to divorce. The "No preference" group seems somewhat "overrepresented," if we can take seriously the estimate of distribution for the whole city that is given above. We would expect the "No preference" population to be somewhat overrepresented in the divorce courts.[3] However, even this assertion is not unquestioned, since the impact of various types of religious preferences, or intensities of preference, upon marriage has not been ascertained by any reliable field studies in this country. Nevertheless, even if all sects are beginning to be similar in their

---

2. Monahan and Kephart, *ibid.*, p. 460, report the same result.

3. In regard to this point see Harvey J. Locke, *Predicting Adjustment in Marriage: A Comparison of a Divorced and a Happily Married Group* (New York: Henry Holt & Co., 1951), p. 221: ". . . many happily married couples are highly religious as contrasted with the divorced group. Three factors appear to be involved: (1) Religion is an indication of conventional and conforming behavior. (2) It is significant that the friends of this couple were religious

divorce behavior, we would still expect the Catholics for some time to have a somewhat lower divorce rate than others.

A "scientifically selected" area sample survey of the Detroit area was done through the Survey Research Center of the University of Michigan in 1952. Referring to only the female adults, and only to the two religious groups of Protestants and Catholics, they found Protestants to be 62% of the total, Catholics to be 38% of the total. Our figures for 1948 were: Protestant divorcees, 65%, Catholics, 35%. Thus, our results are in close accord, suggesting nevertheless a slightly greater divorce rate among Protestants.[4] As can be seen, however, the contribution of Catholics to the total divorced population is *not* much less than their proportion of the total population.

The religion of the couple, as distinguished from that of the divorced wife only, has a more complex distribution, but some part of its meaning seems fairly clear.

RELIGION OF COUPLE

Same	Percent	Cases
Protestant	39.5	168
Catholic	18.4	78
Jewish	2.1	9
Eastern Orthodox	.5	2
No preference	2.8	12
Subtotal	63.3	269
Different		
Protestant/Catholic	11.5	49
Protestant/No preference	14.1	60
Catholic/No preference	8.5	36
Other combinations	2.6	11
Subtotal	36.7	156
Total	100.0	425

Our information almost always comes from the respondent, for the husband was not interviewed. Our "No preference" category was probably increased substantially, then, by cases in which the wife simply did not know her husband's preference, but said that he had no preference. On the other hand, if the wife really did not know the religious preference of her husband, then that preference could not have been very strong. Consequently, little injustice is done to the husband's religious choice by putting it into the category "No preference." Since "Not known" or "No preference," is asserted for 23.1% of the husbands, a substantial proportion of our couples consists of a wife with a religious preference, and a husband with none. The data also document to some extent the often asserted nonreligiousness of the American male.

---

and that their religion is opposed to divorce. Consequently, the pressure and support of a circle of religious friends with their expectations that families will stay together, determined, in part, the unity of this family. (3) In many of these families in which religion is significant, the members engaged in praying together and reading the Bible together, and these serve as common activities, which psychologically unite the husband and wife. One of the functions of religion in these homes is to cause the couple to reinforce each other religiously and thereby create conforming attitudes with reference to the maintenance of the family."

4. *Some Social and Economic Characteristics of the Detroit Area Population: 1952* (Ann Arbor: 1953), p. 50. A similarly small difference is reported in Howard Bell, *Youth Tell Their Story* (Washington, D. C.: American Council on Education, 1938), p. 21: 6.8% of 13,500 youths were from Protestant broken homes, 6.4% from Catholic.

Because of differing procedures and categories, we cannot compare adequately our data with those of Bell, Weeks, and Landis, with respect to the importance of mixed religion for marital stability.[5] However, their data suggest, as do ours and those of Monahan and Kephart, that the mixed Protestant-Catholic marriage is more prone to divorce than that in which both spouses have the same religion. Lacking adequate distributions by religion for the "ever married," we cannot demonstrate this notion, but later on we shall offer more complete data on this point.

Church Attendance. Nevertheless, religion has an ambiguous status as an independent variable in contemporary social analysis, because we do not have systematic data concerning its impact. Numerous essayists of the day have asserted that the differences between religions continue to lessen in our generation. In this study we usually found only small differences in the behavior of different religious segments. On the other hand, differences in church *attendance* might well be correlated with other differences in behavior, since it might indicate some differences in exposure to the pressure of religious groups. We therefore attempted to find out about the church attendance of our respondents. It must be kept in mind, however, that we were then asking about behavior at the time of the interview. A question as to religious *preference* has, on the other hand, a more ambiguous time reference, and in some cases it tells us no more than which church it was that our respondent *once* considered her own. The question as to church attendance, then, has a more specific time reference and a more precise meaning, although it is not a genuine "background" item.

CHURCH ATTENDANCE OF RESPONDENTS
(Time of Interview)

	Catholics %	Protestants %	Other or None %	Totals %
Weekly	49	26	12	32
Occasionally	31	48	33	41
Never	20	27	56	28
Total	100(135)	101(247)	101(43)	101(425)

We are now able to compare the church attendance of our female divorcees with that of the general Detroit population. An area sample was obtained by the Survey Research Center in 1952, which recorded church attendance for the female adult population. Almost exactly corresponding to our apparent relationship, Catholics were about twice as likely as Protestants to attend church weekly, or to attend 1-2 times monthly. On the other hand, in conformity with our expectations, a higher percentage of *both* Protestants and Catholics in the Survey Research Center sample attended church frequently: 77% of their female adult Catholics claimed to attend weekly, against 49% of our Catholic *divorcees;* 33% of their Protestant females, as against 26% of our Protestant *divorcees.* The categories of lesser frequency do not show such great differences.[6]

5. Bell, *op. cit.*, pp. 21, 193-194; H. Ashley Weeks, "Differential Divorce Rates by Occupation," *Social Forces* 21 (1943), 334-337; Judson T. Landis, "Marriages of Mixed and Non-Mixed Religious Faith," *Am. Soc. Rev.* 14 (1939), 401-407. Also, Monahan and Kephart, *op. cit.* pp. 457 ff. Also, G. J. Schnepp, *Leakage from a Catholic Parish* (Washington, D. C.: Catholic University, 1942), pp. 142, 143, *et passim.*

6. *Some Social and Economic Characteristics of the Detroit Area Population: 1952* (Ann Arbor: University of Michigan Press, 1953), Table V-20, p. 50.

We can not of course know whether our Catholics are divorced *because* they did not usually attend church as frequently as other Catholics, or whether they do not usually attend frequently because they have been divorced. The same question might be raised for the Protestants. We are inclined to believe that both relationships exist. The divorcee may feel less welcome at church, but, on the other hand, those who do attend church frequently, whether Catholic or Protestant, are under much stronger pressure to avoid divorce as a solution to marital conflict. We know that the doctrinal conflict, both within the Catholic respondent herself and between the respondent and the priest, is of some importance, since it was mentioned spontaneously by many of our Catholic divorcees.

Nevertheless, it is quite clear that Catholic divorcees do attend church *after divorce,* and with greater frequency than do our Protestant divorcees or respondents falling into the "Other or none" categories. We see also that the differences are systematic. Those who are Catholic are *least* represented in the "Never attend" category, while the "Other or none" religious groups (mostly the "No preference" group) are *most* represented in the "Never attend" group. Correspondingly, we find the Protestants and the "Occasionally attend" group most closely associated. We will later show how important church attendance is for postdivorce adjustment.

Race. We have already shown why the Negro divorcee is included in our sample. Of the entire sample, 81% were White, and 19% were Negro. The Negro population of Detroit in December, 1948, was estimated to be 15% of the total population.[7] It seems likely, then, that Negroes are overrepresented in the divorce population of Detroit, as they are in the national divorced population generally. We have asserted elsewhere that Negroes are more prone to divorce than are Whites, and in a later chapter we shall present more of the essential facts. They may be summarized as follows:

(1) To the extent that economic factors create an inverse relationship between income-occupation and divorce proneness, we would expect the Negro group to exhibit a higher divorce rate: Negroes in the lower economic and occupational strata will approximate the divorce behavior of those strata, while in point of fact Negroes are overrepresented in the lower strata.

(2) We would, however, expect the Negro-White differential to show considerable variation (a) over the decades, and (b) by urban-rural origins. These variations would result in part from variations in procedures for keeping divorce records, particularly in the rural South. In part they are genuine indices of culture change on the part of Negroes as they gradually approximate more closely the marital patterns of Whites (as to *both* marriage *and* divorce). Thus, the Negro-White differentials have changed. Even if the data had been accurately recorded, Negroes would have been nationally *under*-represented in the divorce courts (but not the Census) of, say, the 1890's. Similarly, we would expect Negroes to continue to be underrepresented in the

---

7. Estimate obtained from Richard Marks, Research Director of the Detroit Interracial Commission. Because the influx of Negroes since 1940 has been heavy, the Census data are not adequate. Census data are somewhat difficult to analyze in any event, since metropolitan Detroit encloses several municipalities. Part of the urban spread includes essentially urban sections tabulated under Wayne County only. The Detroit Area Survey gives 11% for 1952; *op. cit.,* p. 40,

rural divorce courts (North and South) until a somewhat *later* period than in urban courts. Since Negroes have been preponderantly from the South, and rural, and since the recording attitudes of Whites have been generally and until recently that a Negro divorce need not always be made a legal matter, we would expect (a) regional, (b) rural-urban, and (c) secular time trends to be closely associated. Of course, the period when the *major increase* in Negro divorce rates occurred might also be different among urban Northern Negroes as contrasted with urban Southern Negroes. That is, the urban Negro-White divorce rate differentials may have changed at different times in the South and North.

(3) We also expect to find that the Negro-White *differential* varies with the depression cycle. Divorce rates generally increase during prosperity and decrease during depression. Doubtless this fact is one of the sources for the general but erroneous belief that the lower strata and the Negroes have lower divorce rates than do the upper strata and the Whites. Now, the *economic position* of the Negro has exhibited a secular upward movement relative to that of the White, during the past two generations. However, it has *also* shown violent ups-and-downs during prosperity, war booms, and depressions, *relative to that of the White*. Consequently, we would expect the Negro-White differential to change, too, even though we would not predict how this ratio will shift (if at all) during future economic cycles.

The data on these points seem fairly conclusive, except for assertion No. 3. The data from the Decennial Censuses, the Sample Surveys, Glick's Census study on remarriage, and my own study, are in substantial agreement on these points, and it seems quite clear that at the present time the Negro divorce rate is higher than the White in (a) urban, (b) rural-nonfarm, and (c) rural-farm categories for the nation as a whole. This debate has, of course, a long history, but the facts for the contemporary situation seem to offer no possibility of further debate. The basic facts are clear, and we require only further specifications as to the conditions which create the rate differentials. We shall present detailed data in a later chapter.

Education. The education of husband and wife is presented in the following table:

EDUCATION OF HUSBANDS AND OF WIVES

	Husbands %	Wives %
College:		
completed	3.5	1.9
some	9.4	6.8
High school:		
completed	20.9	30.2
some	38.4	46.9
Grammar:		
completed	13.2	9.2
5-7 years	10.4	4.2
1-4 years	1.2	0.7
No formal schooling	1.4	0.2
Unknown	1.7	
N = 425	100.1%	100.1%

Although a slightly higher proportion of men than of women has had at least some college education, a higher proportion of men than of women also falls at the other extreme, in the category "No high school." In general, there is a concentration of cases in the high school and lesser educational categories. We shall in Chapter IV take account of the marriages between spouses of lesser or greater education. We can not compare our data with the Detroit "ever married" for specific educational achievement, because we have been unable to uncover such figures. The Detroit Area Study for 1952 gives educational breakdowns, but not by age categories.[8] Since *both* education and divorce proneness vary by age, a comparison without age breakdowns is useless. In a later chapter, we present national comparisons.

Age. The median age of the woman at the time of marriage was 19.4 years, while the mean was 19.5 years. We do not have comparable figures for the husband. The age distribution for the wives at marriage is given in the following table:

AGE AT MARRIAGE

Age Group	Percent
Under 15 years	2
15-19	57
20-24	34
25-29	6
Over 30	1
N = 425	100%

It is clear that the average age at marriage for our divorced group is substantially younger than that of the "married once only" segment of the population. Of our sample, 59% fall into the age bracket "less than 20 years."[9] A Census Bureau Sample Survey taken in April, 1948, found that 77.8% of all women who were married *once* only had married at ages under 25 years.[10] Our sample has 93% in this category. That Survey included persons of previous generations as well. We would suppose that any random sample of the divorced urban population would contain a similarly high proportion of those who were married at very early ages. On the other hand, when we compare our divorcees with women who married in 1953, the difference is small: our divorcees were younger: 19.4 as against 20.4 years for first marriages of women in the U. S. registration area.[11]

The mean age of the woman at the time of divorce was 28.2 years, while the median age was 28.4 years. Again, it is instructive to compare these with

8. *Some Social and Economic Characteristics of the Detroit Area Population: 1952* (Ann Arbor: University of Michigan, 1953).

9. Burgess and Cottrell, *op. cit.,* p. 388, found that those who marry *very* young have less chance of high marital adjustment scores, although in general age at marriage was not an important predictive factor. Tarver, however, shows that for Wisconsin the under-20-year group who divorce have marriages that last as long as those of the divorced who married at ages over 20 years. See J. D. Tarver, "Age at Marriage and Duration of Marriages of Divorced Couples," *Soc. and Soc. Research,* 36 (1951), 102-106.

10. *Current Population Reports—Population Characteristics,* Series P-20, No. 23, 1949, p. 21. The total sample was 25,000. The married once only category was calculated to be approximately 31 million females.

11. Registration area was 18 states. *Vital Statistics-Special Reports, National Summaries, Marriages,* 1953. Vol. 42, No. 5, p. 92. National Office of Vital Statistics, Washington, D. C., 1954.

the Sample Survey data, showing that the median age at the time of divorce for all males was 35.9 years, while that for all females was 32.2 years. However, the distribution shows clearly that the reason for our lower figures lies in the fact that we have imposed an upper age cut-off of 38 years on our sample. When we recalculate their median age of the female at the time of divorce, using age limits as close to ours as possible, we find their median age to be 28.9, almost exactly our figure. We would expect the length of marriage for our couples to be slightly longer, on the other hand, since all of ours have children, and marriages with children do last longer.

With these brief comments on the background characteristics of the couple, we now turn to a more complex set of relationships, the broad socio-economic aspects of divorce in our society, and the social meaning of those aspects. Following Chapter IV, we shall turn to further social and economic factors in the marriage, before analyzing the divorce conflict itself.

SOCIOECONOMIC FACTORS
AND DIVORCE

IN THIS CHAPTER we explore the general relationship between socioeconomic rank and marital stability in the United States. These analyses should help us to understand certain elements in American marriage beyond those of the personal interaction between the spouses and help us see who is involved in postdivorce adjustment.

Our purpose is broader than simple description. We seek to place our economic facts in a sociostructural framework where possible, and to look for their *social meaning*. At many later points, following this aim, we shall show that the impact of an apparently "pure" economic factor is mediated and interpreted by its social dimensions and meanings.

At our contemporary development of social science, we are often forced to use economic factors directly, simply because we are not yet able to locate the mechanisms and processes by which the economic creates its sociological effects. Consequently, we cannot neglect certain economic elements, even when we are not yet capable of isolating their sociological meaning. Thus, we can at at least point to the *direction of effect* created by certain economic items, on types of both marriages and divorces, and on the larger kinship structure of this society.

In sociological analysis, we ordinarily move one step beyond the use of an apparently economic factor, such as occupation or income, by using the framework of stratification. Unfortunately, the present-day development of that framework has not yielded the theoretical guides we continue to expect. Partly, this failure is due to a preoccupation with the *indices* of class to be used, such as education, occupation, or income. The failure is also traceable to a lack of serious theoretical analysis of stratification. Too often, the researcher may be satisfied when he finds that most phenomena he looks into *are* differentiated by class strata, and thus fails to ask *why* even food tastes are class-stratified. As a consequence, we do not possess, for *sociological* phenomena, an adequate description of the *styles of life* that are followed in different strata.

Now, the corollary is that we often use a simple *class index,* such as occupation, in order to organize our observations of family behavior, because we lack unambiguous indices of stratification that are more fruitful for sociological theory. Unambiguous indices of life styles would, for example, be closer in the cause-effect chain to family patterns than is occupation.

However, we must at present use the tools at hand. Since these are neither empirically refined nor theoretically sophisticated, the results are not so sharp as we desire. Nevertheless, we can take several steps forward. In the present chapter, an important step is to recognize fully that there is a rough *inverse* correlation between class position and rate of divorce. We emphasize that this is not a matter of simple economic causation, but is the resultant of the family patterns at different strata. Moreover, we know that even the correlation is not simple. As we move toward the lower strata, the divorce rate *increases,* but the relationship is different for different *indices* of class: occupational rank, income, education. Nevertheless, the general increase is observable. Although this conclusion has not emerged from every study of marital conflict and divorce, it *has* emerged from every study in which there is a *fair approximation to a representative sample.* Since this fact has not been accepted generally, we recapitulate the relevant data in the succeeding analysis.

Previous Studies of Economic Position and Divorce. We note, to begin with, that we were not the first to report this important fact, although we did learn it independently. Our first discovery of this inverse correlation occurred in the spring of 1948 in a pretest study of postdivorce adjustment. We had failed to see it prior to that time because we had accepted Bossard's own interpretation of his 1934 data, based on the 1930 Census. This ecological study placed 5644 divorced Philadelphia women in 404 census tracts, following the data of that Census.[1] It demonstrated clearly the relationship between low income and a high divorce rate. High mobility, dense population, and anonymity characterize the tracts with high divorce rates, and it is almost unnecessary to point out that these are also areas of low income. Bossard interpreted these facts of *location* as due to *mobility.* A common hypothesis of that period was that the divorcee, a kind of social failure, simply "drifted" into such areas. Of course, the Census data furnished no data on the movement of divorcees, and now we know that such a hypothesis is unnecessary. It is true that after divorce some divorcees do move into low income areas, as they do to other areas of similar or even higher income, but the net direction of movement has not, to my knowledge, been calculated by anyone. The residence and movement data from my own study are not good enough to permit such an analysis, but a reading of these data suggest that the lower income groups *are* most mobile, (as they are generally in our society) but they simply move to *other* low income areas. The decline of income for most divorcees is not so great as to cause more than a low net mobility to low income areas.

Schroeder's study shows similar results.[2] Burgess refers to Schroeder's sample as "predominantly of low economic, low educational, and low social

---

1. J. H. S. Bossard, "Spatial Distribution of Divorced Women," *Am. J. Soc.,* 40 (1935), 503-507.

2. Clarence W. Schroeder, *Divorce in a City of 100,000 Population* (Peoria: Bradley Polytechnic Institute Library, 1939).

status." Since the study was a Ph.D. dissertation at the University of Chicago, we assume that Burgess is correct, as far as the *field interview* sample is concerned. The study does not contain enough information to permit a test of Burgess' conclusion, but the list of occupations represented is consistent with his judgment.[3]

Fortunately, however, an apparently satisfactory sample of 1163 cases was obtained from the complete divorce records of Peoria for the period March, 1930 to March, 1934, and Schroeder placed these cases in their respective enumeration districts. Then, using an ecological technique, he related divorce to various social variables such as average rent, annual income, home ownership, delinquency, etc. He traced his cases by the use of the City Directory, and thus any bias from losses would have been in the direction of *over*representing the upper strata. Correspondingly, more losses would have occurred in the lower strata where there is more anonymous mobility. Without attempting to present details, we note that the following correlations were found.[4]

FACTORS CORRELATED WITH DIVORCE

	Degree of Correlation
Juvenile delinquency	.69
Relief cases	.61
Average rent	−.29
Average annual income	−.32
Percentage home ownership	−.53

Similarly, he comments (p. 63) with reference to two districts with *low* divorce rates, "In practically all the measurable factors they produce an opposite picture from those with high rates."[5]

Weeks' study obtained questionnaires from almost the complete secondary school population of Spokane, Washington. The 5490 students in the sample, from both public and parochial schools, answered questions relating to occupation of father, religion, etc., and these items were used to compute the number of divorces per 100 families in each sub-stratum.[6] Some error is always to be expected with reference to both occupation and divorce when children answer, but this error should not be great. The relationship of divorce to occupation (of male) follows:

---

3. Ernest W. Burgess, "Predictive Methods and Family Stability," *Annals*, 272 (1950), 49. Schroeder, *op. cit.*, pp. 83-84.

4. *Ibid.*, pp. 50-51. He also finds a correlation with "percentage male population," and the latter is an index of the "deteriorated neighborhood."

5. One apparent exception to this conclusion is found in his partial correlations in which the relationship between divorce and relief is fairly low (.06, cited on p. 56) when *delinquency* is held constant. However, for all the other factors held constant, the relationship remains high. It is difficult to know whether partial correlations are meaningful for certain of the factors in this total complex. That is, they may not actually be independent. In any event, since delinquency and divorce are also in close association, one would not expect striking further gradations of association between divorce and relief. Certainly delinquency does not cause either, as might be inferred from such a curious statistical test.

6. H. Ashley Weeks, "Differential Divorce Rates by Occupations," *Social Forces*, 21 (1943), 334-337. On the other hand, the lower stratum children are *under*represented here, since a high proportion drops out before high school. Thus the actual proneness to divorce is higher at the lower levels than Weeks' figures show.

NUMBER OF DIVORCES PER 100 FAMILIES, BY OCCUPATION

Professional	6.8
Proprietary	8.4
Clerical	10.4
Skilled	11.6
Semi-skilled	13.4
Unskilled	7.3

Glick's study used data from the sample surveys made by the Census Bureau, and is a comparison of the "remarried" with the "married, but never remarried."[7] Most of the remarried are also "ever divorced." The remainder are the widowed or widowered. A similar pattern is shown, although a detailed cross-tabulation by occupation is not given: The remarried fall into somewhat lower strata than those who stayed married.

We have made independent calculations from the Sample Surveys, with a still more detailed demonstration of this thesis. These Surveys use a random, national sample of about 25,000, and the "divorced" category will ordinarily be no more than 400 (about 2%). However, the results are consistent from one Survey to another. For April, 1949, we calculated an index of "Proneness to Divorce," using the same lumping procedure because the tables are so arranged. This index expresses the relationship between the *proportion* or percentage of "Other Marital Status" (than single or married) in any given occupational category, to the proportion of "Married, Wife Present" in that same category. That is, the index expresses the relationship,

$$\frac{\% \text{ OMS}}{\% \text{ MWP}}$$

The major urban occupational groupings showed the following indices of "Proneness to Divorce" for April, 1949:[8]

Professional, semi-professional	67.7
Proprietors, managers, officials	68.6
Clerical, sales	71.8
Craftsmen, foremen	86.6
Operatives (semi-skilled)	94.5
Service workers	254.7
Laborers (except farm and mine)	180.3

Calculations from the data for 1948 *(Current Population Reports, Population Characteristics,* Series P-20, No. 23, March 4, 1949, p. 17; and Series P-50, No. 11, Table 4) yield similar results. The rankings calculated from the 1940 data differ from the above table only in that "Professional" and "Proprietary" shift places (Series P-50, No. 22, Table 5). The data, therefore, give us a consistent picture.

---

7. Paul C. Glick, "First Marriages and Remarriages," *Am. Soc. Rev.,* 14 (1949), 726-734.

8. As the reader will see, the index is a way of stating whether the number of broken homes in any given group is as much as, or more than, expected, in view of the proportion which that group is of the total population which *could* divorce (i.e., the married). For the data from which these calculations were made: *Current Population Reports, Labor Force,* Series P-50, No. 22, April 19, 1950, Table 5.

Our basic occupational distribution was as follows:

OCCUPATIONAL DISTRIBUTION, DIVORCED HUSBANDS

	Percent	*Cases*
Unskilled	8.2	35
Semi-skilled	40.5	172
Skilled	18.6	79
Agriculture	1.9	8
Service:		
protective	4.7	20
other	3.5	15
Clerical and sales	10.6	45
Proprietary	3.1	13
Professional	7.3	31
Managerial	0.2	1
Other (unemployed, unknown, etc.)	1.4	6
Total	100.0	425

Although the concentration of the divorced in the lower categories is evident, we calculated again the "proneness to divorce" indices for these categories. These were:

INDEX OF PRONENESS TO DIVORCE, BY OCCUPATION

Professional and Proprietary	67.7
Clerical, Sales, Service	83.2
Skilled, foremen	74.1
Semi-skilled, operatives	126.1
Unskilled	179.7

The indices were calculated as in the case of the Sample Surveys, except for these differences: (1) Our sample contained no widowed, and were "ever divorced," rather than "still divorced." These differences of definition are of some importance. (2) The divorces were related to all males in the labor force, rather than married males. The latter would have been preferable. Thus, the index was:[9]

$$\frac{\% \text{ divorced husbands in any given occupational group (my sample)}}{\% \text{ male in that category, Metropolitan Detroit}}$$

Hollingshead has focused his attention on "marital instability," i.e., including desertion, separation, divorce, and marital conflict, and suggests that the greater instability is found in the "working" and lower classes (presumably, upper-lower and lower-lower), with the lower-upper ("the fast set") coming next in order.[10]

Kephart also obtained an inverse correlation, in accord with the above results.[11] His study was based on a 4% random sample of Philadelphia di-

---

9. The data for Detroit were obtained from *Current Population Reports, Labor Force*, "Labor Force Characteristics of the Detroit, Michigan Metropolitan District, April, 1947," Series P-51, No. 19, July 28, 1947, Table 3.

10. August B. Hollingshead, "Class Differences and Family Stability," *Annals*, 272 (1950), 39-46. Data are not given for the design of these aspects of his larger study, but he assures me privately that these will be forthcoming in later publications.

11. William M. Kephart, "Divorce—A Philadelphia Project," paper read at meeting of the Eastern Sociological Society, New Haven, March 21, 1951. See also his, "Desertion and Divorce in Philadelphia" (with Thomas P. Monahan), *Am. Soc. Rev.*, 17 (1952), 710-727. Also: Monahan, "Divorce by Occupational Level," Eastern Sociological Society, April 2, 1955. Monahan's data are from Iowa.

vorces granted between 1937-1950, classified by occupational categories. In terms of proneness to divorce, the ranking was as follows, in *decreasing* order: (1) Labor-Service, (2) Semi-skilled; (3) Skilled; (4) Clerical; (5) Professional-Proprietary.

As is seen, there are some differences of ranking. These seem to be due to the following factors: (a) Differences in occupational classification, or grouping of occupations. For example, "unskilled" is a peculiarly unstable category, and "service" may include factory guards (who are lower class) with hairdressers (who may be lower-middle class in culture). (b) Differences in definition of who is to be considered "divorced." As we have noted, we may use "Other Marital Status" (Glick), "Ever Divorced" (Goode, Kephart), or "Now Divorced" (Census, Weeks).

Finally, (c) whether there are Negroes in the sample will be of great importance. A sample from a city in which the Negro population is *low* will shift the ranking of the "Laborer" group, since the urban Negro divorce rate is higher than that of the White. At the risk of introducing an extraneous line of argument, it seems useful to present the data which appear to demonstrate this conclusion, so contrary to common belief.

Negro Divorce Rate. If we are correct in asserting a higher divorce rate for Negroes, then the slightly different position of the unskilled in various tables of "proneness to divorce" seems understandable. Since a much higher proportion of Negroes than of Whites is to be found there, wherever there is a high proportion of Negroes in the total urban population, the unskilled may well be more prone to divorce than the semi-skilled.

However, this proposition has implications for our understanding of stratification, and for the cultural differences between our two major racial groups. Moreover, after we published our assertion of this fact, it has been called into question, and behind both assertion and counter-assertion there is a long history. We shall not review this history.[12] Leaving aside the work of Wright and Willcox, Groves and Ogburn, and T. Earl Sullenger, we note that Kephart and Monahan recently commented (in answer to our previous statement) that

"Not much is known, factually, about the relationship between the white and nonwhite divorce rates . . ."[13]

They go on to quote from the February, 1948, *Current Population Reports* to the effect that the proportion of divorced persons among the non-Whites does not differ significantly from that among the Whites, and to report that their own Philadelphia data show no overrepresentation of non-Whites among the divorced.[14] As we shall show in a moment, in the same issue of these *Reports* from which they quote there are data which contradict that interpretation. As for the Philadelphia data, there can be no question about the result. We believe that it is caused by the *time periods* included, for during

---

12. See Walter F. Willcox, *The Divorce Problem (1891)*, cited below, and the summary in J. P. Lichtenberger, *Divorce* (New York: McGraw-Hill, 1931), pp. 123-127.

13. William M. Kephart and Thomas P. Monahan, "Desertion and Divorce in Philadelphia," *Am. Soc. Rev.*, 17 (1952), 724.

14. *Ibid.*, p. 725.

much of that period in the United States the divorce rate of the non-Whites *was* very probably *lower* than that of Whites. Apparently, the effect of the depression was to change for a period the relationship between the divorce rates of Whites and Negroes. Doubtless, we shall in the future be able to specify with much greater precision the regional, urban-rural, and socioeconomic conditions under which one or the other of these two population segments has had the greater divorce rate. Moreover, over time it is reasonable to suppose that the *differentials between White and Negro will disappear.* For the moment, we are only concerned with the general relationship between the two rates. Let us look at the data.

In the succeeding table, the proportion of the total population and of each of the two sub-segments, White and non-White (of whom over 90% are Negro) who claimed the marital status of "divorced" is presented:

PERCENT DIVORCED, BY COLOR: 1890 TO 1950[15]

	1890	1900	1910	1920	1930	1940	1950
Color:							
White	0.29	0.37	0.51	0.67	1.2	1.5	2.2
Non-White	0.36	0.62	0.85	1.02	1.8	1.4	2.3
Difference between White and Non-White	0.07	0.25	0.34	0.35	0.6	−0.1	0.1
Total	0.30	0.40	0.55	0.71	1.2	1.5	2.2

It is clear that except for 1940 (a postdepression year) the percent of Negroes divorced is consistently higher than that for Whites.

Now, there are factors which might invalidate these data. First, the Census data only report the marital status at the time of the census. These are the "still divorced," and not the ever divorced. Many who were divorced in the previous decade have remarried by the time of the census. Thus, if the Whites remarry more rapidly than the Negroes, then their representation among the "still divorced" would be lower by the time of the census. Available evidence presented by Glick does not bear out my contention, but only because he has failed to see that his result could have occurred because of a higher Negro divorce rate. For 1910 and 1940 he suggests that the percent of remarried White women was approximately three and two times that of remarried non-White women.[16] My data suggest the remarriage rate is about the same. There-- fore, it is unlikely that this factor invalidates our general conclusion.

Secondly, prior to 1940, there was no Census category for those married but not living together. These were lumped with all who claimed to be still

15. The data in the table are adapted from the figures given in the following: Table 4, "Marital Condition of the Population 15 Years Old and Over by Sex, Color, and Nativity for the United States: 1890 to 1930" in Chapter 11 ("Marital Condition") of *The Fifteenth Census of the United States: 1930, Population, Volume II, General Report, Statistics by Subjects.* The figures were arrived at by dividing the number in the marital status of "divorced" by the relevant total population, age 15 and over. Table 6, "Marital Status of the Population 15 Years Old and Over by Age, Color, and Sex for the United States Urban and Rural: 1940 and 1930," in *Part 1, United States Summary, Population, Volume IV, Characteristics by Age, Sixteenth Census of the United States: 1940.* See also footnote 20.

16. Paul C. Glick, "First Marriages and Remarriages," *Am. Soc. Rev.,* 14 (1949), 728-9, 733.

married. The results of these procedures are complex. Possibly, many who might have once claimed to be "divorced" admitted in 1940 that they were really married but not living with their spouses. On the other hand, many who were actually divorced and obviously living with no one were thus given the opportunity to claim that they were still married, but only separated from their spouses.

More fundamentally, all these reports are based on the statements given to the Census interviewer, who has no way of testing their accuracy. On a commonsense level, it is doubtful that in the 1890's the Negroes were sufficiently used to the White courts to resort to them more frequently than the Whites. We assume, with no possibility of test, that many Negroes claimed to be divorced when actually (a) they had never even been married; or (b) if married, they certainly had not got a legal divorce. On the other hand, if they claimed to be divorced (even if not legally) we have a fair index of the stability of the union. Consequently, if a higher proportion among Negroes than among Whites claimed to be divorced, we have little reason to believe that their marital stability was not lower.

Finally, there seems equally little doubt that Negroes are increasingly resorting to the courts for divorce action. Kephart and Monahan report this in Philadelphia, and even cite their own data (an upswing in the divorce ratio for the late 1940's) as suggestive evidence. Willcox, however, had suggested an upswing in the 1890's.[17] We believe that their "upswing" is merely a return after the depression years to the normally higher Negro divorce rate. In the future, as a higher proportion of Negro marital instability reaches the courts, the apparent divorce rate of Negroes ought to increase relative to that of Whites. But—to complicate the picture—further, as they take on such a "White" cultural pattern, as using the courts, the *differentials* ought to *decrease*. And, as we show in our study, there are few differentials in postdivorce adjustmental patterns between these two segments.

With these substantial reservations regarding the adequacy of the available data, we may ask whether there are differences by sex or urban-rural residence, which need to be considered. In the succeeding tables, we present the available data, using the same procedure as in our previous table.

PERCENT DIVORCED, BY COLOR AND SEX: 1890 TO 1940[18]

	1890	1900	1910	1920	1930	1940
Sex — Male						
White	0.24	0.32	0.46	0.62	1.1	1.3
Non-White	0.24	0.41	0.64	0.77	1.4	1.0
Total	0.24	0.33	0.48	0.64	1.1	1.3
Sex — Female						
White	0.35	0.43	0.56	0.72	1.3	1.7
Non-White	0.49	0.83	1.1	1.3	2.1	1.7
Total	0.37	0.48	0.62	0.78	1.3	1.7

17. Kephart and Monahan, *op. cit.*, p. 725; Walter F. Willcox, *The Divorce Problem* (Ph.D. thesis, Columbia University, 1891), pp. 21-32.

18. Fifteenth Census, *loc. cit.*, and Sixteenth Census, *loc. cit.*

PERCENT DIVORCED, BY COLOR AND RESIDENCE: 1930 AND 1940[18]

	1930	1940
Residence — Urban		
White	1.4	1.78
Non-White	2.2	1.75
Total	1.5	1.8
Residence — Rural — Non-Farm		
White	1.1	1.30
Non-White	1.9	1.39
Total	1.2	1.3
Residence — Rural — Farm		
White	0.59	0.71
Non-White	1.2	0.74
Total	0.68	0.72

As is seen, these data do not contradict our previous assertions, and merely specify the variation in the Negro-White ratio.

In turning to more recent data in order to see in particular whether or not the apparent reversal in relative positions in 1940 is maintained, we must be disappointed. The differences in data from the sample surveys contained in the *Current Population Reports* are not significant at the 95% level,[19] though once more the Negroes show up in higher proportion.

However, we now have data from the 1950 Census, and can thus calculate ratios for the censuses 1890-1950. Since there appear to be no very interesting sex differences, we present only the ratio between the proportion of Non-Whites divorced, and the proportion of the total population divorced. In other words, we are stating whether the given category (White or Non-White) has more than its population share of the divorced. If the ratio is 100, then both segments produce as large a proportion of the divorced as they form of the entire population. For 1950, we have a more exact comparison, since we can compare the divorced in a given stratum or segment with those in that stratum who are married *and* living with their spouse.[20]

RATIOS OF PERCENT NONWHITE DIVORCED TO PERCENT WHITE DIVORCED, 1890-1950

	1890	1900	1910	1920	1930	1940	1950[20a]
Ratios:	1.24	1.95	1.67	1.52	1.50	0.95	1.05

It therefore appears that 1940 represents a deviation from an otherwise constant pattern: proportionately there are more Negro divorcees than White. It is fairly clear, then, that in all likelihood the Negro divorce rate is higher

---

19. And thus the *Current Population Reports* (p. 3) cited by Kephart and Monahan is *technically* correct. The differences exist, but the data are not statistically reliable. *Current Population Reports, Population Characteristics*, Series P-20, No. 10, Feb. 6, 1948, pp. 14-15; *ibid.*, Series P-20, No. 38, April 29, 1952.

20. Data from the 1950 Census are calculated from: *United States Census of Population, 1950. Vol. IV. Special Reports. Marital Status* (Washington: U. S. Bureau of the Census), Part 2, Ch. D, Table 5, pp. 41-43.

20a. If we use a more exact comparison, married *and* living with spouse, the ratio in 1950 is still higher: 1.25.

than the White. Consequently, where the proportion of Negroes is high in any divorce sample, we shall expect the divorce rate of the unskilled to be higher than where the proportion of Negroes is low (as in Weeks' Spokane study). In our own data, as we have already noted, Negroes make up 19% of our sample, but only 15% of the Detroit population.

Let us now continue with our analysis of stratification and divorce rates.

A Contrary Study. One study has been cited innumerable times, usually with the interpretation that the differences between the divorce rates by occupation are only the result of differences in (a) social and geographical mobility and (b) in chaperonage. This was a major compilation of the U. S. Bureau of the Census, based on data collected for the years 1867-1906.[21] Because no major Census study of this kind has been carried out since that time, it must be considered here.

Occupation was recorded for 226,760 husbands, 24% of the males divorced during the period in question. For three states, New Jersey, Pennsylvania, and South Dakota, this datum was recorded for over 50% of the cases. Unfortunately, there is a definite over-enumeration, which cannot be measured, of occupations with higher incomes. Occupation was more likely to be recorded when alimony was granted, and this is correlated with higher income.[22] We ignore the general problems of recording at that time, and only note that even now, half a century later, we have a satisfactory procedure for national divorce registration in barely half the states in this country.[23]

Citations of this study have usually selected one or more occupations, such as medicine, with a high divorce rate, and offered some explanation (e.g. lack of chaperonage) for such a high rate. However, if we look at *all* the 39 occupations listed, we find that the rankings vary sharply from state to state, so that no clear pattern seems to exist. Perhaps this is not surprising, since the then Director of the Census, S. N. D. North writes of the study, "Returns so incomplete can hardly be accepted as typical."[24]

We have made many test recalculations of these data. Particularly, we regrouped the 39 occupations, and tried to calculate a Proneness to Divorce index by this formula:

$$\frac{\%\ \text{which a given occupational category forms of the total No. males divorced, 1887-1906}}{\%\ \text{which the category forms of the total No. married males in the 1900 Census}}$$

We then obtained the following ranking, in order of *increasing* proneness to divorce:

1. Skilled and semi-skilled
2. Proprietary, managerial
3. Professional
4. Service, protection
5. White Collar
6. Labor, not specified.

21. *Marriage and Divorce 1867-1906*, 2 Vols. (Washington: U. S. Bureau of the Census, 1909).

22. *Ibid.*, p. 44.

23. Hugh Carter, "Improving National Marriage and Divorce Statistics," *J. Am. Stat. Assoc.*, 48 (1953), 455 ff.

24. *Op. cit.*, p. 42.

Unfortunately, we tested this ranking by using the *same procedure* for the 9 states with "better data" (p. 46), and obtained a *different ranking:*

1. Skilled and semi-skilled
2. Professional
3. Labor, not specified
4. Proprietary, managerial
5. White Collar
6. Service, protection.

When we attempted to analyze the data further, we found that they remain somewhat unsatisfactory: (1) The total number of divorces for which occupation was recorded is given for all the states in the study, but this figure is smaller than a total of the individual figures given for the 9 states analyzed in detail (pp. 42, 44); (2) Rankings of Proneness to Divorce calculated from different tables (pp. 43, 46) seem too variant to be accounted for by sampling differences; (3) Apparently "labor, not specified" is used in different senses (pp. 43, 46), and in some cases must have included an unknown proportion of agricultural labor; (4) Regrouping the 1900 Census occupational categories into our own classes is only roughly possible.

Finally, we suspect (5) that there is a different divorce pattern in our time. Considerable evidence exists that divorce has gradually been substituted in our time as a solution for conflicts that two generations ago would have ended in only desertion or separation.

Although my own repeated attempts at recalculating these data have resulted in no discernible sociological order, it is possible that analysis of the original sources might be more productive. Until the task is done, however, we can no longer rely upon these data.

Income and Education. Let us look at additional data to make our propositions certain. We have most often cited items that related to occupation and divorce. There are Sample Survey data for the national population, relating income to divorce. We calculate the following "proneness to divorce" table, by the formula:

$$\frac{\% \text{ of the divorced in a given income category}}{\% \text{ of the ever married in that same category}}$$

That is, we relate the proportions divorced to the proportions ever married, in each income category.[25]

PRONENESS TO DIVORCE, BY INCOME (MALE)

Income Category (Annual)	Divorce Proneness Index
Under $500	189
$500-$999	216
$1000-$1999	109
$2000-$2999	106
$3000-$3999	69
$4000 and over	45

25. Table calculated from *Current Population Reports, Population Characteristics,* Series P-20, No. 23 (March 4, 1949), Table 10, p. 20.

The 1950 Census contained, for 3% of the population, questions relating to income. We can therefore calculate a similar "proneness to divorce" index by income categories for male heads of primary families. In the following table we present the indices for those roughly in the age groups of our own divorced husbands.

PRONENESS TO DIVORCE INDEX, BY INCOME
AGED 25-44 YEARS, 1950[26]

Income (1949)	Index
$0	199.0
$1-$999	188.6
$1000-$1999	134.8
$2000-$2999	92.9
$3000-$3999	89.2
$4000 and over	66.7

Finally, we make similar calculations for education, for the same age brackets, but this time we separate Negro from White, since an interesting fact emerges from this additional breakdown:

PRONENESS TO DIVORCE INDEX, BY EDUCATION,
WHITE AND NON-WHITE (MALES) AGED 25-44 YEARS, 1950[27]

	Index	
Education	White	Negro
No School	92.7	55.9
Grammar School	101.9	80.2
Some High School	109.5	131.0
High School Graduate	95.0	141.5
College	86.1	140.2
(Not known)	(183.7)	(141.8)

If we ignore the "Not known" and the "No School" categories, we see an irregular and small decrease in the index with increasing education. If the "Not known" category is not an interviewing problem, we assume that these are the men with very little education, in depressed urban areas mainly—and with a high divorce rate. The "No School" segment occurs almost entirely in the rural, isolated areas, where the tradition against divorce is likely to be strong. In any event, the pattern is not striking, though clear.

By contrast, *among Negroes,* with *increasing education* there appears to be an *increasing proneness* to divorce. Since we have kept within one age segment, this is not a *generational* change, that is, the older people without education and with a strong objection to divorce, compared with the younger, better educated, whose predispositions are more liberal. We forego the obvious lines of guessing what this datum suggests, such as the perception of the White patterns as social models; urban disorganization with increasing education; or differential frustrations in the Negro middle and upper classes, and so on. At this moment, we see in this datum no more than the greater utiliza-

26. *Census of Population, 1950. Vol. IV, Special Reports.* Part 2, Ch. D, Table 6, p. 47.

27. *Census of Population, 1950. Vol. IV.* Part 5, Ch. B, Table 8, pp. 63-65.

tion of the divorce courts by the more educated, and a greater cultural differential between the educational classes among Negroes, than among Whites. Whether indeed there is a significant problem in this datum, we shall see in the next few years.

Summary. In the present chapter, we have given apparently conclusive evidence that the Negro divorce rate is higher than the White. We have also presented rather full evidence for the notion that divorce is inversely class stratified. In the next chapter, we analyze more fully the meaning of these facts.

CHAPTER V

THE MEANING OF
CLASS DIFFERENTIALS IN
THE DIVORCE RATE

IN THE PRECEDING CHAPTER, we presented considerable evidence that the lower classes have a higher divorce rate, and that the Negro divorce rate is higher than the White. A class differential divorce pattern is not, as we noted in detail, to be found only in our own data. We have returned to previous studies which contained similar data, although to our knowledge no one has previously taken theoretical account of the fact, or even noted that the fact was contrary to previous assumption. In the present chapter, it seems useful to pursue further the *meaning* of these apparently economic facts. Let us begin by recalling the work of family analysts who have studied marital happiness. Of course, marital unhappiness is not the same as divorce, but the two are doubtless associated in our society. Moreover, these studies offer some corroboration of our data, and in addition show that the social aspects of the economic data must be taken into account.

Studies in Marital Happiness. It would be unfair to the pioneer work of Burgess and Cottrell to dismiss their results merely because they did not have a random sample. Actually, their data are not basically in contradiction with our own conclusions. True, their *emphasis* is inconsistent with our own, and later analysts have taken over that emphasis in citing their work. We shall summarize the facts on this issue.

1. First, the earlier work of Lang, a graduate student at the University of Chicago under Burgess' leadership, shows clearly at pattern of higher happiness ratings as one moves up the occupational rankings.[1] There is not, of course, a point for point correlation, but the conformity is striking.

2. When there is great homogeneity within a sample, many correlations are substantially reduced. This is a formal characteristic of statistical analysis, and as a consequence we would expect in the work of Burgess and Cottrell,

---

1. Richard O. Lang, *A Study of the Degree of Happiness or Unhappiness in Marriage as Rated by Acquaintances of the Married Couples* (M.A. thesis, University of Chicago, 1932). Lang did not have a random sample, but did obtain happiness ratings on 22,000 couples.

Terman, Burgess and Wallin, and Locke that socioeconomic factors would not exhibit high correlations with happiness. All of these, for different reasons, were homogeneous with respect to socioeconomic factors. As Burgess and Cottrell comment (p. 325), ". . . it must be remembered that our sample is essentially one economic class." Further (p. 29): ". . . the sample . . . is a roughly homogeneous, young, preponderantly nonneurotic, middle class, native-White American urban group." Although Terman's study is particularly weak in its exclusion of class factors, he comments on his own sample (p. 13), that it is ". . . reasonably representative of the middle and upper-middle classes of urban and semi-urban Californians."[2] The most important subsequent study is that of Harvey J. Locke, who attempted to obtain a representative, random sample of the divorced. Because he failed to take into account the class pattern of divorce, however, he tried to make his happily married sample correspond to the characteristics of the divorced.[3] Thus (p. 17) ". . . an attempt was made to distribute divorced and married cases evenly in the different districts of the city and county." Thus, the "representativeness" he sought was with reference to the wrong population. Since he was thereby "controlling" to some extent the class differences, it is not surprising that he often fails to find such differences between the two populations.

3. Such homogeneity ought to reduce considerably any inverse correlation between class rank and divorce rates, or a correlation between class and marital happiness. Such a correlation, if indeed it exists, ought not to disappear entirely.

We now assert that had any of these three studies developed their hypotheses within a framework of class-linked family patterns, the authors would have seen such differences within their own data. Moreover, this assertion specifically means that *their own reports* contain data substantiating our proposition that such differences are class linked. Let us look at the data.

4. First, a Thurstone multiple factor analysis showed in Burgess and Cottrell's data that there was one cluster of clear importance for the marital adjustment of the husband (pp. 319-20). This was made up of the length of time he had held his position, regularity of employment, the amount of income, the amount of savings, and the age of the husband. As against our assertion, however, when partial correlations were made to test its importance, this cluster seemed to have little independent power. Specifically (p. 324), when other factors were held constant, the "economic role" factor had a correlation of only .04 with marital adjustment. This is low, indeed, and the fact has been frequently cited since that time (1939) as proof of a general lack of connection between the economic or socioeconomic, and marital adjustment.

However, the other clusters *also* show an almost negligible correlation when the remaining sets were held constant: Cultural impress, .14; social type, .18; psychogenetic, .20; and response patterns, .20. Nothing higher than .2 is achieved.

5. More important, however, is the fact that in these other clusters there are

2. Lewis M. Terman, *Psychological Factors in Marital Happiness* (New York: McGraw-Hill, 1938).

3. Harvey J. Locke, *Predicting Adjustment in Marriage* (New York: Holt, 1951), pp. 13 ff., 36, 40.

also class factors. Thus, in "social status, social contacts, and participation" (p. 320), we find education of husband, husband's occupation, and number of organizations of which husband is a member. Earlier (p. 78), for a factor called "cultural background," of the 9 items used 4 are class items: occupation of father, education, economic status, and social status. These items, of course, do show correlations with marital happiness.

6. Perhaps still more fundamental is the fact that Burgess and Cottrell *did* understand that it is not the purely economic factor that is important, but its *social meaning*. Thus, they can show (pp. 270-271) that education is correlated with marital happiness. Further, it is not so much the income *per se* that is important (although the low income occupations are concentrated in the lowest quartile of the marital happiness ratings), but the low degree of mobility, the high degree of community control, and the income security, to be found in the upper categories (p. 143). Again, it is occupation rather than the amount of income that is important (p. 157).

Terman's work failed even to have a glimpse of these class factors, except for two asides: Thus, (p. 167) "It is well known that more divorces occur in the higher classes . . ." and (p. 183), "The underprivileged, briefly schooled, and immigrant classes are those most likely to resort to a court of domestic relations [instead of a divorce court]." His failure to include the factors necessary to test the presence of class-linked family patterns prevents any serious analysis here. He did, of course (pp. 188-9), find a relationship between the husband's education and marital happiness, and a slighter relationship for the wife. True enough, there are statistically significant differences between the happy and less happy husbands and wives with reference (p. 85) to the complaint of income, management of income, and other items that might be class linked, but he spends a chapter trying to prove that these domestic grievances are of little importance. Also, he found almost no correlation between income and happiness scores (p. 169), except for wives in the professional group, and notes (p. 169-170) that there is great homogeneity of income in his sample. He finds no relationship between happiness and occupation of husband, but 56.5% of his sample is professional, executive, and managerial, and he groups the semi-skilled with the small proprietors and clerks. The unskilled form 1.1% of his sample.

Thus, we cannot ascertain much from his data, except for the class factor of education. For occupation and income, the results are inconclusive statistically.

7. Although Locke's sample is not entirely adequate, it is the best sample so far obtained in this area of research. To what degree his sampling method also controlled economic factors, and thus wiped out any real class differences in marital happiness, we cannot say. Nevertheless, it is clear that even in his study many indications of class-linked patterns exist. First, he fails to find, in his comparison of the happily married with the divorced, any relationship between marital adjustment and occupations of fathers, occupations of men at the time of the marriage, and the employment of the wife outside the home. Since most of these divorced were matched by neighborhood or area with the happily married, he may have wiped out these differences.

On the other hand, he follows Burgess and Cottrell's lead in emphasizing economic security (p. 297). He also found that the professional or semi-professional positions are more likely to show higher marital adjustment scores. "Good houses . . . as measured by higher than average rents, higher than average values if house was owned, having modern plumbing, and having a furnace," were also associated with marital adjustment (p. 297). Further, he uses several class items as indices of social factors: having a telephone, as an index of sociability; taking a newspaper, as an index of wide interests; owning such items as home, electric refrigerator, electric washer, and radio, as indices of homemaking. Finally, the regularity of the husband's employment, and the feeling that the income was adequate, were associated with marital adjustment. These are all, of course, indices of higher economic status.

We do not, then, dismiss these contributions as irrelevant. Indeed, we rather suggest that a theoretical awareness of class-linked family patterns would, even with a less than random sample, show marital happiness to be related to class position; and that at many points these studies bear out our contention even though they are often cited with a contrary interpretation.

Social Meaning of Socioeconomic Factors. These facts do not require us to think only of class-linked patterns. Other factors are of great importance. Nevertheless, the socioeconomic factors doubtless exert general structural pressures on marriages, in different degrees at different class levels. Consequently, one may not ignore them. The results of empirical study seem to demonstrate what common sense asserts, that economic factors are of importance in marital stability. We can not be surprised, then, that economic matters occupy the top frequency position in Terman's list of husband-wife complaints, or that Schroeder's list of "real causes" gives economic factors as first or second in frequency, depending on how they are regrouped.[4]

Now, students of marital conflict once thought sexual conflict was very important in marital troubles, but have come in recent times to believe that sexual problems are usually an *index* rather than a cause of basic interpersonal conflicts. Thus, when a wife complains that she finds no pleasure in her sexual relations with her husband, one begins to probe for deeper conflicts between the two individuals, with the expectation that these conflicts actually cause the sexual incompatibility.

Naturally, then, similar transformations have been suggested for conflicts about economic matters. More particularly, conflicts about economic factors may sometimes be interpreted as *personality* failures: a "mature" personality will not be affected by such things, and the apparent conflict is simply thought to hide a more basic personality weakness. It cannot be denied, of course, that an "economic complaint" may indeed hide something deeper. It is nevertheless a poor research practice to *assume* the deeper meaning without analyzing the matter. The parlor Freudian dictum, "Things are never what they seem; indeed, the opposite" seems almost a cynical response to observation.

Unfortunately, then, "personality" assumptions often lead into the same kind of stultifying pseudo-explanations that were characteristic of the heyday of

---

4. Terman, *op. cit.,* p. 96; Schroeder, *op. cit.,* p. 106. Other studies such as those by W. P. Meroney, Ernest R. Mowrer, E. T. Krueger, etc., in spite of different emphases, also suggested at times the importance of such factors. Few until recently thought in terms of class position or rank.

instinct-theory. Having pointed to personality problems as a possible cause, the search can stop.

It is at least possible to maintain that since (a) those who obtain divorces represent such a large segment of the population, and (b) the cultural structure of our time contains so many factors reducing the stability of the family, we ought not to search *first* for personality causes. Whatever contribution personality "weakness" makes to marital instability—and no study has achieved such a measurement—the *social meaning* of the economic can nevertheless be studied with some profit.[5] This is not, to repeat, a substitute for personality analysis; it is on an entirely different theoretical level. If we can show through what avenues the socioeconomic seems to affect marital relations, we are at least a step further toward an adequate understanding of divorce and postdivorce adjustment. We shall attempt at many points to present data toward this end.

Burgess and Cottrell granted that economic factors might be of importance through the *stability* of income. Now, stability may be defined in purely economic terms, but of course it has sociological dimensions: not only are the stabler incomes to be found in (a) particular kinds of occupations, but stability of income is likely to be associated with (b) a different way of life. Furthermore, stability of income is associated with (c) *size* of income, particularly over longer periods of time. And the latter factor is also one of the determinants of larger social patterns in our society.

Finally, neither stability nor size of income even when viewed sociologically exhausts the social *meaning* of the economic. *Who earns* the income, and *who controls* the income, are further aspects of the economic factors which must be considered when we look at the American family.[6] We have called the association between socioeconomic factors and divorce a "rough" one. We have done so to call attention to the fact that the economic factor does not act directly, but is mediated through other factors, mainly sociological. We can more easily measure the socioeconomic than these other factors, but we suppose that when we have better techniques we shall have higher correlations between these social factors and divorce than between any purely economic indices and divorce. That is to say, it will be the social *meaning* of these factors which will discriminate between instability and stability. The socioeconomic, then *is* important, but *interactionally,* and not as a simple, direct causal element. We cannot of course present a sophisticated analysis now, but we can at least point to some of the sociological dynamics that appear to play a role. Later on, we shall document these assertions further.

---

5. See, however, the attempt by Erik Allardt, *Miljöbetingade differenser i skilsmässofrekvensen, Bidragtill kännedom av Finlands Natur och folk, Finska Vetenskaps-Societetan*, 96 (Helsingfors: 1953). However, criticism may be directed against his "measures" of personality deviation.

6. To ask about the *social meaning* of the economic, in larger structural terms as with reference to particular families, is a beginning step, but an important one. This notion was used, without later development by other writers, in research on the family in the depression. Thus, Komarovsky found that loss of income had a weakening effect on the stability of certain types of families, while strengthening that of other types, depending upon their definitions of the loss of income, e.g., whether it was viewed as a failure by the head of family, etc. See Mirra Komarovsky, *The Unemployed Man and His Family* (New York: Dryden, 1940); and Samuel A. Stouffer and Paul F. Lazarsfeld, *Research Memorandum on the Family in the Depression* (New York: Social Science Research Council, 1937).

Perhaps the most fundamental set of symbolic relationships is that between the stability of the family, the unity of the family, the role of the husband as breadwinner, and his role as family head. Now, during the 1940's there was a large increase in the proportion of married females actively working; the increase in 1940-1946 was about 50%. By 1953, of the female labor force, married females formed 56.6%.[7] There is certainly more toleration of the working wife. Further, there is no widespread opinion that a family will not survive even if the male head fails in his role as breadwinner. Nevertheless, there is little evidence that the female *as breadwinner* is beginning to emerge as a social role. To the extent that there is folk belief about the matter, on the other hand, it is phrased in a negative fashion: the expectation is that failure of the husband in this respect may help to make the family unstable. When the married woman works, the work generally carries a negative social evaluation in contemporary America (a) except under specifiable conditions of need or (b) unless redefined in *nonbreadwinning* terms.

For example, a crisis situation justifies such work. If the husband, say, is incapacitated for a long or short while, the wife may work. For many strata the wife's work may be defined in terms of need: "saving a nest egg," or "to pay off the furniture," or even "we can't get along without it."

In the upper educational strata, the work may be defined in nonbreadwinning terms: "expressing the wife's personality," or "giving the family a wider range of experiences," or "to keep the wife from stagnating." As we might expect, when such verbal responses express a genuine conviction, it is possible that for such groups we may find as high a "happiness score" as in other families in the same strata.[8]

We believe, then, that toleration or even approval of the working wife are most often given a justification of (a) necessity or (b) essentially *non*-breadwinning aims. By contrast, no explanation at all is called for and no redefinition in terms of "higher" values is required if he *is* earning an adequate income, i.e., is fulfilling his role and his wife is *not* working. Even in those small circles in which it is felt that the wife *ought* to hold a job, this is an ethic that is carefully distinguished from the mere earning of money.

Now, as to the *use* of the money, the husband's income is supposed to be earned for *all* the family. The male head of family is responsible, according to our values, for the support of the entire group, and legal prescriptions underscore these values. This legal responsibility carries correlative headship rights with it, and while the actual patterns of domination are much more complex and often contradictory, open and public failure to keep this headship must be explained or husband and wife will be censured. There are, indeed, various deprecatory terms in our slang to describe a husband in this situation (e.g., "henpecked," "Milquetoast").

If certain earlier comments may now be placed in this context, it is obvious that personality problems can be displaced into economic problems. As the simplicist formulation of parlor psychoanalysis has it, the "stable personality" will not be affected by such economic strains as we have just noted,

---

7. *Current Population Reports.* Series P-50, No. 50. November 30, 1953, Table 1, p. 6.

8. See Harvey J. Locke and Muriel Mackeprang, "Marital Adjustments and the Employed Wife," *Am. J. Soc.*, 54 (1949), 536-8; and Locke, *op. cit.*, pp. 288 ff. who offer partial data to substantiate this hypothesis.

or by any others; while the immature will complain of economic factors in the marriage when the "real" trouble is emotional. Nevertheless in our society the material goals of comfort, medical care, style in clothing, homes and furniture, size and newness of automobiles, are widely accepted, while the actual distribution of *income* is far more skewed. Put in another way, although the material and other aspirations of lower socioeconomic strata *are* lower than those of the upper, the *income* of lower strata is relatively even lower. Consequently, the feeling of socioeconomic strain is greater in the lower strata. Some evidence on that score may be found in Kornhauser's study of class attitudes, in which there seems to be less contentment in these lower strata than in the upper.[9] Many studies report at least a greater occupational contentment among the upper strata.[10]

If the foregoing considerations are correct, then in some cases *economic strain may also be displaced onto noneconomic relationships* such as sex and marital adjustment. Perhaps a general theory of personality will finally emerge which will be able to describe the psychodynamic patterns even when the source of strain is economic, or hunger, or glandular deficiency, not alone when it is "sexual."[11]

Tracing the pattern of strain further, whenever discord from whatever source becomes chronic, the withdrawal of economic support can be one major expression of waning loyalty. This denial of breadwinning obligations and of family unity may be met by a denial of headship. It may be supposed that these changes are economically less catastrophic in the lower economic strata. The upper and lower may be contrasted in this fashion: (1) A higher proportion of the upper strata income is committed to long time "investment" expenditures such as annuities, insurance, houses, etc.; and thus has little flexibility; (2) a higher proportion of the lower strata income, when it is committed at all, is given over to consumer goods such as cars, television sets, etc.; (3) consequently, there is less censure and less catastrophe at withdrawal of support in the lower than in the upper. Moreover, the difference between the husband's earnings and the wife's potential earnings is on the average greater toward the upper strata: thus she is more helpless, and withdrawal of support creates far more problems. Willful failure in the role of breadwinner is often met by willful destruction of the sexual and social unity.

Thus, we often found the wife complaining about "drinking, staying out, and helling around," and of course such behavior means substantially less money for the family. The husband was spending his time and money elsewhere. However, the purely economic matter of unpaid bills was not the

---

9. Arthur Kornhauser, "Analysis of 'Class Structure' of Contemporary American Society— Psychological Bases of Class Divisions," *Industrial Conflict* (S.P.S.S.I., 1939), esp. pp. 242 ff. See also the insightful theoretical analysis of certain consequences of this fact, in Robert K. Merton's "Social Structure and Anomie," in *Social Theory and Social Structure* (Glencoe, Ill.: The Free Press, 1949), pp. 125-149.

10. See, for example, the *Fortune* Survey by Elmo Roper, *Fortune*, 35 (1947), 10. For comparisons: Robert Woppeck *et al.*, "Job Satisfaction Researches of 1946-1947," *Occupations*, 27 (1948-9), 167 ff.

11. Our suspicion of simplicist personality notions about money and family strain is in part derived from Benjamin Franklin's suspicion of the common homily that people can be just as happy though poor: if the conclusion is so obvious, why do people have to spend so much energy trying to prove it in innumerable essays?

theme of such responses. Rather it was the *role-meaning* of the behavior, expressed in such comments as: "What's the good of having a husband, if he won't support you?" or, "When I saw that he wasn't interested in his home any more, I decided he was no good." It was the withdrawal from the unity of the family, and from the role of breadwinner, which was paramount, although, of course, there was no lack of recognition of the debt problem.

Moreover, as we shall see later, the factors of stability of income, type of job, control over expenditures, and social roles influence the postdivorce adjustment of these wives: it is not alone the absolute amount of money available that matters in even *economic adjustment,* but also the social relations of the woman.

We have thus carried our presentation of these symbolic and economic relations beyond the data we have available, to indicate the line of theory we are pursuing. In the following section, we want to show further how the stability of the family can be investigated, with a proper attention to a broader range of variables.

Accounting Scheme for Divorce Rate Differentials. The several social dimensions of income and occupation relating to marital interaction and stability should be placed in a schema which would facilitate the larger sociostructural analysis of the family unit. That is, the inverse relationship between socioeconomic position and divorce proneness is not caused by the direct impact of education, occupation, or income on marital relations. Spouses do not usually divorce on the grounds that marriage does not pay well. Socioeconomic indices conceal a complex of interrelated sociological variables which we must learn to measure more adequately if we are to understand how these socioeconomic factors operate. Until we have the crucial facts, it is as reasonable to suppose that economic strains are displaced onto personal relations, as to suppose that personality strains are displaced onto economic relations.

We know, in any event, that we cannot explain most of the divorce rate differentials between various groups by an appeal to economic factors alone. In the succeeding analysis we wish to broaden our inquiry in an effort to suggest other dimensions that are needed to explain and predict marital instability. Thereby, we can eventually give economic factors their proper weight, and also understand better just how the inverse relationship between socioeconomic position and marital stability comes about. As will be seen, we merely offer a simple version of an accounting scheme that is widely used in decision analysis.

Now, we have used several measures of socioeconomic position. When we use occupation as our class observable, we are also recording the *prestige ranking* of the occupation. But there are many factors other than income and social prestige that are in part determined by occupation. The income and prestige of the physician are at the top of any occupational ranking, but physicians seem to have a very high proneness to divorce, perhaps among the highest of all professions. We would expect to find professors in small colleges and clergymen, by contrast, at the opposite end of a divorce proneness scale. These segments of the professions have relatively low incomes, but may claim at least a medium social prestige ranking. We would expect to find a low rate of divorce among farm owners. We cannot continue these predictions indefinitely. Unfortunately, there exist no reliable data for divorce in specific occupations for the country as a whole. There might nevertheless be some point in stating our *predictions* about the relative divorce-proneness of occupations if we could derive our rankings from some unified theory. We would then have to specify those cultural characteristics of various strata or occupations which are most relevant for family stability. Lacking such a theory, we are likely to "explain" a high divorce rate among physicians in terms of (a) the *internal strains* which a physician's professional life creates. However, we would "explain" the low divorce rate among farmers and academicians in terms of (b) the *external* pressures of the groups or communities in which these people are to be found. Clergymen, on the other hand, are thought to be guided by (c) a set of strong (internal) moral predispositions or values *against* divorce. Clearly, if a different "explanation" for each variation is necessary, we have done no more than bring out the apparent fact that sociological factors might help us in understanding rate differentials.

A clue to one fruitful approach is the association of different occupations with different *ways or styles of life*—educational levels, child-rearing practices, reading habits, membership in formal organizations, aspirations, tastes, or even political attitudes.

The data necessary to describe the class or "subcultural" distribution of major family patterns are not available, and therefore the further distinctions necessary to describe the differences between the family patterns of various occupations and professions can not be made.

We ought, therefore, to outline the *kinds* of data which would be necessary to explain the *differences between the divorce rates* of classes or other strata and groups in our society, at any given time, *or over generations*. The problem of simple "causes" of divorce must be laid aside, for divorce must be thought of as a formal and legal resultant of several different types of pressures in a complex interaction, by which a particular boundary-maintaining social unit is destroyed. We therefore need those types of data which would allow us to explain differential rates between strata, groups, or generations.

At the minimum, distributions for the following data are needed:

1. Predispositions in the economic or social stratum toward or against divorce
2. Internal strains on, and satisfaction from, the marriage
3. Alternatives outside the present marriage
4. External supports for, or undermining of, the marriage on the part of the relevant social groups
5. Precipitants of conflict, or of the decision to divorce

These data must be comparative or historical, so that in some manner the differences between classes, groups, or generations along these dimensions can be weighed. Even if quantitative indices of each item cannot be developed, we would at least hope to be able to rank familiar aspects of the "cultures of groups" along these dimensions.

Such a set of dimensions might be used, for example, to analyze the change in divorce rates in the United States since the Civil War. Quantitative data for these categories do not exist, but we can obtain by historical investigation the macroscopic social changes which have, for instance, made for an increase in the available *alternatives* to existing marriage: new marriages, occupational opportunities for the wife, geographical mobility. Similarly, some historical data on the increased *predispositions* toward divorce over these generations, can be obtained, among different religious sects and ethnic groups, and perhaps comparable data for our other categories.

To make an analysis of contemporary divorce rate differentials, similar data are needed, but more exact observations, perhaps of a quantitative order can be obtained. Until then, we can only guess as to the facts that would be found. However, the line of investigation seems a clear one, and the major categories of questions seem obvious. As a by-product, of course, a great deal more would then be known about the distribution of marriage patterns in our culture.

Let us for a moment follow our hunches about what might be found. We would suppose that such an investigation would uncover few large *class* differences with respect to the *predispositions* toward or against divorce as a solution to marital conflict. Perhaps the middle and upper strata might even show a greater predisposition toward acceptance of divorce as a solution. Possibly the common belief that these strata have a higher rate of divorce is due to their verbal "liberality" toward divorce. However, we also suppose that there are far more *external supports* to marriage within the sub-groups of these upper economic strata. There are, of course, particular occupations in these strata that are peculiarly subject to strain. It is likely, for example, that the marriages of physicians (and to an even more extreme degree, those of psychotherapists) are under very great strain because of the total and complex impact of the transference phenomenon in the physician-patient relationship, and the sacrifices of home life to the demands of the profession.

However, these strata exist as networks of interdependent social groups whose livelihoods and ways of life are based upon great continuity of social relations. The job continuity of the factory worker, by contrast, is dependent upon his relationship to the factory and upon his social relations with factory personnel while he is in the factory. The continuity of the social and economic life of the professional or the managerial official is far more dependent upon his total network of social relationships, many of which are not strictly professional. Divorce is never an anonymous matter in these strata. Furthermore, child support can almost never be evaded, since the career line of the middle and upper strata is very close to a matter of public record. The factory worker can "disappear" (as an alternative) in answer to a child support judgment, as the professional man cannot. And, of course, the disruption of the family estate—actual or potential—is a genuine likelihood for the middle and upper strata, while this problem is almost irrelevant for the factory worker.

It is almost certain that the social groups of the former strata are in general more stable than those of the lower strata.[12] Since the family as a *whole* is more involved in these networks than in the lower strata, and divorce is a disruption of existing relationships, there is more external opposition to any impending divorce. Since friendship and social patterns in the lower strata

---

12. See the review and report on this point by Leonard Reissman, "Class, Leisure, and Social Participation," *Am. Soc. Rev.,* 19 (1954), 76-84.

are much more likely to be between individuals of the same sex, and less likely to be between families as a whole, divorce is not such a group threat, and thus the external group supports for marriage may be less strong. We leave aside the external support of religion (though here again membership is higher toward the upper strata[13]) since we are not attempting any systematic sketch of all the relevant factors.

We have to enter the realm of guess even more deeply if we ask questions about class differential, internal strains within marriage. Let us at least note some of the possible directions to look for such differentials. One suggestion might be to ascertain whether the lower class husband's attitudes have changed less in the last generation than those of the wife. He may make role demands upon the wife that were acceptable a generation ago, while the wife has come to wish for the somewhat greater equalitarianism and freedom that have come to be characteristic of our time. (The question is: Is this discrepancy greater in the lower strata?) It is also possible that the widely accepted material values of our time cause many internal strains, since the lower strata cannot obtain many of these material comforts, but want them. We would suppose that many of these economic strains have important social meanings, and that conflicts of this kind may be displaced onto the individual relationship between spouses. Thus, conflicts with economic sources may appear under other guises. As against the fact that the sexual adjustment of the lower class woman may be slightly less, we would expect to find less romantic attachment, and less emotional involvement, between spouses in these strata. Indeed, this greater freedom actually creates alternatives to the present spouse. There is also less willingness to share confidences, a greater segregation of sex roles, and more openness of aggression, in an era when the values of the society, and especially of the wives, have moved in the other direction. Finally, there is a higher proportion of working wives, creating more internal familial strains than in other strata, because the lower-class husband is less willing than the middle- or upper-class husband to share the burdens of housekeeping. Further, the job that is held outside the home brings few satisfactions except money.[14]

If many of these guesses turn out to be correct, we can no longer be surprised that there is a higher divorce rate in the lower occupational strata. We must leave aside the interesting question of the historical trend. That is, if we assume that divorce has "percolated down" from the upper strata, as did the use of contraceptives, at what point did the rate in the lower strata become higher than that in the upper? Or, rather, has there been a higher rate of marital instability in the lower strata for several generations, and a gradual acceptance of the divorce court as a solution instead of separation and desertion? There is some evidence that the latter process has occurred, at least for the total divorce rate.[15]

Implications of the Inverse Association. Since we have allowed ourselves

13. Reissman, *op. cit.*, pp. 78, 80. See also William G. Mather, "Income and Social Participation," *Am. Soc. Rev.*, 6 (1941), 380-383.

14. It seems likely that both these factors make for a lessened impact of the wife's job upon the home in professional families. See Harvey J. Locke and Muriel Mackeprang, *op. cit.*, and Locke, *op. cit.*, pp. 288 ff.

15. See Beale, "Increased Divorce Rates among Separated Persons as a Factor in Divorce Since 1940," *Soc. Forces,* 29 (1950), 72-4.

the luxury of the foregoing analysis, it is perhaps appropriate to point out some of the implications of the inverse correlation between class and divorce rate. How rigorously these are drawn must be tested by research, but we may at least raise several questions.

The data suggest, for example, that a revision of certain literary clichés is due. The stereotyped picture of the lower-class family as one of easy warmth, love, and stability, contrasted with the neurotic, psychically aggressive, divorce-prone middle-class family makes for simpler novels, but it is not accurate.

Further, much of the vast effort now being expended in "preparation for marriage"—college courses, books, pamphlets, etc.—*misses* precisely those strata that are most prone to divorce. The middle and upper strata are most exposed to such advice, and entirely aside from its possible impact upon marital stability they are more likely to have unbroken marriages than those strata with no such information given to them.

We might also note that many "pathological" characteristics have been roughly associated with divorce. Some of these are crime, lower life expectancies, juvenile delinquency, insanity, and suicide. However, it is now clear that some part of this association may be spurious, in that these characteristics are also associated with poverty. In any event, we must now attempt to disentangle the mainly "poverty-associated" from the "divorce-associated," instead of accepting what may be in part a spurious causal relation between divorce and these negatively valued characteristics.

CHAPTER VI

ECONOMICS OF
THE MARRIAGE BEFORE
THE DIVORCE

IF THE FOREGOING ANALYSIS is correct, then economic factors may shape in various ways not only the marriage, but also the postdivorce adjustment. If we are to ask how the divorced mother faced her economic problems, then we must ask, at least briefly, what was her economic experience before the divorce. We have already presented the occupational distribution of the husband. In the present chapter we pay attention to the husband's income, his steadiness of work, her job-holding, and the accumulation of property.

Husband's Income. From the occupational distribution given in Chapter IV, we know that the divorced will concentrate in the lower or lower-middle income brackets. The basic distribution is as follows:

WEEKLY INCOME OF HUSBAND DURING MARRIAGE

	Percent	Cases
$0-$29.99	8	33
$30-$44.99	22	95
$45-$59.99	34	143
$60-$74.99	15	63
$75-$99.99	10	41
Over $100	8	35
Subtotal	97	410
Unknown	4	15
Total	101	425

The median income for the 410 whose incomes are known is about $52 weekly, while the mean is about $58. However, the time reference is not precise, or the same for all divorcees. Some of these marriages had lasted for more than twenty years, while others had lasted only a few years. The time of divorce was between 1946 and 1948. Presumably, the chronological time referred to as "during the marriage" is some period during the 1940's. During this war period, wages had risen; but of course they were much lower than at the present time. In any event, the average wage was about that of the semi-skilled factory worker, and the income skew is strongly toward the lower strata.

Although a similar income comparison exists for the wife's father, the comparison is much more difficult to make with any precision, since the only time reference possible was "when you were in your teens." In many cases the answers were guesses, and the main period referred to was during the depression. Thus, these data seem too imprecise to be brought into the picture here.

One further point needs to be noted. Studies on stratification have amply documented the fact that different criteria of class will yield different distributions. That is to say, in a highly mobile society there is no one-to-one correlation between various aspects of group style of life and the indices of class, and this is true even when we utilize such apparently unambiguous class criteria as occupation, education, and income.[1] It is thus worthwhile noting that, although "upper and middle occupational class" and "$60.00 weekly income or over" are associated in our study with a Q of + .55; and "upper and middle occupational class" and "high school education or more" are associated with a Q of + .49; "high school education or more" and "$60.00 weekly income or more" are associated with a Q of only + .25. That is, occupation and income, and occupation and education, are more closely associated than income and education.

This means that some items used for class comparisons are less likely than others to yield sharply defined tabulational results. This, however, is in the nature of things in present-day American society, with its class-mobile patterns and its lack of sharp lines between classes. We can erase these apparent anomalies by spuriously precise "class indices," but all of these fail to get at what we really want to study when we are investigating class differences. These are the differences in style of life, in marital process, in value patterns, in types of moral decisions, etc. Until we have charted these latter with greater precision, any of our class indices will yield broad areas of ambiguity. And, of course, once we have charted such factors, the "class" indices we now use will be of much less theoretical importance.

Nevertheless, from these data we can understand that even *during* the marriage the average respondent had *relatively little income* with which to manage her household. And, of course, there were children to be supported with this income. Consequently, the divorcee is likely to have had some economic problems even before the divorce. They are often intensified after the divorce, since in many cases there is still less money with which to run the household. In any event, even without precise comparisons, it seems clear that the divorcee with children is more likely to be found in the lower occupational and economic strata than is the average nondivorced spouse.

Steadiness of Work. As we have already commented, one important dimension of the economic factor is *steadiness* of income. In the Burgess and Cottrell and the Locke studies, too, security of income seemed to be more important than absolute income.[2] It then becomes pertinent to ask how steady was the husband's employment during the marriage. The answers to this question are found in the succeeding table:

1. See the test of this notion in Godfrey Hochbaum *et al.*, "Socioeconomic Variables in a Large City," *Am. J. Soc.*, 61 (1955), 31-38.

2. Burgess and Cottrell, *op. cit.*, p. 416; Locke, *op. cit.*, p. 297.

STEADINESS OF HUSBAND'S EMPLOYMENT

	Percent	Cases
Always had work	49	210
Always had work, except for unavoidable layoffs	20	84
Frequent layoffs	13	57
Never worked for long periods	17	74
Total	99	N = 425

The main time reference for this question was the war-boom period in an industrial city. Without entirely discounting the fact that even during such a period there may be considerable labor turnover that is not under the control of the worker, it is striking how high a percentage of these men did not bring in a steady income. A high proportion of these people were in semi-skilled jobs, but even if we combine those who always had work and those who had work except for unavoidable layoffs, there remains a segment of 30% of our sample whose economic contribution to the family was unsteady. Of course, the impact of this factor cannot be assessed here. Its impact would be different, as between a war-boom period and a prolonged depression. Even though in the latter case the worker himself may feel strong self-doubts and considerable guilt about his personal failure, after a fairly lengthy period of the depression there is usually some recognition by the family that unemployment is not merely a personal failure.[3] During a war-boom period this softening of the possible accusations would not occur nearly so frequently.

The possible bias of the wife was discussed earlier. Even if some wives have viewed their husbands' work record as less steady than it actually was, unless we assume genuine lying we must conclude that many divorced husbands have an unsteady work record.

Numerous rationalizations can be used by both husband and wife, when both have considerable faith in one another. Nevertheless, the exacerbating effect of prolonged unsteadiness of employment might be expected to be fairly strong.

Working Wife. American family research has not yet disclosed the impact of the wife's job-holding upon the marriage. The increase of women in the national labor market has continued during the present postwar decade, as it did during the war, when many women had entered factories and other business establishments in response to government pleas or in response to immediate income needs on the part of the family. Between 1940 and 1947, there was an increase of 50 percent in the number of married women in the labor force. Over half the women in the labor force in 1947 were married.[4] Correspondingly, the proportion of married women who were employed also continued to increase.

Whether there is an increase in the proportion of married women *permanently* employed outside the home is much less certain.[5]

---

3. Cf. the studies by Komarovsky, and Lazarsfeld and Stouffer, *op. cit.*

4. Paul C. Glick, "Family Life and Full Employment," *Am. J. Soc.*, 54 (1949) p. 527. Also, see *Current Population Reports*, Series P- 50, No. 5, "Employment Characteristics of Households and Married Couples, April, 1947."

5. Theodore Caplow, *The Sociology of Work* (Minneapolis: Univ. of Minnesota Press, 1954), p. 234, emphatically denies such an increase.

The trend toward mothers working, whether or not temporary, continued so that by 1953, 37% of the Detroit area mothers with children 6-18 years of age were working,[6] while 27.1% of all U. S. married women (mothers or not) were in the labor force in 1953.[7]

Although popular opinion suggests that when the wife works the family is less likely to be stable, there is no conclusive evidence on this point. The research by Locke and Mackeprang, and by Locke, indicated that there was no great difference in the marital happiness scores when wives worked. Nearly a generation ago, Katherine B. Davis found a slight positive relationship between marital happiness and the wife's *not* working.[8]

One can reason in either direction, with respect to the impact of this factor upon family life. For example, in a society in which the wife is urged to have a career, many women actually come to feel the need for such a career, and take great enjoyment from its pursuit. Such women are likely to be happier if they work. Correspondingly, many women who do not work might feel that their family life does not give them sufficient challenge and scope for their talents, and might thus be somewhat less happy.

On the other hand, whatever the *immediate happiness* of the wife, such working may in the long run weaken marital stability. Few husbands are able to accept a relationship of equality in which their responsibilities for housework are the same as those of their wives.

The attitudes of the husband are likely to be shared by his circle. Consequently, the wife is under some pressure to take on more home responsibilities than she can meet. In most cases the wife actually does respond by trying to conform with the pressures. Nevertheless, no adjustment can change the basic facts of time, space, and energy. If there are children, they are likely to be her responsibility, as is the administration of house affairs. No matter how much she may enjoy these activities, only the rare individual will have enough energy, or enough freedom in time allocation, to be able to take care of both job and home adequately. The children especially may resent these outside activities, even when they are proud of their mother's accomplishments.

Furthermore, in crisis situations it will likely be the wife who assumes responsibility, not the husband. If children are sick, usually the wife will stay home. When there is a job opportunity for the husband, requiring him to move, it is assumed that the move will be made regardless of its effect on the wife's job. Her motivation is thus undercut. Interviews among such women might disclose considerable resentment against this state of affairs.

Nevertheless, it is difficult to judge whether this resentment becomes of any great importance in marital stability. When arguments can so easily run in either direction, it is likely that the important causal factors in this complex have not been located.

The foregoing comments refer, in the main, to the wife who holds a professional or semi-professional job. However, the situation is somewhat differ-

6. *A Social Profile of Detroit, 1953* (Ann Arbor: University of Michigan Press), p. 23.

7. *Current Population Reports,* Series P-50, No. 50, November 30, 1953, Table 1, p. 6.

8. Katherine B. Davis, *Factors in the Sex Life of Twenty-Two Hundred Women* (New York: Harper, 1929), p. 43.

ent for the average wife in the working force. She will more frequently be a nonprofessional, married to a nonprofessional. The personal competition for prestige that is sometimes thought to be characteristic of the professional couple should be less between the average working spouses. In the latter case, there should be little interpersonal competition, and the wife does not generally seek a career. Her entrance into the labor force has a mainly economic cause, or at least the goal is to earn money in order to buy various kinds of material goods (granted that the material goods also have a symbolic importance on the social level, in that the family may wish to have furniture "as good as the neighbors' " and so on). Furthermore, she may claim that it is *necessary* for her to work, in order to balance the budget. The working wife in this case probably views her factory or office jobs as a means to an end, and not as an end in itself. She would probably be willing to leave the labor force if she could afford to. She will usually express the desire to leave the labor force in the future, as soon as the couple has acquired a modest capital or paid for some furniture or a house. In short, the enterprise has much more of an instrumental character, and the wife's job-holding is viewed as a way of increasing the income.

In such a situation there should be far fewer conflicts about the *priority* of values. Both spouses feel that the work done by the wife has little intrinsic importance, compared to the responsibilities of being wife and mother of the home. When there is any unusual demand for the wife's services in the home, there is no question that the job, not the home, will give way.

Correspondingly, such wives are doubtless given even less help than the professional wife in the home tasks they are expected to continue while holding the job. On the other hand, her participation in the work force may allow her to discover that she can support herself, and even that working has a pleasure of its own. Then, if pressures within the marriage become difficult to bear, such a wife may for the first time be able to view life apart from her husband as an economically *possible* alternative.

It does seem unlikely, in any event, that a form of activity which takes up such a substantial portion of the individual's waking time should fail to have some impact upon the daily interaction patterns of the marriage. Whether it has a significant impact upon marital *stability,* is another matter. We are, however, fairly certain that the ways of *behaving* with reference to work and economics are changed before there are significant changes in the *ideal* of marriage or the mutual *rights* of husband and wife. The husband may accede to her work needs, and he may even accept some home responsibilities in view of those work demands, while continuing to hold unchanged his notions about "a woman's place." That is to say, he may not insist upon what he conceives to be his rights, but he does continue to believe they are his rights.

We hazard the guess, however, that the woman's adjustment to the new state of affairs is more easily made. She finds the adjustment to being in the work force rather easy and finds even easier the adjustment to her husband's taking over some of the family responsibilities. It is only the responsibilities of freedom that are hard to assume; its rights are easily accepted.[9]

---

9. A considerable body of poll data, 1940-1950, shows these assertions about sex differences to be correct.

We are not, then, attempting to interpret further our data on job-holding by the wife. We cannot at the present time go beyond merely noting that only 28% of the wives never held a job during the marriage, while 42% always or usually held full-time jobs. Job-holding on the part of the wife is shown in the following table.

JOB-HOLDING BY WIFE DURING MARRIAGE

Type of Job	Frequency				%	Total No.
	Always	Usually	Seldom	Never		
Full time	20%	22%	9%	....	51%	218
Part time	4	13	4	....	21	90
None	....	....	....	28	28	117
Total	24%	35%	13%	28%	100%	N = 425

It is seen that these women were working in higher proportion than married women generally. In 1947, 20 percent of women living with their husbands (including the childless) were in the U. S. labor force.[10] However, by 1953 in Detroit this figure had nearly doubled. Since, typically, the woman in our labor force is paid less than is the man for a comparable job, and since many of these women did not work all the time, their contribution to the family budget was not great (though in some cases certainly crucial).

Accumulation of Property. All of these families had children. Most of them received very modest incomes. Few, then, accumulated much property. Indeed, when we combine the equity in whatever houses they owned with their estimated value of furniture, bonds, etc., the amount remains very low, as can be seen in the succeeding table:

PROPERTY DIVIDED AT DIVORCE

Amount	Percent	Cases
$ 0.00	40	172
$ 1-$ 249	5	20
$ 250-$ 499	6	27
$ 500-$ 999	9	39
$1000-$1999	14	58
$2000-$3999	8	33
over $4000	18	76
Total	100	N = 425

These are estimates. It is very difficult to estimate the value of furniture. When the respondent answers "Nothing at all" to this question, she may simply be giving expression to her disgust at the fact that there is nothing left in material goods when the marriage is broken up. Probably in such cases some small property had been accumulated—perhaps a radio or a set of furniture. On the other hand, these items have usually been bought on time, and the equity is small. In some cases, they are returned to the seller, or are given away.

In any event, the actual value of such goods is probably very small, when it is not exactly zero. It must be kept in mind, too, that we are not merely

---

10. Glick, "Family Life and Full Employment," *op. cit.,* p. 528.

reporting the answers of the wife regarding her *own* property; this is the amount of property which she reported as *available for division* between the two. It is true that in some cases she will not have known how much money the man had accumulated in his own bank account, or how many bonds he may have bought out of his savings at his place of work. Yet wide discrepancies between the reality and the guesses of the wife are probably not common. The wife almost always knows very well the income of her husband, even when she has little control over how he spends much of it. The wife might actually exaggerate the amount of property available, in view of some of the resentments expressed by the wife against the husband, and accuse him of taking it away. We do not believe, therefore, that this table is far from the reality. We shall comment further on these estimates when we discuss the property division at divorce.

Naturally, couples who divorce during the present inflationary period would have accumulated somewhat more property than these couples. There are also regional differences. On the other hand, the period of marital conflict and separation before the divorce decree is relatively long. During this later period the value of accumulated propertly doubtless declines. The demands of double households, the refusal on the part of one or the other to continue payments on house or furniture, a feeling on the part of both that any property accumulated might as well be expended now, the desire to hurt the other through dissipation of goods or money—all of these factors would reduce whatever value of property there had been before the serious phases of conflict began.

However, the amount of property "accumulated by time of the divorce" is not an adequate reflection of the *level of living* during the course of the marriage. The family may have been living relatively well, even though, when debts are liquidated and the furniture goes back to the furniture company for failure to make the payments, there is absolutely nothing left in the bank and the couple may be said to have accumulated no property at all. The respondents may tell us about their level of living, but we could not be satisfied unless we could actually see the family in operation as it was before the divorce conflict began. Then we might have a clearer notion as to the economic life of the couple, or the more specific class aspects of the economic life.

Summary. In the present chapter, it has been shown that the divorced, in conformity with their occupational distribution, are concentrated in the lower income brackets. In addition, it seems clear that the divorced husband is likely to have experienced considerable unsteadiness of employment. This finding is in agreement with studies of marital happiness. Some 40% of these divorced women always or usually held full-time jobs during the marriage, and 17% always or usually held part-time jobs. These figures seem to be higher than the average for all married women in the U. S. Finally, it is clear that very little property was accumulated by the divorced couple prior to the breakup of the marriage. Forty percent claimed that there was no property at all to be divided at the time of the divorce. Consequently, whatever economic problems the average divorced mother faces *after* the divorce, she has already had a long history of economic difficulty even *before* the divorce.

CHAPTER VII

ACQUAINTANCE, ENGAGEMENT, AND FAMILY APPROVAL

THE BACKGROUND social and economic factors just under discussion have some importance for both marriage and the postdivorce adjustment. In the present chapter, we shall discuss factors that seem to have little effect on postdivorce adjustment, but do have some effect on the marriage. We thereby help to validate previous findings with respect to length of acquaintance and of engagement on marital stability, and also give a fuller picture of the premarital experience of the divorcee. We shall, in addition, begin to see the relationship between the divorcee and her circle of friends before the marriage took place, with respect to class differences, length of engagement, and approval of the marriage.

Length of Acquaintance. A minority of our respondents made the acquaintance of their husbands only a short time before marriage. The majority had known their husbands for some years prior to the marriage. Collapsing both our table and that of Terman[1] so as to obtain comparable categories, we find that the two distributions are as follows:

LENGTH OF ACQUAINTANCE

Period	Terman	Goode
0-1 year	16%	30%
1-3 years	34	39
3-5 years	22	16
5 years	28	15
	100%	100%

Over four-fifths of Terman's sample rated their marriages as above average in happiness. If the factor of long acquaintanceship differentiates with respect to marital happiness or marital stability, then our sample should have a somewhat higher proportion whose acquaintance was *short*. The above table bears out the expectation. It is true that Terman's sample is not a representative one, but this deviation from randomness may not affect substantially the association between marital adjustment and length of acquaintance. Our data thus

---

1. Lewis M. Terman, *Psychological Factors in Marital Happiness* (New York: McGraw-Hill, 1938), pp. 197 ff.

support Terman's conclusion. The Burgess and Cottrell categories cannot be meaningfully compared with ours.

Length of Engagement. The factor of length of *engagement* would operate in somewhat the same fashion as that of length of acquaintance. Of course they overlap each other in time. These items, like those of social and economic origins, are genuinely *background* characteristics: that is, they are characteristics of the individuals and the relationship *prior* to their entering marriage. Just what dynamics of later marital interaction come to differentiate those who remain married and those who get divorced have not been made clear in the published material on this problem.

The studies that have compared couples with respect to length of engagement do agree roughly with one another that a short period of being engaged is associated with marital unhappiness.[2] Now, the connection of marital unhappiness with proneness to divorce is fairly clear, although other factors may be equally important in the prediction of marital instability. In any event, the association between length of engagement and proneness to divorce also seems apparent.

In the present study, then, a relatively short engagement seems to be characteristic, as appears in the following table:

LENGTH OF ENGAGEMENT FOR DIVORCING COUPLES

Never engaged	19%
0-2 months	17
3-6 months	35
7-11 months	6
12-23 months	14
24 months and over	8
Not known	.2
Total	99.2%

Over 70% of these divorced couples were engaged for 6 months or less. Although we cannot compare precisely our categories with those of Locke's divorced sample, 13% of his sample were engaged 12-23 months, as against 14% of ours; about 10% of his were engaged 24 months and over, as against 8% of ours. And 55% of his were engaged 0-5 months, as against 70% of ours for 0-6 months (inclusive). Moreover, a cumulative curve drawn for the two distributions follows the same pattern, with no deviations of significance.[3]

We may conclude, then, that this distribution of length of engagement for the divorced is not far from reality.

Let us, by contrast, array this distribution against populations of mainly (four-fifths) happily married couples.

In the following comparative tables we use data from the Burgess and Cottrell and the Terman studies. It is not possible to compare the categories used in the Burgess and Wallin study of engagement for this purpose.[4]

2. See Terman, *op. cit.,* p. 199; Burgess and Cottrell, *op. cit.,* p. 94.

3. Locke, *op. cit.,* p. 94.

4. Ernest W. Burgess and Paul W. Wallin, *Engagement and Marriage* (New York: Lippincott, 1953). They find no decisive relationship between "engagement success" and length of engagement (pp. 316-317); Terman, *op. cit.,* p. 199, Burgess and Cottrell, *op. cit.,* p. 407.

LENGTH OF ENGAGEMENT

Period	Burgess & Cottrell Percent	Goode Percent
Not engaged	6	19
0-2 months	14	17
3-23 months	62	56
24 months and over	18	8
Total	100	100

LENGTH OF ENGAGEMENT

Period	Terman Percent	Goode Percent
0-2	15	36
3-11 months	35	42
1-2 years	38	14
2 years and over	11	8
Total	99	100

From both tables it is clear that our sample of divorced couples has substantially shorter periods of engagement than did the people in the two studies cited, in which four-fifths of the couples claimed to be happily (or very happily) married. Thus our data corroborate their results.

We are far from an adequate understanding of the process of engagement and its effect upon marriage. There are at least two main dimensions to the effect of length of acquaintance and engagement upon stability of the marriage. As a merely classificatory item, long engagement ought to be associated with a complex of attitudes characterized by a rather serious commitment to marriage in general, and a somewhat conservative background. This is, of course, a mere probability statement. The second dimension is that of a *sieving* process. That is to say, if the engagement is long, the chances are greater that individuals who are unsuited to each other will come to that conclusion during the period of engagement. It is not to the point to say, "This long period gives them a chance to become acquainted." This is, after all, what might also happen in marriage. Becoming acquainted is important because it leads to weeding out the incompatibles; in the apprenticeship to each other's service, one or the other fails to acquire the necessary skills.

The Class Meaning of Engagement. Now engagement seems to have a different meaning in different strata of the population. Certainly it has a variant meaning from one clique to another. In some circles a formal engagement becomes very close to a commitment to marry, and breaking the engagement is a serious social matter. In such circles, the engagement is in some sense a public affair, at least for the families concerned. In other circles, engagement means little more than that the couple are now "going steady" or that they have decided to indulge in somewhat more physical intimacy than is normally permitted to those who are merely dating one another. In these latter circles, engagement is perhaps a decision made by the couple only, and announced to very close personal friends and, as almost an afterthought, to the parents concerned. In such circles, too, we would expect the two sets of relatives to do little about it, and to make no great effort toward becoming more closely acquainted with each other.

Some suggestion of the differences that probably do exist may be found in the following table:

LENGTH OF ENGAGEMENT, BY HUSBAND'S OCCUPATIONAL CLASS

Husband's Occupational Class	Length of Engagement			Totals	
	Less than 3 months	3-6 months	More than 6 months	Percent	No.
Upper	29%	31%	40%	100%	45
Middle	35	33	32	100	159
Lower	39	37	24	100	214

N = 418

As can be seen, the upper strata tend to have somewhat longer engagements. But our "upper" class contains a large proportion of people who would be classed as "upper-middle" or even "middle" in a study whose population represented the general population of the city. In such a larger sampling range the differentiation by occupational class would probably be even more striking. We now suggest that there is a difference in (a) average length of engagement by stratum and also in (b) the emotional meaning, (c) the intensity of commitment, and (d) the social pressures in the various strata. Occupational class is our indicator in this comparison, but similar comparisons might be made with other indicators of class.

Length of Engagement and of Acquaintance. It might be thought that there would be no particular relationship between the length of acquaintance and the length of engagement. Perhaps those who have *known* each other for a very long time might, upon deciding to get married, feel that they already know each other well enough to marry. One supposed function of a long engagement would be little served if the individuals already knew each other well. However, as we see in the following table, those who became engaged after a long period of acquaintance are also more likely to have a long engagement. If we use as cutting-off points for our engagement period the two categories "less than six months" and "more than six months," and for acquaintance, "less than three years" and "more than three years," then the Q of association is .60.[5]

What this means for predicting marital adjustment seems clear. It is possible to use length of engagement to help differentiate those who will remain married, because a longer acquaintance between the individuals is in turn associated with a longer engagement. Both long acquaintances and long engagements presumably affect the relationship in the ways already commented upon, (a) by selecting those who are predisposed to stay married; (b) by weeding out the incompatibles; and (c) through the class-differential group and family pressures that are associated with length of acquaintance and engagement.

---

5. As the reader will recognize, in part this is a spurious association, since to some degree these are overlapping periods.

LENGTH OF ACQUAINTANCE, BY LENGTH OF ENGAGEMENT

Length of Acquaintance	Length of Engagement		
	Less than 3 months	3-6 months	More than 6 months
Less than 1 yr.	47%	29%	8%
1-3 yrs.	30	49	38
More than 3 yrs.	23	22	54
Total	100%	100%	100%
Number	153	150	121 N = 424

It is an assertion of folk wisdom, as against the claims of the romantic love complex, that family and friends are better judges of a couple's mutual suitability than is the couple involved. This is a partial injustice, since it is unlikely, in any culture in which the young have some choice in the matter, that they choose with no regard to the present and future usefulness of the potential spouse. Sometimes this judgment is shrewd; often it is forced by their peer group.[6] The claim of folk wisdom also ignores the *self-fulfilling* aspect of the judgment; family and friends may also *help* the couple to adjust, or to fight.

Approval and Disapproval of Marriage by Various Groups. The approval of friends and families can be seen as a merely *classificatory* item in that it is useful in predicting a mutually more satisfactory married life than would be the lot of a couple judged by family and friends to be unsuitable. Along this dimension certain factors, seen or sensed by friends and families, would be the dynamic elements in a future conflict situation, and people's disapproval or approval simply *reflects* their judgment about the future. To the extent that this judgment has any basis in fact, it might serve as a *differentiating* item. On the other hand, a *selective* process is also involved, in that families and friends who approve the marriage would be more likely to continue in close contact with the couple and support that marriage in moments of crisis and strain, or even to punish in one way or another the fiance or spouse who seemed to be deviating from the norm of marital stability.

Put differently, approval or disapproval by family and friends expresses a commitment or lack of commitment on their part to helping or hindering the continuity of the marriage.

There are, then, two main lines of analysis for future research on this point: the relationship of approval and disapproval to a) various known or unknown background items of the couple, and to b) the active help by families and friends toward the achievement of a stable marriage by the couple.

In an urban society not all one's friends and family would take some part in this approval or disapproval, or would have an opinion. Further, even when everyone actually *has* an opinion, the young man and woman marrying might not *know* of that opinion or might pay so little attention to it that they simply fail to note it. Furthermore, for questions about family and friends, "family" is sometimes an almost empty category. One or the other of the fiancés might not have seen his or her family in months or years, and the answer of "approve" might mean merely that a relative wrote a congratulatory letter upon receiving the news that his kinsman was to be married. Similarly,

---

6. For a discussion of these judgments, see Burgess and Wallin, *op. cit.*, ch. 7.

the closeness of a friendship circle will vary from one individual to another. Finally, the individual's knowledge about approval *by his fiancee's friends* may be sketchy at best.

Where possible, these complexities will be analyzed in this study. We queried our respondents with respect to several categories of circles who might have been interested in the marriage. These answers are given in the following table:

ATTITUDES OF VARIOUS CIRCLES TOWARDS THE MARRIAGE

Question: "Would you try to tell me, *in general*, what these people thought about your marriage several years ago, when you were beginning this marriage?"

						Don't Know	
				Attitudes		or	
	Approval				Disapproval	No Answer	
Circles	Strong	Mild	Indifference		Mild Strong		Total
Husband's family	36%	19%	11%		12%	13%	9%	100%
Wife's family	28	18	11		17	23	3	100
Husband's friends	26	25	20		3	2	24	100
Wife's friends	26	30	20		8	8	8	100
Mutual friends	21	24	22		5	3	25	100

N = 425

Perhaps of greatest immediate interest is the large proportion of "Don't knows" in the case of (a) the husband's close friends and (b) mutual friends. These women really did not know their husbands' close friends well enough to know what their opinions were about the marriage. Neither did they know the opinions of mutual friends; or perhaps they actually lacked such friends. In half the cases there was no knowledge as to the attitude of any religious advisor.

We see then, the extent to which the urban divorcee entered a marriage that did not have strong support from an interlocking network of friends. Phrasing the matter somewhat differently, the marriage was so little a subject of serious discussions between the respondent and her circle of acquaintances that she knew *well* only the opinions of (a) her own and (b) her husband's families, and (c) of her own circle of friends. One line of analysis seems suggestive at this point. Let us look at the differences in the *definite* attitudes towards the marriage among various circles of friends and relatives. This is seen in the following table:

DEFINITE ATTITUDES TOWARD THE MARRIAGE AMONG VARIOUS CIRCLES

			Attitude		
				Don't Know	
				or	
Group	Approval	Disapproval	Indifference	No Answer	Total
Husband's family	55%	25%	11%	9%	100%
Wife's family	46	40	11	3	100
Husband's friends	51	5	20	24	100
Wife's friends	56	16	20	8	100
Mutual friends	45	8	22	25	100

N = 425

Several facts emerge from this table. As we see, (1) there are only slight differences between these various circles of families and close friends as to *approval*. About half of husbands' and wives' families and husbands' and wives' close friends are reported by the respondents to have approved the marriage either mildly or strongly prior to its occurrence. (2) On the other hand, we see that the differences in *disapproval* are much more striking. We note that 40% of the *families of these women* expressed strong or mild disapproval of the marriage, while the same respondents reported that only one-fourth *of their husbands' families* disapproved of the marriage prior to its occurrence. (3) The same comparison shows up between the two sets of friends. Of wives' friends, 16% showed disapproval of the marriage, as against only 5% of the husbands' friends. It seems safe to say that this difference expresses not so much an *objective* difference in attitude on the part of these circles as it does a difference in the perception or knowledge of the respondent. The difference is a function of the *wife* reporting. That is to say, she actually *knew* the disapproving attitudes of her own family and her own friends, while she guessed or supposed that her husband's family and friends felt approval unless she had the contrary evidence. Usually, then, she believed that they actually approved of the marriage.

When we turn to the matter of indifference or the "Don't know" answers, we see other interesting comparisons. We note once again that the respondents have reported (4) approximately the same percentage of indifference on the part of husbands' and wives' families and husbands' and wives' close friends. It is noticeable here, however, that (5) the indifference is much greater for the circles of *friends* than for the families concerned. This we would expect, since we would suppose that in general the circles whose destinies are less immediately concerned would also be less likely to have strong feelings about the coming marriage. On the other hand, (6) when we turn to the "No answer" or "Don't know" group, we see once again that there are sharp differences between the husband's and the wife's circle. The wife knows the opinions of her *husband's* family far less often than she knows the opinions of her *own* family, and this is also true for her husband's friends as against her own friends. The ratio is about 1:3. With reference to the category "mutual friends," we would expect this to fall in the direction of the "Don't know" answers, since this category probably includes many people who are not close friends but who are merely acquaintances held in common. For husband's friends and wife's friends, we specified *close* friends. However, in our urban society, "mutual friends" merely means that both members of the couple know the same person. In this case the respondents seem to have been unable to report those opinions, if any; presumably, they simply did not know what they were. In this connection we note (7) that both approval and disapproval are low for this circle of mutual friends, while the "Don't know" or "No answer" response is high.

That our previous interpretation of engagement and approval is roughly correct may be seen in the following set of tables, in which *length of engagement* is run against (a) approval, (b) disapproval, and (c) a combined category of indifference and "No answer." We have, that is, attempted to find out whether there are significant differences in the amount of approval, disapproval, or indifference, between (a) engagements that were very short or nonexistent, and (b) those that lasted a longer period of time. As can be seen from the tables, the pattern is almost completely consistent throughout. That is to say, (1) *approval* steadily increases over time, for the four categories of

(a) husband's and (b) wife's families, and (c) husband's and (d) wife's friends. Furthermore, (2) the amount of disapproval decreases slightly. On the other hand, (3) the amount of indifference *also* decreases. Since one effect of the longer engagement is to allow the couple to learn of these attitudes, the *indifference* decreases. Since a selective process is at work, the amount of *approval* increases over the longer period of time.

APPROVAL OF MARRIAGE AMONG VARIOUS CIRCLES, BY LENGTH OF ENGAGEMENT

	Length of Engagement		
	0-2 months	3-6 months	More than 6 months
Husband's family			
Approval	49%	55%	64%
Disapproval	27	25	23
Indifference, D. K.	24	21	13
Total	100%	101%	100%
Wife's family			
Approval	41%	46%	53%
Disapproval	42	41	37
Indifference, D. K.	16	13	10
Total	99%	100%	100%
Husband's friends			
Approval	47%	53%	55%
Disapproval	4	5	7
Indifference, D. K.	49	42	38
Total	100%	100%	100%
Wife's friends			
Approval	51%	56%	63%
Disapproval	18	15	15
Indifference, D. K.	31	29	22
Total	100%	100%	100%
Number	(153)	(150)	(121)	N = 424

These tables also throw some light on the selective process of engagement, and on the reasons for the apparent rough association between length of engagement and marital stability. Increasingly these circles are committed to the marriage, as the length of engagement increases. At the same time, this commitment is only one of many factors that go into the marriage, and it has only a rough predictive value. Even though there is a greater approval of marriage for couples with longer engagements, it must be kept in mind that this approval could not alone save the marriage. After all, every one of these individuals did divorce, in the face of such claimed approval.

In the Burgess and Wallin report, slightly over 80% of their total sample reported that the parents (father *or* mother separately) approved the union. On the other hand, for those who married and later separated or divorced, the percentages are somewhat closer to our own data, allowing for the obvious discrepancy in categories. They report roughly 70% of the separated and divorced couples had the approval of *both* parents, and 21-24% of the couples had the disapproval of one or both parents.[7] Their proportion of indifference is much less. However, it must be remembered that their sample is largely composed of middle-class couples, and we would suppose that these couples made greater efforts to ascertain the opinions and to obtain the ap-

7. Burgess and Wallin, *op. cit.*, pp. 560-562.

proval of their respective families. With reference to the approval of friends, we cannot equate our category of "circle of friends" and theirs of "closest friend." Presumably, the "closest friend" would either approve the marriage, or would run the risk of losing to some extent his position as closest friend. On the other hand, the engaged person does not have the same control over his *circle* of friends. He may continue his relationships with them even in the face of their mild or strong disapproval of his marriage. Furthermore, it is rare that the engaged person does not know the opinion of his closest friend regarding his own coming marriage. On the other hand, the *circle* of friends may participate generally in preparations for showers and for the marriage itself, and even do so with some good nature, when there has been no great approval of the impending marriage.

In the Burgess-Wallin study the closest friends approved the coming marriages of those who were *ultimately to be separated and divorced* even *more than* (a) those marriages which were to be relatively stable or (b) those engagements which were to be broken. Apparently, the friends of our own respondents were somewhat more realistic. Certainly these circles of kinsmen and relatives were considerably more *accurate* in their implicit predictions as to the outcome of the marriages.

By contrast, Locke reported whether the spouse's parents approved the prospective mate. There were great differences in the approval given by parents as between marriages that ended in divorce and those that were happy. Nearly four-fifths approved the prospective mate in cases of marriages that turned out to be happy. The figures are close to those of Burgess and Wallin. But only about half approved of the prospective mate in those cases that ended in divorce. This figure (52% for men; 46% for women) is almost precisely our figure for the approval of the wife's family (46%).[8]

Summary. We have in this chapter shown that the people who get divorces appear to have both shorter acquaintances and shorter engagements than those who claim to be happily married. This finding is in agreement with previous studies. We have also pointed out several dimensions or aspects of these relationships: (1) the connection between length of acquaintance and of engagement; (2) the connection of both with class; (3) the connection of the latter with various potential group pressures toward marital stability in the various strata—the meaning of engagement, the intensity of the commitment, and the social importance of those networks; and (4) the selectivity of long acquaintance and long engagement. Finally, we have shown how the different circles of kin and friend responded originally to the marriage, and we have corroborated to some extent our notions about length of engagement by relating it to the change in approval or disapproval of various circles. With increasing length of engagement, there is apparently increasing social support for the marriage.

In the next chapter, we turn to certain aspects of the husband-wife interaction during the marriage.

---

8. Locke, *op. cit.*, p. 119.

CHAPTER VIII

SOCIAL INTERACTION OF HUSBAND AND WIFE: DATING AND SHARED ACTIVITIES

INDICES AND CAUSES OF CONFLICT. In the present state of the sociology of the family, we are forced to view many factors as both *indices* and *causes* of conflict. This phase may be viewed as progress, when compared to the past. Perhaps a generation ago many characteristics, such as adultery, absenteeism or desertion, cruelty, failure to settle down, etc., might have been viewed as simple "causes" of divorce. Later, during the 1930's and until relatively recently, when marriage counselors and analysts probed the surface conflict or the grounds given in the divorce suit, they offered the idea that almost *any apparent* conflict was simply an *index* of something that was deeper and more important.

Such a notion was salutary. It is necessary, when analyzing such a complex phenomenon as divorce, to go beneath the immediate answers given by the respondent and to be aware that the apparent focus of conflict is often not the real conflict at all. To a great extent, of course, this insight is derived from psychodynamic theory. We have become acutely aware in our generation that a factor which crystallizes a conflict, or sets off an argument, may be merely a diversion from the main problem. Thus, for example, the wife may complain about the slovenliness of her husband, his poor way of dressing, his table manners, and even his speech; but her basic difficulty may be that she has remained attached to her father in rather deep ways and resents her husband's failure to live up to that model.

Some of these formulations are very old, and are embodied in folk wisdom. One way of expressing this idea is to note that the husband who comes home from a difficult and frustrating day at work may scold his wife about an insignificant item, and his wife, in turn, spanks the child, who kicks the dog, etc. Such insights doubtless go back at least 2000 years in one form or another.

On the other hand, that insight cannot be allowed to remain in such a crude form. The notion that some conflicts are merely *indices* of deeper conflicts is fruitful, but we cannot therefore claim that *all* conflicts are merely indices of some other conflicts. Not only does this logically involve a tail-catching operation, but there is simply no empirical proof of this claim. Furthermore, the form which this latter proposition has taken, that *all* conflict is *only* apparent, turns into a still weaker, simpler idea that all conflict is simply the conflict of different *personalities*. Since the theory of personality is relatively undeveloped, we have no way of knowing whether or not this is indeed the case. In general, however, we have considerable evidence that notions of personality conflict do not afford generalized explanations of social behavior, and particularly marital behavior. Personality theory, particularly as it has been developed within the last two decades, often becomes a parlor game of *ad hoc* hypothesizing when used to explain social patterns.

Meanwhile, it does not seem unreasonable to accept the commonsense notion that some *apparent* problems actually *do* affect behavior and attitudes. It is possible, for example, that, even when the deeper problem is that a wife has really been unable to free herself from her attachment to her father, the slovenliness of her husband (the *apparent* problem) does play an active role in the conflict. Furthermore, she may be of middle-class origin, and may move in circles where neatness, cleanliness, and some conformity with middle-class modes of speech, dress, and manners are required, under the penalty of some deprecation or even ostracism by her friends. In such a case we cannot stop our analysis by some simple reference to "father-attachment." The purpose of a theoretical concept is to allow us to continue with our analysis, not to stop it. We must, therefore, look beyond the notion that underlying some obvious conflicts there may be still other conflicts which are "more real." It is at least worth while to look at those which are there for us to observe. Moreover, as is noted at some length in Chapter V, a broader accounting scheme now yields a more useful model for analyzing the decision to break up a marriage.

A more important, though subtler, comment on this notion must be made here. To the extent that all apparent conflicts, such as adultery, desertion, etc., are viewed as "symptoms of deeper conflicts," we accept a rather peculiar set of value premises. We say, in effect, that no one can commit adultery whose marriage is a "good" one. No one will indulge in selfish spending if his marital adjustment is good, or if his personality is "mature." Now, if that is how "good marital adjustment," or "mature personality" are defined there can be no argument with such propositions. On the other hand, they are empty of content, if it is merely a matter of definition.

If, however, such propositions are to be taken seriously as substantive contributions to our knowledge of marriage and family, then it must be asked whether they can, indeed, be correct. It is a smug expression of "goody-goody" or Pollyanna philosophy, that conformity with a rather narrowly defined set of prescriptions and proscriptions will always occur automatically if the marriage is a happy one. It seems to us an amusingly unsophisticated defense of the *status quo* to believe that husbands and wives whose marriages are really happy, and who enjoy their lives together, and whose personalities are "healthy" might not, under many conceivable circumstances, deviate from this narrow norm. A more complex and complete model of marital dissolution is required.

Furthermore, the norms expressed in such formulations by psychiatrists, psychoanalysts, and psychoanalytically oriented marital counselors form a *middle-class morality*. There is little recognition (perhaps because the distribution of clinical cases is so heavily in the direction of middle-class patients) that there are really *cultural* differences as to the "proper" marital behavior, from one social stratum to another, in different regions, and within various religious and ethnic groups. Adultery and violence, for example, carry a different emotional weight among these various segments of the population.[1]

Consequently, we would be skeptical of such personality formulations which nearly equate moral conformity with marital happiness and emotional health, within middle-class or any other strata, until considerably more empirical evidence exists than at present. At the present writing, such formulations seem to us rather an expression of value premises. We are inclined to the belief that deviation in many respects can be expected from healthy individuals, and that we shall have to know more about the social situations and role definitions involved in such deviations, before we are certain who will and who will not ever deviate, or which kinds of people will or will not put up with the conflict that may result from the deviation.

These arguments, of course, lead to the notion that it is no longer possible to look at all such aspects of the marriage, such as nondating or lack of shared activities, or at the complaints made by spouses, as merely *indices* of conflict. At least, the possibility exists that some of these items play an *active* role in intensifying or crystallizing the conflict, or even in some cases actually "causing" it.

Even if most of the above speculations are incorrect, it is certainly necessary to face the fact that in some cases the behavior that *began* as a mere index of conflict may *in time* take on an autonomous status. The adultery that was an expression of a husband's dissatisfaction with the marriage (or with himself) may in time lead to a serious attachment to a new woman, or to an irremediable conflict with his wife.

Once this possibility is seen, in which any given focus of conflict may develop an autonomous status in the relationship between husband and wife, it is then necessary to embark upon a new and more elaborate research project such as was mentioned in Chapter V, far beyond the scope of the present study. In such a project we would want to ascertain which factors are mere indices of conflict (whether personality or social) for each couple, and which might instead be viewed as more fundamental. We would furthermore wish to observe such families frequently and intimately enough to be able to judge when the status of such factors *shifts*. Both types of shifts may occur in the course of a long marital conflict. That is, some factors that were originally fundamental might come to be of relatively surface importance, mere indices of conflict; while indices in turn may become autonomous and come to play a central role in the conflict. The growth of each individual, the changes that he and she make in their values, their attitudes, friends, the position they hold in their own circle and in the world: their role apprenticeship with each other, would have to be taken into account. At the present time the

---

1. For one analysis of these value elements, see William J. Goode, "Social Engineering and the Divorce Problem," *Annals*, 272 (1950), 86-94. See also Kingsley Davis, "Mental Hygiene and the Class Structure," *Psychiatry*, 1 (1938), 55-65.

techniques we have for making such a study would probably change the behavior and possibly the attitudes of the couple. Nevertheless, it is clear that once we embark upon an attempt to get at "underlying" factors, we must make much more detailed and intimate *processual, longitudinal* observations of family behavior.

Thus, in our own research we have not been willing to assume *a priori* that income will make no difference in a "good" marriage. Income will be one of the items that characterize that marriage, and it would be unlikely that income would have no impact upon it. Otherwise, it might be claimed that most nothing will have an impact upon a "good" marriage—neither the good temper of either spouse, nor the ugliness of one spouse, the slovenly habits of the wife or husband, etc. If we continue to fill such a list, we will soon see that we have listed all the characteristics that go to make up a marriage. Once we have carried out such an operation to this point of substantive absurdity, we are then forced to reverse our assertion, and come to a very simple and old commonsense notion, *that any marriage can break.* This is comparable to the discovery during World War II that, in spite of quite similar notions about the strength and resilience of a "mature" or "strong" personality, *any man can break under some conceivable stress.* There are differences in the breaking point, and there are differences as to which *kinds* of stress, and how powerful a stress, will more easily break either man or marriage. An accounting model comparable to that in Chapter V can be developed for psychological breakdown. We are, then, forced to reexamine our ideas about divorce, and to ask which kinds of stresses lead to early or later divorce. Moreover, we have to specify the social strata and circles involved. As we have already asserted, there are different social definitions of how great a stress a spouse *ought* to bear, and how much support a spouse ought to receive from his or her group if divorce becomes the solution.

The marital relationship, in short, is a social relationship like many others, and under some kinds of internal pressures, external stresses, external attractions, etc., it may come apart. We cannot *a priori* assume any longer that a "good" marriage will not break. What we are then forced to do is to find which of the myriad characteristics that make up a marriage will lead to marital stability or instability, and—at a much later remove in our future research—to achieve some kind of *measurement* of stresses and breaking points.

Dating Behavior. A low frequency of dating *during marriage* may not be a mere index of marital conflict. All these couples did eventually end their marriage relationship. For some of these people, doubtless the fact that they dated seldom was simply (a) an *index* of the fact that they did not particularly like one another's company. In other cases, almost without question the lack of frequent dating was (b) a mere social characteristic of their circle of friends and relatives; that is to say, going out together was simply not a common activity of husbands and wives. In *other* cases—and we do not have the interpretive data necessary for locating these cases in the three categories—the fact that husband and wife did not date (c) actually *affected* their closeness and made one or the other feel less wanted. In the following table it is seen that some 42% of these couples dated relatively rarely, once a month or less.

DATING WITH THE HUSBAND DURING MARRIAGE

Frequency	Percent
Almost never	30
Once monthly	12
Twice monthly	10
Once weekly	28
Twice weekly or more	20
	100%

N = 425

However, let us not deduce too freely from such a table. Failure to date may *express* a couple's dislike for each other's company, or it may be a *cause* for a wife's anger at her husband. On the other hand, dating may be uncommon in some circles, and some couples may even be unable to afford it. It is quite possible, also, that much of the dating between spouses does not bring them more closely together, or even maintain closeness, but instead leads to other emotional attachments or interests outside the family.

Evidence that this last interpretation is partially correct may be seen in the following table:

DURATION OF MARRIAGE, BY FREQUENCY OF DATING

Duration of Marriage	Never	Once monthly to once weekly	More than once weekly	Totals	
0-4 years	21%	50%	29%	100%	72
5-9 years	26	51	23	100	168
10-14 years	35	49	15	99	130
15 and over	38	54	9	101	55
Total	30%	51%	20%	101	425

From this table it is seen that there is a low *inverse* relationship between frequency of dating and the length of marriage. This proposition is not equivalent to saying that frequent dating is a causal factor in *instability* of marriage, although the inference does not seem far-fetched. For (a) the modal group of dating, that is, "once a month to once a week," there are few differences among the various categories of duration of marriage. However, for (b) the very frequent or (c) the almost never group, the relationship seems evident enough. Perhaps, on the other hand, dating is a mere function of income: those date who can afford it.

FREQUENCY OF DATING, BY WEEKLY INCOME

Amount of Income	Almost Never	1/month- 1/week	More than 1/week	Totals	
Less than $45/week	31	55	14	100	128
$45-$75/week	28	54	18	100	206
Over $75/week	28	37	36	101	76
					N = 410

Income is not, of course, the only variable of significance in the frequency of dating. The major differentiation here is between those with less than $75 a week and those above $75 a week. There is little differentiation between the two lower brackets of income.

This table raises the question as to whether a *negative* relationship between duration of marriage and frequency of dating might be *spurious*. We can answer it by ascertaining whether *within* any given income bracket the negative relationship between frequency of dating and duration of marriage remains. As we see in the following sets of four-fold tables, income is a condition for this association; in that, when we hold income constant, there is a low *positive* association between dating and duration of marriage for two of the income groups.

INCOME, BY DATING OF HUSBAND AND WIFE, BY DURATION OF MARRIAGE

Income Duration	Almost Never	1/month- 1/week	More than 1/week	Totals	
$0-$45/wk.					
0 -9 yrs.	30%	51%	19%	100%	67
10 and over	33	59	8	100	61
$45-$75/wk.					
0-9 yrs.	22	55	23	100	126
10 and over	36	53	11	100	80
$75-more					
0-9 yrs.	22	35	43	100	40
10 and over	33	39	28	100	36

Shared Activities. Now, if dating between spouses was actually not frequent, and the relationship between duration of marriage and frequent dating seems unstable under different conditions, perhaps *what* they did and its social *meaning* were also important. Let us inquire into this possibility.

What were the "shared activities" in these dating patterns? For the most part, little more than going to the movies. The two other large categories are dancing and social drinking in bars. These three categories together total slightly more than 60%. The distribution as a whole is seen below.

SHARED ACTIVITIES OF HUSBAND AND WIFE DURING THE MARRIAGE

Shared Activities	Percent	Number
Movies	36	312
Sports:		
Spectator	9	78
Participant	8	72
Concerts	2	17
Work around house	6	52
Reading	4	34
Travel	10	87
Dancing	13	109
Social drinking in bars	12	108
Subtotal	100	869
None		25
Total		894

Now, these different shared activities might have very different meanings. Much has been made of the notion of "sharing in the marriage," and some type of sharing is probably conducive to marital satisfaction. The implied interlocking of actional patterns would also make for the stability of the marriage. Nevertheless, "sharing" can be felt in many ways, often through activities that are not common to both spouses. This sharing may be just as strong as the sharing that is immediate, involving the actual physical presence and co-participation of the other spouse.

The matter might be phrased in this fashion: It is not so much the mere sharing of activities, but the *kinds* of activities that husband and wife take part in, whether singly or together, and their *meaning*. For example, much of the amateur radio-building, cabinet-making, or shop-work that many husbands carry on at home is shared very little by the wife. Nevertheless, we would suppose that such activities are *positive* factors in maintaining the marriage. On the other hand, frequent attendance at dances might be associated with lower stability, even though in this case the activity would be "shared."

Indeed it is possible to claim that the traditional family of two generations or more ago—the "classical" family discussed in Chapter I—was one in which there was relatively little sharing in this direct, physical sense. The areas of co-participation were relatively infrequent, and even narrow. The family ate together, and the wife (we assume that the family lived on a farm) might have taken care of one or two of the farm chores that in some regions were traditionally hers. Thus, for example, she might have taken care of the chickens, since the egg money was to be hers. The family slept together. Further, certain major group activities, such as butchering, sausage-making, smoking hams, etc., were definitely shared. And, of course, recreation was generally shared. However, for the most part, husband and wife went their separate ways during the course of the day, each attending separately to his or her own activity. There was some integration in the total enterprise, but relatively little direct sharing. Furthermore, there was only infrequent recreation, though it is true that in that case the family usually went together. In that traditional family, then, one could not speak of many activities as being immediately shared, even though we all look back with some nostalgia upon the feeling of integration and identity that we impute to those families.

What *was* characteristic of such families, however, was that the activities were "home centered."[2] They either contributed directly to the home, or were part of the management and work that were seen as necessary to keep the enterprise going, whether in the city or in the country. Thus, since all these activities contributed to all family members, one can say there was sharing. It is clear, then, that (a) these activities were centripetal; they *had home-centered meaning.* They were *understood* as contributions toward the health, comfort, and well-being of all members rather than of self.

Furthermore, and certainly of very great importance in contrast with the present age, (b) few such activities brought members into much contact with *those outside the immediate or extended family*. Thus, the family remained the most important element in their lives. When such contacts were made, (c) they were made under the *supervision* of the entire family, not alone that of the husband and wife. It is too much to say that these were "chaperoned" activities, since the very term implies the feeling that chaperoning was necessary.

2. For a beginning test of these notions, see Purnell Benson, "Interests of Happily Married Couples," *Marriage and Family Living*, 14 (1952), 276-280.

It was rather that most outside activities were joint activities of the same circle, and it was very difficult to meet people of the opposite sex within any other context than that of civility and prescribed friendship.

On the other hand, within our own era both dancing and social drinking in bars offer further opportunity for contacts which can lead to commitments and involvements other than those of family friendship. We cannot make the same charge against movies, the most common dating activity of these couples, but it is perfectly clear that movies can hardly be said to be a shared activity, except in the most superficially physical sense. We do not wish here to impugn the emotions and deep feelings that may be felt by a couple in some situations when going to a movie. For example, some couples who have children find that movies are one of the few occasions when they can be really alone. This may be so even when they take the children along. Unlike parties and various kinds of family visits, the movies require far less preparation, and thus need not be viewed with the same kind of alarm which the matron and father may feel when faced with the prospect of cleaning and dressing simultaneously two to four children. It may thus be possible for the couple to escape for an evening, circumscribed in time by the length of the movie, to enjoy a few moments of intimacy, to regain briefly some of their feeling of comradeship. It is not too much to say, either, that for a few couples the movies represent a genuine artistic sharing, since both husband and wife consider the film an artistic medium, and choose each with great care. The movie then becomes a subject of their shared analysis and conversation.

It is hardly fair, then, to dismiss the movies entirely as a simple physical juxtaposition of husband and wife, with no further meaning. However, movies will *usually* fall somewhere between the centrifugal forces to be found in the "sharing" of social drinking in bars and dancing, and such home-centered activities as working around the house, reading together, attending P.T.A. meetings together, taking part in family picnics, etc. That is to say, relatively little will usually be shared in movies, and, in any event, the sharing does not usually lead to any intensification of the forces holding husband and wife together. This does *not* mean that we accept the viewing with alarm to be found in literary reviews, to the effect that the Hollywood myths purveyed in the average movie can only lead to dissatisfaction with one's drab lot, or lead to violence, etc. Data on such points are somewhat ambiguous, to say the least.[3]

It must be kept in mind, however, that we are not attempting to differentiate between activities we approve and those we disapprove. We are not here suggesting that concerts are somehow "better" to go to than movies. We are not here concerned with the moral aspects of dancing or social drinking in bars.

Our real concern is to what extent any of these "shared" activities is more likely (a) to shorten or lengthen a marriage, even if it ends in divorce; and (b) to have an effect on postdivorce behavior. We wish particularly to know which *aspects* of that activity create such a likelihood. We here suggest that it

3. Our own notion (shared by many communications analysts) is that, in general, Hollywood has little hand in making the myth. Hollywood rather locates it, uses it, and expresses it. When the director expresses it very well, that is, when the audience accepts it fully, then the movie is financially successful. Success, then, stems from the fact that the movie expresses a myth shared by many. If anybody is "guilty," it is we, rather than the movies. In any event, the attempts to demonstrate seriously the impact of movies on any substantial segment of the population have not been successful.

is something which we vaguely entitle "home-centered meanings," but we are sure that this is only a first approximation. It seems fairly clear that some of these activities would rank as more centripetal than others. We have no way of judging the concert as an item in this ranking, except that its interruptions during the program create somewhat more of a possibility for husband-and-wife interaction than is the case for movies. On the other hand, we would need considerably further empirical data to judge the effect of: (a) still other activities; and (b) the *variations in social context* which create different effects for various kinds of people.

Locke's data are in conformity with these hypotheses: a higher percentage of divorced than of happily married people reported mutual enjoyment of drinking and dancing; men included gambling; and there was little difference between the two groups for movies.[4]

Unfortunately, we had not anticipated these relationships adequately, and did not develop really pointed questions to get at the social meanings of these activities. Actually, it is only those who stayed at home together, read together, or did nothing, who had marriage of longer duration (11.9 years for the first two categories together; 11.4 for the third). All other types of activity were about the same (8.5-9.7 years duration). Our questions do not come close enough to the social meanings we need for adequate analysis of these factors in marital stability.

Summary. Looking back at the data we have presented with respect to dating and shared activities, there appear to be different marital patterns in different strata even for divorcees. First, it seems likely that it is the *meaning* of the dating that is of central importance, rather than its frequency. Second, since a high proportion of the "dating" is not home-centered in meaning, we would expect (as we found) at least a low negative relationship between frequency of dating in marriage, and stability or duration of marriage.

Third, this negative association is, after all, an association, and does not specify direction of cause. We rather believe that most of this association is due to a much simpler pattern, the gradual decline of dating as the marriage endures and the couple grows older. Of course, the greater the income of the husband, the more dating the couple does. The greater the income, the longer the marriage. But the more dating the couple does, the shorter the marriage. Since frequency of dating, income, and duration seem to be closely related, we can hold each constant: (a) *Holding income* constant, there is a steady *decrease* of dating frequency for each higher category of marriage duration; (b) holding *duration* constant, there is a steady *increase* of dating, for each higher income category; and (c) holding dating constant, there is a less regular increase in duration of marriage with the increasing income. But, (d) the negative association between dating and duration increases with income. That is, the decline of dating with longer marriages is greater for those earning more income. Yet this difference is small and unreliable. We interpret these data to mean: (A) It is more common for couples to date, and to define their shared activities as dating, toward the upper economic strata; but (B) since with increasing duration of marriage these shared activities are less likely to be called dating (i.e., they are more likely to be visiting friends rather than

4. Locke, *op. cit.*, p. 257.

going to a night club), the *felt* decline in dating, with increasing duration, is greater in such upper strata than in lower strata.

Similar, we believe, is the relationship between frequency of dating in marriage, and number of children. Presumably, little more is involved than the economic and time-space problems of caring for children, and longer duration of marriage with increasing number of children. It is true that, with more children one of them is better able to care for the others, and they can be left with less supervision. However, the couple grows older, and is less inclined to date frequently. Thus, only 11% of the couples with three or more children dated more than once weekly during the marriage, but 28% of those with only one child dated this frequently.

We have attempted in this chapter to present some of the reasoning that must be used in interpreting the conflict and interaction of spouses. We have insisted here that at present many factors in conflict must be seen as both causes and indices of conflict. We have also analyzed the dating and shared activities of those couples, so as to see which patterns lead to short or long marriages. Nevertheless, none of the sharing was strong enough to keep these marriages together. All these couples eventually parted. Let us, then, turn to some of the elements in that conflict as it developed, and to the reactions of our divorcees to the conflict.

CHAPTER IX

FURTHER CHARACTERISTICS
OF THOSE WHO DIVORCE

IN THE PRESENT CHAPTER we wish to pursue further some of the structural patterns which seem to tend towards instability of marriage. In the first section of this chapter we wish to take up the structurally important fact that in all known societies those who get married share many characteristics in common, particularly those status characteristics that are structurally central in that society. In commonsense terms this means simply that marriages are likely to be much more stable if those who enter them have already served a long apprenticeship in learning their proper roles, and if they bring somewhat the same perceptions of those roles to the marriage. This is likely to happen, of course, if they come from somewhat the same cultural backgrounds. By contrast, if the marriages are *heterogamous,* that is, their cultural background are different, then the ordinary and predictable conflicts of any union are made still more intense. This does not mean that all such marriages are necessarily unstable. It merely means that statistically speaking marital instability is more likely to be found among heterogamous than among homogamous unions in this or in any other society. It would be indeed surprising if this were not one result of the years of socialization that both spouses have gone through prior to the marriage. This socialization creates certain barriers to upward mobility by making the individual unfit for easy social intercourse in other strata, and by closing certain avenues to social interaction that might lead to upward mobility generally, and to mobility in marriage especially.

In the second part of this chapter we turn in detail to some of the major status attributes or experiences which we have already used to describe our divorced couples. Particularly, we wish to ascertain what is the relationship between any of these attributes and the duration of marriage. We are assuming that in general an attribute which tends toward a shorter duration of marriage also tends in general toward marital instability. Some of these attributes are youth (which we have already discussed), urban background, Protestant background, less frequency of church attendance, and shorter duration of engagement.

Homogamy. The birth of a legitimate child binds three nuclear families in a network of social expectations which are mainly primary relationships marked by a "we-feeling," reciprocity of help, the right to visit and dine together, and a shared lineage and inheritance. Implementing this structure is an underlying set of interlocking predispositions, pressures, and subsidiary decisions in courtship and mate choice, which in this and almost all known societies tend to bring together in marriage those who are *alike* in many characteristics. Notably, spouses tend to be alike in those status characteristics that are structurally central for their society, such as race, religion, rank, education, and income. Cross-class and cross-caste marriages are the exception among the societies of the world. The rules of exogamy do not invalidate this proposition, but only specify its direction of application.[1]

It is not so much that we actually think of these characteristics when we choose a mate in our society. The circles in which we already find ourselves, our own tastes and predispositions, and the cumulative effect of our actional patterns, prevent us ordinarily from even *seeing* real alternatives. If we are White, we do not ordinarily "choose" a White mate. Instead, we simply never think of an alternative. We may discuss generally whether upper-class girls should marry lower-class boys, but in point of fact upper-class girls have little occasion to meet on equal and intimate terms many boys from lower classes. As empirical analysts from Marx to Hollingshead have amply documented, we do not have to be aware of the class structure in detail in order to be moved and shaped by it.[2]

The subsidiary consequences of these facts are many, and include, among others, the fact that in well over one hundred studies of homogamy in mate selection almost *every* characteristic of spouses shows some, albeit low, correlation.[3] These include everything from race to handsomeness and prettiness (but not red-headedness).

It can not be surprising, then that studies of stratification show less mobility "than expected by chance" between generations. Since the group or individual pressures that result from socialization and participation in the kinship structure are strongly against mobility, it is rather surprising that in our society there is so much of it. The important theoretical corollary is, however, that since kinship and stratification patterns are so deeply interlocking, when there is relatively great class mobility (as in our own society), there must be (a) greater freedom in the choice of mate, (b) a development of romantic love, (c) a less intense set of ties between the lineages tied together by marriage, (d) a smaller network of relatives, and hence (e) a lowered marital stability.

Almost all of the work on homogamy in mate selection has merely documented the correlation between the social and personal characteristics of spouses, without any adequate probe into the processes by which this result occurs; and little of it has related homogamy to marital adjustment. The latter

---

1. See, however, the interesting case analyzed by Kingsley Davis, "Intermarriage in Caste Societies," *Am. Anthropologist*, 43 (1941), 376-395.

2. August B. Hollingshead, *Elmtown's Youth* (New York: Wiley, 1949).

3. See Burgess and Wallin, *op. cit.*, Ch. 7. For older bibliographies, see C. A. Anderson, "The Sociological Approach to the Study of Assortative Mating," *International Congress for Studies Regarding Population Problems* 8 (1932), 600-634; and Helen M. Richardson, "Studies of Mental Resemblances between Husbands and Wives and between Friends," *Psychological Bulletin*, 36 (1939), 104-120. See also various works cited in the present study.

statement must be qualified. Hamilton, Terman, Burgess and Cottrell, Ferguson, and Locke dealt with *age differences* between wives and husbands.[4] We know, of course, from demographic data that in most present-day marriages the husband is slightly (about two years) older than the wife. The results of these marital adjustment studies have been generally inconclusive on this point. The best of them, Locke's, reports that age is not an important factor, but that approximate equality of ages is more conducive to marital happiness.

A second exception is that of cross-religion marriages. However, *none* of the standard researches in the prediction of marital adjustment has used this item. Burgess and Wallin used it for broken engagements, and found that 73% of engagements between couples of the same religious affiliation were unbroken, as against 59% for couples with different religious affiliations.[5] The studies of Bell, Weeks, Landis, Schnepp, and Monahan and Kephart, already cited, did not measure marital adjustment directly, but did show that mixed religious marriages tend to be less stable than others.

Finally, homogamy of *education* was used by Terman, Hamilton, Ferguson, Williams, and Kirkpatrick.[6] Terman found no difference in the happiness of husbands, but found that wives were less happy if they had more education than their husbands. Hamilton obtained a contrary result: *men* tended to be happier if more educated than their wives, while the differences between women were very small (they were slightly less happy if they had equal education). Kirkpatrick found that resemblance in education is conducive to better marital adjustment, as did Williams.

On structural grounds, we would expect: (1) Intra-class marriages will occur more frequently than could be expected by chance; (2) marriages that are homogamous with respect to the major status criteria of the society are more likely to be stable than those that are heterogamous; but (3) among heterogamous marriages, the stability of hypogamous marriages (the wife marrying downward) is less than that of hypergamous marriages (the wife marrying upward). This last hypothesis does not seem applicable to cross-religious marriages when social rank is controlled, because such marriages can not easily be classified as hypogamous or hypergamous.

If these hypotheses are correct, then even in a divorced population there would be more homogamous unions than would be expected by chance. On the other hand, we should also find (if we can locate a comparison population of the ever married) that there is *less homogamy* in a divorced population than in the ever married population. Or, that the *mixed marriages contribute more than their share of divorces to the total divorced*. Finally, if we can divide the ever married and the divorced into homogamous, hypergamous, and hypogamous unions, the last of these three should contribute propor-

4. Terman, *op. cit.*, pp. 183-187; Gilbert V. Hamilton, *A Research in Marriage* (New York: Appleton and Crofts, 1929), p. 510; Burgess and Cottrell, *op. cit.*, pp. 161-4, 406; L. W. Ferguson, "Correlates of Marital Happiness," *Journal of Psychology*, 6 (1938), 293; Locke, *op. cit.*, pp. 103-5.

5. Burgess and Wallin, *op. cit.*, p. 289.

6. Terman, *op. cit.*, p. 191; Hamilton, *op. cit.*, pp. 513, 291; Edith W. Williams, *Factors Associated with Adjustment in Rural Marriage* (Ph.D. thesis, Cornell University, 1938), p. 98; Clifford Kirkpatrick, "Community of Interest and the Measurement of Adjustment in Marriage," *The Family*, 18 (1937), 279; Ferguson, *op. cit.*, p. 291.

tionately the largest share to the divorced, and the homogamous the least share. We have not been able to locate adequate data with which to test all these hypotheses adequately, but we can approach a test at certain points.

Homogamy of Religion. If we accept the estimates of the Detroit Council of Churches for 1948, or those of the Detroit Area Study for 1952, for the membership of each religion, then theoretically we would expect Protestant-Protestant marriages to be 30%-31% of all marriages; Catholic-Catholic marriages to be 14%-16%; and Jewish-Jewish marriages to be about 0.06% of all marriages. Mixed couples would make up the remainder. In our divorced sample, these three religiously homogamous types actually made up 40%, 18%, and 2.1% of the total. Roughly, then, the ratios of actual to theoretically expected homogamy are between 1.29 and 1.33, 1.13 and 1.29 (Catholics), and 33.6 for Jews. The total homogamy ratio would be between 1.28 and 1.36, which correspond closely to that of Burgess and Wallin (engagements). The individual ratios seem to be lower than those of Hollingshead.[7] The latter studied marriages rather than engagements. The ordering of homogamy he finds in New Haven might vary in other cities, because the amount of Catholic out-marriage varies. In our divorced population, the Catholics show slightly less homogamy than the Protestants, although all homogamy ratios are above 1.

Since the proportion of mixed Catholic-Protestant marriages varies greatly from one city and region to another, we have no comparison population to test whether *our* proportion of mixed marriages is higher than in the non-divorced population.[8] Thomas claims that Hollingshead's degree of religious homogamy is higher than in most regions and cities of the U. S. Thomas does, however, present data from the Great Lakes and Midwest, which show that in cities of 100,000 and over the Catholic-non-Catholic marriages form 15% of the total in selected parishes.[8a] If he is correct, and his data may be applied to our Great Lakes city, Detroit, then the *mixed Catholic marriages contribute 25% more than their share to the divorced population,* for the mixed Catholic marriages make up 20% of our sample. We have no comparable data for the Jewish marriages and divorces.

Homogamy of Occupation. With respect to occupation, we may use Centers' national sample as a comparison group for marriages.[9] Collapsing his tables so as to correspond with our occupational categories, and then arranging them according to whether the marriages were homogamous, hypergamous, or hypogamous, we find (a) the coefficient of contingency between occupational rank of husband and that of wife's father is $+.44$ ($P<.001$). Although the difference between two coefficients from different samples can not be tested for significance, we would expect, for our own sample, that (b) the two occupational ranks should be associated; but that (c) this coefficient should be *lower for our divorced sample* (since we predict that heterogamous

7. Burgess and Wallin, *op. cit.,* p. 206. August B. Hollingshead, "Cultural Factors in Mate Selection," *Am. Soc. Rev.,* 15 (1950) 619-627.

8. John L. Thomas, "The Factor of Religion in the Selection of Marriage Mates," *Am. Soc. Rev.,* 16 (1951), 487-491.

8a. *Ibid.,* p. 490.

9. Richard Centers, "Marital Selection and Occupational Strata," *Am. J. Soc.,* 54 (1949), esp. 532-533.

marriages are more likely to end in divorce). That is, we have predicted that even among the divorced, homogamous unions occur more often than by chance, but that among the divorced there should be less homogamy than in the ever married population.

Correspondingly, we find that our coefficient of contingency between occupational stratum of wife and of husband is lower than for Centers' population, $+.22$ as against $+.44$ (for both, $P<.001$). That is, the *homogamous unions contribute less than their share to the divorced.*

Thus far, our hypotheses have proved correct. Let us see whether our notions about homogamy, hypergamy, and hypogamy are correct. Using a three-class occupational grouping (including foremen and skilled workers as middle class rather than lower class), we find this pattern for our divorcees:

MARRIAGES BY OCCUPATIONAL RANK OF HUSBAND AND OF WIFE'S FATHER

| Wife's Father | Husband's Occupational Class | | | |
	Upper	Middle	Lower	Totals
Upper	9	26	13	48
Middle	19	74	83	176
Lower	16	57	110	183
Totals	44	157	206	N = 407

We find upon calculation that we could expect homogamous marriages to make up 41% of the total, while actually they make up 48% of the total. Comparing our proportions of the three different types of unions (divorced) with Centers' proportions (married), we obtain this result:

DIVORCED AND MARRIED, BY TYPE OF UNION
(OCCUPATION AS INDEX)

| | Type of Union | | | |
	Homogamous	Hypergamous (wife marries upward)	Hypogamous	Totals
Divorced sample (Goode)	48%	23%	30%	101%
Married sample (Centers)	55	24	21	100

Centers' figure of 55% corresponds closely to that of Hollingshead, who used residential area as his class criterion for New Haven.[10] We see, then, that two of our hypotheses appear to be correct, and the third appears to be probable. The *homogamous* unions seem to contribute slightly *less* than their share of the divorces, since their proportion of the divorced is less than their share of the married. At the other extreme, the marriages in which the wife marries *downward* form a smaller proportion of the married than of the divorced. Put in commonsense terms, in our society the average woman is better trained to handle the family role problems of strata higher than her own, than the man is trained to handle the occupational problems higher than his own. She feels fewer problems if she marries upward, than if she marries downward.

The hypergamous unions do fall between the homogamous and the hypogamous in marital stability, as predicted, but do not contribute more than their share of the divorces.

---

10. Hollingshead, "Cultural Factors . . ." *op. cit.,* p. 627.

Centers' data also confirm a subsidiary hypothesis that is implicit in our thinking about marriages: the *hypergamous* union is slightly more frequent than the hypogamous. This is a corollary of the structural fact that toward the upper educational and occupational strata a *higher* proportion of men eventually marry, but a *lower* proportion of women marry. Since a higher proportion of men toward the top of the strata do marry; but obviously can not all marry the females in *those* strata, since the sex ratios are not greatly different in different strata: Then at least *some* of the men in those strata must marry *outward,* and this means that they marry *downward.* This is a hypergamous union, from the side of the woman. The same reasoning applies toward the other end of the strata, in reverse: a higher proportion of women marry, but a lower proportion of men. This is the result of our status system, in which status is primarily determined by the husband, and most fundamentally by his occupation. Consequently, he stands to lose little by marrying downward, but the woman stands to lose much. Consequently, (a) he is more likely to marry downward than she is; and thus (b) unions in which she marries *upward* are more common than unions in which she marries *downward.*

However, this reasoning, though likely, is not rigorous. It makes these assumptions: (1) An equal proportion of men and women of marriageable ages in a given stratum; (2) an equality of *desire* to marry for all strata and sexes, or at least no large class-linked differences. For education, we know that the first assumption is not correct. For the population as a whole, more women than men go to high school; but more men than women go to college. We suppose, but do not know, that there are still other differences when we analyze education by sex *within* a given social class.

Homogamy of Education. Consequently, our hypothese would have to be specified further for education. We can not do this theoretically at present, but practically we see that if (a) "completed high school" is one breaking point for an educational class; if (b) the proportion of college people in the nation is small; if (c) almost all the college men marry, and many marry downward; while (d) a lower proportion but a majority of women at this level do marry; then it is likely that at the present time there are more hypogamous marriages by education than hypergamous ones. These last two assumptions are correct, and so is the conclusion.[11] However, we do not see how one can respecify these hypotheses so as to derive this last one theoretically from those we have been analyzing.

In any event, we can ask whether our earlier three hypotheses are correct for education. We first note that the coefficient of contingency between educational achievement of wife and of husband is $+.31$ ($P<.001$), for our sample. Thus, it is clear that even among the divorced, homogamy of education is common.

If our reasoning is correct, we ought also to find that, compared with a standard married population, the hypogamous unions contribute proportionately the greatest share to the divorced, and the homogamous least, while the hypergamous unions (wife marrying upward) should fall between. In the

11. See the cross-tabulation calculated by Meyer F. Nimkoff, *Marriage and the Family* (New York: Houghton Mifflin, 1947), p. 416, drawn from *Population Differential Fertility, 1940 and 1910, Women by Number of Children Under 5 Years Old* (Washington, D. C.: Bureau of the Census, 1945), Table 30.

following table, we have used as our comparison population the U. S. native white women, aged 15-49, living with their husbands (1940). We have collapsed the educational divisions into three: (a) completed high school or more education; (b) some high school; (c) grammar school only.

DIVORCED AND MARRIED (LIVING TOGETHER), BY TYPE OF UNION
(EDUCATION AS INDEX)[11a]

	Homogamy	Hypergamy	Hypogamy	Totals
Divorced (Goode)	47%	19%	34%	100%
Married (Census)	64	13	23	100

As we see, there is considerably more homogamy among the still married and living together, than among the divorced. This is according to hypothesis. However, our third hypothesis, that marriages downward (for wives) will furnish proportionately the largest fraction among the divorced, does not hold up. In comparison with the proportion of these unions in the married and living together population, the hypergamous union is overrepresented among the divorced with a ratio of 146:100 (among the married); while the downward marriages have a ratio of 148:100. This difference is, of course, unimportant. On the other hand, almost all these hypogamous unions are between (a) a woman with completed high school, married to a man with some high school; and (b) a woman with 1-3 years of high school, married to a man with some grammar school education. Therefore, it is possible that using finer class divisions, and taking into account the *number* of steps across which the marriage takes place, we would confirm our hypothesis definitely. Such a procedure would get closer to the central theoretical points at issue here: (a) similarity of cultural background is generally conducive to marital stability; and (b) it is the wife who does the most adjusting, and thus the cases in which *she* must "move upward" are likely to be more stable than those in which she moves downward. That is, there is less strain on her, and thereby on the marriage, if she must move upward.

However, the reliability of our cells for such a more detailed comparison seems too low, and we shall not make this further test. It is possible, further, that we should make such a comparison only if we can control for occupational rank, since these are so highly correlated.

Let us now see how certain of these background attributes affect not alone overall instability or stability, but also the duration of marriage.

Duration of the Marriage. Since the mean age at marriage for our respondents was 19.5 years, and the mean age at divorce was 28.2 years, the average length of marriage for these couples was 8.7 years, the median being 9.3 years.[12] There is a difference in duration of marriage for those who were married to veterans. Marriages to veterans lasted a mean length of 8.0 years, as against 10.1 years for nonveterans. Seventy-six per cent of those married *15 years and over,* and 60% of those married 10-14 years, were *nonveterans,* as against 24% and 40% respectively who were veterans in those two classes. It is not certain that the veteran status has any independent effect on length

11a. *Ibid.,* Table 30, pp. 47-51.

12. William M. Kephart, "The Duration of Marriage," *American Sociological Review,* 19 (1954), 290, obtains a median of 10.4 years for *first* marriages ending in divorce.

of marriage, since veterans would thus be younger than nonveterans, and the difference in length of marriage may be no more than a function of different age brackets. However, when we control for age, veterans are still overrepresented in the short duration classes, and underrepresented in those of long duration. For 25-29 years of age, there are no differences.

In an effort to avoid some of the fly-by-night war marriages, only families with children were studied. On the other hand, this does not entirely discount the impact of the war separation, whose effect is not known in any event. Yet there is no way to distinguish the effect of military service upon marital stability, as against the general disorganizing effect of the wartime dislocations that most married people experienced at the same time.

As might be expected, many background factors seem to have an effect upon the duration of marriage of divorcees. Such factors do not often differentiate sharply with reference to family behavior. After all, they are only *one* set of elements going to make up the concrete family experience.

We use them because they are expressive of more fundamental elements. Thus, whether the respondent came from a rural or an urban background, can be used as a differentiating factor, because of the family values and predispositions that are presumably different in the two backgrounds. If these latter could be recorded as easily as the simple datum of "urban-rural background," we would, of course, use them.

The relationship between rural background and length of marriage seems clear. Whether we use all three of our categories for background (rural, small town, and city); or group small town as urban or as rural; and whether we use husband's *or* wife's background as the basis for calculation, the relationship remains. If small town is included with urban, and we use the cutting points of 0-9 years duration, and of "10 years and over," for husband and wife the Q of association is about $+.5$ to $+.8$. Furthermore, the relationship also holds when we consider *couples,* as both nonurban, one urban, and both urban.[13] The following table presents this relationship:

DURATION OF MARRIAGE, BY URBAN — NONURBAN BACKGROUND

Background of-Couple	Length of Time					Totals
	0-4 yrs. %	5-9 yrs. %	10-14 yrs. %	Over 15 yrs. %	%	
Both nonurban	0	15	46	39	100	13
One urban	14	21	43	21	99	56
Both urban	18	43	28	11	100	355

The median duration of marriage was 12 years for respondents with a rural background. It was 10 years for those with a small town background, and 9 years for those with an urban background.

Religion. The background factor of religion is also related to duration of marriage. Although the difference is not great, Catholics tend to have longer marriages than do Protestants or those who have "Other or no religion."[14]

---

13. Burgess and Cottrell, *op. cit.,* pp. 85-86, 376, found the marital adjustment of those with a rural background to be higher. Locke, *op. cit.,* p. 33, found no such difference. However, he may have created this result by trying to "match" his rural divorcees with his happily married rural people.

14. Because of the small numbers of cases involved, we have bracketed all respondents with

DURATION OF MARRIAGE, BY RELIGIOUS PREFERENCE OF RESPONDENT

	Catholic	Protestant	Other or None
Percent married 10 years or longer	49%	41%	39%
Base	135	247	43
Mean duration of marriage (years)	9.4	9.1	8.5
Median duration of marriage (years)	9.9	9.1	8.5

Now, the *particular* religious affiliation might be less important than *regularity* of church attendance, since the latter should be a better indicator of the respondent's acceptance of the church attitudes against divorce. Thus, the couple would stay together longer before ending the marriage. In the case of Catholicism, of course, there is an absolute prohibition. Although Protestants are not all forbidden to divorce, the attitudes of almost all Protestant denominations are very strongly opposed to divorce. Frequency of attendance ought therefore to be associated with duration of marriage. However, this relationship does *not* seem to exist for the entire sample.[15]

On the other hand, the relationship does exist if we consider *only* Catholics. As the frequency of attendance increases, the average duration of the marriage also increases. For Protestants, it seems to decrease, but the difference is small.

MEDIAN DURATION OF MARRIAGE, BY RELIGION AND FREQUENCY OF CHURCH ATTENDANCE

	Frequency of Church Attendance		
Religion	1/wk. or more	Less than 1/week but sometimes	Never
Protestant	8.7 yrs.	8.4 yrs.	10.2 yrs.
Catholic	11.0 yrs.	9.8 yrs.	7.2 yrs.

Race. We have devoted some attention to the higher rate of divorce among Negroes than among Whites. We cannot reason rigorously from that fact to the hypothesis that the average duration of marriage among Negroes is shorter than that among Whites, although we would generally suppose that most factors that increase rate also decrease average duration. We find that the duration of marriage for the two racial groups is almost exactly the same. This we see in the following table:

DURATION OF MARRIAGE, BY RACE

	Negroes	Whites	Total
Percent marriage 10 years or longer	43	44	44
Base	80	345	425
Mean duration of marriage (years)	9.2	9.1	9.1
Median duration of marriage (years)	9.5	9.2	9.3

The differences are very small, although it is seen that Negroes might have a slightly longer duration of marriage than Whites.[16]

It is impossible at the present time to analyze this datum further. We do

---

some other religious affiliation than the Catholic or Protestant in the category "Other or None." This, of course, does some injustice to the Jewish and Greek Orthodox respondents. However, for the most part, the cases in this category are those who claimed no religious preference.

15. We do not have a measure of attendance *during* the marriage. We do know how frequently they were attending at the time of the interview, and we know whether this was then more frequent than at other times.

16. Kephart and Monahan do find a *longer* duration of marriage, but a longer period of separation prior to divorce. See previously cited articles, and Wm. M. Kephart, "The Duration of Marriage," *Am. Soc. Rev.*, 19 (1954), 291.

not have a full enough understanding of the divorce patterns of the two racial groups. There seem to be few significant differences between them. In the present instance there are too many divergent factors that prevent our controlling for all of them in any acceptable fashion. For example, we would suppose that a large proportion of these Negroes are (a) *migrants* from the *South,* (b) and some of these would be from (c) the *rural* South. Having a rural background would increase the length of marriage, but it is also possible that there is some personal and marital disorganization among such migrants to the urban North. On the other hand, we know that (d) *childlessness* among urban Negroes is *higher* than among urban Whites.[17] If childlessness is associated with shorter marriage among Negroes, as it is among Whites, then the average length of marriage among *all* urban Negroes might be slightly shorter than for Whites. It is possible, then, that the remaining marriages—those with children, which are *our* cases—might last longer.

Furthermore, to complicate any future analysis still further, we know that (e) roughly the same class system is to be found among Negro families as that among Whites. Yet, as we showed in Ch. IV, among Negroes there should also be a rough association between higher class position and a higher rate of divorce. We have, however, no data with reference to this possibility: if it is true that divorce was once less frequent among the lower classes, at what phase of this large-scale transition is the urban Negro (who is generally rising in the social scale) to be found? Is he to be compared with, say, the urban White of the 1920's with respect to average duration of marriage with children? Finally, in our present sample, the Negroes have (f) incomes and occupations that are substantially lower than those of Whites, as a group. However, since Negro strata of a *given social rank* have lower incomes and occupations than Whites at the same level, must our Negro sample actually be considered somewhat (g) higher in class position on the average than our White sample?

As stated, there is no way of analyzing these complex interacting factors at the present time. The data do not exist. However, they will eventually become available.

Occupational Class. In agreement with our earlier analysis, duration of marriage is also associated somewhat with occupational class. Although the relationship seems clear enough, and is somewhat regular in its effect through each of the duration categories, it is not strong. The average duration of marriage by occupational class is as follows:

AVERAGE DURATION OF MARRIAGE, BY OCCUPATIONAL CLASS

Upper	10.1 years
Middle	9.2 years
Lower	8.9 years

Length of Engagement. Length of engagement and its relationship to class was treated earlier. Let us now see what relationship may exist between length

---

17. The Negro-White fertility patterns are much more complex than is commonly supposed. The "current fertility" of urban whites is .92 of that of urban Negroes, while tables of completed fertility show the childlessness of Negro families to be higher than that of Whites. See Frank W. Notestein, "Differential Fertility in the East North Central States," *Milbank Memorial Fund Quarterly,* 16 (1938), 186-191; tables 1, 2, 3, in Charles F. Westoff, "Differential Fertility in the United States," *Am. Soc. Rev.,* 19 (1954), 549-561; and Everett S. and Anne S. Lee, "The Differential Fertility of the American Negro," *Am. Soc. Rev.,* 17 (1952), 437-447.

of engagement and duration of marriage. The possible relationship between this factor and marital happiness, as well as, presumably, marital stability, has been discussed frequently in the literature; and we have already devoted some attention to it. However, its relationship with length of marriage is somewhat more complex. As we see in the following table, the average length of marriage increases steadily with length of engagement. To this extent, our data tally with the results of studies concerning marital adjustment.

DURATION OF MARRIAGE, BY LENGTH OF ENGAGEMENT

	Length of Engagement		
	0-3 months	3-6 months	Over 6 months
Percent married 10 years or more	37%	44%	51%
Base	153	150	121
Mean length of marriage	8.7	8.9	9.9
Median length of marriage	8.4	9.3	10.1

However, does length of engagement have a *different effect,* depending on the *occupational class background of the wife?* We discussed earlier why there might be differences in its effect on duration of marriage in the different strata.

As we see in the accompanying table, *length of engagement is* much more important for duration of marriage *in the upper strata.* The differences between middle and lower strata are less, but they are observable. Thus, 75% of the upper class marriages lasted 0-9 years when there was really no duration of engagement, as against 25% in the 10 years and over category. For middle class couples, the corresponding figures were 55% and 45%; for lower class, 53% and 47%.

DURATION OF MARRIAGE, BY LENGTH OF ENGAGEMENT, CONTROLLING FOR OCCUPATIONAL CLASS (HUSBAND'S)

Class	Length of Engagement (months)	Duration of Marriage	
		0-9 years (%)	10 years & over (%)
Upper			
	0	75	25
	1-2	66	33
	3-6	43	57
	7 and over	39	61
	Totals	49%	51%
Middle			
	0	55	45
	1-2	76	24
	3-6	58	42
	7 and over	54	46
	Totals	59%	41%
Lower			
	0	53	47
	1-2	71	29
	3-6	55	45
	7 and over	46	54
	Totals	55%	45%

Number of Children. There were 796 children in these 425 divorces, an average of 1.87 children per divorce. This is close to the reported national average (for divorced couples with children), although both figures may be slight underestimates.[18] In the following table we present the age and sex distribution of the children involved in these divorces:[19]

DISTRIBUTION OF CHILDREN BY AGE AND SEX GROUPS

Age Group	Males	Females	Totals	Percent
0-2 years	38	43	81	10
3-6 years	127	146	273	34
7-12 years	149	143	292	37
13 years and over	69	81	150	19
Totals	383(48%)	413(52%)	796(100%)	100

Wives with a rural background have a higher fertility than those with an urban background. The character of this association may be seen more easily in the following table:

NUMBER OF CHILDREN, BY RURAL-URBAN BACKGROUND OF WIFE

Respondent's Background	One %	Two %	Three or more %	%	Total No.
Rural	18	53	29	100	34
Small town	40	39	21	100	93
Urban	51	32	17	100	298

N = 425

Interestingly enough, however, the differences between our three major religious groups are almost nonexistent. The average number of children for Protestants, Catholics, and the category marked "Other or none" was as follows:

Protestant	1.92
Catholic	1.80
Other or none	1.81

If we control for race, there is no difference at all between Catholic and Protestant fertility among these divorcees. This lack of difference may seem a bit surprising, since there might be at least a spurious relationship. Those who have been married somewhat longer should have more children, and Catholics remain married somewhat longer than non-Catholics. We can *not* expect a higher fertility merely because of Catholic affiliation. As Stouffer and Jaffe have both shown, when urbanism and economic status are controlled, Catholics

---

18. For the national figures, compare: "Divorce and Size of Family," *Statistical Bulletin*, 31, No. 2 (Feb., 1950) (Metropolitan Life Ins. Co.), p. 1; Paul H. Jacobson, *American Sociological Review*, 15 (1950) p. 241. The national figure is 1.78, although it is known that some proportion of the children is not recorded. Both figures, of course, refer only to those divorcing couples with children.

19. *Statistical Bulletin, op. cit.*, p. 2, estimates that two-thirds of children of divorces are under age 10. Our tabulations do not permit an exact comparison, but a rough curve based on our distribution shows the same proportion under the area delimited by the curve 0-10 years. The *Bulletin's* calculations seem to have been Jacobson's.

do not have a higher net reproduction rate than the non-Catholics.[20] We believe, however, that the data indicate that the meaning of children in divorce varies for the two religious groups. Specifically, if one has strong Catholic convictions, the presence or absence of children does not make the sin of divorce any greater. On the other hand, for Protestants, who are not so absolutely forbidden to divorce, the generally stronger social disapproval of divorce when children (especially small children) are involved would tend to reduce the divorce somewhat among families with children. Thus, for our sample, all of whom have children, there should be no great differences in fertility by religion.

The current fertility of urban Negroes may be slightly higher than that of urban Whites, and the proportion of the *childless* married seems to be higher among Negro urban couples than among White urban couples.[21] Since we have specifically excluded all *childless* couples from our sample, we should then expect the fertility of our Negro couples to be slightly higher than that of the Whites. The fertility of our Negro couples is somewhat higher. The average number of children for these couples is 2.16, and for Whites it is 1.81.

Since education is usually correlated *inversely* with birth rate in any age group, we would expect to find the same relationship among these families, even though they have been broken and the childless families are excluded. A confirmation of this expectation is to be found in the following table, which is collapsed from a larger table, in which no differences appear between those who completed high school, and those who went to college; and no differences between the number of children of grammar school and of high school respondents.

NUMBER OF CHILDREN, BY EDUCATION OF WIFE

Number of Children	Education		Totals
	Completed High School or more	Some High School or less Education	
1	47%	53%	100%(194)
2 or more	32%	68%	100%(225)
		Q = +.30	N = 425

Of course, there is a relationship between duration of marriage and number of children. This may not be a causal relationship in either direction. The association is through a complex of factors of much greater importance, such as rural-urban background, the couple's predisposition toward both a greater number of children and a longer duration of marriage prior to divorce, the physical fact that it takes some years to have several children, and so on. The association does exist, but we cannot untangle all its causes here. For the married population as a whole, the childless are about twice as prone to divorce, but most analysts suppose that the same factors that lead to postponing children also lead to divorce. That is, the decision to have children

---

20. Samuel A. Stouffer, "Trends in the Fertility of Catholics and Non-Catholics," *Am. J. Soc.*, 41 (1935), 143-166; and A. J. Jaffe, "Religious Differentials in the Net Reproduction Rate," *J. Am. Stat. Ass.*, 34 (1939), 335-342.

21. Notestein, *op. cit.* That is, fewer urban White married couples fall into the category "childless."

is for many a decision that the marriage is good enough to continue; or, negatively, since the marriage is not going well, there should not be any children just yet. This suggests, then, that the *meaning* of children is important in divorce analysis.

It may be worthwhile, then, to present one aspect of this meaning, as it relates to the impact of the number of children upon the duration of marriage. As a mere rational matter, the prospect of caring for several children might deter husband or wife from seeking a divorce, more than if only one child were involved. Then one might speak of the "causal" connection between number of children and duration of marriage.[22] We cannot, of course, adequately test this notion. We do get suggestive data, however, by comparing urban and nonurban strata with respect to the impact of a greater number of children upon the duration of marriage. We have calculated Q's of association for various combinations involved here, attempting to control for urban and nonurban backgrounds, as well as for number of children. What seems to emerge from this analysis is the following set of notions:

(a) Nonurban couples are more likely than are urban couples to have longer marriages, as well as to have more children;

(b) The number of children involved is associated with the length of marriage; however,

(c) the associations differ somewhat. The difference between average duration of marriage in *urban* groups between couples who have *only one child* and those who have *several children* is somewhat *less* than the comparable difference in the rural group. The data are shown in the following table:

AVERAGE DURATION OF MARRIAGE BY NUMBER OF CHILDREN, BY URBAN ORIGIN

Urban Background of Respondent	Number of Children		Difference in Duration
	One	Two or more	
Urban	7.2 yrs.	10.1 yrs.	3.0 yrs.
Nonurban	7.7 yrs.	12.7 yrs.	5.0 yrs.

Apparently the number of children involved seems to have a slightly smaller impact upon the duration of the *urban* marriage than upon the duration of the *nonurban* marriage. This was contrary to our predictions. *Ad hoc* explanations for this result are possible, of course, but they need not be presented here.

There appear no significant differences in the fertility of occupational strata by occupation of husband.

Summary. In this chapter, we have brought together two main bodies of data bearing on the characteristics of the divorced. One dealt with the tendency of people to marry others who are alike with respect to major status attributes: race, religion, occupational class, and education. We have recalculated data from various sources to show that homogamy is also found among the divorced, but that heterogamous marriages seem to have more than their share of divorces. This was true for occupational class, religion, and education. Among heterogamous marriages, we hypothesized that hypogamous marriages (wife

22. Paul W. Jacobson, "Differentials in Divorce by Duration of Marriage and Size of Family," *Am. Soc. Rev.*, 15 (1950), 239-244, shows that this supposed effect has been greatly exaggerated. In any event (p. 239) the average number of children increases with duration of marriage.

marrying downward) were still less stable than hypergamous marriages, but our data did not confirm this notion.

Continuing with the characteristics of the divorce, our second body of data dealt with factors that are associated with a shorter duration of marriage: urban, Protestant background, lower occupational class, short engagement (mainly for upper class), smaller number of children (for Protestant and urban couples). In the course of this last discussion, we also analyzed the apparent meaning of fertility among different groups.

In the following chapter, we analyze the themes of complaint in these divorces.

CHAPTER X

THE CONFLICT PROCESS— THEMES OF COMPLAINT MADE BY THE WIFE

MEANING OF "CAUSE OF DIVORCE." In this chapter, we deal with what were, in the wife's opinion, the causes of her divorce. Now, attempts to understand divorce have been plagued somewhat because often an impossible question was formulated. This question is a commonsense one, and like most commonsense questions it is not useful for scientific research. As generally formulated, it may be phrased, "What causes divorce?" This is similar to the questions, "What causes death?" "What causes crime?" or "What causes society?" The kind of answer that seems to be demanded is one that will essentially say, "Factor X causes divorce, and all divorces may be explained in terms of factor X." Sometimes those who analyze the problem attempt to locate the guilty party. Others may view divorce as the simple resultant of personality failure, or of sexual maladjustment.

The serious student must soon drop this search. Such factors are never found in any other natural phenomena, and should not appear here. The question shifts from, "What causes death?" to defining certain types of necessary biological *activities* which must be carried on, or *functions* which must be served, if an organism is to continue living. It is necessary to specify *conditions,* to attempt to map out types of *interaction* between various *kinds* of factors, and different kinds of phenomena must then be looked at within quite different conceptual frameworks. We begin to look for simple associations between a phenomenon and other phenomena that seem to accompany it. We no longer ask the question, "What causes crime?" but begin to describe the activities of criminals, and to ascertain under what conditions individuals learn the techniques and attitudes of criminality.

There are two different levels of questions here. The first one is: How is it that there is such a phenomenon as divorce? The second is: Under what conditions, within our own time and society, are individuals more likely to terminate their marriages than to continue them?

In neither case is there an attempt to predict the individual's *unique* behavior. This is not done in any science, and sociology and psychology are at much too crude a level of development to be able to surpass other sciences in this respect.[1] Science typically deals with *classes* of individuals, or *relationships among characteristics* of classes of individuals. That is to say, a given *characteristic,* such as church-going or the sharing of home activities by the two spouses, is related to another factor, such as *stability* of the marriage. It is not possible, however, to calculate precisely whether a particular couple will still be married five years from now.

Let us return to our two types of questions, however. The first type is a general theoretical question that can be answered in very rough terms now, and in more precise terms after a more far reaching cross-cultural analysis of marriage and divorce patterns throughout the known preliterate and literate societies of our day and of former epochs has been made. The question, "Under what types of institutional arrangements is divorce to be found?" is comparable to asking for a specification of the institutional patterns under which there will be a pattern of dowry giving, "wife purchase," or "mother-in-law avoidance." In earlier chapters we outlined several directions this research might profitably take.

However, we have also attempted at least some answers to the second type of question: What characteristics are associated with marital stability, or what factors in dissolved marriages were associated with one another? We shall analyze the conflict process in this chapter, but only as a *prelude to the events that took place after divorce.*

We did, of course, ask our respondents why they divorced, and we have asked them some questions about the conflict itself, the advice given to them by counsellors, the attitudes expressed by friends or relatives, etc. We did not at any time believe, however, that we would thus obtain an answer to the question, "What causes the divorce?"

We have rather kept in mind that we were trying to find out how the divorce crisis *was viewed and experienced by the spouse.* We wanted better knowledge about the kinds of complaints made by the wife, because it was these problems that they faced during the marriage, and it seemed likely that the kind of conflict which occurred then would have some effect upon the subsequent adjustment after the divorce.

Grounds for Divorce Suits. The "causes of divorce," however defined, bear only little relationship to the tabulations of divorce complaints as they appear in divorce suits. In general, the rule in such suits is that the *legally most effective* and *morally least accusatory* grounds are asserted in the suit. It is for this reason that newspaper accounts are so replete with apparently trivial grounds for divorce. The divorcee, like the marital counselor, well knows that these complaints were offered in the suit simply because they would be adequate grounds for divorce and would give the least grounds for adverse publicity. It is probably true, as Kephart has noted, that the *incidents* described in most divorce suits actually happened,[2] and when a man is accused of alcoholism, the chances are great that the charge is true. But when milder charges are made, few inferences can be made from them. Moreover, what one spouse com-

1. It is, on a more fundamental level, an axiom of modern epistemology that science can deal *only* with classes of data, and not even the data from many sciences could predict *any* specific, concrete phenomenon exactly.

2. Wm. M. Kephart, "Drinking and Marital Disruption," *Quarterly Journal of Studies on Alcohol,* 15 (1954), 64-65.

plains of is a poor statement of all the major forces that led to the decision. The court is not interested in *cause,* but in *responsibility.*

Thus, it is safe to say that in almost every divorce case there are far more basic conflicts in the marriage than are asserted in the suit, and that these more basic conflicts would have been aired if the trivial grounds had not been accepted by the court. Thus, adultery is not often used as a complaint if it is possible to use cruelty. Physical cruelty need not be asserted if the traditions of the court allow divorce on the grounds of "psychic cruelty." Sometimes the lawyer uses his knowledge of a particular judge to offer the ground of "drunkenness," if that judge is strict in his interpretation of other legal grounds, but has a strong prejudice against drunkenness.

It is possible to obtain the major "themes of complaint" or conflict if we ask the divorcees *outside* of court why they got the divorce. In this section we focus upon these major themes as reported by our respondents. These are the problems as our respondents lived them, and thus they were important in the process of adjustment, before and after the divorce.

However, even if we assume that respondents are able to tell us the "real" reasons for their divorce, our research plan would not give us the causes of divorce generally. After all, we have questioned only those who did get divorces. We do not have any way of comparing the kinds of answers nondivorcees would have given to similarly phrased questions. Perhaps a systematic probe would inform us that those who stay married have the *same kinds of complaints* as those who do not, although divorcees perhaps experienced them with a deeper intensity, or were unhappier about them.

Classifying the Complaints. On the other hand, we *had* no such aim. We were rather concerned with learning what happened *after* the divorce and wanted to know what our respondents saw as the marital problems they had to live through. Some of these will turn out to have less emotional impact than others, but some of those "reasons" are important in the respondents' divorce adjustment.

The relevance of the husband's comments was discussed earlier. These comments are important for a total picture, of course, for they may determine whether the ex-wife must carry on a protracted battle for independence or remarriage afterwards, or whether she has a heavy or light financial burden to carry. From either side, however, "reality" is a shifting and dubious thing, and it is safe to say that we are little closer to the truth when we have added the husband's complaints. If there were a considerable body of research materials on the postdivorce period, the husband's comments would be more useful. However, in a preliminary exploration it is possible to focus on what the wife felt and saw, as important for *her* own adjustment.

Precisely because no one has used an adequate model for analyzing causes of divorce, the problem of classifying answers to the question, "What was the cause of the divorce?" is difficult. Some sophisticated respondents attempted to present a personality diagnosis of their husbands in superficially objective terms. Others felt that the husband personally betrayed them, or suddenly became a drunkard. A few never guessed that a divorce was impending until it happened, while others felt from an early period in the marriage that it would not last. It was not possible to classify each answer on several levels of meaning, as we wanted to do, because each respondent varied in her grasp of these levels. We were forced, then, to stay as close as possible to the literal statements of the respondents.

The answers were varied, but almost all responses fell into these categories:

1. *Personality,* 2. *Authority, or Cruelty,* 3. *"Complex,"* 4. *Desertion,* 5. *Triangle,* 6. *Home Life,* 7. *Consumption,* 8. *Value,* 9. *Nonsupport,* 10. *Drinking,* 11. *Relatives.*

Before seeing what percentages of cases fall into each type, let us make certain that the meaning of each class of answer is clear. This will aid subsequent researchers in their attempts to compare their own results with ours. It will also allow the reader to understand in a more complete fashion just what kind of response each of these labels refers to. We shall begin with the items about which there is *least question;* then we shall analyze the categories which are *more difficult* to apply to the answers given by our respondents. For all categories, of course, we continued with our code-fitting and checking of coding until reliability was at the 95% range or better. Nevertheless, as the experienced researcher knows, some categories fall into this range very easily, while others must be defined with very great specificity before any such level is achieved.

In this coding operation, our unit is the *response,* not the respondent; and, more particularly, it is the single complaint, rather than the total response.

That is, if the respondent stated that her husband ran off with another woman and was emotionally unstable, this total response was coded as *two separate complaints.*

Therefore, if, say, 40% of our respondents gave as a complaint "indifference to home," this can *not* mean that this was the "cause of divorce" in 40% of the cases. All those women listed might have still other complaints. The average number of complaints was over two per respondent, and we have no way of weighing their importance in "causing" the divorce. We can say merely that 40% of our respondents thought that this item was of importance in the breakup of their marriage. Finally, our real aim was to ascertain their impact on adjustment to divorce.

Drinking—Any Mention: If a wife made any mention of her husband's drinking, whether she complained of excessive drinking or merely that he went to the beer garden, this was coded as "Drinking—any mention." Thus, the category is broader than a complaint that "her husband drank too much." We have coded this item in this fashion for two reasons: (1) the item occurs very often as a theme; (2) the wife has chosen this item as one (among others) to be mentioned as "causes for the divorce." It is true that a majority of adult Americans do drink once in a while, and perhaps in most of these cases the husband's drinking would fall into the category of casual drinking. Nevertheless, it would not have been mentioned if it had not been salient in some respect. The mild disapproval of drinking characteristic of our society is partially evidenced by the fact that drinking is mentioned. (We might make the contrast mildly ridiculous but effective by noting that a majority of the adult populace also drives automobiles, but this is *not* mentioned as a complaint. The same might be said of many hobbies—liking for baseball, and reading books and magazines.)

Desertion: Here again coding was relatively simple. If the wife complained that the man ran away with another woman, this was classified as Desertion (as well as Triangle). His behavior was not classified as desertion if the husband merely stayed away from time to time or stayed out each night for weeks on end. In all of these latter cases the husband is clearly *using his home as his base of operation.* In the case of desertion, however, the man stops using the home as his base. Other responses that were classified as desertion are some of the following: "Desertion—left home suddenly." "He left me for five years." "After all, he never came back from the Army."

Relatives, Conflict with: Responses were placed in this category if by statement or context, the claim of *conflict* with relatives is made. For example, these responses were classified as "Relatives, conflict with": "His mother finally told me to leave, so I left." "His stepmother hated me."

This response was a borderline case, just *within* the category: "Difficulty over his family."

On the other hand, the following response was *not* included in this category: "His mother never made him work, so he wouldn't work at all." Here, the claim of actual conflict with the mother is not made.

Triangle—Another woman: It is slightly more difficult to decide whether or not a given response falls into this category, since some adulterous behavior might fall into another category, which we have labelled "The complex." We limited the "Triangle" category to those cases in which another *specific* woman was mentioned as having a love and/or sex relationship with the husband. We included also those cases in which the husband had actually gone with several women, but the wife viewed the case as involving one *definite* woman, sometimes one with whom the wife had actually caught the husband. Typical responses in this category are the following: "There was another woman. He was living with her." "He ran away with another woman." "Another woman—I caught them." "Bigamous marriage to another woman." "We had a happy marriage until he met someone else."

The Complex—"Drinking, gambling, helling around": We shall analyze the meaning of this category more fully at a later point. At the present time we wish merely to indicate what is included within it. The coding difficulty lies in the fact that in the case of any given husband not all of these items may be mentioned. Consequently, we adopted this arbitrary rule: if the wife complained of "running around" or "other women," that response was categorized as "The Complex." On the other hand, if these key phrases were not used, we required that her response contain at least *two* of the following complaints before including it in this category: (1) staying away, (2) drinking, (3) gambling, (4) out with the boys. The complex seems to be a frequent phenomenon. It is also a behavior pattern which arouses strong objections on the part of the wife. This activity invariably costs money which the family cannot usually afford. In addition, the wife may also view this behavior as a rejection of the home. As the marriage clinician knows, the pattern might be no more than an *index* of the marital unhappiness of the husband. On the other hand, as is so often the case for such indices, this activity may become an independent "cause" (or at least a precipitant) of the divorce.

The only coding problem here is that some of these actions, (a) taken separately, or (b) viewed by different wives, might be coded elsewhere. Therefore, (a) when there are items of *behavior* which, taken separately, might also be coded elsewhere, they *are* also coded elsewhere. When a response coded as "The Complex" does include the charge of drinking, it is also coded as "Drinking—any mention." (b) If the behavior can be classed as "The Complex" but is also criticized by the wife as wasting money, then we code this comment *also* as "Consumption Behavior." Unfortunately, this procedure prevents sharp delineation of differences between the consequences of different complaints.

On the other hand, if the wife complains of drinking and "running around with another *woman*" (i.e., not merely "women"), this is categorized as "Drinking—any mention" and "Triangle—'Another woman'."

That is to say, as far as possible in this class all those responses are placed in which the wife was complaining of a particular *mode of life* adopted by her husband, in which he was, to use the classic colloquial phrase, "helling around."

Miscellaneous. We are coding, as far as is possible, *all* complaints made by the wives, including very specific comments. As is generally the case, the closer the categories are to the original responses, the greater the difficulty in fitting all responses into a limited number of categories. Therefore, this category is relatively large. We are, after all, coding responses and not women.

Thus, a given woman may complain of her husband's personality, non-support, desertion, etc.—and also admit that she had seizures of epilepsy which she viewed as some part of the cause of her divorce. This last item, the epilepsy, we classified as "Miscellaneous."

In this category, then, we included all highly idiosyncratic responses, and some less idiosyncratic answers which could not easily be fitted into our major classes. In one unusual case, the husband had been married before, but had divorced his wife. However, both he and his second wife belonged to a church which forbade divorce. Thus, in the eyes of their church, he had never been divorced from his previous spouse, and thus he and his second wife were, in their own eyes, living in adultery. Consequently, after some discussion, they decided that they would become legally divorced, and did so.

All cases of physical defects were put into this category, such as deafness, fatness, etc. In addition, cases of venereal disease were put into this category.

Another group, also too small for analysis, was made up of those women who admitted a premarital pregnancy that led to a forced marriage to which the wives themselves objected from the beginning.[3]

Thus, we have included in this class (1) some highly idiosyncratic cases, (2) cases of physical defects, (3) complaints of venereal disease, (4) triangles in which the wives were the guilty party, and (5) cases of an unwanted but forced marriage because of premarital pregnancy. In addition, two other groups are included: (6) felonies by the husband, leading to penal sentences, and (7) sexual problems.

With reference to our decision to place "sexual problems" as a complaint in the category of "Miscellaneous," the following comments are in order. As every serious survey has shown, sexual problems do not form any large pro-

---

3. We believe Christiansen has shown conclusively that a high proportion of marriages in this country *follow* pregnancy, possibly as high as one-fourth. We also have fair data to suggest the divorce rate among such couples is *very* high. See Harold T. Christiansen, *A Comparative Study of the Time Interval Between the Marriage of Parents and the Birth of Their First Child.* (Ph.D. Thesis, Brigham Young University, 1937).

portion of the "causes" for marital disruption. This was also the case for our own study.

Nevertheless, we did code this item separately at an earlier stage of our analysis. We wished to ascertain, with this sample of the divorced, whether sexual problems were statistically frequent. Having found out the frequency of this complaint (17 cases), and made a few cross-tabulations so as to check our conclusion that this factor is indeed of little importance, we then eliminated "sex" as a separate complaint, and included it in the category of "Miscellaneous." Thus, we used the item as much as it seemed worth, but thereafter freed a punch in our card column.

Nevertheless, we shall indicate what we thought of as being meant by the class, "Sexual problems." Our criterion was simple and easy to apply. If the woman made a complaint about the specifically sexual behavior of her husband, we coded it as "Sexual problems." Thus, if she complained that he was over-sexed, or that there was sexual incompatibility, this type of response fell into this category. Similarly, if she complained about sexual "perversion," the response fell into this category. In one case the women stated that after a hysterectomy her husband felt that she "would not be any more use to him sexually."

We are not, then, concerned with the deeper psychodynamic levels at which doubtless many personality problems might be traced to various sexual problems. We were not either concerned with the simpler psychodynamic relationships in which unconscious or unmentioned sexual incompatibilities appeared only as other types of conflicts. In general, as the sophisticated clinician knows, most problems of continued frigidity and sexual incompatibility are basically conflicts at quite other levels, and appear to be sexual conflicts only because this type of conflict can easily be mentioned nowadays.

We do not take seriously the possibility that our respondents did not wish to mention sex, since they mentioned sexual behavior in a frank manner in other connections.

The following categories remain to be discussed: (1) Nonsupport, (2) Consumption behavior, (3) Home life, (4) Values, and (5) Authority. Since we see these as closely connected, they must be analyzed together.

Economic role-playing. The economic role-obligations of the husband are many. Most of them, however, may be placed under two headings: (a) *providing* money with which to support the household, and (b) helping to *manage* that money with some regard for the needs and desires of the family members. A husband may fail in one of these and not in the other.[4]

With respect to the first of these categories, "Nonsupport," the complaints were that the husband "underplayed" the role of *provider*. In most cases, we have no objective proof that the family had insufficient food, clothing, etc., due to the husband's failure to provide. In some cases, as every harassed husband would know, the wife complains that the bills cannot be paid, when the general level of living is actually rather high. We confined ourselves, however, to the complaints made by the wife, since it is her world that we are attempting to explore. If she claimed that she could not pay her bills at a wage level of

4. See Michael Young, "Distribution of Income Within The Family", *Brit. J. Soc.*, 3 (1952) 305-21, who cites several relevant studies and avers that "primary" poverty may not be as important as "secondary" poverty. In particular, the British husband's wages seem to have risen more than his money allowances to the family.

$60 a week, while many families manage to survive on $50 weekly, we must nevertheless classify this case under the heading of "Nonsupport."

Similarly, if she complained that he would not work, or that he would not bring his paycheck home, that response was classified as "Nonsupport." Again, if the complaint was that he "failed to provide a home for the family," the response was considered "Nonsupport." In short, the complaint had to be that the husband was not bringing enough money home, or making enough, to provide adequately for his family, whether the provision mentioned was food, medical expenses, house, or clothing.

Generally, disapproval of the husband is somewhat greater in our society if he fails as provider (particularly if it is willful) than if he fails in the second task of his economic role, that of *manager*. As manager, he may spend too much on entertainment, and thereby leave insufficient money for food and rent. He may be charged by the wife with "throwing money around," being wasteful, or gambling his money away. We labelled charges of this type "complaints about consumption behavior."

The Playing of Noneconomic Roles. This broad area of husbandly behavior could be reliably coded into five main categories, two of which we have already discussed. These categories are: (1) General absence of emotion for the home and its occupants; (2) The Complex; (3) Triangle; (4) Harmony and integration of wife's and husband's notions as to style of life, values, goals; and (5) Authority of husband. These areas bear some relationship to one another, but they can be coded independently.

These behavior patterns may be viewed under two main headings: (A) Husband invests strong affect or emotion in the home or its occupants; and (B) Husband has little emotional involvement.

With respect to this first class, the disagreements of husband and wife fall under these sub-headings:

A. STRONG AFFECT IN HOME OR HOME ROLES

VALUES	AUTHORITY
Disagreement with wife concerning way of life, goals, education, religion, occupation, etc.	Disagreement concerning permissible degree of dominance over wife. (Cruelty, beating, jealousy, wanted to have own way.)

With respect to the second class, these sub-headings seem appropriate:

B. LITTLE EMOTIONAL INVOLVEMENT WITH HOME OR HOME ROLES

No Outside Attraction Mentioned HOME LIFE			Outside Attraction Mentioned Husband Goes Out Without Wife COMPLEX	TRIANGLE
Indifference toward home, emotional neglect	Did not want children	Would not take wife out	Peer group: "the gang," "the boys," "dating group"	Another woman

Although the relationships shown in the diagrams above are useful theoretically,[3a] even if this is not the case, the items may be separately coded. Let us now look at these categories separately.

3a. The relationship most open to attack would be that between Triangle and "Little emotional involvement." Some unknown but substantial proportion of spouses involved in *serious affairs* may also have deep emotional commitments to their homes.

Values—Harmony and Integration of Values, Behavior, and Way of Life of the Two Spouses. Here, the complaints were that the husband may have had a strong interest in the home, but different views of what was right, good, beautiful, etc. Husband and wife disagreed about the right style of life, education, manners, entertainment, the arts, religion, etc. Also in this class are to be found those complaints in which lack of harmony is expressed, but little detail was given: "We couldn't get along." "We couldn't agree on anything." "Intellectually, he wasn't satisfying." "There were misunderstandings all the time."

Now, the main problem of classification is that almost *any* kind of disagreement between wife and husband might be viewed as a "Value conflict." If the husband refuses to work, and the wife opposes that behavior, then one might speak of a value conflict. However, this does not cause difficulty, since we applied two criteria: (1) We kept close to the actual complaint of the wife, without interpretation, and, if she made her complaint in terms of their differing goals or standards, the response fell into this category; (2) When it is possible to classify a given conflict under a more specific heading, that is done. Thus, if the complaint is nonsupport, we suppose that the wife and husband did fight about it, but we are not free to infer this conflict, and there *is* a specific category of nonsupport. Similarly, if the husband thought that he had a right to beat his wife, and did so, we would usually guess that a value conflict existed, but we already have a specific class for "Authority—cruelty."

Consequently, we classified a complaint as "values" only when the wife reported that these various disagreements were a basis for *conflict*.

Authority: Dominance over Wife. In this category, too, the husband showed no lack of emotion about wife and home. We might almost say that she complained about his "overplaying" one element in the husbandly role, that of family head. We explained above why we do not code this as a value complaint.

On the other hand, we ought to consider whether a charge that the husband was domineering ought to be treated as a *personality* complaint. Perhaps the husband was insecure, or perhaps he displaced his self-aggression onto his wife. Now, doubtless some substantial part of this behavior was due to personality problems. On the other hand, we cannot assume that personality factors are at work if the husband is charged with beating his wife. We must stay as close as possible to the complaint as she sees it. If she only reports his maltreatment, we cannot classify this as a "personality" theme of complaint.

Moreover, we must also keep in mind that in our society wives and husbands are very likely to be found at different points along the dimension of acceptance of the husband's dominance. We suspect that, on the average, *husbands* would prefer to have *more* control over their wives' behavior, while wives would prefer them to have less control, than they actually maintain. Since the complaint grows out of this discrepancy or gap, we have no right to assume a personality problem.

Finally, in different strata and groups, the husband may be permitted different control techniques. For example, the middle-class male will very likely be censured more if he uses force to control his wife than if he uses the techniques of nagging, jealousy, or sulking. On the other hand, there is a strong reservoir of attitude on the part of the American male generally, that he has a *right* to tell his wife what to do. This attitude is given more overt expression, and is more frequently backed by force, in the lower strata. It is not so much that beating and cruelty are viewed as an obvious male right in marriage, but only that this is one of the techniques used from time to time, and with little or no subsequent guilt, for keeping control over the wife.[4] This attitude is given much less overt expression in the middle and upper strata, where a philosophy of equalitarianism is often given lip service. Nevertheless, we guess that most wives would be surprised if they knew to what extent even the middle-class male thinks wistfully back to an older family system in which the male was given great authority over his wife's behavior.[5] In our society, the husband who successfully asserts his dominance does enjoy some approval and even a modicum of envy from other males. Male dominance is to some extent *actually approved*. Of course, wives who refuse to accept the moral rightness of male dominance may sometimes view this assertion of authority as a kind of selfishness. Psychodynamically oriented wives may see it as male "immaturity." However, the complaints in this category of "Authority" are specifically to the effect that the wives were not allowed to run things in their own way or to make decisions as they chose, and instead had to cater to their husbands' wishes.

Home Life: Lack of Affect for Home and Occupants, No Outside Attraction Mentioned. Here the complaint was that the husband simply showed little interest in the home, the children, or the wife. This was not reported by the wife as active fighting, but as his failure to be interested in the home. This is a *range* of behavior, from cases of apparently complete disinterest in the home and wife, to simple refusals to go out with the wife. In these data, there is no way of analyzing at any deeper level the origins of this pattern. Doubtless, in some cases, the husband was by personality little given to expression of emotion. In other cases, the refusal to exhibit any emotional involvement was an index of the coming dissolution of the marriage. That is, some husbands "went out with the boys" (Complex), while others stayed at home but acted as though they were no part of the home (Home Life). Typical responses in this category would be the following: "He never seemed to care for the children." "He didn't want the children." "He would not take me anywhere" (i.e., lack of interest in companionship role). "He did not seem to love me at all." "He showed no interest in being married."

Personality: In the context of marital problems, the category of "Personality" is often amorphous, unstable, and frustrating, unless there is a fairly reliable personality diagnosis made through some standardized diagnostic devices, such as the Rorschach test, TAT, etc. The diagnosis of "personality" is not usually reliable if the analyst has only the data from a direct face-to-face interview, and is not himself specifically trained in psychodynamic diagnostics. These are, after all, complaints made by wives, who were not experts in this craft.

4. We should perhaps also remind the reader that violence is generally more common in the lower strata. It might be very difficult to learn which of the two spouses struck first in some of these "beatings." Usually, of course, the man will win. Consequently, the woman can complain that she was beaten.

5. One index of this sex difference might be found in attitudes toward the so-called Victorian age. We predict that more males than females will be found to look back nostalgically to such a period.

Here, then, we classified the item as "Personality" if the wife used terms which clearly indicated her *belief* that the fundamental problem was one of personality. In the main this kind of comment was of the following type: "He was emotionally immature." "Our personalities were just incompatible." "Neither of us ready to get married—our personalities clashed." "He was irresponsible, couldn't settle down." "He wasn't reliable." "Change in my husband's attitudes and personality after being overseas in the war." "He had moody spells and didn't talk to me for months at a time."

We have not, then, attempted an analysis of the husband's character. We have not attempted to find the "cause" of his behavior. His childhood background or sexual experiences which might have led to a neurosis or a psychosis were ignored. We have simply classified the wife's responses in this category when she has herself used a term which emphasized his personality—or in few cases her own. In this fashion we have managed to get consistency between the coding of the same responses by different coders. On the other hand, analysts who hold to a personality theory of social action will be dissatisfied by our reluctance to depart from or to analyze further the comments made by the wife herself as to the "cause" of the divorce.

Distribution of Complaints. We have outlined in detail our criteria for classifying these responses under the headings used. As can be seen, we have stayed close to phrases and comments made by the wife herself, and have, as far as possible, used *all* of these comments. We were attempting to ascertain how the *woman herself* viewed the problem, not to pinpoint a "cause of divorce." We wanted to understand what she saw as the problems of her marriage. We believed, and we shall attempt to show that this is the case, that certain of these responses are associated with differences in postdivorce adjustment, particularly in its early phases. We believed that once we could see the problem as the respondent viewed it, we would have some grasp of her position and complaint when the divorce occurred and thus some understanding of why she acted as she did later. Let us now turn to the actual distribution of these responses.

WOULD YOU STATE, IN YOUR OWN WORDS, WHAT WAS THE MAIN CAUSE OF YOUR DIVORCE?

Complaint Theme	% Responses	% Respondents
Non-support	13	33
Authority	12	32
Complex	12	31
Drinking	12	30
Personality	11	29
Home Life	9	25
Values	8	21
Consumption	8	20
Triangle	6	16
Misc.	4	12
Desertion	3	8
Relatives	2	4
Number	1110	N = 425
Total	100	

Vocabulary, Behavior, and Reference Models. Were these complaints the truth? Even if we grant that in such an emotionally charged relationship we would not get all "the" truth, is there at least some "felt truth" in these charges? If there is, we should find that these complaints are not made accidentally or at random, but have some pattern and direction; for they affect, or are affected by, behavior and attitudes of husband and wife. By presenting some of these relationships descriptively, the validity, meaning and importance of these complaints can be seen.

Great differences in the distribution of complaint themes for most variables, such as occupation, income, or rural-urban origins, are not to be expected. These background variables do not structure husband-wife interaction enough to create many sharp differences in the distribution of complaints. The distribution of themes is determined by many factors, and we are not certain what all of these are. For example, complaints about Authority, i.e., that the husband dominated the home or wife too much, are only slightly more frequent in families in lower occupational strata than in those in upper strata. Now, this distribution may (1) reflect the *fact* that husbands in such strata actually are only slightly more inclined to be dominant. However, there is an alternative possibility, that (2) wives in such strata complain in the *vocabulary* of authority. That is, they speak of the "bossiness" of their husbands. A wife in the upper strata, with a different training, might describe the *same behavior* with a different set of words, such as "personality immaturity." Finally, even when the *husband's behavior is the same,* and the vocabulary is not very different, (3) wives in a different strata may have different *responses.* A higher proportion of males in the lower strata may be dominant, but their wives may be less inclined to complain about the behavior, since in their group it is more acceptable. Therefore, if (A) there are far *more* lower-strata husbands who are authoritarian, but there is *less* objection by the wives to this behavior; while (B) such behavior by husbands is *less* common in *upper strata,* but their wives are *more* likely to object to it if it does occur; then, the distribution of the Authority theme would exhibit less differentiation by occupation than would the distribution of actual behavior.

Since we cannot prevent these factors and others from affecting the distribution of verbal responses, we cannot always expect great differences generally, and some of the apparent differences in theme of complaint distributions may reflect: (1) real differences in behavior, (2) differences in wives' vocabularies, or choice of words, (3) differences in the responses of wives to similar behavior of husbands. Finally, since all wives made more than one complaint, the categories are not exclusive. Among those who complained about Nonsupport will be found wives who also complained of Authority, Personality, or Complex. Thus, the associations between a given complaint and other behavior may not be sharp. To the extent that we wish to understand the *wife's* problems, these problems of interpretation will exist in any such investigation.

Authority, Nonsupport, Personality. The wife from an urban background was more likely than the wife from a rural background to complain that Personality was the main cause of divorce: 31% of urban wives complained of Personality, as against 21% of rural wives. Those wives from small towns fell in between (27%), although in general the distribution of complaint themes was almost exactly the same for the small town group as for the urban group. On the other hand, the wife of rural origin was a bit more likely to complain of "Authority" than was the case for the urban wife (38% versus 30%). In a parallel fashion, the husband of rural origin was more likely than the husband of urban origin to have the charge of "Authority" brought *against* him. The comparison may be seen in the following simple table:

WIVES' COMPLAINT OF HUSBANDS' DOMINATION, BY RURAL-URBAN ORIGIN OF HUSBAND

Origin of Husband	Respondents Who Complained of Authority %	Base
Rural	44	48
Small town	28	112
Metropolitan	31	264
Total		424

Correspondingly, if the husband was of rural origin, the complaint of Personality was less likely to be made against him (21%, if rural; 30% if small town; and 30%, if metropolitan).

Whether personality problems are indeed more frequently found in urban than in rural divorcees, is not known. It does seem likely that the woman of urban origin or of slightly greater education is more likely to view the domineering behavior of her husband as due to his personality structure. The simpler (but not necessarily less accurate) view of the rural wife with lesser education is that her husband is simply self-centered, overbearing or bossy. Similarly, we suppose that the rural husband is more often complained against because he is more likely to follow traditional patterns of male dominance.

Now, if our reasoning is correct, then these differences should appear more sharply if we arrange these marriages by the rural-urban origins of the *couples*.

WIFE'S COMPLAINTS OF PERSONALITY AND AUTHORITY, BY RURAL-URBAN ORIGINS OF COUPLE

Origin of: Wife	Husband	% Complaining of Personality	% Complaining of Authority	Base
Urban	Urban	30%	30%	356
Urban	Rural	23	43	35
Rural	Urban	24	33	21
Rural	Rural	15	46	13

Here the "small town" people are grouped with those from a large city, since in our tabulations they are closest in characteristics to the latter. We see that our notions are borne out partially, but not entirely: (1) The urban wife married to the urban husband is more likely than any other to complain of her husband's personality. (2) By contrast, the rural wife married to the rural husband is *least* likely to make that complaint (although the numbers are very small). (3) The other two combinations fall between these extremes. Further, (4) the urban wife, unaccustomed to the *rural patterns* of greater male domination, is very likely to complain of Authority—but (5) the *rural wife* married to the *rural husband is just as likely to make that complaint*.

We had not anticipated this last result, for we had forgotten to take into consideration the fact that, though the rural couple might indeed have as an *original* reference model the rural family, they are *actually* living in an urban setting (metropolitan Detroit), so that almost any social circle would present an urban reference model. The wife from a rural background would, then, measure her rural husband's behavior by that standard and find him just as overbearing as would the urban wife married to a rural husband. We noted earlier that somewhat the same husband behavior might be viewed as Personality or Authority, if one made no reference to the behavior as seen by the wife. That these wives saw these actions very differently is attested by the *negative* association ($Q = -.25$) between Personality and Authority complaints.

We had expected to find a somewhat similar relationship between the rural-urban origins of the couple and the complaint of Nonsupport. Twenty-six percent of the rural wives complained of Nonsupport, as against 32% of the urban wives. Moreover, 42% of the rural husbands had that complaint made *against* them, as against 33% of the urban husbands. If the complaints were at all valid, income differences would play a part: 41% of those husbands making less than $45 weekly had this complaint made against them; 34% of those making $45-$60; 24% of those making $60-$75; and 21% of those making $75 and over.

However, standards of reference might also play a part. If so, then rural wives with somewhat lower standards for husband's income might complain less than urban wives. The differences are small, but in the predicted direction.

But when these *couples* are arranged by rural-urban origins, once more there is only partial predictive success: (1) The rural wives married to urban husbands (i.e., lower standards as against higher performance) complained *least* about Nonsupport (14%). (2) The urban wives married to urban husbands (higher standard, higher performance) fell between (33%); and (3) the urban wives married to rural husbands (higher standard, lower performance) were more inclined to complain of Nonsupport (40%)—but, once more, (4) *rural wives married to rural husbands* were just as inclined to make this complaint (46%). Again, we interpret this by supposing that her standard of reference is no longer the rural background, but the urban circles within which she now moves.

Home Life. Now, with reference to both Authority and Nonsupport, the rural husband could be expected to differ from the urban husband in a direction that the wife would *not* usually approve, i.e., by being more domineering, and by producing less income. However, the contrary could be expected for *Home Life.* Coming from a more intensely home-centered background, he could be expected to give more love and attention to the children, and more interest to the home, than the urban husband. Correspondingly, the wife from a rural background could be expected to have higher standards for husbandly behavior in this area.

The wife from a rural background is only slightly more likely than the urban wife to complain about Home Life (29% *vs.* 24%); and this complaint is more likely to be made *against* the urban husband (25% *vs.* 17%) than against the rural husband. Remembering that in this area the rural husband is more likely to have a higher performance, let us once again arrange our couples by their origins. Then we find that the rural wife (higher standard) married to the urban husband (lower performance) is most likely to complain of Home Life (38% made this complaint). By contrast, the urban wife (lower standard) married to the rural husband (higher performance) is *less* likely to make this complaint (17%). However, in this case, the rural-rural marriage is just as unlikely to give rise to such a complaint (15%), perhaps because now the reference model is the urban patterns, and by this reference the rural husband performs well. The urban-urban couple falls between these two extremes, with 25% of these wives making this complaint.

Similarly, wives who marry *downward* educationally are least likely to make this complaint (18%), as compared with those who marry at the same level (26%) or those who marry upward (33%).

Race and Religion. Although the absolute figures are not great, Negro husbands are twice as likely as White husbands to be charged with desertion by their wives (14% *vs.* 7%). This corresponds with fairly reliable data from other sources.[6] (In general, however, the Negro-White differences are minor: e.g., 30% of White wives complained of Personality, as against 24% of Negro wives).

In general, differences in religious preference affect the distribution of complaint themes very little, whether we distribute by religion of husband or wife separately, or by marriages of like or unlike religious backgrounds. The reason for this negative result may be seen in the fact that there are no important differences between the religious groups with respect to *permissible* as against nonpermissible themes of complaint. The Catholic prohibition against divorce is absolute, while the Protestant is not, but neither suggests gradations of marital difficulties so as to allow a judgment as to what kinds of problems "justify" a divorce.

The consequence is that the few differences by religion seem expressive of income and educational differences, rather than of genuine doctrinal differences. The Catholic population has a slightly lesser occupational and educational attainment than does the Protestant. When we tabulate by religion of husband, we find that the Protestant husband is more likely than the Catholic to have the complaint of Personality made against him (30% of Protestant husbands as against 21% of Catholic husbands). This pattern is like the differences in theme of complaint by education. However, a similar tabulation by religion of wife shows no such difference. A tabulation by like-unlike religious backgrounds shows a very slight difference. On the other hand, the Protestant husband is more likely to have the charge of Value Conflict made against him, and the Protestant wife is more likely to make that complaint. Again, these differences are small: 22% of Protestant wives versus 18% of Catholic wives; but 26% of Protestant husbands as against 13% of Catholic husbands.[7]

Nonsupport, Consumption, and Steady Work. Since the complaint of Consumption refers rather to the handling of money (overspending, gambling, etc.) than to a basic failure to provide enough money, only a low association exists between this complaint and that of Nonsupport ($Q = +.20$). On the

---

6. See the summary of data by Thomas P. Monahan and William M. Kephart, "Desertion and Divorce in Philadelphia," *Am. Soc. Rev.*, 17 (1952), 719-727. However, their percentages are higher, because they include all cases in which desertion was charged so that the wife could get a support order from the court.

7. When we drop the religious category and use instead the category of frequency of church attendance, these differences are slightly more regular but, nevertheless not large enough to be

other hand, since this latter complaint reflects standards and not only absolute amounts of money, it might be related to whether the wife married upward or downward educationally. Although the differences are negligible, 18% of the wives who married upward educationally did make this complaint, as against 19% who married at their own level, and 23% who married downward.

The distribution by income ought to relate to the complaint of Nonsupport. We noted previously that the complaints of Nonsupport drop steadily as we go from low incomes to high incomes. Since, however, many husbands seemed not to work steadily, it seemed likely that using this last attribute would also be relevant. Indeed, only 13% of those (a) who had steady work *and* received $60 weekly or more had the complaint of Nonsupport made against them. This percentage increased to 24% for those (b) who had steady work but received less than $60 weekly when they did work; and increased to 55% for those (c) who worked unsteadily and received $60 or more weekly. Finally, 63% of the wives complained of Nonsupport, (d) whose husbands worked unsteadily and also received less than $60 weekly when they did work.

This ranking is reversed for the complaint of Consumption, when we consider those who complained of Consumption, but *not* of Nonsupport: only 2% complained of Consumption *only,* whose husbands worked unsteadily and received less than $60 weekly; 6% of those in the category of unsteady work and more than $60 weekly; 16% of the category, less than $60 weekly with steady work; and 17% of those whose husbands got $60 or more weekly and also worked steadily. That is the proportion of Consumption *only* complaints increases with economic well-being.

And, since the pattern we call Complex is one in which the husband spends much of his money (and time) away from home, there is a moderate association between the complaints of Complex and Consumption ($Q = +.47$), and between Drink and Consumption ($Q = +.44$). Because the complaint of Triangle is emotionally so overriding in its effect, there is a negative association ($Q = -.65$) between Consumption and Triangle.

Duration of Marriage. Since the themes of complaint are not to be seen as the causes of these divorces, there is no simple relationship between them and the duration of marriage. Furthermore, since all of these marriages ended in divorce, complaints which are serious are not easily separated from those which are not. However, some perhaps predictable patterns do emerge. We note, for example, that the complaint of Personality is associated with a short duration of marriage:

COMPLAINT OF PERSONALITY, BY DURATION OF MARRIAGE

Duration of Marriage	% Making this Complaint
0-4 years	42%
5-9 years	28
10-14 years	28
15 years and over	18

To the extent that the complaint of Personality is *actually* associated with personality problems, we should expect such marriages to have a shorter duration than marriages with certain other kinds of complaints. In general, personality disturbances would be a consistent and continuous source of conflict within the marriage, and would begin with the marriage itself. Complaints about Home Life, on the other hand, are associated with a longer duration of marriage, for this type of complaint reports a negativeness, a passivity on the part of the husband, a failure to perform. A personality disturbance is much more likely to issue in a definite form of positive, if disturbing, behavior. For the complaint of Home Life, the increase is small but steady through each category of duration of marriage (22% for the 0-4 years category, to 29% for the 15 years and over category).

On the other hand, the category of duration of marriage in which there is the highest proportion of complaints about Value Conflict is the marriage that lasts 5-9 years. From this point on, there is apparently a slightly lesser chance that the wife will complain about Value Conflict (though, of course, she will complain about other things, since she always gives some reason for the dissolution of the marriage). The differences may be seen in the following table:

PERCENTAGE OF WIVES COMPLAINING OF VALUE CONFLICT, BY DURATION OF MARRIAGE

Duration of Marriage	%
0-4 years	22%
5-9 years	26
10-14 years	18
15 years and over	15

As a matter of common sense, we would expect that claims about value disagreements would decrease over the years of marriage, and this does seem to be the case. However, we are studying a group in which there are many possibilities of complaints. We might phrase the matter journalistically by saying that those marriages in which there is high conflict from the beginning are likely not to get to the second stage, in which matters of value conflict seem important. Once this latter phase has been worked through, the chance of a marriage ending because of value conflict will be lower.

On the other hand, the complaint of Home Life increases steadily for each category of duration of marriage, as do the complaints of Drinking, and Complex:

COMPLAINT OF NO HOME LIFE, DRINKING, TRIANGLE, AND COMPLEX, BY DURATION OF MARRIAGE

Duration of Marriage	Home Life	Drinking	Triangle	Complex
0-4 years	22%	26%	10%	22%
5-9 years	24	27	15	32
10-14 years	25	32	17	32
15 years and over	29	40	25	33

Although the cynical might comment, looking at these data, that long marriages apparently drive men to drink or to helling around, a simpler explanation seems applicable.[8] Since all of these marriages ended in divorce, but certain of these types of complaints (such as Personality, Value Conflict,

---

8. One study of 7000 broken Catholic marriages also found that the last three of these four "causes" were associated with longer marriages. See John L. Thomas, "Marital Failure and Duration," *Social Order*, 3 (1953), 24-29.

and Relatives) will decrease in frequency over the years, either because such marriages are eliminated or because the spouses will grow accustomed to the differences, the range of possible complaints decreases with time.

Moreover, the complaints that are associated with a longer duration of marriage are to be divided into two categories. That of Home Life is *par excellence* made by the wife who comes increasingly to feel that she is simply not getting enough out of the marriage, because her husband is not putting enough into it. Such a charge is somewhat difficult to formulate, since it often is directed against an *attitude* rather than any particular *behavior*. The husband himself is often puzzled by this kind of charge, and may ask helplessly, "What do you want me to do?" The answer is, of course, that the wife wants him to *feel*, not *do*. We are assuming here that in this complaint the main variable is the wife's slow formulation of the complaint, and her decision to do something about it. In addition, we suppose that the change over time also reflects a change in *his* behavior. We shall analyze this matter later, when we discuss the strategy of divorce conflict. In particular, both Drinking and Complex are likely to be part of a strategy in which the husband forces her to ask for a divorce. This is behavior over which he has some control, while it is difficult to make the same statement about Triangle.

It is worth commenting that these four items are only partially independent. Complex and Drinking are, of course, associated ($Q = +.50$). But Complex is not associated with Home Life. And Home Life is *negatively* associated with Triangle ($Q = -.36$), while Triangle is negatively associated with Drinking ($Q = -.74$). Finally, when there is a higher frequency of dating during the marriage, there is less likelihood that the charge of Home Life will be made: 17% of the wives who dated more than once weekly made this charge; 22% of those who dated once weekly; and 30% of those who dated twice monthly.

As noted before, it is possible to claim that the husband will not take part in such behavior as drinking, gambling, staying out, or having an affair, if his marriage is "good." This is to some degree a matter of definition. On the other hand, it is quite clear that the husband who does indulge in such activities will increase the statistical likelihood that he will eventually *wish* to destroy his marriage, or that his wife will wish to do so, however good either thought it was before such behavior began. Sooner or later, he is likely to lose his emotional attachment to his home, or to develop another attachment outside it. We are leaving out of consideration the possible *changes* in the wife's response over time, although we shall devote some attention to it in our discussion of divorce strategy.

As we have already noted, it is the urban wife who complains more frequently of the personality of her husband as grounds for the conflict. The wife of higher education is also more likely to make such a complaint, and the urban husband, or husband of higher education, is also more likely to have that charge made against him. Similarly, if the wife marries *upward* educationally, she is more likely to make that complaint (33% of the hypergamous wives, *vs.* 30% and 26% of homogamous and hypogamous wives).

As noted previously, Protestant husbands are more likely to have this complaint made against them, as are veterans (35%, *vs.* 23% of nonveterans).

Wives who marry downward are more likely to complain of the domineering behavior of their husbands. Similarly, as we noted, rural wives (in urban social groups) are also more likely to make this complaint of Authority. Wives of lesser education are more likely to make this complaint, but the differences are very small. Husbands against whom this charge is made are also more likely to be charged with drinking ($Q = +.42$). On the other hand, those who complain of *Authority are less likely* to complain of Personality ($Q = -.25$); of Desertion ($-.33$); or of Triangle ($-.71$). Husbands from rural origins, or with lesser education, are more likely to have this charge made *against them*.

It seems consistent with the patterns we have analyzed that women with more education are more likely to complain of Value Conflicts. However, the only significant difference is between college women (35% made this complaint), and those with less education (20-21%). And husbands of upper occupational strata are more likely to have this charge made *against them* (33% of the upper, *vs.* 21-19% of the middle and lower). Protestant husbands have this charge made against them more frequently (26% *vs.* 13% of the Catholic husbands); and steady workers as compared with unsteady workers (23% *vs.* 15%).

There are, however, three bits of data that seem not to fit well with the foregoing analyses, although it is equally possible that their importance is minor. *Rural* wives complain *more* than urban wives about Value Conflict (35%, as against 20%), and Negroes more than Whites (26% *vs.* 20%). Occupationally hypergamous wives make this complaint more often (25% *vs.* 18% of those who marry downward). Of course, these are *not* significant differences. And from rural-rural marriages and marriages of rural wives to urban husbands, more complaints of Values seem to grow (38% and 33%, *vs.* 9% for urban wife/rural husband, and 21% for urban-rural marriages). Since we usually expect those toward the upper occupational strata to make their values more explicit, to argue about them more, and to use them as justifications for conflict; and since we have the same expectation for (2) Whites as against Negroes, and (3) urban as against rural spouses, these small differences seem to be somewhat anomalous. However, until we have come to understand better the relationship between the complaints made by husband and wife, and the entire structure of events that lead to divorce, we shall not attempt to offer any harmonizing interpretation for these facts.

Summary. Since these complaints do reflect the wife's problems and complaints as she viewed and experienced them, we can expect that various characteristics of their postdivorce experience are affected by them. We shall at various points in our analysis of this experience comment on these apparent effects.

Nevertheless, these complaints were not the causes of the divorce—after all, every *still* married wife could very likely make one or more of these charges against her husband. They are only *one* of the elements leading to instability. Correspondingly, however salient and poignant a woman's complaint against her husband seems at the time of the conflict and divorce, she will find that other items, such as her age or dating behavior, will shape her later postdivorce experience far more definitely. In subsequent chapters we shall not lose sight of these themes of complaint, but they will fall into a more modest perspective over time. Here, we have concentrated upon these complaints so as to contribute some analysis of the themes that are used by divorced women when explaining the "causes" of their divorce. We have also related these themes (a) to various background attributes, including homogamy and heterogamy; and (b) to each other.

CHAPTER XI

STEPS TOWARD THE DIVORCE

IN THIS CHAPTER we analyze the role patterns of the husband in our society, and come to the conclusion that (a) the husband more frequently than the wife is the first to desire a divorce; and (b) it is the husband more often than the wife who adopts (whether consciously or not) a line of behavior, a "strategy," which forces the other spouse to suggest a divorce as the appropriate solution.

We then analyze this overt step toward divorce, the first suggestion that a divorce be obtained, as well as who continued to insist after the first suggestion. We shall take note of factors that are associated with the first suggestion, and in later chapters will show that who first suggested continues to be important for postdivorce adjustment, including even the rapidity of remarriage.

The Strategy of Divorce Conflict. The average respondent tried to tell the truth, but the limitations on her understanding, and on the skill of the interviewer, are too obvious to need further comment here. However, she did not need to hide what she could not herself know, the *total structure* of influences playing on her. Though doubtless the husband had his own complaints, she is reporting her problems, as she understood them. In many cases she may have failed to see the strategic pattern of the overall conflict.

The reader should be struck, even within this context, by the apparent fact that most wives felt sinned against. Almost no wives claimed that the divorce was mainly their fault. A few divorcees did make such a confession as this: "I guess he didn't like it when he came back from the service and found that I had a baby." Such an admission, however, is a rarity. Even when the wife admitted that she had faults, she was not likely to admit that she was the *major* offender.

Now, even granting that we cannot now get at the ultimate reality of so intimate a conflict, it is worthwhile speculating as to how far these claims represent the facts. We believe that, whatever counter charges the husbands would make, the complaints of the wives *were also mainly true,* and that *it was more often the husband than the wife who wanted first to break up the marriage.*

We start with two major institutional facts. (1) The male has a dominant position in this, as in all other known cultures.[1] (2) The attitudes of wives,

---

1. With the possible exception of the Tchambuli. See Margaret Mead, *Sex and Temperament.* Although Mead's stay among the Tchambuli was short, her report would indicate that the female plays a dominant role in that society. Whether later investigation will confirm this in detail

and women generally, toward this lesser power are changing more rapidly than are the attitudes of men in the society. Perhaps a close parallel may be found in the relationship of other subordinate groups to ruler groups, such as Negroes in American society, or colonial peoples generally. People accept new liberties more quickly than the loss of power. One consequence of these major institutional facts is, of course, a conflict in the definitions of the appropriate roles to be played by husband and wife, with each spouse pressing in somewhat different directions. We leave aside the ethical problem as to the correlative responsibilities that go with increased freedom and privilege, since we are concerned rather with the predictable attitudes and behavior of the two sexes.

The dominance of the male exhibits itself not alone in the realm of the family, where typically the male assumes the right (even when he does not always exercise it) of making most major decisions, but more fundamentally in the area of occupation. Here we point to the obvious. When both husband and wife work, it is assumed that major changes in family organization or geographic mobility are to be decided mainly by reference to the husband's, not the wife's, occupation. The class status of the family usually stems from the husband's occupation, not from the wife's attainments in that or any other sphere. For the same type of work, the male receives more income than the female.

More fundamental, however, is the fact that the job is considered a legitimate *major* interest for the husband. This is the case even when he has no great aspirations for business or occupational success. It is assumed in our society that the husband has a right to absent himself from home and children for at least eight hours or more a day for at least five days a week for most of the weeks of the year; and he expects to be given some deference and respect for this activity. This expectation exists even when he has no great liking for the job. Toward the upper educational strata, the claims of the job or business are given even greater scope. These facts have several complex ramifications. One of them is that the male always has legitimate interests away from the home, and in all major civilizations it has been taken for granted that home, wife, and children were secondary considerations, though the latter have been lauded in poetry, and eulogized in speeches. The characteristic epigram is the Byronic phrase, "Man's love is of man's life a thing apart; 'tis woman's whole existence." This means, then, that the man actually has much of his energy diverted away from the home. To this extent, his dedication to home and family, particularly in terms of overt behavior, will be less than that of the woman, who is socialized to feel that *her* major dedication is to home and children.

Moreover, even in commonsense terms, the greater physical mobility of the man, and the fact that a greater segment of his waking hours need not be accounted for, mean that he has a much wider scope of activity. He meets more people, both male and female. Perhaps much more significant, however,

---

remains to be seen. Other societies have been variously reported to be "matriarchal," but later investigation disclosed that this was not the case. Such reports were particularly made for societies in which there was a matrilineal inheritance of property, as, for example, among the Zuñi. It is even possible that a reinterpretation of Mead's own data would suggest a somewhat different picture.

is the fact that in perhaps no society is his behavior with members of the opposite sex *more restricted* than that of wives, and usually it is less restricted. Thus, for example, the middle-class male may go to any bar and drink alone. This is not the case for the middle-class woman, who is expected, even under the freer dispensation of our era, to go to "cocktail lounges." Behavior which is considered legitimate and innocent for the husband, would be considered questionable for the wife.

We are not now concerned with a moral evaluation of this socially accepted nonequalitarianism. We merely point out the differences and some of their consequences. One obvious consequence is simply that the husband is much more likely than the wife to become involved in pleasurable activities away from the home, and with members of the opposite sex. Putting it differently, the wife is much more likely to be scolded, criticized, reported on, gossiped about, and even chastised, at an *earlier* stage of her deviation from home-centered activities than the male.

Of course, these are large-scale institutional pressures, and within such larger patterns all sorts of deviations are possible. These pressures seem to add up to these rough facts: (1) The male is much more likely than the female to be less interested in the home and to be more easily attracted away from it. (2) The male is much more likely than the female to become involved in external complexities of an emotional nature, from drinking and club behavior with the boys, to extreme dedication to an occupational task. (3) In our generation, the wife increasingly views these matters by an equalitarian standard. However, (4) even when she does not do so, she may nevertheless object to the *consequences* of inequality: the failure of the husband to appear for meals, his spending of money on drink, his failure to dedicate himself to his family, or his involvement with another woman. The major consequence is, then (5) that in our generation an increasing proportion of wives have strong complaints to make against their husbands. There may be counterbalancing attractions, but the complaints remain to annoy her, and perhaps to threaten the relationship.

Now, from the husband's side a different picture emerges. Since the husband takes his prerogatives for granted, he can use them without guilt. He may feel guilty at the *consequences* of frequenting bars, but within rather wide limits he is permitted to be there. He may feel guilty about becoming involved seriously with another woman, but he has a much lesser sense of guilt about taking part in the steps *preliminary* to the involvement. More significant perhaps is the husband's lesser involvement in the family as the center of his world and his *statistically greater exposure* to attractive stimuli, which may lead him away from dedication to the family.

This leads to an obvious conclusion: Although the wife will have fairly serious charges to make against her husband, we believe that in our generation it is more often the husband who first wishes to escape from the marriage. If this is true, then the process of divorce decision may be analyzed to some extent in terms of a *strategy of conflict.*

On the other hand, it is likely that our respondents are telling the truth when they say in over 60% of the cases that they first *suggested* the divorce. The resolution of this apparent paradox is obvious: The husband must make himself so obnoxious that his wife is willing to ask for and even insist upon a divorce. From our data, it is not possible to know in what proportion of cases this is the situation, or even in what proportion of the cases the husband was aware of what he was doing. We guess that often the husband is not aware that he is following out any such plan or tactics. But his behavior is not unconsciously motivated; he is simply unaware of the total pattern. He would see it if it were pointed out to him.

Precisely because the wife, in general, makes more adjustments in her marital life than does the husband in his in order to make a marriage successful, and because, in general, it will be the husband who has strayed first, the husband has a guilt load to bear. This guilt load is less for men than for women for most deviations from the marital norm, but it seems likely that very few mothers and fathers[2] divorce without real problems of guilt. Happily for the husband, the institutional structure permits him to remain within the limits of male decency and respectability, while being rather offensive in the eyes of his wife. The reasons for this are fairly clear: (1) The society actually permits him a wider range of behavior, and (2) it is mainly the wife who will be able to see the *pattern* of his behavior. Thus, for example, he is allowed to have a drink in the bar after he finishes his workday, and he will receive no criticism for this. On the other hand, this may mean that he is often late to dinner and thus makes his wife feel that he does not care at all for his family. Alternately he may go from his office to parties within the city, and not take his wife, on the plea that it is difficult to get a baby sitter, or the transportation problem is hard to solve, etc. For this behavior he is not scolded, although he may be joshed.

Indeed, we may range most of these complaints along a quasi-continuum of social knowledge: (a) Behavior that is mainly observable by the wife, leading to complaints such as Home life, Consumption, Values; (b) behavior that is observable by and known to both the wife and her very close friends or kin, leading to such complaints as Complex, Personality, and Authority; and (c) behavior that can not be hidden from a still wider circle, such as Nonsupport, Desertion and Triangle. He may follow any of the patterns in these first two categories without incurring more than mild censure from his group, but with a considerable impact upon his marital relations. The patterns in the last of these three categories effectively destroy the husband-wife role system.

Among the many consequences, of course, will be her responses: scolding, nagging, conflict, loss of emotional attachment to the husband, jealousy, etc., so that she begins to take seriously other alternatives to continuing the marriage.

We suggest, then, that in our society *the husband more frequently than the wife will engage in behavior whose function, if not intent, whose result, if not aim, is to force the other spouse to ask for the divorce first.* Thereby the husband frees himself to some extent from the guilt burden, since he did not ask for the divorce. A by-product of this process frees him still more: The wife's repeated objections to this behavior will mean that there are family

---

2. We use the criterion of parenthood here only to emphasize roughly those marriages in which there has been at some time a fairly definite emotional commitment. Perhaps some other criterion would be equally useful.

squabbles, and one almost constant result of repeated family squabbles is a lessened affection between husband and wife. In particular, of course, these squabbles mean that the husband can begin to think of himself as also aggrieved, as also sinned against. Although this is not the only possible way of ridding oneself of guilt, it can be fairly effective.

Finally, class differences in permissible behavior mean that different strategies may be used by different classes. The lower-class husband can more easily use physical cruelty or overbearing behavior, while the middle-class husband may instead have to show indifference to the home—or even have to ask for the divorce *first,* because the behavior he and his group considers permissible is not effective enough to force her to suggest the divorce first.

We do not have data to prove all these assertions, but some of our data bear on them. They are predictions from institutional theory, and can of course be tested. Let us now, however, turn to some of the more overt steps toward the divorce, including the initiation of the divorce decision.

Consideration to Filing Suit. Although we shall be concerned more with the separation and postdivorce phases of the total marital conflict, we must at least take notice of the *manifest steps* toward the divorce, including not only the consideration and decision phases, but also such matters as marital counseling and talks about the divorce between the spouses.

An arbitrary but obvious set of steps would be these: (1) serious consideration of the divorce as a possibility; (2) final decision; (3) filing suit; and (4) obtaining the decree. Although the separation usually occurs *after* the final decision and *before* the filing of suit, it may occur anywhere in this series. Indeed, it may not occur even after the decree, under extreme circumstances. Since its personal and social consequences also appear to be emotionally more important than any of these four steps, we shall discuss it later when we deal with other processes immediately following the decree itself.

Many American (and foreign) jokes suggest that divorces in this country are precipitate and based upon whim. The evidence is clear, however, that divorcees do not characteristically dash for the nearest divorce lawyer when the first spat occurs. Divorces are preceded by a long period of conflict, and the final action is the result of a decision and action process that lasts on the average about two years.

TIME FROM FIRST SERIOUS CONSIDERATION TO DECREE[2a]

Time (in months)	Percent	Cumulative Percent
0- 5	6%	6%
6-11	15	21
12-23	30	51
24-35	23	74
36-47	17	91
48 and over	10	101%
Total	101%	
Number	410	
Not known	15	
Total	425	

Median $=$ 23.8 mos.

2a. "First serious consideration to decree," and "serious consideration to final decision" are

This tabulation represents the total time elapsed, from the first serious consideration of divorce to the legal end of the marriage. Let us break this into the steps we listed above.

Time (in months)	SERIOUS CONSIDERATION TO FINAL DECISION		FINAL DECISION TO FILING	
	Percent	Cumulative Percent	Percent	Cumulative Percent
0- 1	36%	36%	31%	31%
1- 2	9	45	18	49
3- 4	7	52	12	61
5- 6	6	58	13	74
7- 8	4	62	3	77
9-10	2	64	2	79
11-12	4	68	10	89
13-23	8	76	5	94
24 or more	23	99	5	99
Total	99%		99%	
Number	423		423	
Not known =	2		Not known = 2	
	425		425	

The median time for the consideration phase was 4.6 months, while the median time from decision to filing was 3.2 months.

The period from filing the suit to the final decree is not so much in the control of husband and wife as are the prior steps. Either may delay the progress of the suit by failing to cooperate, but in general they cannot hasten it much. The minimum period for obtaining a divorce in Michigan is sixty days. As can be seen in the following table, few obtain it in so short a time. On the other hand, about one-third of the cases did not obtain their divorces until one year after filing the suit. One out of ten took over two years to get the decree.

TIME FROM FILING TO DECREE

Time (in months)	Percent	Cumulative Percent
2	5%	5%
3- 5	24	29
6- 8	27	56
9-11	10	66
12-23	23	89
24-35	7	96
36 or more	3	99
Total	99%	
Number	412	
Not known	13	
N = 425		
Median = 8.3 mos.		

In general, the time taken in any *one* of these steps appears to be *independent* of the time taken in any of the others. For our population as a whole, those who take longer for, say, consideration of divorce, are distributed rather

---

constructed from answers to the questions about time from final decision to filing, from filing to decree, and from first serious consideration to filing. Mid-points of the intervals were added or subtracted to obtain the further time data presented. The errors in the result should not be great, but the figures are approximate.

evenly in the next step. Some sub-segments show minor differences, which we shall discuss briefly. There is a very slight, statistically significant, but not entirely consistent *positive* association between (a) length of time for the move from decision to filing, and (b) the time from filing to the decree.

Serious Consideration to Filing. Since the period from first serious consideration to filing the suit is much more a function of actions and attitudes of the couple than the period after the matter has entered the official machinery of the courts, let us see whether there are any factors which tended to delay or hasten these steps. This distribution is as follows:

TIME FROM FIRST SERIOUS CONSIDERATION TO FILING OF SUIT

Months	Percent	Cumulative Percent
0- 1	13%	13%
1- 2	8	21
3- 4	8	29
5- 6	9	38
7- 8	5	43
9-10	2	45
11-12	10	55
13-23	12	67
24 or more	33	100
Total	100%	

N = 425

Median = 12.0 months

Background Factors in Time from Consideration to Filing. Many of the background factors in the lives of the spouses appear to have little to do with whether the time given to these two steps toward divorce is long or short. Thus, these items were all *unrelated* to the length of time for first serious consideration to the filing of the decree: occupation of the husband, husband's income, education of husband, wife's religion, husband's religion, and the church attendance of the wife.

On the other hand, (1) the rural-urban backgrounds of husband and wife do make a difference. In addition, (2) there is a small difference that appears to be associated with race. Also, (3) the steadiness of the husband's employment is of importance. We shall present the first two sets of data now, and afterwards analyze other factors in the marriage which seem to overshadow these in significance.

TIME FROM SERIOUS CONSIDERATION TO FILING DECREE, BY RURAL-URBAN BACKGROUND OF HUSBAND AND WIFE

	Median no. months from serious consideration to filing	No.
Husband:		
Rural	19.3	48
Small town	12.2	112
City	11.4	265
Wife:		
Rural	22.6	34
Small town	13.4	93
City	11.3	298

When these couples are grouped according to whether *both* spouses are from city backgrounds, or noncity ones, or from different backgrounds, parallel differences are seen. Moreover, of the 13 couples in which *both* husband and wife were from rural origins, 11 of them took *longer than 12 months* for this period of consideration, decision, and action; and 9 of them took longer than 2 years. The 2 cases taking less than 12 months were both precipitate divorces, in which the total time elapsed was less than 1 month. Analysis of such precipitate cases will be presented later. We are now simply emphasizing the apparently slower development of the divorce action when either spouse is from a nonmetropolitan background, and the very small difference between city and small town backgrounds. Although we do not reproduce the tables here, *both* duration of marriage and rural-urban background affect the time from serious consideration to final decision. Holding either constant, the effect of the other is less, but definite.

Negroes take *longer* from serious consideration to filing than do Whites. The median time was 15.6 for Negroes, 11.7 for Whites. Since, however, rural-urban background seemed to be important, we wished to know whether the apparent Negro-White difference was due to a difference in backgrounds. There was no marked association between rural background and being Negro, for our sample. On the other hand, when we do control for rural-uban background, the Negro-White differences are inconsistent. The White from a rural background took *slightly more* time (over 24 months, vs. 18.5 for rural Negroes), while the Negroes from small towns took *considerably* more time (22.2 months vs. 12.0 for small town Whites). The urban Negroes, finally, took about the same time as the urban Whites (11.3).

Alternatives to Marriage, and Situational Elements. It seemed likely that the *existence* of *alternatives* to the existing marriage might be associated with a *shorter* period of time for these steps toward divorce. Thus, if the wife was in love with someone other than her husband prior to the divorce, or she held a job during the marriage, she would feel freer to divorce without a long period of consideration and decision. Both these predictions were wrong. Job-holding of the wife during the marriage is not associated at all with a shorter period of time. Moreover, when the wife was in love with someone else prior to the divorce, the time given to these steps was much *longer*. The median time was 20.7 months when she was in love, but only 11.7 months when she was not in love. We shall devote some further attention to the in-love patterns when we discuss the first suggestion of the divorce. Let us now make only this comment: In some cases, her being in love prior to the divorce occurred *after separation,* and when the divorce was no longer in doubt. She began dating other men, just as her husband was dating other women, and in only a legal sense were they still married. Thus, we cannot be always certain that she had fallen in love while the marriage was still a reality.

More important, we believe, are the factors analyzed at length in the section on the strategy of divorce conflict. Specifically, there are two sets of factors which might prolong the period from first serious consideration of divorce to filing suit even if the wife is in love with another. The first is (A) the complex of social values, group pressures, and emotional involvements and commitments which mean the wife-mother will more intensely and more frequently than the husband-father feel disposed to stay in the marriage even under unpleasant marital conditions. The second set (B) relates to her role obligations, which give her a narrower range of actions that might make the marriage difficult for her husband without appearing to her kin and friends as a neglectful wife-mother. If the husband does not quickly agree, and she is unwilling to neglect her home or to create a scandal, she has to attempt a strategy of attrition, wearing down the husband's resistance by her actions (nagging, contempt, refusing him sexual access, etc.) *within* the home. Consequently, there will be a much greater delay between first serious consideration and the final filing of suit when (a) *she* is in love, than when (b) *he* is pushing for the divorce, or than when (c) *both* have come to an agreement about the need for a divorce. However, we had not thought about these factors prior to our analysis, and thus predicted incorrectly the impact of her being in love on the time given to carrying the conflict through to filing suit.

Of the various situational factors in the marriage, neither the anticipated effects of the divorce on the children, nor the prior approval or disapproval of friends and kin of the marriage itself seems to have had any effect on hastening or slowing the movement through these steps toward the divorce. On the other hand, (1) duration of marriage, (2) number of children, (3) ages of children, and (4) age of respondent are all associated with the length of this time period. Since only one of these (duration of marriage) appears to have a consistent effect, we can mention the others briefly. Moreover, it is clear that all four of these items are somewhat associated: with a longer duration of marriage, there are more children, and they are likely to be older. With a longer duration of marriage, the wife herself is also older. Finally, it must be kept in mind that the marriages of couples with rural backgrounds are more likely to last longer, and a rural background is associated with a longer consideration time. Consequently, we may be locating an important determinant with complex aspects.

When there is only one child, the median time is 11.2 months, but when there are three children the time is 15.7 months. Thus, there appears to be an increasing amount of time for implementing the conflict when there are more children. On the other hand, when there are four or more children, the time drops to 11.2. Moreover, we might expect that with *increasing* age of children, the time would be shorter, since the mother is released somewhat from the immediate, constant demands of the child, and thus somewhat from the moral demand to stay in the marriage. This hypothesis is incorrect: with *increasing* age of children, the time taken for carrying out these steps is *greater*. Moreover, as we noted already, the ages and the number of children are not independent factors, and both are to a great extent a function of duration of marriage.

Now, it might be reasoned that with increasing age the wife is *less* willing to leave the marriage, because alternatives become scarcer. In addition, there may be less energy and decisiveness, or less optimism about meeting the problems that divorce creates. Such factors might be theoretically isolated on biological, psychological, or social levels. On the other hand, with increasing duration of marriage, it could be expected that the web of *family* friendships (as against merely personal friendships) would be stronger and more definite. There is also an increasing commitment to the marriage itself, and doubtless a greater tolerance of husbandly foibles, personality irritations, values, etc.

It is not surprising, then, to find that (a) with increasing age there is a longer time to move toward the actual filing of suit; and (b) with increasing duration of marriage there is also a greater amount of time to move from serious consideration to filing suit. Thus, wives aged 20-22 years took only 5.0 months for this period, as against 20.7 months for wives aged 37 or more. And marriages that had lasted from 0-2 years moved from first serious consideration to filing suit in 4.5 months, as against more than 24 months for marriages lasting more than 15 years.

Since these two factors are associated, are they independent in effect? Perhaps one of them is at least partially spurious. Indeed, this is what we do find. When we control duration of marriage, age continues to have its effect (higher ages take a longer time) only up to a duration of 9 years.

However, at 10 years duration of marriage and over, the relationship between age of the wife and time for these steps toward divorce becomes inconsistent. For example, the wives 35 years of age and over who have been married 10-14 years took only 12.0 months, as against 15.4 months for the wives 20-29 years of age who had been married the same length of time.

By contrast, when we hold *age* constant, the median time for these steps is consistently *higher for each category of duration of marriage*. This relationship is presented in the accompanying table. Thus, we suggest that, for marriages lasting less than 10 years age has some apparently independent effect, it is overshadowed by the effect of duration of marriage.

TIME GIVEN TO THE STEPS FROM FIRST SERIOUS CONSIDERATION
TO FILING SUIT, BY DURATION OF MARRIAGE, HOLDING
AGE OF WIFE CONSTANT

Age	Duration of Marriage (Years)	Median Time (Months)	Number
20-24	0- 4	5.3	48
	5- 9	9.0	22
25-29	0- 4	6.0	17
	5- 9	11.9	98
	10-14	16.1	32
30-34	0- 9	10.3	46
	10-14	19.6	58
	15 or more	24 or more	16
35 or more	0- 9	12.0	9
	10-14	12.0	39
	15 or more	23.2	39

Space does not allow us to present a similar table for the relationship between rural-urban background, duration of marriage, and time for implementing the divorce suit. (1) When we hold rural-urban backgrounds constant, the duration of marriage still has a rather consistent effect by lengthening this period of time. On the other hand, (2) when we hold duration of marriage constant, there are no differences between urban, rural, and small town backgrounds in the time given to these steps, when duration is 15 years or over. Moreover, there are three other minor deviations from what we would expect if rural-urban backgrounds acted entirely independently. We conclude, therefore, that this factor does have some effect on the time given to carrying out these divorce steps, but it appears to work mainly through its association with duration of marriage, which in turn remains as a most important factor.

Complaints and Time from Serious Consideration to Filing Suit. Of the various complaints, only two appear to have any connection with the length of time for these steps toward divorce, Triangle (8.5 months) and Authority (15.4). There are no significant differences among any of the rest, all close to the median of 12 months. Since Authority usually represents a drawn-out battle of wills between the spouses, this greater length of time is not surprising. On the other hand, we know already that Triangle is a complaint made when the *husband* has become emotionally involved with another woman, and has usually announced that he wishes to be free. He is thus openly pushing for the divorce, and we have already noted in detail how much greater pressure he is able to create toward breaking up the marriage, than the wife can. Consequently, we would expect to find that in many or most of these cases it is the husband who shortens this period of time.

However, there is an apparent puzzle in these facts. Why is it that the complaint of Desertion is not associated with a much longer period of time? We find the answer in the fact that many of the wives who complained of Triangle also complained of Desertion ($Q = +.65$). Thus, our group of Desertion complainants contains wives who complained only of Desertion, as well as those who made both complaints. Reciprocally, there may be Triangle cases which were only Desertion cases for a long period of separation, and later became Triangles, when the separated husband finally became involved with another woman. It is possible then, that the median time for all Triangle complainants (8.5 months) is shorter than it is for those who have only this complaint to make, with no charge of Desertion; and correspondingly the median time for all Desertion complainants (12.5 months) is longer than for those who have no accusation of Triangle behavior. This relationship holds only for marriages of less duration.

SERIOUS CONSIDERATION TO FILING, BY COMPLAINT, FOR MARRIAGES
LASTING LESS THAN TEN YEARS

Complaint		Median Time for Consideration to Filing	
Triangle	Desertion	Months	Number
Yes	Yes	18.5	7
Yes	No	2.2	25
No	Yes	10.0	13
No	No	9.2	195
Yes or No	Yes	12.0	20

Duration of marriage, then, has a complex relationship with the length of time given to the period from serious consideration to filing suit. Duration reflects a complex web of personal and social commitments, the changing age status, rural-urban backgrounds, race, and the number and ages of children, and reflects to some extent even the themes of complaint. Most of these factors have some independent effects upon the length of time from serious consideration to filing suit, but they operate differently under different combinations to shorten or lengthen this period in which a personal conflict becomes an official action.

Who First Suggested the Divorce. The importance of the Triangle theme suggests, because it spotlights the *husband's* role in the marital dissolution, that we turn to a factor which is more centrally a part of the conflict itself than is duration of marriage, i.e., who *first suggested* the divorce. Since the husband can implement his suggestion more effectively than can the wife, without losing standing in his circles, we would expect that the time given to these steps toward divorce is shorter when *he* is first to suggest that they divorce. This effect might appear to be somewhat less accentuated in our data than it actually was, since it is possible that some wives claimed they themselves suggested first, or both suggested together, when in fact the husband suggested first. Thus the apparent differences would not be as great as the real differences.

Indeed, when the husband was *admitted* to have been the first to suggest the divorce, the median time was 5.4 months, but when the wife claims that she first suggested the divorce, the time was 12.9 months, and when there was mutual suggestion, the median time was 18.5 months. We may break this down in more detail, as in the table following.

TIME FROM FIRST SERIOUS CONSIDERATION OF DIVORCE TO FILING DECREE, BY WHO FIRST SUGGESTED DIVORCE

Who First Suggested	0-2 months	3-12 months	13 or more months	Total	Number
Husband	43%	29%	29%	101%	105
Wife	13	38	49	100	264
Mutual	18	29	54	101	56
Total	21%	34%	45%	100%	425

This association was tested by controlling for (1) rural-urban backgrounds, since the latter seems to have some independent effect on the haste or slowness in filing suit. The factor of who first suggested the divorce is independent of these backgrounds. Similarly, (2) it is independent of age, although there is a slightly greater chance that the wife suggested first if she is in the younger age bracket, and that the husband suggested first if she is older. Since, finally, (3) duration of marriage appeared to be more important than either of these items, we held duration of marriage constant to see whether who first suggested the divorce continued to have the same effect on length of time to move through these steps toward the suit. The effect is maintained, except for couples with the shortest duration of marriage, 0-4 years. For this class, the time was shortest for divorces in which the suggestion was made by both (4.0 months, as against 5.5 when the husband first suggested, and 6.2 when wife first suggested). These are, in general, also the younger couples, most of whom would doubtless be classifiable as cases of "mutual incompatibility". (It was in the marriages of shortest duration that the complaint of Personality was most frequent; 40% who had been married only 0-4 years made this complaint.)

Otherwise, who first suggested the divorce is independent in its effect. Keeping in mind this single exception, we present here the relationship between these two factors.

TIME FROM FIRST SERIOUS CONSIDERATION OF DIVORCE TO FILING DECREE,
BY WHO FIRST SUGGESTED DIVORCE, HOLDING CONSTANT THE DURATION OF MARRIAGE

Duration (Years)	Who Suggested	Serious Consideration to Decree			Total	Number
		0-2 months	3-12 months	13 months or more		
0-9	Husband	46%	35%	19%	100%	54
	Wife or mutual	18	42	40	100	186
	Total	25%	40%	35%	100%	240
10 or more	Husband	39%	22%	39%	100%	51
	Wife or mutual	7	29	63	99	134
	Total	16%	27%	57%	100%	185

As can be seen by internal comparison both factors have an independent effect.

Factors Affecting Who First Suggested the Divorce. As noted in our analysis of divorce conflict, most of the wives claimed that they first suggested the divorce. Over three-fifths (62%) of the wives made this claim, while 25% admitted that the husband suggested first, and 13% stated that the suggestion was made "mutually." Now, this factor is of importance in hastening or slowing the time from first serious consideration to filing suit. We shall later show that who first suggested the divorce is of importance in the social adjustment of the divorce. However, which factors are associated with who first made the suggestion?

Certain items either seem *not* to have any relationship with who first suggested, or have *no consistent* relationship. These are: (a) rural-urban background of wife; (b) race; (c) religion of husband; (c) religion of wife; (d) occupation of husband; (e) education of the wife; (f) type of work the wife did, if she held a job; (g) duration of marriage; and (h) number of children.

Religion and Who First Suggested the Divorce. Although the religious affiliation of the wife seemed to have no effect on who first suggested the divorce, *frequency of church attendance* did have some effect.[3] We have usually found that frequency of attendance is a better predictor of differences by religious behavior, than is church preference. However, we here find (as in several other relationships) that frequency of attendance is a better indicator for Catholics than for Protestants. That is, (A) the frequently attending Catholics differ more from the infrequently attending Catholics than (B) do the frequently attending Protestants from the infrequently attending Protestants. Specifically in the present context, it is mainly the Catholics who almost never attend church who are different from all the rest of our wives: far more

---

3. We remind the reader once more that "frequency of church attendance" is a *post*divorce measure. We do not know how often these women attended church during the conflict itself. We know how often they were attending at the time of the interview, and we know whether this frequency was highest during the marriage, the final separation, at the time of the divorce, or at the time of interview, or always the same. It seems a fair measure of the divorcee's acceptance of church pressures generally.

of those who rarely attend made the first suggestion toward divorce: 81% of this group made the first suggestion, as against approximately 61% of all other categories (frequently attending Protestants or Catholics, Catholics or Protestants who attend only occasionally, Protestants who almost never attend). The suggestion is tempting, that when the Catholic wife does not have the frequent guidance of her church, she is more likely than the Protestant to deviate from church teachings. There are, of course, some theoretical bases for this suggestion, but our only relevant data are contrary: those who now attend infrequently are more likely to claim that they attended more frequently during the marriage. Corresponding to the higher proportion of these "non-attending" Catholics who made the first divorce suggestion is the very low proportion of mutual suggestions (4%) among them, and the lower proportion of husbands who made the first suggestion (15% as against approximately 25%-27% for other categories of religion and attendance).

Class and Who First Suggested the Divorce. The education of the wife had no consistent relationship with who made the first suggestion, but the education of the husband made some difference. This is partially corroboratory of our analysis of divorce strategy. We suggested that in our society it is the man more often than the woman who first wishes to leave the marriage, and that the range of his role definitions permits him to be generally more obnoxious to his wife than she can be to him, without undermining his standing in his small circle or larger community. We also analyzed the various factors which frequently lead him to adopt, consciously or not, a behavior pattern which will lead *her* to *ask him* for a divorce. These hypotheses were developed further: just as the general role definitions in this culture give a *differential* range of socially permissible but maritally unpleasant behavior *to the two sexes,* so are there comparable differences *between social circles and strata.* Thus, helling around with the boys and physical violence to the wife are less acceptable in the middle and upper strata than in the lower. We believe that failure to provide well is also condemned more toward the upper than toward the lower strata. This further hypothesis is difficult to test, until we have an adequate *sociological* chart of family differences between strata. These differences, like many others already noted, are not immediately derived from income or occupation, even though these latter two do have a certain limited use.

Our hypothesis predicts, then, that with a lesser range of such permissible but unpleasant behavior the middle- and upper-strata husbands who do wish to dissolve the marriage will find this task more difficult. Consequently, these husbands will succeed less frequently in forcing their wives to ask for a divorce first. We should find, then, that there is either (1) a higher percentage of husbands who make the first suggestion, or (2) a higher percentage of mutual suggestions.

Now, if we use *occupation* as our class indicator, this prediction is only partially borne out. Wives of men in the upper occupations *are* slightly less likely to make the first suggestion, and the husbands slightly more likely, but the differences are small and not statistically significant. Moreover, this small conformity has to be taken still less seriously when we uncover a further item that helps to determine who will first suggest: In general, wives are less likely to make the first suggestion if they are married to husbands *with steady incomes*—and the upper occupational levels are more likely to have steady incomes. Thus, 56% of the wives married to husbands with steady incomes made the first suggestion, but 75% of those married to unsteady workers suggested first. Correspondingly, 29% of the wives in the first group admitted their husbands suggested first, as against 15% of the wives married to husbands with unsteady incomes. Thus, an additional factor enters to confuse the test of the prediction. That is, we predicted that men toward the upper strata will *more* frequently than men in the lower strata have to ask their wives for the divorce first, but since the former are also more likely to have steady incomes, these wives are still *less* likely to ask for the divorce first. Since both factors have the same direction of effect, we cannot easily test our prediction.

However, let us bring in both the education of wife and of husband, which might intensify the effect of our predicted cultural differences in divorce strategy. If both have some college education, we would expect that the mutual suggestions would be proportionately higher, and a lesser proportion of wives would be forced to initiate the divorce suggestion, since within the limits of the husbands' values there is less tactical freedom for any obvious divorce strategy. Moreover, we are inclined to believe the commonsense observation that those with more education are more likely to express overtly their satisfactions and dissatisfactions with the marriage.

We maintain that in general the husband in our society has the greater choice and control in the strategy of divorce. Consequently, when the education of husband and wife is different, the proportion of wives suggesting *first* ought to be in conformity with the *husband's* education. That is, for hypogamous marriages (the wife marries downward educationally), the proportion of wives suggesting first ought to be about that of homogamous cases in which the education is high school or less (for if the marriage is hypogamous the college wife is married to someone with high school or less education).

This is indeed what we do find, as we see in the following table.

WHO FIRST SUGGESTED THE DIVORCE, BY HOMOGAMY-HYPERGAMY-HYPOGAMY OF EDUCATION

Who first suggested	Both College	Hypergamy	Both High School	Hypogamy	Both Grammar School	Totals
			Marriage Patterns by Education			
Wife	47%	53%	64%	65%	73%	62%
Husband	35	27	23	23	27	25
Mutual	18	20	13	11	0	13
Total	100%	100%	100%	99%	100%	100%
	(17)	(64)	(209)	(98)	(30)	(418)

Reading across from left to right, we see (1) a steady increase in the proportion of wives suggesting the divorce first. We also see that (2) when the woman has married upward (hypergamy) or downward (hypogamy) educationally, the proportion follows that of the husband's education. Correspondingly,

(3) the proportion of mutual suggestions steadily increases from right to left (with increasing education). To the extent that our data permit, then, our notion is confirmed.

Complaints and First Suggestion. The younger wives (who in our generation have more education) were slightly more likely to have made the suggestion first than were older wives. However, the age of the wife does not have a strong association with her suggesting first, and it is not statistically significant at the 5% level.

Of course, in some considerable (but unknown) proportion of cases the wife not only asked for the divorce first, but did so because she really wanted to escape the marriage first. At a minimum, 13% of these wives admitted they were in love with another man prior to the divorce. We do not, then, assume that she was merely passive, responding to the husband's pressures. We *do* assert that the data suggest the real initiator to be more often the husband than the wife. Within this institutional context, then, we may ask which of the various behavior patterns reported as complaints *could* be used by the husband as pressures on the relationship. If we are correct, then a higher percentage of wives should have suggested first when such behavior patterns were reported. That is, the husband was *able* to use these in order to force her to take the initiative.

Testing this notion is not entirely possible, since few wives made single complaints. The heaping of complaints is doubtless the reality of almost all divorces, but such complexities prevent a nice testing of theoretical analyses. Let us nevertheless get as close as possible to a test, in order to push our hypotheses as far as can be done. We start with the notion that the behavioral patterns reported as Personality, Authority, and Values, are *not* under the control of the husband. They are deep expressions of his social and personal background, and of his personality. With the best of good will, he cannot change these much. If his wife dislikes their manifestation, he can make only a partial adjustment. Correspondingly, with the worst of bad will, he cannot use them much as tactics, since he cannot change them much, and their impact is dependent rather upon *her* response.

Secondly, Triangle cannot be easily used as a tactic, since the husband cannot *will* himself to be in love or to become emotionally involved with another woman. Desertion, as we noted earlier, is more complex. It is usually associated with Triangle. Moreover, the husband often "deserts," *after* suggesting a divorce; so that desertion *can be a tactic* for persuading her to divorce, but empirically it may *follow* or even be itself the first suggestion.

Third, we believe that only four of these major themes represent behavior that is clearly usable as tactics, while a fifth theme may be so considered. The four are Drink, Consumption, Complex, and Support. The fifth is Home Life. To the extent that this last complaint is made because the husband is by personality structure incapable of giving emotion and attention to his home, wife, and children, the husband cannot (because he has no great control over such emotional patterns) use them easily as tactics. On the other hand, we believe that in at least some cases this complaint is made when the husband *is* capable emotionally of enjoying and contributing to family living, and uses open disinterest as a conflict technique. These cannot be separated, since only the wife's report is available, and the husband's report would be equally useless as an evaluation of his own personality.

The data do not, then, answer our own question adequately. However, the four behavioral patterns that are most clearly under the control of the husband as possible conflict tactics *are* the themes in which the highest percentage of wives made the first suggestion: For the four themes of Drink, Consumption, Complex, and Support, the percentages are respectively 76%, 70%, 69%, and 67%. At the other extreme is the complaint of Triangle. In this context, this behavior pattern has two significant characteristics: (a) it is not easily usable as a *tactic;* and (b) unlike Personality, Values, or Authority, it cannot within our society simply "be adjusted to" by the wife. The husband need not *adopt* a strategy of conflict; he has already become attached to another woman, and thus has in most cases already effectively denied the existing marriage. Consequently, only 37% of wives reporting this complaint claimed that they had first asked for the divorce.

Our two complaints with two dimensions, Home Life and Desertion also fall toward this extreme. Desertion is most often associated with Triangle, and 54% of the wives who made this complaint asked first for the divorce. Home Life, which we view as a rejection of our hypothesis, is next with 56%. In general, the differentials are between husband and wife suggesting; the only two complaints with a higher proportion of wives reporting "mutual suggestion" are Values and Authority (17% and 19%, *vs.* 13% for all other complaints together), and these differences seem unimportant.

Insistence on the Divorce, After Suggestion. Now, even if one spouse does suggest the divorce first, the other may have also wanted the divorce without having said anything about it. The first to suggest, moreover, may not desire the divorce seriously, making the suggestion only as a verbal attack. Thus, some spouses both suggest first and continue to insist on the divorce. Others suggest first, but do not continue to insist. Since these patterns throw some light on the process of divorcing, we might look at them briefly.

In 55% of these divorces, the wife claimed that she *both* suggested first *and* continued to insist. Fourteen percent were husband-husband cases, and all others made up 31% (mutual suggestion—wife insisted; mutual suggestion —husband insisted; husband suggestion—wife insisted; wife suggestion—husband insisted). Church preference or attendance, occupation, and income are unrelated to these patterns. There is a very slight tendency for women who held jobs during their marriage to suggest first and insist, more than those who rarely or never held jobs. When the husband was *not* a steady worker during the marriage, there is a greater likelihood that the wife both suggested and insisted, than when he *was* a steady worker (68% *vs.* 50%). And if the husband was a steady worker, he was more likely both to suggest and insist, than if he was not (17% *vs.* 6%).

Although we shall look at the attitudes of approval and disapproval of the divorce in more detail in the succeeding chapter, it is relevant here to ask how such attitudes relate to who first suggested and insisted on the divorce. In the following collapsed table, we see several interesting facts.

ATTITUDES OF WIFE'S CIRCLES AND HUSBAND'S CIRCLES, BY FIRST SUGGESTION
OF, AND INSISTENCE ON, THE DIVORCE

Social Group	Attitude toward Divorce	Who Suggested and Insisted		
		Wife/Wife	Other	Husband/Husband
Husband's Family	Approving	36%	32%	30%
	Indifferent	32	36	25
	Disapproving	32	32	45
	Total	100%	100%	100%
		(235)	(132)	(58)
Wife's Family	Approving	68%	55%	41%
	Indifferent	17	20	28
	Disapproving	15	25	31
	Total	100%	100%	100%
		(235)	(132)	(58)
Husband's Friends	Approving	27%	23%	31%
	Indifferent	58	58	43
	Disapproving	15	19	26
	Total	100%	100%	100%
		(235)	(132)	(58)
Wife's Friends	Approving	63%	58%	46%
	Indifferent	30	31	25
	Disapproving	7	11	29
	Total	100%	100%	100%
		(235)	(132)	(58)

At least two kinds of social cleavages are visible here. One is, of course, the allegiances of *her* circle of family and friends, as against *his*. The second is the different interests of *family,* as against *friends.* The family of orientation (parent's family) has, above or aside from the immediate allegiances to their child, a set of generational interests. The wife's and husband's parents are the grandparents of the children in the divorce, and make moral judgments about the divorce and its consequences, centering on family ties, the grandchildren, and the children-in-law. The divorced woman was for a while a member of the husband's parents' family. They feel some responsibility for the grand-children, and will see the divorce as a threat to their relationship with the grandchildren. Since the mother usually gets custody, their access to the child is made more difficult. Consequently, they are much more likely to judge the divorce and the divorcing spouses by traditional family values than by the happiness of their own child (the husband). They may have a fierce loyalty to their child, but may nevertheless condemn the divorce because of its family consequences. Therefore, we expect to see two major social cleavages in these data, not one.

To turn to the more obvious cleavage, however, we note first, (1) that when the suggestion and insistence both came from the wife, her family and friends are more approving than his. Both her two circles are more approving of the divorce than either of his. (2) Secondly, within all these circles except *his friends,* the percent approving is highest when suggestion and initiation came from her, than when it came from the husband. (His strategy was suc-cessful, but they have observed it.) Correspondingly, as the ex-wife saw it, (3) the disapproval was *least* when the wife both suggested and insisted, greatest when husband both suggested and insisted, *for all four circles.* This we can understand, for in these last few cases the husband's action was likely to be precipitous and was less likely to be accompanied by a long process of "adjustmental conflict" through which the husband makes the wife really want to be free. In these cases, then, his behavior is more likely to have been disapproved.

On the other hand, (4) although her family seems less disapproving than his, and her friends less disapproving than his, it is also true that *his family* is more disapproving than *his friends;* and *her* family than *her* friends. Granted, in many or even most cases the friends are closer to the conflict than the parental families. But more fundamental, we believe, is the fact that families are more likely to disapprove of divorce among their children than among their friends. Different role sets are relevant, and the traditional values are more likely to be asserted.

From data already considered, it can be supposed that in the cases in which the husband both suggested and insisted, the time between first serious consideration and filing suit would be shorter. Thus we find that the median time between (a) consideration and decision, and between (b) decision and filing, was 0.8 months for this type. But when the wife suggested and insisted, the duration was 5.6 and 3.9 months. The "Other" category is very close to the wife/wife type with 5.0 and 3.3 months. Similarly, the wife's reconsideration of her decision is less likely when the husband both initiated and insisted (91% stable) than when the pattern was mixed (81%), or when the wife both suggested and insisted (74% stable). Of course, the "stability" of decision when the husband pushes for the divorce is *his* stability rather than hers.

In-Love Patterns. Since the first initiation and continued insistence might at times be stimulated by either spouse being in love with another, we may see whether such a relationship is indeed apparent. The following table seems self-explanatory.

WHO FIRST SUGGESTED, *AND* INSISTED ON, THE DIVORCE, BY WHETHER
EITHER SPOUSE WAS IN LOVE WITH ANOTHER

		In-Love Patterns				
Husband in love:	No	Yes*	No	Not known	Yes	
Wife in love:	Yes	Yes	No	No	No	Totals
Wife suggested/ and insisted	72%	65%	63%	46%	43%	55%
Mixed pattern	22	31	27	42	34	31
Husband suggested/ and insisted	6	4	10	12	23	14
Total	100%	100%	100%	100%	100%	100%
	(32)	(23)	(182)	(52)	(136)	

N = 425

*Because size of cell is small, this class includes 7 cases in which husband's attachment is not known.

Stability of Decision. We asked our divorcees whether the decision to divorce was stable, once the "final" decision was reached. Only 9% said that indecision occurred frequently. Twelve per cent stated that this happened several times, while 12% reported that only rarely were there times when the spouses decided not to divorce. The remainder, 67%, asserted that there *never* were such periods.

Thus, about 79% of these wives claimed that there was almost no serious hesitation, once the final decision was made. As might be expected from the preceding analysis, ordinary status or background items were either unrelated, or inconsistently related, to stability of decision. Thus, (a) rural-urban backgrounds were unrelated, as was (b) religion of husband or (c) of wife. Similarly, (d) occupation had no association with stability of decision.

Other items more closely related to the marriage itself were also of little importance for the instability of decision. (e) Age of the wife was unrelated, as was (f) duration of the marriage. Moreover, (g) the number of children was unimportant, although either might have been thought to be at least indirectly associated. We had originally thought that the dating of husband and wife during the marriage might have served as an index of their earlier closeness, and thus might be associated with instability of decision. However, as we have already pointed out, mere frequency of dating is ambiguous, in that the kinds of shared activities, and their meanings, are the significant dimensions of dating in marriage, rather than mere frequency of dates. (h) Frequency of dating during the marriage is, therefore, not related to the instability of the decision to divorce.

The relationship of religion and church attendance to the stability of the decision is interesting but somewhat puzzling. Let us first look at a collapsed table showing this relationship, together with the factor of who suggested the divorce first.

STABILITY OF DECISION TO DIVORCE, BY RELIGIOUS PREFERENCE, CHURCH ATTENDANCE, AND WHO FIRST SUGGESTED THE DIVORCE

Religious Preference of wife	Church Attendance	Husband suggested the divorce	% Claiming Stable Decision (rarely or never reconsidered the the decision)	No.
Protestant	Once weekly or more	Yes	94%	18
Catholic	Once weekly or more	Yes/No	85	66
Protestant	Less than once weekly	Yes/No	80	184
Other	—	Yes/No	79	43
Catholic	Less than once weekly	Yes/No	74	69
Protestant	Once weekly or more	No	62	45
Total			79%	N = 425

First, the most stable decisions are usually to be found among the most devout, if we may take high frequency of church attendance as a crude index of commitment to religious doctrine and a religious way of life. We commented on a parallel relationship earlier, noting that the movement toward divorce is so serious for the Catholic, that it may not even be considered except in a very difficult marriage. Apparently, the real break with doctrine comes with serious consideration itself. Once that step has been taken, the Catholic moves about as swiftly toward divorce as the Protestant. We now suggest that this relationship may also hold for the devout Protestant, and in the present connection it helps to explain the high stability of the decision among both devout Catholics and Protestants. The moral problem has been faced and answered prior to the final decision; and since only an extreme marital situation could drive either to divorce, the stability of decision is greater than for any other categories.

Within the devout circles of a given Protestant church, the social disapproval of divorce is very strong, but the prohibition is not absolute as it is for the Catholic. There remains an area of possible decision or indecision. Unfortunately, we have no measure of *"degree* of marital difficulty," but suspect that both devout Protestants and devout Catholics are in a more difficult marital situation before turning to divorce, than are other women. Even granting this notion, the devout Protestant differs from the devout Catholic when we consider who suggested the divorce first. The devout Catholic is highly *stable* in her decision once it is made, *whether or not the husband first suggested the divorce.* However, the devout Protestant has a relatively *unstable* decision if it was *not* the husband who first suggested the divorce. That is, if she is devout (by the index of frequent church attendance), her moral problem is not definitely answered by making a final decision to divorce. She has made an answer to the doctrine, but not to her moral problem, because she has not really crossed the divide until the act itself is consummated. Thus, if it is *not* the husband who is the sole instigator of the divorce, then she must continue to wrestle with her conscience. The devout Catholic, however, has already crossed the divide when she makes her "first" final decision. Therefore, for her, who first suggested the divorce makes little difference in the stability of decision.

The less frequently attending Protestants, and those with a religious preference other than Protestant or Catholic, have the same stability of decision as the average for the entire sample. Moreover, who first suggested the divorce has no effect on stability among these women. This is in accord with expectation, since along the two dimensions we see at work here (devoutness and absoluteness of the prohibition against divorce) they fall between the extremes.

However, why are the *less frequently* attending Catholics somewhat *less stable* than the average? Granted, the difference is not sizable or significant, but we have no hypothesis to account for their being at that point, or at any particular point. A partial solution is this: (a) the less frequently attending Catholics are most likely to make the first suggestion (81% *vs.* about 61% for other categories), and (b) the women who suggest first are more likely to have a *less* stable decision.

This, however, simply moves the puzzle backward a step. Why do these women more often suggest first? Our closest approximation to a solution is this: the *now* infrequently attending Catholics are more likely to claim that they attended most frequently during the marriage, and the stability of decision is *lowest* for the *now infrequently* attending Catholics who attended *most* frequently prior to the divorce conflict. Fifty-four percent and 67% of these two cells were stable in their decisions, as against 100% and 92% of the infrequently attending Catholics who attend most frequently now, or whose frequency of attendance never changed. Thus, our presently infrequently attending Catholics are made up of (a) those who were *once more* devout; and these women were unstable in their divorce decision; and (b) those who have *always* been less steady in attendance. These, by contrast, have very stable decisions. As a consequence, the infrequently attending Catholics fall in a position in our preceding table, which could not be predicted. However, with this further breakdown, the effect of religion seems consistent.

In general, however, stability is not greatly affected by the various elements of the conflict, and most of these that matter have to do with (1) the kind of complaint, (2) whether husband or wife was in love with another, and (3) who first suggested the divorce. Since all of these turn on the question of who was actually pressing for a divorce, we need only refer to our preceding analyses of who suggested the divorce, and of conflict strategy.

We have already noted (1) the connection between the in-love patterns and who first suggested; and (2) between initiation and insistence, and stability of decision. The decision is least stable when the wife was in love, or first suggested. Thus, when the husband first suggested the divorce, only 16% of wives reported that frequently or several times the couple had decided not to divorce, while the proportion was 24% when the wife had made the first suggestion. We have already analyzed the factors which put a more powerful and consistent set of pressures in the hands of the husband, when he wants a divorce, and we only note that here again the data are in conformity with expectation.

Summary. We have suggested in this chapter that it is more often the husband than the wife who first wishes to escape from the marriage; and the husband more often than the wife who is able to adopt a strategy of divorce which forces the other spouse to ask first for the divorce.

We have also analyzed the steps toward the divorce, and have shown that these divorces were not precipitate. The median time from first serious consideration to filing the suit was one year. Couples with a rural background were more likely to spend a relatively longer time for these steps than urban couples, and Negroes more than Whites. Couples married a long time, and to some extent older couples, take more time. These relationships are complex, and we have tried to analyze them in terms of predispositional background factors, alternatives to the marriage, the consequences of divorce when the wife's situation is considered (e.g., more or fewer children), and the conflict themes.

We have also shown the importance for the divorce action of the first suggestion of divorce. When the husband first suggests, then action is likely to be rapid, somewhat independently of age, duration of marriage, or rural-urban background. On the other hand, various factors seem to affect who first makes the suggestion. We have analyzed the effect of religion, class, and in-love patterns. Now we turn to the discussions the couple had during the conflict period.

CHAPTER XII

COUNSELING, AGREEMENTS, AND APPROVAL OF THE DIVORCE

WITHIN THE LAST GENERATION, an increasing proportion of people in marital conflict have come to seek marital counseling. In this chapter, we learn that only a minuscule percentage of divorcees in a metropolitan center had any counseling at all.

If counseling is not successful, and the couple insist on the divorce, there are many details of postdivorce arrangements that must be discussed. Often these are discussed only through attorneys, but three-fifths of our group did take part in some last discussion with their husband, about such matters as the children, support, or division of the property. There was generally agreement between them, but we shall see that children are most frequently the subject of such discussions, and proportionately the couples agreed least often about the children. Even if there are discussions and agreement, the spouses may not keep their agreements, and thus we deal with the keeping of agreements.

Finally, in this chapter the patterns of approval and disapproval of the divorce among the circles of friend and kin are analyzed further.

Marital Counseling. Most of our divorcees did not receive any marriage counseling. Compulsory counseling does not (to our knowledge) exist anywhere in the United States.[4] In only a few cities are there even unofficial judicial pressures toward counseling. Most divorces occur without any contact with the insufficient number of counseling agencies in this country. Indeed, our group would have had even more contact with counseling than do most divorcees, since all divorces involving children were required to be investigated by the Friend of the Court. Although this agency is supposed to work toward reconciliation (see *Ladies Home Journal,* November, 1952), and in-

---

4. Perhaps one should now make a partial exception for Conservative Jewry. Effective December 1, 1954, the Conservative Jewish husband and wife must ". . . consult a newly constituted Beth Din, or court—in this case a marriage court—before seeking divorce." (*New York Times,* Nov. 14, 1954, p. 1, Col. 3.) Couples must go to their own rabbi, who will call on the court if he fails to reconcile them. If the wife and husband refuse to obey the court findings, they will be liable to fines.

deed has received considerable publicity on this work, there are not enough trained counselors attached to this agency to handle the task, and most of the supposed "counseling" at the time of our study consisted in (a) recording the fact that both parties were adamant, and (b) ascertaining whether the home situation of the wife might be judged good enough to continue as the abode of the children. This is not, of course, an indictment of the Friend of the Court. It is, on the other hand, an indictment of the numerous facile huzzas that have been given to this agency by writers for popular magazines. The Wayne County Friend of the Court has not had staff enough, or money enough to hire the staff, to carry out its ideal tasks, and perforce the latter have been whittled down to the minimal ones.

That this comment is not extreme can be judged quickly enough. *All* of our cases had been investigated by the Friend of the Court. However, only 29% of the total stated that they had ever *consulted any marriage counselor*.[5] Furthermore, to see clearly what this meant, we asked each of these what *sort* of marriage counselor had been consulted. Half of this group (14% of the total group) listed the Friend of the Court. The rest had talked with a priest or pastor (5.4%), a social work agency (4.0%), physician (3.3%), or other person (3.0%). It is clear that 86% of our respondents had no such experience with the Friend of the Court as to consider the interview "marriage counseling." This conclusion is bolstered by the frequent (though untabulated) requests of our respondents for the name of an agency that would give them marriage counseling, and the expressed wish of still others that there might have been such counseling.

In view of the small number who received any counseling at all, and the varied types of that counseling, we cannot analyze that experience systematically. The type of advice given was as follows:

TYPE OF MARITAL ADVICE GIVEN TO RESPONDENTS

	Counseling Received	
"Patch it up"	7%	
Wait before acting	3	
Separate for a while	2	
Get a divorce	12	
Miscellaneous and not known	5	
Sub-Total	29%	
No counseling	71%	
Total	100%	N = 425

The facilities in Detroit for marital counseling at this time (1948) were not extensive, and in any event were not well known. Consequently, not many respondents would seek or obtain help in their conflicts. However, those who *did* get help from sources other than close friends and kin might differ in certain ways from those who did not. In particular, we would expect the seeking of marriage counseling to be more likely (1) among Catholics, (2) among those with a medium education, and (3) among those who delayed somewhat

---

5. We doubt that the proportion of divorcees who ever obtained marital counseling would be any higher than this in most of the cities of the U. S. We have seen no comparative data.

more in the steps toward a divorce. In the following comparisons we see these guesses borne out, although the differences are not large.

SEEKING MARITAL COUNSELING, BY RELIGION

	Obtained Counseling	Did Not Obtain Counseling	Total	No.
Catholic	38%	62%	100%	135
Non-Catholic	25	75	100	290

SEEKING MARITAL COUNSELING, BY EDUCATION OF RESPONDENT

Respondent's Education	Counseling, other than social work agency	No Counseling	Total	No.
College	13%	87%	100%	37
Completed High School	28	72	100	128
Some High School	26	74	100	199
Grammar School	23	77	100	61

SEEKING MARITAL COUNSELING, BY PERIOD FROM SERIOUS CONSIDERATION TO FILING

Period of Consideration to Filing	Counseling	No Counseling	Total	No.
One year or less	27%	73%	100%	235
More than one year	32	68	100	190

Catholics would seek aid more than non-Catholics, simply because there are greater pressures on the Catholic to avoid divorce. When the conflict is great, then a slightly higher proportion of Catholics might seek aid. This might contrast with the usual differences between Catholics and Protestants with respect to their seeking professional aid in nontraditional areas. More Protestants than Catholics would seek psychiatric or psychoanalytic help, but divorce relates closely to doctrine, and there is greater internal conflict. With respect to education, the more highly educated groups seek counseling less than do those with medium education, and these slightly more than those with less education. We do not as yet know what is the public image of the marital counselor. In general, however, we believe that the public image of the marital counselor is somewhat like that of the vocational counselor. The lower-middle-class child may be encouraged by his parents to seek vocational counseling, but not the child in either of the other strata. At the risk of oversimplifying, we believe the lower strata know little about either type of counselor, while the upper educational strata think they know as much about the subject as either.

It is also worth noting that, since there is a tendency for those who seek counseling to be Catholic, and these are, in turn, likely to have slightly less education than Protestants, the associations of either factor with counseling are not so clear as they would appear under stricter controls. Our cases are too few to permit such controls. We see, then, that (1) relatively few couples obtained any marital counseling at all; that (2) a large proportion of these did not *seek* any counseling but at best got some advice from the Friend of the Court investigator; and that (3) over one-third of those who got any definite advice were told to get a divorce. However, these answers do not refer to the conversations about divorce with kin and friends.

In most divorces there is a relatively long preparatory period. Even if this period is not an "adjustment to divorce," it can nevertheless be called an "adjustment to the *idea* of divorce." During this period the conflict between the spouses does not lessen to any degree. Indeed, if we consider the rather long time period involved, and the lack of any available counseling, it is clear that toward the end of this period the two spouses are likely not to be amenable to any kind of discussion or advice. Counseling after filing suit is rather late, at best.

Indeed, when this later phase of divorce conflict has been adequately studied, it may be learned that it is not so much a period of *intensified conflict* as one of an intensified wish to avoid conflict. Perhaps it may even be found that for a large segment of cases it is a period of "increasing boredom with conflict." That is, the couple find that the conflict no longer interests them greatly. The possibility of emotional or other advantage from the conflict diminishes. As the spouses enter other lives and roles, the denouement has been reached long before the decree. In a sense, couples in these categories no longer care to assert their rights, to prove their rightness, or to excoriate their culpable spouse. When, then, they finally "escape," it is not so much the conflict they escape from, as it is the lack of any end, profit, or zest in the conflict.

Talks About Divorce Arrangements. Nevertheless, by whatever circuit, spiral, or sudden turn they came to divorce, 60% of them took part in some last conversation as husband and wife—a discussion of the divorce arrangements. Perhaps almost all couples discussed this matter in some fashion if they were in any contact with one another during the period of decision or filing suit. However, we were particularly interested in whether there were discussions, thought of and remembered as such, of matters such as the division of property, the effect of the divorce on the children, alimony or child support, etc. So far as we are able to ascertain, domestic squabbles or battles in which such questions were fought over, were not classified as "discussions," so that in approximately 40% of our cases the respondents claimed that there were no talks of this kind. As we shall show later on in this section, these may be differentiated in several respects from those who did have such discussions.

WERE THERE DISCUSSIONS ABOUT DETAILS OF THE DIVORCE?

How Many?	% of Total
Many	16
Some	16
Few	28
None	40
Totals	100%

$$N = 425$$

Few would fall into the "Many Talks" category, whether the divorces were (a) precipitate or (b) long drawn out. The number of discussions would be low in the former cases, because the spouses suddenly move toward divorce without bothering to work out the details; and in the latter because there has been such a long period of conflict and estrangement that there seems little point in further discussions. In the latter case, most of the matters we asked about could, by the time of filing suit, be taken for granted, or were already embodied in the separation agreements; or (the spouses felt) could not be worked out by talks anyway.

DIVORCE DETAILS DISCUSSED BY SPOUSES

Topics	Number of Cases in which Topic Was Discussed	% of Topics Discussed	Of Those Who Discussed, % Who Mentioned Topic
Division of property	67	17	26
Effect on child/children	165	43	65
Support or alimony	100	26	39
Remarriage to others	15	4	6
Seeing each other	15	4	6
Miscellaneous	24	6	9
Total	386	100	

(no discussions: 170 = 40%)

As we see, most of these discussions centered about three types of items: (1) how the property should be divided, (2) what effect the divorce would have upon the children, and (3) the problem of maintenance for the wife and child after the divorce. As every marital counselor knows, most predivorce talks between husband and wife that focus on the divorce actually center on which of the two is at fault. Apparently our respondents classed these as "arguments," since they were not mentioned as items about which there was "discussion of divorce arrangements."

The reader unfamiliar with the conflict between divorcees may have been surprised to learn that almost 6% of the respondents discussed the matter of "remarriage to others." In a legal sense, of course, this was no proper concern of either spouse. They would presumably be free to remarry anyone they chose. One might even think further that spouses would not wish to discuss this matter, on the ground that this would be an area of rather great explosiveness.

These cases seem to represent two groups: (a) cases in which a new spouse for either husband or wife has already been picked out, and the discussions center on that person; and (b) cases in which one spouse demands reassurances from the other that she or he will not marry or will not marry soon. Even in a triangle situation, the spouse who is leaving to marry a new love may derive some emotional strength and courage from reassurance that the abandoned spouse will not marry soon. The attachment between the spouses may continue long after the breakup of the marriage, as we shall see later on. It is worth noting in this connection, although the figures are much too small to be of significance, that there is less agreement between the spouses on this item than on any of the others discussed.

Now, the amount of property to be divided is usually small. On the other hand, (a) *any* accumulation of common possessions comes to be invested with considerable emotion. Furthermore, (b) the property is the only thing that *can* be divided, for the children almost always go to the wife. Finally, (c) arguments about the division of property often become more or less polite ways of bringing up once more the subject of who was at fault, or what will happen after the divorce.

Because of these derivative meanings of property, this item might be mentioned as a point of discussion, even when the amount of property concerned is very small. Indeed, we might even guess that those with little property might be as much concerned about it as those with a greater amount of property. However, this is not the case. True enough, 7% of those with *no* property did mention property as an item of discussion, and there are *no* differences in frequency of mention between those who had $250-$499 worth of property, and those who had $1000-$1999. Nevertheless, there is a Q of association of +.80 between amount of property (more or less than $2000) and discussions of property as part of the divorce arrangements.

Moreover, frequency of talks is in general associated with amount of property, as we now see:

FREQUENCY OF TALKS, BY AMOUNT OF PROPERTY

Amount of Property	Frequency			Totals	
	Many or some	Few or none			
$0-$500	25%	75%	100%	219	
$500-$3999	35	65	100	130	
$4000 and over	42	58	100	76	
Totals	31	69	100	425	

$$X^2 = 9.3 \qquad\qquad .01 > P > .001$$

It may be, on the other hand, that some other factor enters to create this association. For example, property and education are associated (33% of the college husbands had a total of $4000 or more, but only 20% of those with grammar school education had so much). In turn, those with greater education would be more likely than the lesser educated to engage in discussions about any divorce arrangements. The greater the education, the greater the acceptance of the advisability, propriety, and even duty of discussing divorce plans with some semblance of calm and rationality.

Indeed, there is such an association:

FREQUENCY OF DISCUSSION ABOUT DIVORCE ARRANGEMENTS, BY EDUCATION

Education (of Husband)	Frequency			Totals	
	Frequently or several times	Rarely or never			
College	40%	60%	100%	55	
High School	33	67	100	252	
Grammar School or less	25	75	100	111	

Perhaps, then, the apparent relationship between amount of property and frequency of talks is spurious, and exists only because those with more property have more education. Then it would rather be the educational pattern of "talking out" problems that underlies this frequency, rather than some shared interest about which to talk.

In the succeeding table, this notion is tested by holding education constant.

FREQUENCY OF TALKS, BY TOTAL VALUE OF PROPERTY, HOLDING EDUCATION CONSTANT

Education of Husband	Property	Frequency of Talks Many or some	Few or none	Totals	
High School Graduate	Less than $500	19%	81%	100%	67
or over	$500-$3999	38	62	100	45
	$4000 or more	56	44	100	32
Total		33%	67%	100%	144
		$X^2 = 13.8$		$.01 > P > .001$	
Less than High	Less than $500	28%	72%	100%	147
School Graduate	$500-$3999	35	65	100	83
	$4000 or more	32	68	100	44
Total		31%	69%	100%	274
		not significant			

The surmise is not entirely borne out. When education is held constant, among those with *less* than four years of high school there is *no* relationship between total value of property and frequency of talks. But those with completed high school education or more *do* show such an association. Apparently, then, both property and education have an influence upon frequency. If there is low education, then amount of property makes little difference.

Let us, however, make the reciprocal test, by holding *amount of property* constant, to see whether education continues to have an influence. As we see in the succeeding table, when there is little or no property, there are no real differences in the frequency of talks in strata of different education. However, with *increasing* amounts of property, the association between education and frequency of talks becomes sharp. Both factors, then, are independently important.

FREQUENCY OF TALKS, BY EDUCATION, HOLDING VALUE OF PROPERTY CONSTANT

Property	Education	Frequency of Talks Many or some	Few or none	Totals	
Less than	College	28%	72%	100%	25
$500	High School Graduate	14	86	100	42
	Some High School	32	68	100	92
	Grammar School	22	78	100	55
Total		25%	75%	100%	214
$500-$3999	College	42%	58%	100%	12
	High School Graduate	36	64	100	33
	Some High School	37	63	100	49
	Grammar School	32	67	100	34
Total		36%	64%	100%	128
$4000 and	College	56%	44%	100%	18
over	High School Graduate	57	43	100	14
	Some High School	41	59	100	22
	Grammar School	23	77	100	22
Total		42%	58%	100%	76

Agreement on Items Discussed. Whether we measure by the percentage of respondents mentioning the item (65% of those discussing anything) or by the total number of times the item is mentioned (165), the effect of the divorce on the children ranks as the primary item for discussion, and the more so if the parents seriously analyze the problem. There is general agreement in our society, at all social strata, that children need both parents, and opinion is that children of divorced parents are more likely to be unhappy. Juvenile delinquency is associated in the public mind with broken homes, particularly those broken by divorce.

Parents could not be expected to agree about the children in divorce because a solution that satisfies the accepted values of our society is almost impossible. The situation is not one of two individuals battling for an uninvolved and easily definable gain such as money. In such a situation, as in the division of property, there is general agreement about the main principles and elements that are to be considered, and the argument is merely about their interpretation or application. There is some agreement within any given circle on what "generosity" or "stinginess" is; the jockeying between spouses is *where* between these two the final decision ought to be. A wife may insist that she shall have a set of books for her property, since it was her salary that originally paid for them, even though (or because) she knows they would be more useful to the husband. Another wife may leave the entire division to her husband, washing her hands of it, and feeling that all the accumulation was due to his efforts. The actual behavior, then, is widely variant, and often creates an additional conflict factor, as we noted previously: emotions are invested in even small bits of property. However, the fact remains that the main elements, and the rough principles guiding those elements, are generally accepted.

There would be less agreement with reference to the children, however, simply because there *cannot* be any basic agreement concerning the ethical or moral principle to be applied: both spouses are violating the only significant principle, that both should remain together in amity to create a happy home in which the children can grow to adulthood. The children represent an investment of *both* the past and the future. Almost all the property items are at least theoretically replaceable. The children are not, since even new children in a new marriage do not replace the first children. Of course, the disposal of the children is almost automatic in our legal system, in that they will nearly always be given to the mother. However, since the discussion concerned "effect of the divorce on the children," and this effect is not really predictable, such a decision does not aid much in achieving real agreement between spouses.

Between these two extremes of property and children is the item of alimony or child support. In Michigan there is no alimony, but some husbands do make temporary or permanent agreements to help their ex-wives financially. All husbands are by law responsible for their children's support unless these are adopted by others. Husbands can be jailed for failure to provide support and may be extradited from other states if they attempt to flee their obligations. Of course, this does not prevent some of them from escaping. Some succeed merely by refusing to pay, or by paying grudgingly and late, or only when threatened by court action, so that their former wives are discouraged from continuing to pursue them. The court action usually forces them to pay only the back sum owing, and a new action may be necessary if the husband becomes delinquent again.[6]

Although the amount of the support payments is theoretically fixed by the court, it is usually fixed by agreement between the attorneys, or between the wife's attorney and the husband, and merely ratified by the court. However settled, it remains a mortgage on the future earnings of the husband. Since visiting and domicile arrangements almost always favor the mother, the husband may feel less inclined from the beginning to commit himself to heavy payments. It is also obvious that even in terms of monetary rationality the husband can more wisely be generous in the disposal of *accumulated* property than in *future* support payments. (For example, if he agrees to pay $80 a month for the support of two children—an amount which could not furnish minimum living standards, by Bureau of Labor Statistics Standards—and the children are six and eight years old, he has in effect agreed to pay over $10,000 by the time they are both eighteen. A difference of $20 a month amounts to $2400 in ten years.) Since most divorces with children occur when the children are young, the family has usually accumulated very little. The husband has more future income than present savings, and in any event the money will go to his wife. Consequently, he may be willing to disagree about support when he is almost indifferent about the division of property.

On the other hand, the position of the wife is clear. Aside from any wish to punish her husband, she is fixing her future base income for some time. If this base is not sufficiently large, her financial problems will be great.

Consequently, we should expect more disagreements about the matter of support than about that of property division. That is, (1) in the latter case there is an emotional investment and some (usually small) equity to be divided. However, it is replaceable, and there is some agreement about the bases or principles by which it should be divided. It is also an item which has little future, mainly a past. At the other extreme, (2) the effect of the divorce on the children, there is a great emotional stake, but there is no approved solution within the moral and ethical structure of our society. The right of the spouses to be free, and to be happy, are accepted, but so are those of the children to have a complete home. There is no solution, and no amount of jockeying for advantage between spouses will solve the problem. Indeed, the very *definition of what an advantage would be* is not entirely clear. Between these two items, there is (3) the matter of future support payments. Here, the principles to be applied are fairly clear, as is the kind of advantage to be gained; and the argument is over the interpretation and application of the principles. There is not a past investment of emotion, but a very substantial future investment or mortgage of both emotion and earnings. Consequently, we should find that the amount of disagreement is least with respect to the division of property, most with regard to the matter of the chil-

---

6. With reference to support payments, the Friend of the Court has worked out procedures for seeing to it that the husband keeps up his payments. These are doubtless more effective than in most jurisdictions, but we shall see that many husbands nevertheless do not pay.

dren; and the disagreement about future support payments should fall between these two.

DISCUSSION AND AGREEMENT ON DIVORCE DETAILS

Item Discussed	No. Respondents Who Discussed	Of Those Who Discussed, % Who Agreed
Property Division (only those with property)	62	79%
Support Payments	100	68
Children	165	63

However, our predictions were not entirely borne out. There is least agreement on children, as predicted, and most on property division, but the differences seem small and unimportant, possibly because only those couples who were in agreement already could "discuss" such matters.

Keeping the Agreements. When we turn from the *making* of agreements to the *keeping* of agreements, the situations of both spouses have changed substantially. In many important respects both spouses have failed to predict their postdivorce circumstances, not alone because of the ordinary frustrations and failures of living, but also because both spouses are different from the persons they were before. Agreements that were made with the best of will, and made by spouses intent on keeping them, become impossible to keep; or impossible to keep without disrupting still other commitments that have since been made. The wife may have sincerely wished to let her former husband visit the children, but each visit requires much planning and adjustment. Her new husband may be a bit jealous, and she herself is leading a busy life—with the result that she may not directly refuse to permit visits, but may simply make them difficult for her ex-husband and the children. Similarly, the ex-husband may wish to be reasonable about support payments, and may for a while even be willing to help his former wife during an illness, or in starting a small business. However, he may find that living alone is very expensive. He comes to feel that he has the right to entertain his friends once in a while, and begins to resent the sacrifices that he must make. Further, he sees that he does not get to visit his children often, and that they are growing away from him, while his wife receives ample income from her new husband.

There is no intent here to sketch the various types of agreement-breaking. We simply note that the complete circumstances of life *after* the divorce cannot be predicted *prior* to the divorce, and that agreements which seemed easy to keep at an earlier stage become very difficult to keep at a later stage.

To put the matter in a slightly different form: with succeeding months of adjustment, the two lives grow so far apart that their main connection comes to be the agreements made prior to the divorce. It would be surprising if these old agreements were in harmony with the demands of their new lives.

On the other hand, agreements become not only impossible to keep. They also become irrelevant. Some matters over which the couple fought bitterly may dwindle to unimportance after the divorce. A book, a record, a living room suite, a picture album—all the things that had symbolic significance early in the divorce negotiations—may, after a while, seem irrelevant. Similarly, agreements made about visits to see one another, or dating and marrying other people, may come to be broken only in a technical sense: actually neither party cares any more about the agreements.

We rather guess that this is so even with respect to property. Usually such agreements are not broken, since after the division no further action is called for. However, there can be recriminations of various kinds later on, and battles about the matter. We would suppose that in general these, too, become less likely as time goes on.

We shall discuss the children in a subsequent chapter, but let us say now that once the new position of the children is recognized (and in a few cases it never becomes recognized), the spouse who relinquishes the children builds a life in which the children are only on the periphery, and probably does not even visit the children as much as is permitted by the decree (except when visits are only during vacations). Consequently, here again the agreements made about visits are at least partially irrelevant; the party who has the right to demand fulfillment of the agreement will not usually make the full demand.

One interesting consequence of this shift of relevance is that increasingly the meaning of "keeping agreements" seems to become, for the wife, a simple matter of whether or not support payments are continued.

We note, first of all, that the ex-wives apparently included in their "agreements" some agreements which had not been part of their original discussions, since *more* wives spoke of keeping or not keeping agreements than *mentioned agreements having been made*. Some of these added cases were, of course, agreements that were made through the lawyers, or were directives made by the court. Thus, wives could speak of keeping agreements that did not grow out of the predivorce discussions between husband and wife. Most husbands seem to have kept the agreements that were made: 85% of the wives whose husbands made agreements reported that their husbands kept all or some of the agreements.

Although education of husband does have some effect upon whether the agreements were kept, the difference is mainly between (a) husbands with *some* college and (b) husbands with *no* college education, and even this difference disappears if we collapse the possible categories into (a) college—noncollege and (b) kept no agreements—kept all or some agreements. This would make a four-fold table, in which there is practically no association between college education and keeping the agreements. Nevertheless, if we consider only the husbands who had *completed college, all* kept either *all* the agreements made, or *some* of them.

There are no significant differences between Protestant and Catholic ex-husbands in the keeping of agreements, although both these groups seem more likely to keep agreements than husbands with no religious affiliation, or a different one. Thus 65% of Catholic ex-husbands kept *all* the agreements; 59% of the Protestants, but only 35% of the husbands in the "other religion, or none" category kept all the agreements they had made with their wives.

Since continuity of child support payments is of such great significance to the divorcee's postdivorce adjustment, we shall discuss that item at length in our later chapter on economic adjustment. For the present, we merely point out the close relationship between "keeping of agreements," and steadiness of the husband's work. We shall relate this item later to the support payments.

KEEPING OF PREDIVORCE AGREEMENTS, BY STEADINESS OF HUSBAND'S WORK

Agreements kept	Always or usually had work		Frequently out of work		Total	
	%	No.	%	No.	%	No.
All	61	79	40	19	55	98
Some	28	37	33	16	30	53
None	11	14	27	13	15	27
Totals	100	130	100	48	100	178

Attitudes of Various Groups toward the Divorce. During the major period of conflict, the spouses doubtless center much of their attention on each other, and we shall later show that they continue to do this for some period after the separation and decree. In the movement toward disenchantment and disinvolvement, they move to create new lives, but they start from each other as foci.

Both spouses, however, live in networks of relationships with friends and kin, and necessarily these relationships are also a part of their ongoing decisions and activities. Naturally, some of these circles are more important than others. We noted earlier that the wife's knowledge of approval and disapproval of the marriage on the part of friends and kin was structured in particular directions. She seemed to know more definitely the attitudes of her own friends and kin toward the marriage than she knew those of her husband's friends and kin. Moreover, she seemed to report a greater amount of disapproval on the part of her *own* friends and kin than of her *husband's* friends and kin. In presenting these two sets of facts, we viewed them as reciprocally related. That is, the wife's judgment about the approval of her husband's friends and kin seemed to be a reflection of the fact that she did not really know their disapproval as well as she knew the disapproval of her own group.

As the divorce becomes a social fact to be adjusted to by everyone involved, a sharper cleavage appears between the wife's circles and the husband's than appeared at the original marriage. The wife seems to have lost contact with her husband's group, although we do not know whether there was open conflict or merely a drifting apart. The data suggest a process of selective association, by which she comes to lose contact with those who do not sympathize with her troubles, or who do not give her the warmth and friendship of old ties. By the time the divorce has occurred, her circle has become a sympathetic set of friends and relatives for the most part, having gradually lost those who expressed antagonism toward the breakup.

We believe it is for this reason that half of these divorcees report no change in their circle of friends after the divorce. Although the circle of relatives cannot be basically changed, there can be differential associations (a) among her own relatives; and (b) between her relatives and the relatives of the ex-husband. It seems reasonable to suppose that, as a result, she can: (a) report somewhat more approval of the divorce among her relatives than actually exists; and (b) report more approval of the divorce among *her* relatives than among *his*. With reference to proposition (b), of course, it would be surprising if his relatives and friends felt more approval than her own relatives and friends. Her bias, if indeed it exists, is therefore toward asserting a slightly greater disapproval than exists, but we would expect the difference in disapproval between the two circles to be at least in the same direction as she reports.

In the accompanying table, we see the basic distribution of these attitudes of disapproval or approval toward the divorce.

ATTITUDES OF VARIOUS GROUPS TOWARD THE DIVORCE

| Groups | Approval | | Indif- | Disapproval | | Don't Know | Totals |
	Strong	Mild	ference	Mild	Strong	and No Answer	
Wife's Family	44%	16%	17%	9%	11%	2%	99%
Wife's Friends	40	19	22	5	6	7	99
Husband's Family	21	13	18	15	19	14	100
Husband's Friends	16	10	25	9	9	31	100
Mutual Friends	20	16	26	8	6	24	100

N = 425

We analyzed earlier a simpler version of this table, when we discussed the first suggestion of divorce, and continued insistence on it. Here, we wish only to point out these further relationships:

1. Over twice as high a percentage of the wives' families felt attitudes of strong approval toward the divorce, as of the husbands' families (44% vs. 21%).

2. Parallel to this apparent cleavage is the difference between the percentage of *strong* approval among her friends, as against his friends (40% vs. 16%).

3. On the other hand, the differences in *mild* approval between the two sets are small (wife's family 16% vs. husband's family 13%; wife's friends 19% vs. husband's friends 10%), although in both cases her circle is more approving than his.

4. Both *family* circles, that of the ex-husband and that of the ex-wife, are reported less frequently to be *indifferent* to the divorce, than are her *friends,* his friends, or mutual friends (17% and 18% vs. 22%, 25%, 26%).

5. On the other hand, as we move *outward* from her circle of family and friends to his, the percentage of "Don't know" or "No answer" responses increases (her family 2%; her friends 7%; his family 14%; mutual friends and his friends, 24% and 31%).

6. Corresponding to these cleavages, the *mutual* friends express approval somewhat more frequently, indifference about as frequently, disapproval somewhat less frequently, and are somewhat less likely to have opinions that are unknown to the ex-wife, compared to the *friends that are the husband's alone.*

Aside from the social cleavages that are documented in these data, there is also indirect evidence that the divorces were not seen from the wife's side as mere whimsy or arbitrariness. About 60% of her circle of family and friends are reported to have felt mild or strong approval of the divorce, as against the general disapproval of divorce in this country when children are involved. This fact is of some importance in her later adjustment to divorce, since both these circles may become helpful in meeting new people and particularly in meeting eligible suitors. Underlining this essentially particularistic approval, i.e., an approval of *this* divorce because of the woman's particular ties with family and friends, is the fact that there are no differences in approval or disapproval by religion. Whether we relate the husband's religion to his family's approval, or her religion to her family's approval, there are no differences between Catholics and Protestants.

Approval and Themes of Complaint. When we relate these patterns of approval and disapproval to the themes of complaint, we are dealing to some degree with the justifications given by the wife for the divorce, and relating these to the reactions of different circles. Then we see that there are at least two dimensions to "approval." First, her family may disapprove of the *fact* of divorce and be upset that there will be a divorce, but agree nevertheless that the divorce is *justified*. Reciprocally, if the husband's family sides with him, they may disapprove either the grounds for divorce, or the divorce itself.

A second dimension is the extent to which a given type of behavior is *public knowledge* within any of the four main networks of kin and friend. We made reference earlier to this fact, noting that the husband might develop a pattern of neglect in his conflict with his wife, without that pattern being seen as a totality by his friends. Only those who are in very close and daily contact with the social interaction inside the home would be able to see that his neglect forms a pattern. Others may see husband or wife in the role of host or hostess, casual friend, or in other contexts, where an individual item of behavior is not seen as part of a pattern, or not even judged as particularly undesirable. Most outsiders, even members of his own family, might not be able to ascertain that the husband (or wife) actually pays little attention to the family and cares little about home life and children. Our failure to take proper account of these dimensions prevents a neat analysis at this point. Nevertheless, we may see some of them through the themes of complaint, and the attitudes toward the divorce that grew out of those complaints.

Thus, (1) her circles are more approving than his; (2) both families are less approving than the corresponding circles of friends; (3) she sees *his* friends as more inclined toward "indifference" than toward disapproval or approval. Further breakdowns do not now change these general patterns, but there are some small differences that are worth noting.

Of the major themes, Values receives the lowest percentage of approval among all four networks. Just over two-fifths of the wives' families are reported to be approving, as against approximately three-fifths for most complaints. Twenty-two percent of the wives making this complaint reported that their husbands' friends approved, as against about 30% for most complaints. The differences for the other two networks, her friends, and his family, are smaller, but in the same direction. We would not expect great approval on either side, unless his values were highly deviant. Although differences in values may be irritating to the spouses most intimately concerned, they are not defined socially as adequate grounds for divorce in our society. As a consequence, approval is lower for this theme than for most themes.

A slightly different contrast may be seen in the two themes of Complex and Authority. With reference to the first, the husband's helling around would usually be done *with* his friends, so that they are not likely to express great disapproval of such behavior. The complaint of Authority sometimes means physical cruelty, but more often refers to a degree of male dominance to which the wife objected. We would expect his groups, particularly his friends, to see his assertion of male dominance as a proper exercise of husbandly right, so that their disapproval of that behavior would be minimal. But her friends would be more likely to see her as being put upon and bullied, so that they would have a high approval of the divorce. Thus, their approval is higher for these two themes than for any others: 70% for Authority, 72% for Complex. And his friends' disapproval is lower than for any theme except that of Nonsupport: 14% and 15%, and for Nonsupport, 9%.

With reference to this last behavioral pattern, it is possible for the husband to give little money to his family without his friends knowing about this failure. But the financial burden will usually then fall on her own family. Since, further, such a complaint ordinarily refers to a continued pattern, they will feel that the divorce is justified: 71% of the wives making this complaint reported that their own families did approve. On the other hand, though in general his friends are reported (by her) as feeling *indifference* to the divorce, the proportion indifferent for this theme is higher than for any other theme except Home Life (both are 60%). This is not, we suppose, an indifference to the situation. Rather, they do not usually know the situation, and she has too little contact with them either to tell them about it or to elicit a definite attitude.

The complaint of Triangle also suggests differences in social contact and definition. This theme and those of Nonsupport and Desertion are the only themes for which the proportion of wives' families reported to be approving is higher than that of friends. Although Nonsupport creates a burden for her family, both behavior patterns are open violations of minimum role obligations in our society. Either will effectively destroy the family in almost all instances, especially since Triangle usually means that the husband in this situation was pressing for a divorce. Such behavior is a violation of familial norms that cannot be long hidden from either family. We thus find that even his family disapproved in 54% of the cases in which Triangle was the complaint, although for most complaints the ex-wife reports his family to be about equally divided between approval, indifference, and disapproval. Moreover, for this theme the percentage of his circles of friends reported as indifferent is lowest of all themes (45%), and the highest percentage disapproving (26%).

Now, turning once again to approval and disapproval without regard to themes, we note that the frequency of wives reporting approval of the husband's family toward the divorce increases very little with longer duration of marriage (30% for 0-4 years, to 38% for 10-14 years, and then a slight drop). The attitude of disapproval also decreases very little.

There is a slight decrease in the frequency of favorable attitudes on the part of the wife's family, with increasing duration of marriage (68% for 0-4 years, to 57% for 15 years and over); and an increase in the frequency of unfavorable responses (13% for 0-4 years, to 21% for marriages lasting 15 years or more).

This is a complex relationship, which we interpret without having any certainty that we are correct. We believe that when the wife who has been married longer reports slightly greater amount of approval by the husband's family, she merely asserts that the husband's family thinks the divorce is justified. This has a reasonable basis, in that over these years she has worked out a relatively friendly relationship with his family. And the longer the period of the marriage, the greater the understanding she expects them to have. On the other hand, when the wife who has been married longer reports that *her* own family has a greater *disapproval* of the divorce, we believe that she refers to their general disapproval of there being a divorce at all, even when they may approve her reasons for divorcing. Thus, they think of the greater consequences of the divorce for themselves. It is mainly her family circle who will bear the responsibility for her and the children, and who will have to help her to adjust. These problems are greater, the longer the marriage, at least within our age limits. Kin and friends are therefore more likely to express disapproval of the divorce generally, the longer the marriage.

On the other hand, when the wife speaks of the attitudes of the husband's family, she reports mainly her judgment of their sympathy with her and her marital difficulties; and this should increase slightly with increasing duration of marriage.

Divorce rates are higher in the lower strata, and our analysis has already pointed to several apparent differences in social behavior among the strata which might help to explain those differences in rates. If our reasoning is correct, we ought to expect a somewhat greater amount of disapproval of the divorce and a somewhat lesser amount of approval toward the upper strata. This is, indeed, what we find. When we group our occupational strata into three categories, and consider only those who have *definite* attitudes toward the divorce, we find that the frequency of disapproval gradually increases toward the upper strata, and the frequency of approval decreases.

DEFINITE ATTITUDES OF APPROVAL-DISAPPROVAL BY THE WIFE'S FAMILY, BY OCCUPATIONAL GROUP OF WIFE'S FATHER

Occupational Group of Father	Approval	Disapproval	Totals	
Upper	66%	34%	100%	41
Middle	73	27	100	156
Lower	79	21	100	136

It is worth adding that wives from lower-class families are also more likely to claim that they do not *know* the attitudes of their families, or to impute indifference to those families. When we include these categories, however, the differences between middle and upper class families are slight. This lack of knowledge again documents the lesser definiteness and strength of *social* networks among the lower strata, compared with the upper. The relationship is only slightly less regular when we make a similar table for the attitudes of the *husband's family* according to the *occupational group of the husband:*

DISTRIBUTION OF DEFINITE ATTITUDES OF HUSBAND'S FAMILY TO DIVORCE BY OCCUPATIONAL GROUP OF HUSBAND

Occupational Group	Approval	Disapproval	Totals	
Upper	39%	61%	100%	31
Middle	53	37	100	124
Lower	51	49	100	130

On the other hand, the differences in attitudes of husband's friends, grouped by occupational class of husband, are too small to be important.

Summary. Nevertheless, whether or not kin or friends approved the divorce, all these wives did go through with the divorce action. We have in the preceding chapters analyzed the overt steps toward a final dissolution of the marriage. In the present chapter, we have noted that only a minority of these respondents received any kind of help that could be called marital counseling, and the most frequent advice was to get the divorce. We pointed out that Catholics are somewhat more likely to have obtained some counseling, as are those with a medium amount of education.

Attention was also paid to the types of items that were discussed between husband and wife, and the agreements that were reached. Apparently, children were discussed most frequently, but there was very slightly less agreement on this item than on other items. Most of the husbands seemed to have kept their agreements, which may mean in part that many agreements become irrelevant after the divorce.

Finally, as part of the divorce experience, we dealt with the approval and disapproval of the friendship and kinship circles of both spouses. Again, we find a cleavage between her circle and his, and between family and friends. In addition, certain of the themes of complaint appear to have a complex relationship with the response of approval and disapproval.

CHAPTER XIII

SEPARATION AND TRAUMA: THE FINAL DISSOLUTION

AT THE PRESENT TIME, we have relatively few systematic data on the emotional meaning of separation. We shall in the succeeding sections offer both our speculations and the facts we have found for our divorces. Unfortunately, we do not know whether certain of our speculations are correct. The period of separation is experienced by many couples as an approximation to divorce. However, when we wish to go beyond such a simple fact, we must draw upon unsystematic observations and protocols. Such couples may feel the unhappiness of living apart, and have a first recognition of the loss they will suffer if the conflict continues. For them, the separation is not so much a part of the divorce as it is a symptom of the depth of conflict. They separate because the conflict is too severe to bear, but there may be strong ties binding them to one another. We have already discussed some of the factors that play a role in this decision process when it leads to divorce.

Now, all of our respondents who once felt this internal hurt at separation nevertheless came ultimately to divorce, but this is certainly not true for most who separate in this country. In this chapter we explore the meaning and impact of the final dissolution of the marriage.

Separation as a Step toward Divorce. When couples separate, the spouses may find the separation painful, and thus wish to come together again as man and wife. The social pressures of the usual kinship and friendship group do press toward some kind of maintenance of the relationship during a separation, and usually support a reconciliation. Separation may be even more burdensome than divorce. In divorce, the relationships between the ex-spouses are at least spelled out in part by the decree itself. The parties are free to find substitutes for each other. They may be able to find emotional security or at least solace with other people. The situation has become officially defined, even though there are major gaps in the institutional definitions. The legal rights and obligations are definite, if minimum. In separation this is not usually the case, and it may characteristically serve as a temporary measure to alleviate severe conflicts. The assumption of their group may be that, after a while, they may possibly live together again as man and wife.

There are no data as to what proportion of separations ultimately end in divorce. A guess may be made by comparing the Decennial Census and the Sample Surveys data on the numbers of households which appear to exhibit a separation against the tabulations of divorce decrees. Nevertheless, the definition of what is a separation in these circumstances is not always clear, and we cannot follow the separated over any period of time to see what becomes of them. It is certain that the number of divorces in any given time period is considerably less than the number of separations for any comparable previous time period.[1]

Of course, the phrase, "We're separated now," sometimes becomes a euphemism for "We plan to get a divorce." Nevertheless, when the term is not euphemistic, "being separated" is not viewed as a permanent measure, and it has none of the advantages of such a minimum specification of duties.

Here, then, is social improvisation in an ill-defined situation. Both parties have all the duties and burdens of parenthood and spousehood except that of interaction with one another. "Being separated" is socially different from "going to get a divorce," as it is from "having been deserted." Obviously, in the latter case the offended spouse can count upon help, perhaps even from the departed spouse's circle. Separation does not, however, allow either party to establish a new life. There is no extended kin to whom either spouse may return with full knowledge that most problems of support and emotional security will be met or alleviated. Both parties are merely social appendages.

Consequently, it is not too much to say that the American social structure pushes the separated spouse into a decision, and we guess that in most cases that decision is toward reconciliation.

On the other hand—and it hardly needs to be emphasized that we are merely sketching obvious alternatives—the separation may for a smaller proportion of couples represent such an alleviation of the pain of conflict that the decision moves toward divorce. Each contact with the other spouse must mean a prolonged discussion of problems both present and past. These ordinarily precede any solutions for the future, and prevent any enjoyment of each other's company as "strangers first and well met." Such contacts may merely re-arouse the ancient wrongs and recriminations, leading to a continuance of the separation, a failure to solve the conflicts, and a weary or bitter decision to end the ambiguity by getting the divorce.

Since the separation cannot be viewed as one of the formal and necessary steps toward the divorce (though, rarely, it is also in itself a formal, legal step), separation as an action needs to be separately examined. We shall look particularly at its emotional meaning, to the extent that we can do so.

The fact that we do not have a clear picture of separation prevents an adequate analysis of the factors that are associated with it. We cannot view it as always a preliminary to divorce, or place it in one particular place in the sequence of steps leading to divorce. On the other hand, it is also a *real decision,* and we know its emotional impact is on the average greater than that of the divorce decree itself. We therefore propose to analyze this period together with the immediately postdivorce period. For the divorcee who carries out the final decision to divorce, this total period is viewed as "the

---

1. See Beal, *op. cit.;* and Wm. F. Ogburn, "Marital Separations," *Am. J. Soc.,* 49 (1944), 316-322.

final separation and divorce" period. We must, then, analyze the trauma of divorce in these sections as well.

Types of Separation. Before analyzing the predivorce or postdivorce separation activities and emotions, let us attempt to outline what appear to us as the main types of separation. Since these have been derived only after our data were in, they are suggestions for future research rather than theoretically rigorous hypotheses about our divorcees. We believe the experienced marital clinician will recognize familiar patterns, even though we cannot show how frequent any of them are.

Let us begin with what we may call a "rational model" of decision and action. We would suppose, in this ideal pattern, that separation would occur some time after the decision to divorce had been made, close to the time of filing suit. The couple would not decide to divorce until they had considered the problem adequately. They would not decide to separate unless it became clear that they could not work out an adequate mode of life together. Having made that decision, they would then decide to separate. Within this "rational model" the filing of suit and the actual decree are merely a resultant of the decision taken at an earlier stage. The couple would not live together any longer than would be necessary to make satisfactory living arrangements apart, since it was the inability to stay together in contentment that led to their final decision.

Now it is quite clear that a substantial proportion of individuals does not follow this model. True enough, 40% of our respondents separated from their husbands after the final decision and before filing the decree. However, 6% did not separate until after the decree. Equally strikingly, nearly two-fifths of the cases separated *before the decision was reached,* that is to say, in the period that we have called "Serious Consideration to Final Decision." In certain of these cases, the separation actually occurred before the wife gave any serious consideration to the possibility of a divorce.

Using our rational model for comparison, there are two main types of deviation with respect to the point in the total conflict when the separation occurred. There are the cases (a) where separation occurred before any final decision had been made, and (b) where the separation occurred a considerable time after the suit had actually been filed.

Let us then look at several facts which seem to structure the separation pattern. We must remember that (1) there are great differences in the *happiness* of the two spouses, whether the marriage continues or ends in a divorce. There may even be great disagreement from one spouse to the other with respect to some of the basic facts about their relationship.[2] In extreme cases one spouse believes that the marriage has been very happy, while the other believes that it is an unsatisfactory marriage in all basic respects. One spouse believes that they share decisions and communicate with one another about all important problems, while the other believes no such thing. Even in families where there is some emphasis upon "democratic patterns," it can often be shown that no one but the father believes that a truly democratic pattern is followed. The rest of the family believes that the father makes all

---

2. See Terman, *op. cit.,* ch. V, for an analysis of the disagreements between spouses as to the "facts" of their relationship.

of the decisions autocratically. We would suppose, then, that in families in which there is a sharp difference in the happiness ratings by the two spouses the meaning of separation would be different for the two.

(2) There are also great differences in the willingness of different couples, or of each spouse, to *use divorce as a solution* for some kinds of marital problems. Sometimes these come from differences in religious beliefs, but often the differential willingness is caused by particular family histories or the beliefs and pressures of friendship circles. In any event, the spouse who is *more* unhappy may be *less willing* to use divorce as a solution to the problem. This difference in willingness to use divorce would, then, have an effect upon when the separation occurs, and upon its meaning for the two spouses.

(3) There are also differences from one couple to another with respect to the difficulty of the problems that have to be faced if a divorce does occur. The two *spouses* always face a different set of problems, because of the different sex statuses. The differences between *couples* may lie in such areas as possible help from kin, how separate and independent their lives have become, property and income, number of children, available money for divorce expenses, and so on. For example, some families may believe that a given couple has tried seriously to solve its marital problems and has simply been unable to do so. The family might have an extended kinship network, with substantial property, so that the breakup of the couple would not occasion great difficulty in the way of new housing and income. On the other hand, another couple may face fairly complex property claims and counterclaims, or the father may be unable to furnish enough money to his wife and children when the household dissolves. They may then delay separation for some time while these practical problems are being solved, even though the divorce conflict during that period may not lessen in bitterness; or, by contrast, a couple may have gradually come to lead separate lives in fact, while sharing the same house. Then, the final separation may come at almost the same time that serious consideration takes place.

(4) It is perhaps useful to separate the previous set of differential problems from another set, which involves more specifically *social pressures.* Pressures from priest, pastor, and the network of kinfolk and friends may have a different impact on different couples with respect to the time of separation and the meaning of separation. If a couple is strongly Catholic, for example, they may be willing to separate because of the bitterness of conflict long before they are willing to consider the possibility of divorce. On the other hand, in some circles of friends the notion of divorce might be so disapproved that a couple might attempt to keep up a brave front until very late in the divorce conflict, unwilling to admit to anyone that the divorce was impending, until the decision had been reached and the actual suit filed.

(5) A further factor that might be of some significance in separation would be the difference between couples in their ability to remain together once the difficulties have been crystallized by a final decision. The avoidance of violence among the middle and upper classes, and the greater habituation to "politeness and manners," might *allow* a couple to remain together—if there were any other practical factor which prevented their separation—*longer* than would be the case for families in lower strata, or at least families with a lesser

ability to live together on a merely civil level of intercourse and communication. This factor might be considered a negative one. It does not act except to *permit* remaining together, if there are any reasons for doing so after the decision has been reached. On the other hand, it is not in itself a positive factor in keeping the couple together during any period of conflict.

Finally, (6) we must consider the *impact of the complaint* itself. To take a common example among our divorcees, if the divorce is caused by the desertion of the husband, then in most cases there would be no final decision taken until after the separation has occurred. On the other hand, we may be unwilling to consider this a "separation" in the ordinary sense. Another kind of case might be that of a sudden disclosure in which one of the spouses learns that the other has been having an affair, or is actually unhappy. In such a juncture, there may be almost no time given to serious consideration, and a separation follows immediately upon the announcement, before consideration or decision. Finally, there are certainly some cases in which the two have grown bored with one another over the years, and have decided to divorce merely because there are some mildly attractive alternatives of freedom or job plans, without any great emotion involved. In some of these cases the couple may for convenience continue to live together until the actual time of the decree.

We are not insisting that these are the sole factors at work. We do believe that these are the main organizing factors which determine when the separation will occur among the several phases of the divorce conflict, and we can show that certain of them have some effect on the emotional meaning of that separation when it does occur.

We may therefore summarize what seem to be (A) the important types of separation; and (B) the main factors associated with these types, in the following fashion. We suggest that there are five main types of separation, four of which are among our sample. (1) First, there is the "rational model," the *separation as a divorce preliminary,* which we have just discussed. The separation comes after a decision to divorce. The couple decide that they cannot bear living together, for whatever reasons, and thereafter implement that decision with reference to the various problems of housing, child or wife support, etc. Ordinarily, they *will* separate before filing suit, since the lawyer will point out that they cannot maintain the necessary allegations about their fundamental conflict, if a court investigator comes to their home and finds them still living together. A few couples, because of their home reorganization problems, may delay separation until the suit is actually filed, but in general almost all these couples have separated by a month or so after filing suit. Since 40% of our couples separated *between* the final decision and filing suit, and some additional couples stayed together until only a short time after the suit, we *estimate* that separations of this type, separations preliminary to divorce, form about half of the total.

A second type is the *separation as substitute divorce,* and technically (because all our separations ended in divorce) we have none in our sample. These are couples who find living together very painful, but who cannot or will not divorce. Thus, they try to alleviate the conflict by temporary separations (which may become very long separations) without deciding to divorce.

Doubtless, few of these separate without *considering* divorce, but *all* separate before a final decision to divorce. We believe that this kind of separation is very common in the United States. We cannot give a numerical estimate, since our definition is based upon the *intent* of the couple, but it is worth commenting that separations in 1940 were 5.4% of the number of married couples living together.[3] Of course, some unknown percentage of these couples finally decide to divorce, anyway, but with our data we have no way of separating these from the rest of our sample. Certainly, many of them become desertions. All these, in any event, would be part of our 39% who *separated* before final decision.

A third type of separation is the *one-sided* divorce, in which one spouse simply announces the decision to divorce without the other having seriously considered the possibility of a divorce. The separation occurs, then, either simultaneously with serious consideration, or immediately afterwards. We have already commented on this pattern, and shall later have more data on it. A fourth type, but one which we cannot identify with precision, is the *drifting separation,* in which the two spouses gradually build lives separately, with little thought about divorce as an important step. They have considered divorce, but have failed to make a final decision simply because there has been no important precipitant or open conflict. These couples are separated a long time before a final decision, but move swiftly once the decision has been reached, since neither spouse is emotionally very involved with the other. Neither separation nor the decree itself makes much difference in their lives.

A final type is the *delayed separation,* formed by those couples who separate only *after the decree,* or not at all (almost 7% of the total). In spite of their decision to separate their lives, they remained together until after they were legally unmarried.

Now, we shall not emphasize these types. because we have arrived at them intuitively after a study of many divorces, and did not build into our interview the questions that would have classified each separation properly. On the other hand, this seems not to be a substantial gap, since in only *two* of these types does the *kind* of separation appear to make a real difference: Type 3, the one-sided divorce or separation, and Type 5, the delayed separation. This difference is significant for postdivorce adjustment in two major areas: (a) the *trauma* that is experienced; and (b) dating and the steps toward remarriage. Specifically, the women who experienced a one-sided separation or divorce also had a higher trauma index and were slower to re-enter courtship; and those who delayed separation until after the decree had a lower trauma index and moved more rapidly toward remarriage. These data will be presented later.

When the Separation Occurred. Since we are interested in the separation mainly because of the changes it creates in the life of the divorcee, we shall devote most of our succeeding analysis to what happens afterwards. Since, however, the separation *is* often the dividing line between "before" and "after" the divorce, let us first ascertain at what phases in the process of divorce these separations did occur.

The separation may occur at any phase of the marital conflict. It may

---

3. See Wm. F. Ogburn, "Marital Separations," *Am. J. Soc.,* 49 (1944), 317.

occur before both of the spouses have seriously considered divorce, or may not happen until after the decree. Indeed, three of our couples had not yet sepated at the time of the interview.[4]

WHEN DID THE SEPARATION OCCUR?

Conflict Phase	Percent
Before final decision	39
Final decision to filing	40
Filing to final decree	15
After final decree	6
Not by time of interview	.7
Total	100.7

N = 425

As we see, 4/5 of the separations occurred while the divorce was still being considered, before a final decision had been reached; or after a definite decision had been reached, and as a preliminary to filing the suit. In order to keep in mind the period of chronological time we are considering, let us also ascertain when the separation occurred with reference to the decree itself:

WHEN DID THE SEPARATION OCCUR?
(Time before decree)

	Percent
After decree	6%
Less than 4 months before	15
5- 6 months	10
7-10 months	17
11-12 months	10
Over 1 year, less than 2	17
2 years or more	23
No answer	2
Total	100%

N = 425

Thus, 40% of the separations occurred over one year prior to the decree, and 50% occurred over 10 months prior to the decree. In a *social* sense, then, *adjustment to divorce has begun long before the decree* for perhaps most divorcees.

As noted previously, there is no strong relationship between the time taken for any one of these conflict phases, and the time taken for any other: If the time for seriously considering the divorce is short or long, and the time from filing the suit to the final decree may be short or long. If the time from final decision to filing suit is short or long, the time from this last step to the final decree may also be short or long—*with the single exception of those who take a very short time for consideration.*

---

4. These may have believed they were still married. One certainly did. In 1948, an interlocutory divorce law went into effect in Michigan, by which couples were not permitted to marry again until six months after the decree. They were not, however, required to appear again in court. Thus, failing to reappear meant that the divorce became final. However, some divorcees misunderstood, and thought that if they did not reappear, the divorce was not final; or, that they were not "really divorced" until six months afterwards. This particular divorcee, then, insisted that she was not really divorced, because she and her former husband had decided to live together again. Legally, they were divorced, but socially and by self-definition they were still married.

The effect of this single exception is felt throughout all these phases, for these are mainly the precipitate divorces in which the husband has suddenly demanded a divorce, and insisted on getting one soon. This action also has an effect on the subsequent social adjustment of the ex-wife. Separations in this type of marital dissolution are not only more likely to occur *early* in these phases; often they occur before the wife has given any serious consideration at all to divorce.

Let us see what factors seem to affect when the separation occurs. (1) Duration of marriage is *not* associated with either late or early separation, and (2) the frequency of dating during the marriage has no effect. (3) The number of children has no apparent relationship, either, although we had supposed that these three items might tend to keep the spouses together until a somewhat later period of their conflict. We had also guessed that (4) the divorcee's judgment after the divorce, as to whether things would have been worse or better if no divorce had occurred, might be associated with the time of separation. That is, if she still thought, after the divorce, that things would have been better if there had been no divorce, then perhaps the separation would occur later. However, this guess was wrong; no such relationship appeared.

The factors which are associated with early or late separation are two main sets: (1) The factors that determine class position, such as education, income, occupation, and amount of property; and (2) who initiated the divorce. With reference to the first set, we shall not reproduce all the relevant tables, since they essentially parallel one another, suggesting in each case that toward the upper strata a later separation is found than toward the lower strata.

Separations in which the wife's education is higher, the husband's income or occupational rank is higher, or the amount of property accumulated by the couple is higher, are more likely to occur *later* in the phases of conflict. These findings are in conformity with the earlier discussion in this chapter, pointing out that practical problems of new households or the division of property might make an early separation difficult, and the culturally imposed "rationality" or civility of the upper strata might *permit* couples to remain together without violence, even though they have decided to break up their marriage. However, we had only expected that such factors would cause a *late* separation. We had not supposed that these factors would have any effect on *separation after the decree,* or delayed separations. Let us, in any event, present a table drawn from these factors, showing the relationship between time of separation and the amount of property.

WHEN SEPARATION OCCURRED, BY AMOUNT OF PROPERTY ACCUMULATED BY COUPLE

Amount of Property	Time of Separation				Totals	
	Before Decision	Decision to Filing	Filing to Decree	After Decree		
None	50%	40%	8%	2%	100%	172
$1.00-$1999.99	41	34	17	8	100	144
$2000 and over	18	47	24	11	100	109
Totals	39%	40%	15%		101	N = 425

In general, these differences are consistent. The education, income, occupation, and amount of property are slightly higher among those who separate late, or who separate *very* late, in the phases of divorce.

There are two apparent relationships that deserve brief mention here: (1) When there are young children (0-2 years), separation is likely to occur later; and (2) when there have been long absences (12 months or over), on the part of the husband during the marriage, separation is likely to occur earlier. Both are obviously spurious: (1) If separation has occurred *early,* the biological chances of there being very young children are reduced; and (2) when there have been such long absences, these merge insensibly into the separation proper, and thus the respondent speaks of "separation before decision" as her experience.

Of real importance, on the other hand, is our second set of factors, relating to who first made the suggestion to divorce. We shall only summarize these facts here, since they are in conformity with our data in Chapter XI, on first initiation, stability of decision, whether either spouse was in love with another, and the length of time for the various phases of the conflict.

These facts are as follows: (1) When the husband first suggested the divorce, it is more likely that the separation occurred early rather than late. In almost 40% of all our cases, the separation occurred before the final decision. In about one-third of these cases, it was the husband who first suggested the divorce, as against a proportion of one-fifth in the cases where separation occurred *after* the decision. In the succeeding table, we present the pattern of separation by who first suggested the divorce, with the further refinement that we have included *both* first suggestion and later *insistence* that the divorce take place.

WHEN SEPARATION OCCURRED, BY WHO FIRST SUGGESTED AND WHO INSISTED

Who Suggested and Who Insisted	Before Decision	When Separation Between Decision and Filing	After Filing Suit	Totals	No.
Husband/Husband	47%	31%	22%	100%	58
Mixed	39	35	26	100	132
Wife/Wife	36	44	20	100	235
Totals	39%	40%	22%	101	425

Furthermore, as we would expect from our previous data, (2) an *early* separation is associated with a slightly *more* stable decision, just as the latter is associated with the husband suggesting the divorce first. Thus, of those who separated *before* the final decision, 28% reconsidered this decision at some later period; but of those who separated *after* the final decision, 38% later reconsidered the decision. We cannot assert, however, that there is a tendency for these early separations to be associated with the husband being in love with another woman. In fact, the proportions of husbands in love with someone else, and not in love, are the same among those who separate *before* any final decision is reached and those who separate afterwards. Much higher, on the other hand, is the proportion of husbands whose wives *did not know* whether or not the husbands were in love with another (54% of the "Don't Knows" are in this pre-decision separation group, *vs.* 36-37% of those who *definitely* were either in love or not in love with another). Of course, this is due to an association between (a) the husband having moved out of the wife's life, and (b) her not knowing about his being in love. He separated from her before any decision was reached, so that her not knowing is associated with early separation.

Emotional Consequences of the Marital Dissolution. We have probed to some extent into the social relationships which center on *when* the separation occurs. However, we now wish to turn to the more immediate emotional experiences of the divorcee at the end of her marriage. In these sections, then, we shall treat mainly of the so-called divorce "trauma."

Our kinship institutions very likely create a greater personal disorganization in the lives of divorcees than other systems do. The nuclear family of our general society, without strong extended kin relations, and based to only a limited extent upon religious foundations and to a very great extent on romantic love or the expectation of happy affection, is structurally unstable. Yet there are sufficient moral commitments to an older pattern of marital stability that (1) there are few direct institutional patterns to dictate the postdivorce behavior of divorcees, and (2) the divorce as well as the divorcee is under some moral censure. It is at least partly derivative from this latter factor that divorce is supposed to be an emotionally trying experience. The participants are expected to be unhappy, and to exhibit various patterns of personal disorganization. Although it would be reckless to phrase this expectation as a "widespread opinion," it is at least fair to say that when we hear of a recent divorcee, male or female, who is drinking heavily, indulging in some sexual laxity, failing to meet the demands of his job or career, or giving vent to bitter and melancholy complaints against the world, we are not at all surprised. Indeed, we may hear such behavior "explained" as being due to the divorce.

We shall not be able in this study to explore all the dimensions of these notions about the immediate effects of divorce. We shall be able to touch on some of them, and will try to keep sharp the line separating our data and our speculations.

Let us begin by commenting that we still have not succeeded in making any deep probe into the emotional meaning of the divorce as a *finality*. We are referring to one particular element, its character as an *official, definite* (though not entirely irrevocable) conclusion to a marital relationship. We have enough unsolicited comments from our own respondents and from other sources, to know that many spouses do indeed fail to accept the reality of their decision until the final appearance in court. A few are unwilling to accept even that as a finality. For a much larger group, it seems likely that (a) the court appearance, in which after all only one of the spouses usually participates, and (b) the decree itself are emotionally anti-climactic. That is, the stages of serious consideration and reconsideration, final decision, filing of suit, and separation, *have long defined the situation as one of divorce*. The final decree is merely the official, external cognizance of a cleavage that has already become a part of the ongoing reality for the two spouses.

For our respondents, of course, the larger group is not in this precise category. After all, these wives were in most cases the spouses who appeared in court. Most husbands do not. Consequently, the court appearance itself would be expected to arouse many old emotions, to cause them to re-live old conflicts and hurts. The situation is, then, structured toward giving a maximum emotional finality to the decree. We did ask them about their feelings toward the actual court process. We know that many participants found the swift, mechanical flow of prearranged suits to be a violation of the personal significance of the individual case. The press of court business means that in most cases the judge must ask merely legal questions, and ignore the deeper problems of the divorce.

With respect to their feelings toward the divorce process in court, our wives grouped themselves in the following fashion:

FEELINGS OF THE WIFE TOWARD PARTICIPATION IN THE DIVORCE PROCESS

	Percent
Best thing, glad to get it over with	30
Hated idea of divorce	16
Nervous about process	14
Nervous in general	14
Worried about child	14
Did not want it	8
Never worried	7
Ambivalent	3
Other	14

N = 425

Of course, these include multiple answers. When we combine all those who stated both bad and good reactions, we obtain this distribution:

Negative only	52%
Ambivalent	8
Positive	31
Other, irrelevant	9
	100

As we see, these answers do not extract the meaning of the divorce as a finality, but they do show that for half the wives the court process or appearance was an unpleasant experience.

These feelings toward the court process do suggest to some degree how the respondents reacted to their new status as divorcees. In part, this is not entirely a "new" status, since they have experienced some elements of it through the approval or disapproval of family and friends. Nevertheless, the major area of adjustment to the new status must be the divorcee's *continuing* experiences. Let us look at two such areas: (1) social discrimination against her, and (2) postdivorce trauma.

Social Discrimination Against the Divorcee. Social isolation is difficult to achieve, even when it is desired. The divorcee must come into contact with kinfolk, neighbors, storekeepers, etc., and the divorced mother cannot keep her divorce hidden. If there is strong anti-divorce sentiment in the society, she thus runs the risk of being discriminated against. The journalistic literature on divorce reports numerous incidents in which the divorcee is treated badly, because people know that she is a divorcee. These accounts range from incidents in which the man she was dating believed that her morals were loose, because she was a divorcee, to the refusal by a priest to allow a divorcee to take confession. It is difficult to evaluate such reports. Such incidents do occur, and doubtless they occur more often in some groups than others. On the other hand, we must keep in mind that the situation of the divorced person in our society is gradually changing, and that discrimination of this kind is becoming less likely.

Moreover, some of these incidents are not related to the divorce itself. For example, much of the sexual mythology about the divorcee does not derive from the divorce itself but from the fact that (1) such a woman has definitely had sexual experience. Furthermore, (2) she is likely to be an adult, and (3) she is unattached. Even the average male makes statistical judgments about the likelihood or lack of likelihood that a given woman might be interested in sexual activity and these factors are given some weight. Of course, the divorce itself may have its effect, too: her sexual appetite may be unsatisfied, and she may wish to express her bitterness in rebellion.

It is worth remarking that somewhat the same mythology used to be widespread with respect to the widow. Since, however, such mythologies are likely to be a generation or so out of date, males in their innocence may give too much weight to the divorce, and as a consequence "discriminate" against her. Possibly the mythology is destined to disappear, simply because in our generation sexual access to adult women becomes increasingly possible, and the differentiation among the single, widowed, and divorced begins to blur.

The fact is that, when we asked our respondents, "Have you ever been in a social situation in which you felt that someone thought less of you when he or she found out that you were divorced?", 70% said "no." In general, there were very few differences between various categories of our respondents in their answers to this question. The youngest group, those *under 24* years of age at the time of interview, reported a slightly greater frequency of discrimination. In this youngest age bracket, 40% said "yes" as against 27% in the 25-29 year bracket, 30% in the 30-34 year bracket, and 23% in the 35 years and over bracket. We are rather inclined to interpret this difference as suggesting that the "social situation" in which this apparent discrimination was felt was the ordinary dating and sex situation; and that the discrimination itself was simply the male's notion that the woman might be willing to engage in sexual intercourse with him. One might turn the proposition around by saying instead that it is the youngest groups who have the *opportunity* to be discriminated against in this situation, while fewer males make the *attempt* against the older group. On the other hand, 42% of the respondents who thought there was discrimination described it in only very general terms: people "make remarks," "behave differently," "look down on you," etc.

Moreover, although those with grammar school education reported a slightly lesser frequency of discrimination (23% vs. 30% for higher education), and those who remarried earlier a slightly higher frequency (39% vs. 25% for those not remarried), these differences suggest no more than that those who have more social contacts are somewhat more likely to experience discrimination.

Trauma of Divorce—When it Occurs. The "trauma" of divorce has interested some theorists because divorce and bereavement seem to be structurally similar, and both may be traumatic experiences. Theorizing has not gone beyond the point of describing these similarities (status change, loss of spouse, economic difficulties, sexual deprivation, etc.), and suggesting that the widow unlike the divorcee obtains social support and has a well-defined role to play. One might conclude from the comparison that the divorcee may undergo more personal disorganization than the widow, or that the experience is more difficult to incorporate in one's life. Nevertheless, the biological finality of death causes a parallel social finality, and to this extent divorce is different from the death of a spouse. Moreover, the divorce is preceded by a long period of conflict whose effect is to reduce the emotional attachment between the spouses, and thereby to make the finality of the divorce less upsetting than that of bereavement. Of course, the marriage ending in divorce has no monopoly over marital conflict, but it is at least safe to guess that the average amount of conflict is (a) more frequent, and (b) more intense between divorcing spouses than between spouses whose marriage ends through death. It is likely, therefore, that the emotional attachment of divorcing spouses is less than that of spouses whose marriages end through death, and that therefore the trauma of divorce would be less. There are, moreover, certain psychodynamic processes which would accentuate the emotional hurt of death. We make explicit these fairly obvious comments, since we do not believe that a comparison between these two types of terminations to marriages is theoretically fruitful for the analysis of trauma, or even for the trauma of divorce.

Unfortunately, the term "trauma" is not adequately defined in any of these analyses of divorce. It becomes a literary term. Even the medical usage from which it originates contains some ambiguity. The term is possibly misapplied in divorce analysis, and in any event ought to be more rigorously defined if it is to be kept. It was introduced, of course, because some individuals who divorce do go through a period of deep emotional disturbance, disorganization of habits, and failure to carry out role obligations. Perhaps a few even go through a period of "emotional shock." The term might usefully be confined to only this last type of case.

However, we might instead define the term so as to *include less extreme* behavioral deviations as well. For most divorces, as we have already seen, the process of divorce conflict is a relatively slow one, in which the bitterness of the interaction serves gradually to estrange the parties from one another. They are "being divorced" for months before the decree. Divorcee habits are gradually formed, as each spouse fails to give as much emotional support, cooperation, friendship, or understanding as before. For most if not all of these cases, we can speak of unhappiness, bitterness, or perhaps a feeling of misfortune during some period, but certainly most of it is created by the conflict and the unraveling of marital habits rather than by the final divorce itself.

However, we need not specify exactly which causes the "trauma": the divorce itself or the marital conflict. Those who divorce do usually feel that they have been through an unfortunate experience. We therefore believed that if we asked them directly about the intensity of the experience we would be simply stimulating them to exaggerate the experience. On the other hand, there would be no point in using any of the standard personality diagnostic tests, such as Rorschach, TAT, etc. These are mainly useful in ascertaining basic personality structures and processes, and accepted theory is that these do not change much under the impact of the ordinary tragedies of living. Consequently, such tests would not measure the trauma of divorce.

It seemed more useful, then, to introduce the subject of unhappiness in divorce conflict, and how that affects the *actions* of those who go through it. Then we could ask, for example, "If there was some increase in smoking, was it most apparent during the period of: (a) final separation; (b) final decision; (c) first filing; (d) final divorce decree; (e) at present time; (f) never any increase?" We selected six such behavioral items which might be supposed to vary somewhat under the impact of the conflict. Thus, we have adopted as our operational definition of "high trauma-low trauma," whether or not the difficulties of any period showed up in specific behavior or (in the case of loneliness) feeling. These items lent themselves to both Guttman scaling and latent structure analysis. In particular, it was possible with the Lazarsfeld technique to substruct to an attribute space, and thus confirm our intuitive notion that these items could be viewed as rough indices of the same phenomenon, the upset caused by the final marital conflict and divorce.

Let us first see where the *concentration* of trouble seemed to occur, if at all.

BEHAVIORAL INDICES OF DIVORCE "TRAUMA"

Behavior	Final Decision	Final Separation	Filing of Decree	Final Decree	Time of Interview	Never any Increase*	Total	
Difficulty in Sleeping	16%	27%	11%	4%	4%	38%	100%	425
Poorer Health	15	26	16	5	5	33	100	425
Greater Loneliness	11	29	12	10	5	33	100	425
Low Work Efficiency	8	16	11	5	3	57	100	425
Memory Difficulties	6	11	6	3	6	68	100	425
Increased Smoking	4	11	8	3	4	70	100	425
Increased Drinking	1	5	4	3	3	84	100	425

*Includes "No Answer"

Several conclusions appear to be reasonable, on the basis of these data:

1. The so-called "divorce trauma" is not universally to be found in our cases, even though we would expect our group to have more intense problems of adjustment than divorcees without children: 37% of our respondents were "low trauma" cases.

2. Also, there appears to be *no one time period* in which there is great personal disorganization for all divorcees. Naturally, it can not be assumed that these indices of health, smoking, etc., are the only ones possible, but we would expect the textbook trauma to show up under *some* of these forms. As to the possibility that these women minimized their troubles, the interview would rather afford them such an opportunity for talking out their problems, that there would instead be some tendency to exaggerate personal suffering. The impact of divorce seems, then, not so sudden and devastating as to be labeled a "traumatic episode" in even half the cases.

3. Nevertheless, it is evident that at *some* time or another a *considerable* proportion of these cases *did* show evidence of personal difficulty: 63% were high or medium trauma respondents.

Thus, approximately two-thirds had a greater feeling of loneliness or being friendless, or had poorer health, or greater difficulty in sleeping some time during these several phases. For three of the seven items, drinking, smoking, and forgetting, the predominant majority of cases failed to show much disturbance. However, for one of these items, drinking, there is likely to be a hesitation about admitting that it did increase. For the third, forgetting, we would expect that most individuals would have some difficulty in remembering any given period as one in which forgetting was increased, unless it was very pronounced. In short, although no unequivocal and universally predictable period of personal disorganization can be asserted, there is ample evidence that for a substantial proportion of the divorcees there is disruption of personal organization at *some* period.

4. However, it is equally clear that the *period* immediately *following the final decree*—the "postdivorce" period—is *not* the point of maximum "trauma." Indeed, this period is hardly different from the point of interview, with respect to the percentage of women showing indices of disorganization (3—10% *versus* 3-6%). We showed earlier that the time from the earliest conflict to the decree itself is long, and here we see that considerable "adjustment" has apparently occurred before the decree itself. At least, the decree itself is not marked by a higher percentage of women exhibiting "trauma."

5. The point of *greatest disturbance* appears to be the time of *final separation*. Roughly one-fourth to one-third of the cases in which there was trouble, experienced this period as one of greatest disturbance, for each of the seven items. From the data already presented, this conclusion is not entirely surprising. The long period over which the marital conflict extends would suggest that the point of greatest trouble would lie somewhere between the final decision and the decree, when the divorce becomes legally a part of their lives. Our original guess was that the point of first filing would exhibit the greatest unhappiness, since it represents a kind of formal and public acknowledgment of marriage failure. In the light of our data, we see what might have been apparent at an earlier stage in our research: the filing of the suit is indeed a formal, public act, but the *public concerned* is an essentially distant, even artificial, entity called "the government." This *public is not nearly so important as the social groups within which the future divorcee is known:* her own and her husband's families, and their circles of friends. Within such groups, the fact of conflict is not hidden, and this is especially the case if the conflict continues over an extended period. However, since most couples fight occasionally, the conflict itself is no admission of marriage failure, nor is the confession that a divorce is being considered. On the other hand, *the separation is a public act for the reference groups involved,* even though it has no legal standing. Both husband and wife have to begin playing the role of divorcee to some extent, once they have broken up their common household, and the change cannot be hidden from their families and friends.

Furthermore, the physical separation, symbolic of the social one, has further consequences, in that the changes *legally expected* after the decree must *actually* begin to be made at this point. New households must be set up and patterns of visiting with friends together, eating together, shopping, etc., are necessarily changed. Sexual access to one another is decreased, or is stopped altogether. Common plans for the future become less meaningful, and the spouses begin to understand for the first time how many areas of their lives had been intertwined even within the conflict, and thus how many areas now require new decisions that formerly could be taken for granted.

In short, the final separation seems to represent the formal announcement of the impending divorce to the reference groups of the spouses, and thus has more impact upon the spouses than either the filing of the suit or the handing down of the final decree.[5]

6. Finally, although the usefulness of each item as an index varies, we note that the *"curve of trouble" seems to be parallel for all of the items:* The impact or disturbance rises from (a) the point of final decision to (b) a high point at a final separation, then (c) tapers off very gradually to the point of first filing, and (d) drops somewhat further to the point of the final decree. For five of the seven items, there is (e) a further drop to the time of interview, but this is not an unequivocal datum, since for Group I (one-fourth of our cases) the final decree and interview were separated by no more than a month or two.

It must be emphasized, of course, that for all these "time points" *chronological time* is not our reference, but *events* in the resolution of conflict. We use these particular events, because they seem to be markers in the lives of divorcees, mentioned by the divorcees as well as by the society. It is worth noting that "separation" can occur at almost any point, and thus is not necessarily in "chronological order" as are the other events. There is no simple correction for this, although in general it does occur at the chronological point where it is placed in the table.

Summary. In this chapter, we have attempted to explore the emotional meaning of separation, and in so doing we have suggested five different types of separation, as well as the major factors which seem to structure them. *When* the separation occurred among the various overt steps toward the divorce was also analyzed, and it was shown that the two main sets of factors that make for early or late separation are (a) class items, and (b) who first suggests the divorce.

The emotional consequences of divorce were also brought into focus, particularly the feelings of the wife during the court and divorce process, and her perception of social discrimination. About half reported mainly unpleasant feelings at the court process, but about 70% reported no experiences of discrimination against them as divorcees.

Finally, we began to explore the so-called divorce "trauma," and found that over three-fifths of the respondents did appear to show various kinds of personal disorganization, but that the main time of emotional impact was not the decree itself, but the final separation. Moreover, it seems that the "trauma" is not so overwhelming as to disorganize most divorcees.

In the next chapter, we continue this exploration of the divorce trauma, looking for the factors that seem to make for high or law trauma.

---

5. Perhaps it should be emphasized that often the final separation and the filing of suit occur closely together in time. This fact underlines the importance of our tabulation, since the revealed differences in the data show how differently the two occurrences are experienced.

CHAPTER XIV

FACTORS ASSOCIATED
WITH TRAUMA

AS SHOWN IN OUR structural analyses of divorce, divorcees are under many conflicting forces. "Trauma" is then not merely the result of "personality failure." In this chapter we ask which experiences and characteristics are associated with a high or low degree of trauma. The degree of trauma should, in turn, be related to different patterns of postdivorce adjustment.

As noted previously, we used the Lazarsfeld latent attribute technique, substructing to an "attribute space" that we assumed was "trauma," using as responses the answers given by respondents about the occurrence of memory loss, work inefficiency, poor health, or sleeping.[1]

Types of Factors Related to Trauma. Let us classify on a common sense basis the main sets of items or experiences that might affect degree of trauma. Our data do not yield adequate measures of all these, but in several instances approximate indices are available. They are as follows:

A. Values, predispositions, backgrounds.
   Possible measures: religion, rural-urban background, occupation, length of marriage.
B. "Objective" characteristics of the prospective divorce situation.
   Possible measures: economic problems, number and age of children, age of wife.
C. Incidents of the Conflict itself.
   Possible measures: who first suggested the divorce, vacillation in divorce decision, attitude toward divorce process, themes of conflict, length of decision process.

---

1. These calculations allow the inference that these questions do tap, or yield an index to, the same attribute space or latent dimension, and we have assumed that this characteristic measured is that of "trauma." We dropped "lonesomeness" from our calculations, since these answers did not yield a higher reproducibility. That is, the item adds very little to the reproducibility index. We shall therefore treat lonesomeness separately. The response patterns for health, sleeping, work efficiency, and memory (in that order) follow a Guttman grouping. The result of the latent distance operations was five classes along the apparent dimension or attribute of "trauma." The four items used turned out empirically to have approximately equal "weight." We then collapsed the two extreme classes at each end, so that three classes finally resulted:
   (a) "High trauma": ever having manifested at least *three* of the four responses (poorer health, sleeping, work efficiency, or memory);
   (b) "Medium trauma": ever having manifested *two* of the four;
   (c) "Low": ever having shown one or none of the four.
The average mean scale score for these three sets of response patterns was, respectively, .75, .49, and .21.

D. Objective alternatives to the marriage.
> Possible measures: social activities, whether dating before divorce, retrospective judgment as to how her life would have been without a divorce.

E. Social pressures of her group.
> Possible measures: approval—disapproval of kin and friend groups, experiences of being discriminated against, whether friends divorcing.

F. Attraction toward husband.
> Possible measures: Desire to punish husband, willingness to wipe out divorce, attitude toward his remarriage, whether still in love at time of interview.

Let us now look at each of these.

Backgrounds, Predispositions, Values. Our "measures" for this set of characteristics are less satisfactory than for any other set. Although no large social groups in this country definitely approve of divorce, some disapprove of it less than others. Respondents were not, unfortunately, asked about their more fundamental values or predispositions concerning divorce, although even that response (thus coming after the divorce itself) might not have been an adequate index to their intensity of disapproval of divorce. In any event, Catholics probably disapprove of divorce more strongly than do Protestants, and those with rural backgrounds more than those with urban backgrounds. Mainly by inference, we supposed that those with middle or higher occupational backgrounds and high school or higher education would disapprove of divorce more strongly than those with lesser education or from lower occupational backgrounds. In general, higher disapproval of divorce would lead more often to higher trauma, since the divorce is a violation of basic values.

These expectations were borne out, but the differences were smaller than we had guessed. In some instances the differences were not statistically significant. Thus, 45% of the Catholics fell into the "high trauma" group, as against 40% of the Protestants; 33% of the Catholics were "low trauma" as compared with 38% of the Protestants. We are not comparing directly their disapproval of divorce, but the apparently greater Catholic disapproval of divorce might be supposed to cause high trauma more often than would be the beliefs of the Protestants. On the other hand, the Catholic who divorces would perhaps have been originally *less strong* in her attitude against divorce, and this greater tolerance both (a) paved the way for the divorce, and (b) created less shock in her personal life. In any event, we noted earlier that the apparent Catholic tendency toward divorce (as measured by estimated divorce ratios) is not much less than the Protestant, so that perhaps great differences could not be expected.

The rural-urban comparison is similar. Exactly half of the wives from rural origins were high trauma cases, as against 40% of the urban women, and 48% of the women from small towns. When we look at the other end of our grouping (low trauma), we find that the differences are similar, but so small as to be unimportant: 29% of the women from rural origins were low trauma cases, as against 35% of the women from small towns, and 38% of the women whose origins were urban.

There are no differences by occupational class of father. By occupational class of the husband the differences are again in the expected direction, but small: 47% of the divorcees whose husbands had middle and upper class occupations were high trauma cases, as against 38% of those with lower occupational class origins; at the low trauma end of the scale were 34% of the middle and upper group, and 38% of the lower group.

As we see, the differences at *both* ends of the scale are in the expected directions. This congruence gives a higher reliability than would a comparison of mere dichotomies, but the differences are small.

They are somewhat larger for the characteristic of education. The differences are to be found, however, in the medium and low trauma classes, as against high trauma:

TRAUMA, BY EDUCATION OF RESPONDENT

| | (Degree of Trauma) | | | | |
	High	Medium	Low	Total	Number
College	43%	32%	24%	99%	37
High School	42	21	36	99	327
Grammar School	46	13	41	100	61

As is clear, there are no statistically significant differences in the percentage of cases falling into the high trauma class. The differences that do exist are definite enough, but are only between medium and low trauma. Here, too, the consistency of the differences gives a statistical basis for accepting the direction of influence—these characteristics *do* have the effect predicted—but the differences are so small that we do not believe we have tapped any important factors.

Since the previous factors would also be predictive of a longer *duration* of marriage, let us see whether duration is associated with trauma in any way. Thus we move from strictly background factors. On the other hand, a longer duration of marriage may itself be a test of the impact of such predispositional factors. In either event, the relationships are complex. We assume in a commonsense way that a long marriage ending in divorce means greater disorganization in the lives of the participants than does a short marriage. Yet it is also clear, both from common sense and some research, that long marriages may become over time more like associations between friends than love relationships. "The old shoe" is doubtless very comforting in and of itself but most of us in its later years are not crushed by its loss.

That we can reason in either direction suggests a weakness in our theorizing. Apparently the habit cage of marriage is strong, however, for a longer duration of marriage *is* associated with a greater traumatic effect of the divorce. Short marriages have the lowest percentage of high trauma cases, and the highest proportions of medium and low trauma cases.

TRAUMA, BY DURATION OF MARRIAGE

| Duration of Marriage | (Degree of Trauma) | | | | |
	High	Medium	Low	Total	Number
0- 4 years	29%	26%	45%	100%	72
5- 9 years	42	21	37	100	168
10-14 years	48	20	31	99	130
15 and over	47	15	38	100	55
Totals	42	21	37	100	N = 425

However, a longer duration of marriage is not only created by many background factors, such as religion, class, or rural-urban backgrounds. The length of the marriage in turn *creates* other associations: the spouses become older, and thus longer marriages usually have older spouses in them. The number of children is likely to be (at least curvilineally) higher; the accumulation of property is likely to be greater, etc. In the next section, therefore, we shall see whether this apparent relationship continues to hold when we remove the effect of these other factors.

Objective Elements of the Situation. If a longer duration of marriage is associated with high trauma, then it may be asked whether this apparent association does not *hide* the effect of still other factors that normally are themselves associated with duration of marriage. For example, the age of the respondent is also associated with a higher degree of trauma. As the following table shows clearly, with each increase in age the proportion falling into the high trauma class also *increases,* while the percentage falling into the low trauma class *decreases.*

TRAUMA BY AGE OF RESPONDENT

| Age of Respondent | Degree of Trauma | | | Total | Number |
	High	Medium	Low		
20-24 years	31%	23%	46%	100%	71
25-29 years	38	18	44	100	147
30-34 years	48	24	28	100	120
35 and over	52	20	28	100	87

N = 425

At the same time, however, the percentage of *high* trauma cases is also *higher* for respondents *having two or more children* than for respondents having only one child: 48% versus 36%. At the other end of this scale the relationship is reversed: 32% of those with two or more children fall into the low trauma class, as against 43% of those with only one child.[2] We cannot here reproduce the partial association tables, but we may summarize the relationship between these characteristics as follows: Age does play an important factor, but its effect is masked or overridden by other factors at times: for example, (a) when people are young it seems *not* to be much more traumatic to be divorced with (1) two or more children than to be divorced with (2) only one child. However, in general, (b) having two or more children *is* associated

2. A further comment must be made here. Although we have been somewhat disappointed that sharper differences did not emerge, it is, on the other hand, true that for such a period of time as we are analyzing, some of these "difficulties" are the normal experiences of living for all of us over any comparably long period. Thus, it is possible that not all of these so-called difficulties can be ascribed to divorce or marital conflict. As a consequence, *the differences* between one segment of the population and another may be relatively small, when the cross-tabulating characteristics are those we have used here. Actually we do not have a genuine comparison group. It is one of the points in the study at which it might be useful to have data for the general population as a basis for comparison.

Furthermore, several steps are necessary in order to get even these comparisons: (a) Some but not all respondents *had* such traumatic difficulties, or experienced the difficulties that we are using as indexes to trauma; (b) Some but not all of these would be *aware* that they were experiencing such difficulties, since they may have been preoccupied with other matters; (c) Some but not all of these would *remember* that there were such difficulties; and (d) of course, not all of these would in turn necessarily *report* accurately what had happened. Indeed there may be some pride in maintaining that there were no real difficulties. These steps or phases might tend to reduce, or even enhance, the differences between various sub-groups such as class, age, etc.

with a higher trauma index. And (c) when there is *only one child, age is not* closely associated particularly with a higher trauma index, but (d) when there are two or more children, more wives at the *higher* ages do exhibit a high trauma index.

Perhaps a still more interesting pattern may be seen in the fact that (e) for *younger* people there *is* an association between a long marriage and a higher trauma index. However, (f) for *older* people this pattern is reversed; a long marriage seems to be less traumatic. Our only solution for this complexity at the moment is the possibility that in the case of older people the marriage has itself become somewhat stale and there are relatively few attractions in it for them. On the other hand, (g) when the *marriage* is a *short* one, there is little association between age and trauma.

We had supposed that we would find a negative association between the *length of time* given to the conflict process and the index of trauma. Those who took a long time to come to a decision and to take definite action toward getting a divorce might have thereby had enough time to become adjusted to the difficulties of the divorcing process, and thus to have absorbed the experience in their lives without much disorganization. Actually, however, there is relatively little association between these two factors. For example, of those who took *less than one month* between their first serious consideration of a divorce to the time of filing the suit, 46% fell into the high trauma group, exactly the same percentage of high trauma individuals as was found in the group who took *more than two years* between serious consideration and the actual filing of the suit. This might lead us to a guess that in general those people divorce fast *who are able to do so,* that is to say, the adjustments that have gone on in their lives *allow* them to move relatively quickly, and at the same time prevent them from feeling much disorganization.

This interpretation is not destroyed by an apparently contradictory set of facts: when we narrow our focus somewhat and look at only the period from *final decision to filing the suit,* those who took less than one month are more likely to be found in the high trauma class than those who took more than one month for this process. Similarly a *higher* percentage (39%) of those who took *more than one month* are to be found in the *low* trauma group than of those who took less than one month (32%). On the other hand, these "quick actors" were not acting quickly because *they* were ready to divorce. These women were most likely to have husbands who had simply "announced" a divorce decision. Consequently, although the wives acted quickly, they were not prepared. There was, then, little or no time given to consideration, so that these facts are not contradictory to those in the previous paragraph, stating that the length of time from *serious consideration* to filing suit is not associated with trauma.

Incidents of the Conflict. Thus, as we suspected from commonsense considerations and from our previous data, *who* first suggests the divorce is important for the intensity of the trauma. Apparently the *least* trauma pattern occurs when the wife reports that the suggestion was first made mutually. When the wife made the first suggestion, the proportion falling into the high trauma group is somewhat higher, and when the husband made the first suggestion the percentage is still higher. This we may see in the following table.

TRAUMA, BY WHO FIRST SUGGESTED DIVORCE

| Who first suggested | Trauma Index | | | | |
	High	Medium	Low	Total	Number
Mutual	37%	20%	43%	100%	56
Wife	41	21	38	100	264
Husband	49	22	29	100	105

One element in the complex association between the length of the conflict process and trauma seems to be whether the wife has adjusted somewhat to the idea of divorce, in commonsense terms is "ready" for the divorce. This *readiness* might be of more importance than the length of time involved, and indeed this readiness may often *determine* the length of time given to this conflict process. This suggestion is borne out in part by the association between a lack of decisiveness, or vacillation of decision to divorce, and the degree of trauma. We see in the following table that when the respondent reports that there were frequent occasions when they decided *not* to carry out the decision to divorce, the trauma index was likely to be higher. Correspondingly when the respondent reported that there *never* was such an occasion, the proportion having a *low* trauma index was greater.

TRAUMA, BY STEADINESS OF DECISION TO DIVORCE

| Frequency of Decision Not to Divorce | Trauma Index | | | | |
	High	Medium	Low	Total	Number
Frequently	65%	15%	20%	100%	39
Occasionally	44	24	32	100	102
Never	38	21	41	100	279

When the decision to divorce is not steady, then it seems likely that there are factors involved which make either the marriage itself somewhat *more attractive,* or the alternatives to marriage somewhat *less appealing.* Perhaps these factors increase trauma, too.

We do not find any systematic relationship between the themes of conflict and the trauma index. There are, of course, some obvious connections, but few that are orderly. This seems to be due in part to the fact that themes themselves cannot be viewed as precipitants in any strict sense; they may rather be the tone and coloring of much of the married life. Moreover, they overlap concretely. Consequently, there are few clear-cut associations of a single theme with degree of trauma. For one or two of the themes there are rather clear connections. The class of themes with the highest proportion of high trauma cases (54%) is, of course, what we have called the Triangle. Next is the complaint that there was no Home Life, 49% showing a high trauma index. Following that is what we called the Complex (47%); this is the "drinking and helling around" pattern. A theme with a low proportion of high trauma cases (34%) on the other hand is the complaint of Nonsupport. This, of course, we would expect from our previous discussion, since Nonsupport is a theme used when the marriage has deteriorated over the years. In general, a role failure of this type is one which does not create trauma for the woman, though of course it creates great inconvenience. By the time divorce has become a reality, the woman has long since reorganized her life around other requirements of economics, space, and time, and the marriage itself may be said to have ceased long before the decree. The other themes fall in between these extremes, with little variation among them in the amount of trauma they seem to cause.

As a partial internal test of our index of trauma as well as of our question relating to the actual experience of the divorce process, particularly the time of court appearance, it is worth noting that the highest proportion of high trauma cases is to be found in the group who claim they were "ambivalent" toward divorce, i.e., felt torn internally about it. At the other end are those who claim that they never worried about the matter, that it was the best thing that could happen, or that they were glad to get it over with. These differences are summed in the following table, showing the relationship between trauma and attitudes toward the divorce and the divorce process.

TRAUMA, BY ATTITUDES TOWARD DIVORCE AND DIVORCE PROCESS

Attitude	High	Medium	Low	Totals	
Ambivalent	64%	17%	19%	100%	36
Negative	47	24	29	100	221
Positive	30	19	51	100	129
Other, Irrelev., D. K.	36	15	49	100	39

Alternatives. Since the period we are talking about is toward the end of the marriage and the beginning of the immediate postdivorce phase, not many of our respondents could be said to have available and waiting another potential husband. Only about 10%, for example, admitted that they were in love with another man prior to the divorce. On the other hand, all of these people did have the problem of adjusting their social lives to the absence of a husband, and we therefore asked them how they filled this gap. As we expected, some of them (32%) were already dating or began dating at this period, even before the divorce decree. We shall later show the relationship between these and other social activities as they lead to a new marriage. For the moment we are only concerned with the relationship between such social activities and the degree of trauma experienced by the wife. In general we find that those activities which were most likely to help in finding new friends, and finding eligible men (thus leading ultimately to remarriage), are also associated with a *low* proportion of *high* trauma cases. Alternatively, the kinds of social activities that apparently did not lead in these directions were more likely to be engaged in by women with a *higher* proportion of *high* trauma.

Thus, women who "fill this social gap" with women's club activities (48%) or who did nothing at all (9%) or who filled the gap with church activities (11%) were more likely to be high trauma cases: 47% of those who mostly engaged in women's club activities, 47% of those who did nothing, and 49% of those who mainly engaged in church-going were also high trauma cases. At the other end of this grouping are to be found (a) those who had *already* been dating, (b) the one-third who went to movies alone, and (c) those who began dating at this time: 36%, 37%, and 43% were high trauma cases.

It is not easy to interpret the "movies alone" category. We are inclined to be somewhat cynical about this response. We believe in general these were women who had adjusted somewhat to separation from their husbands and who were at least passively open to flirtations and new relationships with men. That is, this response does not mean that all these women were going alone to the movies in some despair, in order to obtain private solace. Doubtless, there were some cases of this kind. On the other hand, since all of these women did have children there were many other activities that could have engaged their attention: 43% claimed that they gave greater attention to their children. Since their husbands no longer were there to help, or to distract the attention of these wives by fighting, it seems likely that they actually did give greater attention to their children. By contrast, going to the movies is an excuse for getting out of the house, and it at least opens the door to possible meetings with other men, particularly meetings which would not be under the surveillance of one's friends or family. In general, then, we interpret this response as meaning that these women were to a considerable extent ready for the divorce, and were also ready for an alternative to their ex-husband. On the other hand, it does not *assure* new social relationships.

There is another sense in which we can speak of "alternatives." We asked our respondents what would have been their situation if there had been no divorce at all. Some answers showed concern about the child's welfare, or expressed the wife's unhappiness. Most of these answers suggested that things would have been very bad indeed had there not been a divorce. However, some did think that their situation would have been better had there not been a divorce; and there are certain differences even in the remaining categories. These differences may be seen in the following table:

TRAUMA BY ANSWERS TO QUESTION, "HOW WOULD THINGS HAVE BEEN
IF YOU HAD NOT GOT A DIVORCE?"

	Trauma Index				
If no Divorce?	High	Medium	Low	Total	Number
Better financially	66%	17%	17%	100%	18
Better generally	57	18	25	100	28
Health worse	53	23	24	100	99
Better for child	50	18	32	100	22
Worse for child	43	22	35	100	103
Respondent unhappy	41	23	36	100	129
Other, D. K.	41	14	45	100	22
Same as before	40	19	41	100	109
Worse financially	37	20	43	100	111

Although in general this table is self-explanatory, one or two comments are in order. First, it is to be noted that when the respondent believed that *finances* would have been *better without* the divorce, the percentage of high trauma cases is highest, 66%. At the other extreme are those who said that things would have been *worse financially* if there had not been a divorce; only 37% were high trauma cases. Whether these two comments may be interpreted as materialistically as seems apparent we cannot say. (Certainly some of those whose finances are *now* better were desertion and support cases, so that the period of adjustment prior to divorce was long). It is also to be noted that 53% of those who thought that without the divorce their *health* would be much worse also fall into the high trauma group. These respondents thought that it was better to have got the divorce, but their situation during the marriage conflict was so unpleasant for their mental and physical health that the period was experienced as one of trauma (in our limited sense).

Finally, about one-fourth of our respondents stated that things would be "the same as before" if there had been no divorce. This group has an average proportion (40%) of high trauma respondents. Apparently these women believed that nothing would have been changed if there had been no divorce, that is, the situation would not have been improved. On the other hand, they did not experience that period as one of great personal failure. By the time of our interview they had thrust the experience and the situation into the category of things which cannot be changed, but can only be accepted as bad. Since they had a chance to leave the situation, they did so, and their very acceptance of its unchangeable reality is an index of their own internal resistance to it.

Social Pressures in Various Groups. The divorcing woman might be predicted to experience less trauma if she has a considerable amount of social support from her kin and friends. In the traditional comparisons between the trauma of bereavement and the trauma of divorce, this social support given by the relatives and friends of the bereaved spouse is alleged to allow her (or him) to continue to play the necessary roles, to carry out ordinary obligations, in short to hold on to his or her personal organization. It is, then, generally supposed that such support would reduce the amount of trauma in both situations of bereavement and divorce. However, the reasoning that leads to this hypothesis may lead to an alternative formulation: that the *amount of social support* given in any case of predicted trauma is in part a function of the groups' *judgment as to how much support is actually necessary*. To use an older comparison, if the bereaved spouse has been separated long from her or his spouse for a long period before the death, if the surviving spouse shows clearly that only a modicum of social support is necessary to see that ordinary role obligations are fulfilled, then we would suppose that in general much less support will be given by kinfolk and friends.

Corresponding changes in our predictions about social support and divorce trauma are in order. Unfortunately, we cannot yet *specify in advance* who will or will not support the spouse. A further complexity is introduced by the fact that "support" may have two major emphases: (a) it may mean that the relatives or friendship groups actively believe the spouse in question is *morally right* and has conducted herself properly and therefore deserves support; (b) it may simply mean that the group feels that the decision to divorce was *rationally correct* in view of the difficulties of the marriage. Unfortunately the importance of this distinction was not seen until it was too late. Consequently we have only the data as to the "general approval or disapproval of the divorce," and there is an inherent ambiguity in the answers that suggests caution in interpretation. Even so, whether or not there is definite affect is of real significance.

A simple corollary of the distinctions mentioned in the previous paragraph is that when there is high approval or disapproval then we may suppose that the difficulties of the marriage, *or* the involvement of kin and friends in the conflict, are likely to be great. This general notion was examined in our first presentation of data concerning approval and disapproval of the divorce.

Consequently, the *most favorable situation for low trauma is one in which the major reference groups are viewed by the respondent as being relatively indifferent to the divorce.* (40-50% are then low trauma cases.)

Correspondingly, when they definitely disapprove *or* approve the divorce the respondent is likely to have a higher trauma index. Finally, the highest proportion of high trauma cases is to be found when these various groups actively *disapprove* of the divorce. Then, over half are high trauma cases. There is high consistency in these patterns for all the major groups. In general, when the *husband's* family disapproves the divorce this should mean that they disapprove at least partially of the wife's behavior and her decision. Alternatively we have supposed (and it must be emphasized that we do not have supporting data for our interpretation) that when the *wife's family* disapproves the divorce they rather disapprove the former husband's behavior *and* the situation as it has developed. We summarize these patterns in the succeeding table.

TRAUMA EXPERIENCED, BY ATTITUDES OF VARIOUS GROUPS TOWARD THE DIVORCE

Attitudes to Divorce	TRAUMA INDEX				
	High	Medium	Low	Total	Number
Husband's Family:					
Disapproval	54%	21%	25%	100%	143
Approval	41	21	38	100	144
Indifference	32	20	48	100	138
Wife's Family:					
Disapproval	52	20	28	100	87
Approval	41	21	38	100	256
Indifference	35	23	42	100	82
Husband's Friends:					
Disapproval	57	22	21	100	76
Approval	47	21	32	100	111
Indifference	36	20	44	100	238
Wife's Friends:					
Disapproval	52	29	19	100	48
Approval	44	21	35	100	253
Indifference	34	18	48	100	124

It might thought that there is some association between the reported experience of discrimination and the trauma index. That is, those who experience trauma to a considerable degree might be more sensitive to slight and rebuffs, and might ascribe them more frequently to their status as divorcee. Reciprocally, the rebuff or slight might itself be one of the experiences that create a feeling of trauma. This association, whatever the casual direction, was indeed found. 50% of those who reported *some* situation of discrimination were high trauma respondents as against approximately 38% of those who claimed that they had met with *no* such discrimination.

Another type of social support might also be found by the respondent. She might find relatively little support in her *existing* social groups, but might actively seek the friendship of *others who are divorcees.* Alternatively, she might feel a lesser degree of trauma if her circle of friends already included some friends who were divorced or divorcing. With reference to the first hypothesis, that divorcees *choose* friends who are divorced or divorcing, the proportion of such cases is, as we shall show later, much less than one might suppose from reading the classical qualitative accounts of this process. Apparently few people drift to other friends who are inclined to divorce, or who might be considered "lesser in quality" than existing friends.

The second hypothesis, that there is some relationship between having friends who are divorced or divorcing, and a lower trauma index, finds slight support in our data, and the relationship is statistically *not* significant: 35% of those who had "some friends" who were divorced or divorcing were found in the high trauma group as against 46% of those who had *no* friends in these categories. A similar relationship is found at the other tail of this scale: 44% of those in the "some" category are low trauma respondents as against 31% of those who had *no* friends divorced or divorcing. The differences are not great and seem relatively unimportant, even though they are in the direction postulated.

Trauma and Emotional Involvement with the Ex-Husband. We would suppose, of course, that if the ex-wife is still in love with her former husband after divorce, then the emotional loss would be expressed in various ways and that some of these ways would be the forms of disorganization we are here using, such as memory loss, lowered work efficiency, and so on. At the same time, a particularly difficult conflict period ending in divorce might lead to a great amount of dislike or even hate on the part of the wife toward her husband. Then, the varied conflict which *led* to the divorce and created the feeling of dislike *would also be* essentially a traumatic experience. The trauma would not be caused only by having lost a beloved husband. It might also be an *effect of the same conflict and difficulties that led to the divorce and the hatred*.

As a consequence, a wife with a strong or even relatively mild emotional attachment to her former husband would feel a sense of loss, and go through some type of trauma (in our limited sense). Also, wives who still *disliked* their husbands after the divorce would have a higher trauma index. We do not believe that in the present state of theory it is possible to specify just which degree of love or hate leads to which degree of trauma. Present theory cannot even settle the question as to which of the two, love or hate, should be most traumatic in the divorce period.

For our limited descriptive facts in the following table, the time reference is the period of interview. We are then relating the *residual* emotional involvement with the husband to the *prior* experience of trauma. We do not have data on how much the wife loved the husband before the divorce.

TRAUMA INDEX, BY (POSTDIVORCE) ATTITUDE TOWARD EX-HUSBAND

Attitude toward Ex-Husband (time of interview)	High	Medium	Low	Total	Number
Positive	51%	29%	20%	100%	106
Negative	44	18	38	100	131
Friendly or Indifferent	36	18	46	100	187

As is seen, those who were positively emotionally involved with their husbands after the divorce were not only more likely to have a high trauma index. Among them were also a higher proportion of medium trauma cases.

Here we have combined the two categories, "friendly but not in love," with "indifferent." Later on, we shall separate them. We cannot, however, separate what we believe are *two* dimensions in this "indifference" response. These are: (a) the relative indifference to the husband which *comes* from having gone through an adjustmental period prior to the divorce, so that the divorce itself and the difficulties relating to it were not felt to be very traumatic. That is, the respondent was then "ready for the divorce." (b) In some cases, however, it is simply true that the *conflict with the husband was not* harrowing or emotionally trying whether or not the wife herself was adjusted to the idea of divorce. That is to say, the stress was not great, and therefore there was little trauma. The former dimension refers to an indifference that was prior to the divorce, and was a defense against the stress. We cannot disassociate these two major elements at the present time.

When we tabulate the index of trauma by the wife's willingness to punish her ex-husband *at the time of the divorce,* a higher proportion of the high trauma women were "frequently" willing to punish their husbands at the time of divorce, than of low trauma divorcees (34% *vs.* 23%). Correspondingly, 64% of the low trauma women *never* wished to punish their ex-husbands at the time of divorce, as against 45% of the high trauma divorcees. Somewhat similar results are obtained when we ask our respondents whether they are now willing to punish their ex-husbands. Both of these questions were, of course, designed to ascertain whether the experience in the conflict process was so difficult as to leave a desire to punish the husband for his behavior. We had initially thought that the desire to hurt or punish the former husband would decline with time (as it did slightly) and would thus furnish a measure of adjustment of the wife. Actually, only slightly more than one-fourth of all respondents admitted that they "frequently wanted to punish their ex-husbands at the time of divorce," and thus the reduction in proportion is not so great as we had originally expected. Nevertheless, trauma *is* associated somewhat with this desire to punish. Naturally, it is not the trauma which creates this desire, but the experience of the divorce conflict which (a) made the conflict itself traumatic for the respondent and also (b) made her willing to punish her former husband. However, we shall analyze later and more fully the postdivorce relations of the wife to her former husband.

One is almost led to the conclusion that the "return to normalcy" of the divorcee has occurred only when she can look at her ex-spouse and her former life with *indifference.* It seems clear from various data that "indifference" is usually associated with an easier transition. We have already noted the complexities in the interpretation of this datum. At this point we merely note the association once more. When we asked the wife what her attitude *would be* toward his remarrying, or what it *was* toward his remarriage, there was a strong association between indifference towards this event and a low trauma index. More specifically, when she was definitely unhappy at this prospect or had experienced the event with unhappiness, she was most likely to have a high trauma index, while her claim that she was quite happy at this turn of events fell between unhappiness and indifference in its association with trauma. Again the indifference has the double dimension of expressing a relatively easy conflict period *or* a real readiness to leave the marriage. We cannot tease out the contribution of these two elements to the total association.

WIFE'S TRAUMA, BY HER ATTITUDE TOWARD HIS REMARRIAGE OR HIS REMARRYING

Attitude to His Remarriage or Remarriage	Trauma Index			
	High	Medium	Low	Totals
Unhappy	53%	27%	20%	100% (93)
Happy	45	21	34	100 (123)
Indifferent	36	18	46	100 (209)
Total	42%	21%	37%	100%

N = 425

Q of association between indifference and low trauma = +.35

Of course, an extreme question was the query whether the wife was "willing to wipe out the divorce." Since the proportion of women who were willing to do this was so small (12%), we could not make detailed comparisons. It is worthwhile noting, however, that 80% of those who answered "yes" to this question were either high (54%) or medium (26%) trauma respondents.

Summary. We have attempted in this chapter section to analyze the association of trauma with other characteristics of the divorcee's life. In general most of the associations are as one might expect. It is nevertheless of some utility to ascertain that our expectations were correct. In addition it is useful to have some specification of the *degree of trauma,* when cross-tabulated by various characteristics, so that we have a more definite notion of the *degree* of difference between the impact of various factors. It is also clear that several of the factors that we had supposed to be of great importance are only of fair importance. That is to say, the differences appear in the *direction* expected, but the differences are not great.

It also seems likely that readiness to divorce may lead to a quicker implementation of the divorce action, and to somewhat less group support, so that speed of implementation and low support need not be associated with high trauma. Who first suggested the divorce, the judgment about what might have happened if there had not been a divorce, and the postdivorce emotional involvement with the ex-husband, seem to be closely related to trauma.

Since the data on trauma suggest that the final separation itself is the major line of emotional and social demarcation between "predivorce" and "postdivorce," we have in the previous two chapters explored the emotional meaning of separation, and the factors associated with a more or less intense emotional hurt. During this phase, then, and in many cases much earlier, the divorcee is "being divorced." We have throughout emphasized the importance of the institutional structure in shaping those experiences. Let us in the next chapter analyze further the quasi-institutional structures that force adjustment upon the divorcee.

CHAPTER XV

THE INSTITUTIONALIZATION OF POSTDIVORCE ADJUSTMENT

WE MAY COMMENT on postdivorce adjustment with an old phrase, by saying that it is not the impact of tragedy that is surprising, but the deadly insistence with which the old, habitual round continues to make its demands afterwards. The death of Antinöus caused Hadrian to weep, and to vow and decree that his cities should weep, but the life of those cities went on. A poet is indignant that the sun and moon do not darken at his sweetheart's death, that people chaff and barter in unconcern, but an old network of habits soon draws him into the same conversations with the same friends about the same subjects, between similar meals and patterns of repose.

Perhaps this truism might be changed slightly, to take note of the fact that others *expect* the participant in tragedy to modify his life, while the participant himself learns with some surprise that such a modification is more difficult than anticipated. Indeed, their expectation is embodied in constant pressures to force the participant to continue his former habits, or to start new ones only on the foundations of the old. Social scientists have analyzed the customs of bereavement in these terms, noting that the kinfolk rally to the bereaved, offering material and emotional support during a period of disorganization. At the same time, these kin are pushing the bereaved into the specified rituals of burial accepted by the group, and also toward a resumption (with group support) of old obligations and habits. That is, their actions embody an assumption that the bereaved *would* change much of his life if they did not help.

Divorce occupies a very particular place among the predictable tragedies of living. Of the participants, only the children may make *moral* demands on the extended kin. The adults may in fact make particular demands on their kin, but the grounds are likely to be those of friendship, or the claim that they were sinned against, not the grounds of moral right. Further, this particular tragedy is viewed as the willed result of a definite decision by the participants. They have violated a civil contract to remain together, broken a moral compact of monogamy, and assailed the myth that the romantic love of marriage must continue throughout life. If, in addition, there are children of the marriage, the parents have (in cold blood, anger, or desperation) decided to destroy their prospect of a permanent home. This the parents have done with the merely selfish aim of personal happiness, or the avoidance of unhappiness. The tragedy is, then, one they have wished on themselves.

We have just analyzed in detail certain aspects of this tragedy, the emotional impact of the final marital dissolution. However, this dissolution does not end the drama. These actors must go on living. We are then interested in the further pressures which shape their continuing decisions. They have been reared in a particular institutional structure, and continue to live in it, even though it makes little specific room for these deviants from the norm. How, then, does it shape their further action?

Meaning of Institutionalization. We have already uncovered many regularities in what might seem a most personal and individual form of behavior, the dissolution of marriage and its aftermath. As we unfold still further patterns in postdivorce behavior, we must ask whether we may speak of "postdivorce institutions." In our first chapter, we analyzed in some detail the proposition that contemporary American kinship institutions fail to define the proper behavior for the divorcee, male or female. That is, we think of institutions as made of interlocking systems of role obligations and rights. But just what the divorcee ought to do, or may demand, in the familial area of action is not specified. We noted also the importance of these institutional gaps for the behavioral and emotional responses of the divorcee in the new situation. Lacking such prescriptions, many participants in marital dissolutions could be expected to undergo considerable personal disorganization. Since the divorced mother appears to face more problems of this type, she might exhibit an even greater amount of personal disorganization than would other divorcees. Although we could not, with our data, make such a comparison, we did analyze at length the emotional impact of the final marital dissolution.

In many societies there are institutional arrangements to take care of the various problems which necessarily arise when a family nucleus disintegrates. Now, in our own, with a steadily high divorce rate, there may be a process of institutionalization going on: such institutions *are growing*. But what kinds of measures are adequate to ascertain just when an institution can be said to exist, or to be in the process of growth?

Space does not permit a full theoretical exposition of this problem, and definitions of institutions are in any event currently undergoing reanalysis.[1] Nevertheless, we have attempted throughout this study to view divorce and adjustment to it in their institutional framework, and should therefore devote some comment to the points at which we can say that postdivorce patterns are institutionalized. In order to ascertain these points, we should present our own view of this broad matter.

1. First, the social institutions are the structures by which the needs or requirements of any society (e.g., production, distribution, creation of the

---

1. See, for example, Talcott Parsons, *The Social System* (Glencoe, Ill.: The Free Press, 1949), pp. 36 *et passin;* and S. F. Nadel, *The Foundations of Social Anthropology* (Glencoe, Ill.: The Free Press, 1953), Ch. VI.

next generation, etc.) are met, in that the institutions specify the role obligations of the individual. These are immediately required of the individual; the larger structural requisites for the maintenance of the society are not. The institutions translate these broader needs into actional requirements for the member of the group or society.

2. To the extent that the institutions serve these needs, a much more fundamental societal requirement is met, the creation of common patterns or regularities in the behavior of the individuals in the society. There must be a considerable integration—we do not know how much—of this behavior, unless there is to be a great loss in time, energy, materials, etc. This is of course true not alone for human social groups, but for all animal social groupings. Human groups, however, meet this need through the social structures known as institutions. It is characteristic of institutions, then, that they not only *are* regularities; they also help to *create other* regularities.

3. Institutions are thus complex, interlocking structures or sets of role obligations and rights. These are not usually, or even often, mutual; what the father owes to the child is not what the child owes to the father. What each has the moral right to expect is not what the other may expect. They are, however, complementary and interlocking; they consistently specify the other's behavior. What *one* may morally *expect* is what the *other owes*. Thus, institutions or parts of institutions (such as father-child statuses and roles) have the further characteristics that they are backed by *moral sentiment*.

4. The moral sentiments backing these behavioral patterns *vary in intensity*. Some actions are only permitted; others are simply preferred. Still others may be proscribed, or prescribed. There is thus both prohibition and injunction, of varying intensity.

5. Institutions are, within the view now being presented, *both* ideal and action, comment and behavior, aspiration and fulfillment. The institutional demands are not mere formulas. If there is deviation, there is also punishment, of various types and intensities. And there are also rewards for conformity.

6. But if there are deviations, or varying degrees of meeting these role demands, then we must view an institutional pattern in *statistical* terms. All norms are violated at times, and all of us violate certain of the milder norms at times. We do not know, either theoretically or by test, how high a frequency of violation a given pattern will bear, before it is converted with a change of ideal into a different institutional pattern. According to our present view, however, the statistical distribution of action and ideal does tell us at what point the *pressures against deviation* will be found, i.e., how far from the ideal one may stray without being punished; as well as at what point along the distribution one might be rewarded.

7. Necessarily, socialization in any society, whether it is the socialization of children or of adults, focuses on inculcating both the action and emotion required in particular role sets.

8. Although we are most accustomed to thinking of the larger, embracing institutions such as kinship and religion, various *sub-groups* within a society will *also* have institutional patterns. Some of these, such as criminal gangs, or ethnic or regional sub-groups, may possess institutions, i.e., interlocking

role patterns, that are in conflict with those of the enclosing, larger society. Similarly, there may be very specific role sets within a larger institution, such as those of a religious order.

9. A structural requirement of any system of interlocking role sets is that there is a "third party" to any particular set. Thus, the institutions of property center about any object, (a) claimed by one person, as against (b) the actual or possible claims of one or more other persons, but between these claims or potential claims is (c) the society as a third party, supporting one or the other. Similarly, the role set of husband and wife in the kinship institutions implicitly includes the society as interested party. Consequently, the marriage "contract" is *never* a pure contract between spouses in *any* society. Now, the structural, consequence of this fact, and of our previous assertion, is that *just which is the third party will vary* according to which institutional pattern we look at, according to which larger or embracing group or sub-group we study. In some marital institutions, for example, the *families* of both spouses, rather than the *larger society,* make up this third party (or fourth, if we separate the two families). In analyzing any institutional pattern, then, we must explicitly or implicitly also locate and study this third party.

10. Finally, we are usually analyzing concrete behavior patterns in sociology, rather than abstractly isolable variables and attributes. This means that we find regularities whose order and pattern is not entirely, or even mainly, and immediately due to institutional definitions, but due (a) primarily and immediately to other structuring elements in the society, or (b) *indirectly* to still other institutional pressures. That is, the social items and elements that are somehow "given" also structure other patterns indirectly, by making deviation difficult and inconvenient. This is not, of course, a new insight. Marx was not expressing a kindly bias toward the 19th Century capitalist when he noted that the entrepreneur was caught in the demands of the capitalist economic structure, which gave him only two alternatives: systematic and rational exploitation of labor; or going bankrupt. Similarly, we cannot assert that many of our modern suburban and commutation patterns are supported directly by institutional sanctions. Nevertheless, within the framework of existing work patterns, the ideals of "country" living, bridge and train connections, and so on, it may be difficult for the individual suburbanite to work out a pattern of going to work that is greatly different from those of his fellow commuters. Small, cumulative *indirect institutional pressures may create as much regularity* as larger, direct institutional definitions; and the latter always require the former for effective pressures on members of the society.

Institutional Factors in the Divorcee "Status." When we assert that the divorcee status is ambiguous and relatively noninstitutionalized, we do not mean, therefore, that it is unpatterned or unstructured. We have, indeed, already analyzed some of these structuring factors. It was one of our assertions above, that social behavior *must* be integrated with reference to time, space, energy, materials, and so on, if the society is to continue. We ask, then, what kinds of institutional patterns and pressures (indirect or direct) must exist, if a high divorce rate is to continue without creating major disruptive forces in the society? We cannot answer this question in such general terms, but we can begin to answer it for our own society.[2] We must also leave aside just how high, under any conceivable postdivorce institutional arrangements, the divorce rate could become without disrupting the kinship institutions.[3] We are only asking what are the institutional patterns, whether we call them quasi-institutions or indirect institutions, that serve to minimize the disruption stemming from a failure to define clearly the role of the divorcee. We have noted these institutional gaps in detail, but we do not believe that our high rate of divorce creates great *societal* disorganization. That it creates considerable personal disorganization we have already documented. Is it, then, possible, that there are various structuring factors which serve to keep the kinship institutions functioning in our society, even with a high divorce rate and a failure to define appropriate role behavior for the divorcee?

We start with the fundamental fact that there is at least *apparent* structuring. *There is a great regularity in the behavior pattern of most divorcees: they are reassimilated to the status of "married."* Indeed, their remarriage rate is even higher than the marriage rate for single people in the ages beginning with the late twenties. Apparently about 94% of women divorcing at age 30 will eventually remarry.[4] Although we cannot give so precise a figure for our own sample, since we did not follow them over a period of years, 54% of these divorced mothers aged 20-38 at the time of the divorce had remarried in our Time Group IV (interviewed 26 months after the divorce), and 50% of the rest have a steady date. Moreover, as we shall note later, the "rate" of remarriage actually seems to be higher when there are more rather than fewer children. And, for reasons we shall present in this chapter, we are rather convinced that the remarriage rate of divorced mothers is not much lower than that of female divorcees generally.

Much of our analysis of kinship institutions documents the structural importance of children. The theoretical notions underlying this focus are to be found in the existing literature on the family.[5] The nub of these considerations is that the focus of kinship institutions is the status and care of the child, specifically, the procreation, maintenance, status placement, and socialization of the child. The infrequency of generalized sexual chastity as an ideal demonstrates that kinship institutions do not have the "control of sex" as their primary function. Most prohibitions and injunctions that deal with the spouses *also* serve to define the proper care of the child, and to fix responsibility for such tasks. Finally, it is an obvious theoretical proposition, and not a paradox, that this *apparent* concentration on the child must be interpreted as a *real* concentration on the *adult world:* It is by fixing the place, role, tasks, destiny, and relationships of the child, that such matters are also determined for the adults, who are connected by the biological and social fact of the child. It is *because* the child creates these connections of responsibility—role obligations and rights, i.e., institutional relationships—between adults, and families of

2. Of course, many contemporary analysts do maintain that our high divorce rate does create major disruptive forces in the society.

3. Kingsley Davis, "Statistical Perspective on Marriage and Divorce," *Annals,* 272 (1950), 9-21, asserts that our divorce rate will not continue to rise, but will level off.

4. *Statistical Bulletin,* 26, No. 5 (1945), 1-3.

5. For a particularly good, succinct presentation of this position, see Kingsley Davis, *Human Society* (New York: Macmillan, 1949), Ch. 15.

adults, that the kinship institutions concentrate upon the child. Consequently, our concentration on the "indirect postdivorce institutions" that relate the child to the parents is not due to our having only divorced mothers in our study; it is due to the great theoretical importance of these relationships in any analysis of kinship institutions.

In our own society the structural disruptions created by a high divorce rate without *explicit* postdivorce institutions are accentuated by (1) the fairly general disapproval of divorce, particularly when children are involved; and (2) the perhaps increasing structural importance of the nuclear family as the primary kinship unit, that is, the family composed of parents and children, and with few strong ties with further generations or collateral relatives.

Now, the divorcee is not entirely without normative guides, even if for the most part these do *not* refer to the *status* of divorcee. Some of these guides are to be found in the extensive body of marriage and divorce laws of the states. Within each state the law undertakes to define the legal responsibilities of the husband for the care, if any, of the wife, care of the child, and sometimes, reciprocally, the responsibilities of the wife for the husband. In addition, of course, the law defines *her* responsibilities toward the children, if there are any. Finally, there are rather elaborate laws relating to property ownership within the family, including inherited property, as well as gifts and purchases. Since the family is a major institutional focus for the inheritance and enjoyment of property, the corpus of family law overlaps considerably with other bodies of law.

The Primary Status of Parent. In general, these legal prescriptions are attempts to enforce or to define in some detail the statuses and roles of husband and wife, and of father and mother, but not usually those of divorcee. Often the problems of legal specification become so involved that it is difficult to find a clear foundation or origin for them in the normative prescriptions of the kinship structure, as seen and understood by the average adult. Nevertheless, it is safe to say that few, if any, legal prescriptions relating to the family are without some such foundation and origin.

Both the legal and the social definitions of the status of divorcee are somewhat ambiguous. However, the *legal and social definitions of parent (divorced or not) are much clearer*. Indeed, one must find very particular circumstances in order to locate exceptions to the general clarity of duties and rights of parents. Such exceptions might be the situation in which a child becomes a serious juvenile delinquent, or exhibits symptoms of psychosis or severe mental retardation. In such cases, just what the parent is supposed to do is not clearly prescribed by the norms of the society (although the legal rules are relatively clear). And, of course, it is hardly necessary to comment that there are many details of these rights and duties about which there is much argument in our time. Thus, for example, whether the parents have much, if any, right to interfere in the choice of spouse by the children; just how late the children may stay up; and even the control over comic books, television, etc., are highly specific points about which there is great argument within parental circles. It is perhaps true, then, that the *rights* of parents are often unclear, at least in contemporary society. Nevertheless, we believe that, in general, the *duties* of parents are fairly clear.

The ambiguity of role is reduced even more if we turn from the general role of "parent" to that of "mother." Although we have few survey data with respect to the *behavior* of mothers, and only isolated bits of knowledge about variations in the attitudes held by the population with respect to maternal behavior, the *ideal* institutional pattern can be formulated in at least rough terms. The commercialization of this ideal, as seen in such manifestations as Mother's Day, would not be possible if there were not a substantial and relatively univalent set of ideals about the approved role behavior of the mother. It is not useful or relevant here to analyze in any detail the sometimes amusing journalistic notions regarding the "mother-complex" in this country. It is sufficient to note that the ideal behavior of mother has its mirror image in a set of ideal expectations as to *children's* responses to the maternal behavior. For example, sons are supposed to revere their mothers, protect them, etc. This set of complementary role expectations is fairly well defined. The position of mother in our society is complex. Without denying that complexity, we would nevertheless assert that "mother" is a "primary" status, and contains less ambiguity of role expectations than even the status of father. This "primary" character may be seen in several sociostructural nexuses. One connection is with the egalitarian tendencies of the movement for the emancipation of women. Here it is sufficient to note that the attitudes toward a *single* woman's being in the job market are relatively permissive, and are less so for the married woman without children. However, the attitudes against the mother's working are much stronger.[5a] Furthermore, much of the verbal approval of the mother's working is likely to be hollow in actuality. That is to say, within almost every social group the working mother is under strong pressures to take care of her children and to leave the job market. Her claim that the extra salary is absolutely needed for survival is viewed with considerable skepticism, even when the claim is not openly rejected. This general disapproval becomes relatively strong in precisely those middle-class strata where the egalitarian notions are held most strongly, because in such strata and groups the recent psychodynamic justifications for child freedom, child affection, breast feeding, security in mother love, etc. have become most fully accepted.

The primary character of the status may be viewed in another way: all other role obligations are *residual,* compared to this, and must wait until those of mother are satisfied. Everyone occupies several statuses. One may be father, physician, friend, cousin, neighbor, member of the board of education. Thus, he has other roles to play, and responsibilities to meet, than paternal ones. This is true for the mother as well. However, compared with other major statuses, that of mother is more likely to be viewed as exclusive, and other roles as residual. The maternal obligations have first call on her energies. The legitimacy of *non*maternal responsibilities is questioned unless it can be shown that the maternal responsibilities themselves are being properly met; and the clarity and moral force of this prescription are greater than for her other statuses.

We may phrase the situation in a slightly different fashion. We are all

---

5a. Corroborating data are in Hadley G. Cantril and Mildred Strunk, *Public Opinion 1935-1946*, Princeton, Princeton University Press, 1951.

more surprised in our "anonymous" urban society, when a woman fails to let us know that she is a mother, than when she does not tell us she is *married*. We accept the fact that she may wish to be considered single or may feel herself to be unmarried in all but legal senses. We suspect, however, that she has rather basic personality problems if she attempts in any way to hide her motherhood.

This greater definiteness and weight of the motherhood role is apparently not confined to contemporary society or even to Western society. There are many psychodynamic and socio-structural factors which make the pattern a cultural universal. We are not concerned with those at the present time. We need only note the basic fact that the status is primary and unambiguous, in several senses and with respect to most areas of behavior.

One may differentiate further and suggest that there is least ambiguity of status with respect to (1) widow-mother; while (2) wife-mother and (3) divorcee-mother follow in order of *increasing ambiguity*. This further differentiation does not undermine the essentially greater clarity of the basic mother status as against that of other kinship statuses.

Different "Mother Statuses." Now, in spite of the general failure of the society to define closely the appropriate differences in behavior for the divorcee or for the divorcee-mother as against that of the nondivorcee-mother, there are some differences in the social attitudes toward the three categories of widow-mother, wife-mother, and divorcee-mother, and very great differences in their positions in the social structure. Only the second of these continues to act in a complete family. The wife-mother is related to a husband-father, and the two form a couple, in various senses and with respect to an immense network of relationships and social definitions. This cannot, of course, be the situation of either the widow-mother or the divorcee-mother. As several analysts have pointed out, various structural factors in the social positions of the spouse are similar for the widowed and the divorced. On the other hand, the widow enjoys considerably greater sympathy, unquestioned help, rallying of friends and kin, etc.[6] We have noted this before and repeat it here as contrast.

Its immediate relevance here is that the widow has a completely unambiguous status, and her corresponding role expectations are relatively clear. This is true for the ideal case, and the complexities of daily living simply redefine this ideal pattern without changing it greatly. For example, the widow may actually have to be a worker in addition to being mother because of financial problems, but this qualification is already envisioned in the fuller statements of the ideal widow-mother.

Solution for the Institutional Ambiguity. Now, both the lesser approval enjoyed by the divorcee-mother, and the greater amount of status ambiguity, press in the same direction: toward remarriage.

There are few solutions to the institutional ambiguity and all these are only partial solutions. The mother may rid herself of her children by giving custody to some member of her family. This presents legal complications in some cases, and women are socialized to find this solution rather unacceptable. The mother may instead attempt to work out an unambiguous role in a

6. Becker and Hill, *op. cit.*, Ch. 22.

Bohemian group or in a relatively anonymous urban situation. Anonymity is almost impossible when there are children. The Bohemian solution is difficult for the majority of mothers and in most cases will be only a temporary solution.[7]

The most frequent solution, and the one that is institutionally clearest, is to marry again. The greater clarity of role definition that results is easily seen. So far as strangers are concerned, there is no particular reason to question the new marriage. There is a father for the children, and a common domicile. The mother is once more wife-mother, and the lesser events, problems, solutions, etc., of daily life are very similar to those in families where there has been no history of divorce. The social position is somewhat more complex when there are visiting rights and custodial battles. However, both visits and battles decrease in importance as time goes on. And, in any event, they are only intermittent in all but a very small proportion of cases.

Finally, the reconstitution of a full household gives the woman a strong hand in dealing with her ex-husband. She usually has custody by law and now offers her children a home that is apparently normal to the outside eye. Both children and mother are likely to be sensitive to this social aspect of the situation, and thus the mother is better able to resist the otherwise potential power of the husband to divide the children's loyalties in some substantial manner.

We have emphasized the factor of status ambiguity in the pressures toward remarriage. Commonsense factors press equally in the same direction. Nevertheless, even some of these can be grouped under the general category of institutional ambiguity. The most important commonsense factor is, naturally, that of money. The female earns less money than the male in our society for the same type of job. Even without listing other aspects of the problem of the female divorcee's income, it is clear that she is in a precarious financial situation after the divorce. It is true, of course, that she may have been in a disadvantaged financial condition prior to the divorce also, but she could do very little about the problem at that time. Once she is divorced, she has a *further* alternative, that of remarriage. Even remarriage with a husband at the same job level as her own allows her greater financial security. There are then no added expenses for child care.

The same kinds of comments may be made with respect to the general problem of energy allocation in the care of children. It is difficult for one person alone to take care of children. Not only are there many occasions when the adult must be absent for such activities as shopping, but illness of the adult or of one child may disrupt even the most cleverly organized routines and schedules. At such times, the presence of another adult to share the time and energy burdens is of very great importance. In addition, the psychic strain of caring for children, whose energy and energy-recovery are likely to be greater than that of the adult, requires help at various times from another adult. Institutional prescriptions do not define clearly how the divorcee mother is to solve this problem, but other people are not morally required to help her. Our kinship system permits divorce, but does not provide for its consequences.

---

7. Waller, *op. cit.*, Ch. IV.

The only institutionally sanctioned solution for this problem is marriage, although various other social arrangements or speculative possibilities exist—for example, cooperative arrangements among widowed and divorced mothers, the use of extended kinship networks with or without remarriage, or various forms of polygamy.

Further Pressures toward Marriage. In addition to these pressures that are intrinsic to the situation once the primary role responsibility of the mother is accepted, there are *direct* social pressures toward marriage which vary in intensity and explicitness. Some of these pressures occur as direct criticism and advice. Most of them occur, as is so often true for many powerful social pressures, in relatively minor, but recurrent and insistent, experiences of friction and incongruence between the demands of any given social circle and the needs or possible behavior of the divorced mother. These are, then, further elements in institutional integration. For example, adult informal groups are made up of *couple* relationships. Almost everyone in our society gets married, and even the unisexual social groups of neighborhood and work, such as sewing circles, or office bowling groups, may rest in part upon additional ties between couples. When they do not have such a basis, they are likely to be compartmentalized as to time, place, and importance. The unmarried person, whether divorced or single, finds as he becomes older that he simply does not fit into his social circle well, unless he brings along a person of the opposite sex as his partner. The adult couple planning to invite friends over finds it a nuisance if they must find a date for an unmarried friend. When the unmarried person is engaged, the problem is partially solved, and this is the case only because such a couple is assimilated to the general married-couple pattern. Thus, the kinship institutions press the divorcee toward remarriage by making her unmarried status inconvenient.

Furthermore, married couples spend some time and energy in attempting to see to it that their unmarried friends get married, and this pressure increases with increasing age. Some cynics have remarked that these pressures are simply an effort on the part of the married to force others to assume the burdens and troubles of the married. The matter is of course more fundamental in character. All couples spend much of their time together in discussing matters of common interest. To the extent that an individual or individuals are still dating, or for any reason simply do not have the ordinary marital experiences about which conversation turns, the individual will feel somewhat isolated, and cannot contribute adequately to the gossip, or even enjoy it. Alternatively, the couples will generally not be so interested in things outside marriage, and thus the activities of the unmarried are of less concern to them.

This difference becomes greater when there are children, since a major part of couple conversation relates to the activities of children, and the problems created by children.

To some extent it is also doubtless true that the unmarried, whether divorced or single, are viewed by spouses as potential threats. The divorced particularly represent *symbolic* threats, in that their existence demonstrates the possibility of ending existing marriages. They represent an *actual* threat to the extent that they are a potential *alternate* spouse for someone already married. Doubtless one can exaggerate the sexual mythology of the divorcees, and especially of the female divorcee, but this factor is certainly of some importance.

Finally, there is a rather strong feeling, as we have noted before, that children "need both parents." The divorcee-mother is under constant criticism or advice relating to the importance of her acquiring a husband as surrogate father for the children.

It will be noted that in these comments we have laid no emphasis at all upon the romantic complex or the importance of love. We do this, not because there is no residue of romanticism in divorcees, but because the minor and recurring pressures toward remarriage do not generally take this form. The main pressures relate to the moral responsibility of the mother, the status ambiguity of the divorcee, the needs or requirements of social groupings composed of couples, and the problem of allocating money, time, and energy— that is, factors that are mainly the *indirect* effects of the *explicit* kinship institutions.

We might add here, although we have no data on this point, that children also make demands upon their parents to remarry. Children of divorcees are aware of their own status ambiguity, and usually desire to "be like other children." We do not in this connection discount oedipal ties or the more general possessiveness of children in postdivorce situations of instability and divided loyalty. Nevertheless, there is romanticism in children as well, and a perception of kinship structures, and we would speculate that a majority of children sooner or later suggest to their divorced mother that she remarry. We are not certain that this would be the case for divorced fathers, but children's contacts with their fathers are intermittent and of short duration for the most part.

One final pressure beyond the above is mentioned often in commonsense discussions. It is the inconvenience of sexual pleasure outside of marriage. Divorced adults of either sex, unless disadvantaged to an extreme degree by physical handicap or psychic disturbances, find it possible in contemporary American society to locate sexual partners outside marriage. This is the case for a variety of reasons that are not relevant to our discussion. However, such relationships involve far more complications and difficulties than the innocent and the morally strict, with their notions about the "freedom" of the less strict, can possibly believe. Individual cut-and-run sexual episodes may remain undetected; but it is almost impossible for any continued sexual relationship to remain unknown to the social circles of both partners. Any arrangement short of continual and free access to one another is also likely to fall short of satisfying the relatively unchanging sexual demands of the adult, so that the liaison will become well known. It may even approach a quasi-marriage, and thereupon the pressures to legalize the relationship can become strong. This is particularly the case when children are involved, since most adult friends of the sexual partners believe that *parents* should be more moral than nonparent adults.[8]

---

8. Correspondingly, parents with no strong convictions regarding religion may feel that it is their moral responsibility to send their children to church. If they do not feel this responsibility, their *neighbors* believe that they ought to do so.

Furthermore, in our society the woman in particular is conditioned to respond less fully and adequately in a sexual relationship if it is defined as purely for sexual pleasure. It is the statistically rare case when the women feels as comfortable in such a relationship, without a close approximation to a love pattern, as she does in marriage. The man is not quite so inhibited, but for most occupational strata some approximation to sexual probity is asked, and may even be demanded. Furthermore, the problems of time and place make a continuity of sexual outlet fairly inconvenient. Putting the matter in the most awkward way possible, given the boudoir facilities, working hours, and social relationships within any given clique or circle, a couple must carry out detailed and clever plans if they wish to continue a sexual relationship without eventual marriage. The divorcee consequently finds any given sexual arrangements short of marriage increasingly inconvenient.

In the most general formulation, the institutional arrangements with reference to kinship in our society allow *little room* for the adult nonmarried, divorced or single. The patterns of action, the expectations, the types of invitations and conversations, increasingly center (with increasing age) on households and children. The nonmarried, and especially the divorced mothers, find many difficulties in the way of simple living patterns outside marriage. We phrase this negatively, since the participant experiences the situation in terms of difficulties and problems rather than in terms of explicit institutional definitions of the divorcee status. Nevertheless, the principle would seem to be that most of the social actions of the nonmarried with children are made socially difficult within the contemporary American kinship system (and most others as well).

We may phrase the matter differently by noting that with reference to kinship roles most of us have been socialized to feel most comfortable, and to respond without thought most easily, in the married status. Thus almost all roads for the divorcee, even when not so labeled by institutional prescriptions, lead to remarriage.[9]

In this way, then, the institutional problem is solved. The divorcees, male and female, do move to a defined status, in which the role expectations are more clearly defined. We have emphasized the informal and nonexplicit pressures, since we are convinced at this stage of thinking that these play a far more important role than any overt threats, promises, rational compromises, etc. We need hardly comment that this is merely a specific instance of a much broader social theorem, the general proposition that not *only does the society socialize its members to feel more comfortable in the statuses that are already defined,* but *the social structure makes deviant behavior difficult and inconvenient, even when it is not explicitly punished.*

We may further comment that the movement toward a new marriage (a) sets in train and (b) is accompanied by other adjustmental processes. Entering the courtship phase is at once an *index* of adjustment and a *cause* of it. The same proposition may be made with reference to the new marriage itself. That is, the complex pattern of pressures we have just outlined causes

---

9. We are inclined to believe, in addition, that there is a gradually increasing feeling on the part of friends of the divorcee that he or she "deserves a break." That is to say, he or she *deserves* a spouse and a good marriage.

the male or female divorcee to go into the behavior of dating, even when the individual does not really feel emotionally free of the former spouse. The individual may thus be forced into what is suggested as "appropriate" behavior even *before* the emotional freedom supposedly *expressed* by dating has been adequately achieved. On the other hand, the *behavior itself helps* the individual to free himself or herself emotionally of the former spouse. That is to say, in the dating situation the individual is given some emotional response, is treated as an attractive person, etc., and this may help to some degree in assuaging old psychic hurts.

More important is the fact that this behavior *creates a redefinition of status* for the individual. She begins to see herself as "eligible," as an individual. The divorcee no longer needs to look at herself as "wife" or "ex-wife," but as "divorced," or even "not married"—in any event, as a *potential spouse* or as open to romantic interest or involvement. The individual must begin to see herself as *separated* from the previous relationship, and the new behavior itself *offers* her the opportunity of seeing this new definition in the eyes of other whom she dates or sees frequently. To a lesser extent this is the case for male divorcees, as well.

Similarly, although economic problems are difficult to solve, the action of taking a job and working at a job sets in motion various factors that define the woman's primary status (at least on the job) as worker. Even when her primary status is mother, and a secondary status is that of worker, neither of these definitions refers to any great degree to her status as "ex-wife."

The same proposition may be made with respect to other kinds of activities. In other role behavior away from the primary demands of motherhood, *the individual divorcee is gradually seen and judged in other contexts.* She is defined as "girl," divorcee, mother, worker, club member, etc., but she is less and less defined as anybody's "ex." Ultimately, even the "status" of divorcee may at worst become a general status not tied to any particular male.

These complex factors emphasize, therefore, (1) the finality of the divorce and (2) the possibilities of a new status. With reference to this second emphasis, the possibility of new marriage is emphasized increasingly as something that is desirable or important. The new activities and behavior change the divorcee's focus, therefore, from the past, and direct it toward the present and future *as an individual* rather than as a person with a historical connection with a particular man.

Summary. Divorcees, like all of us, are engaged in daily tasks of planning, buying, voting, or working, and in their social contacts they find that far fewer people care about their personal traumas and difficulties than they could have believed. Alternatively, most co-workers and the people in her friendship circles offer her less and less opportunity to remember that there was a spouse. This is so whether the spouse is dead or merely divorced. These circles and networks of acquaintances will not be greatly concerned with someone who is *socially not there.* For the former spouse is socially there only derivatively. He is there only through the behavior and attitudes of his ex-wife. Since her own circles wish to anticipate her actions and behavior (because they are in continual interaction with her and can mesh their lives with hers only by such social prediction) the former spouse becomes from their point of view only an intrusion, to be combatted by pressures on her to build a new life independently of this former relationship.

The kinship institutions do not, then, make provision for the consequences of divorce, *within* its structure. But, *by the very fact that there are no such provisions, no set of status privileges and stigmata, which would allow the divorcee to play easily the mother role outside marriage,* the institutional patterns create pressures toward new marriages, while offering some positive inducements in the same direction. There is thus as yet little direct institutionalization of postdivorce adjustment. But the larger kinship patterns nevertheless force very similar behavior on divorcees, by making difficult or inconvenient any other status than that of married mother.

It is thus that our society has been able to bear such a high rate of divorce without specific, direct kinship prescriptions for handling the problems that are created by the dissolution of a marriage. Although the rate of divorce is high, the existing kinship institutions indirectly move both child and mother back into relatively well-defined statuses, thus fixing responsibility for maintenance, status placement, and socialization of the child. Whatever the degree of personal tragedy in these experiences, for both parents and children, most of these individuals move forward into definite, new kinship units. As a consequence, there is little evidence that our high divorce rate is undermining the larger social structure. Moreover, we see in this extended theoretical analysis an implicit broader generalization: That under most structural arrangements, a high divorce rate in any culture will be accompanied by a high remarriage rate.

CHAPTER XVI

POSTDIVORCE ECONOMIC ACTIVITIES

IN CHAPTER IV, we pointed out some of the complexities of interpreting economic data, and stated that our main interest is in the sociological aspects or social *meaning* of economic facts, in so far as they affect the marital conflict and the divorce situations.

This insistence is not mere pedantry, since the divorcee herself proves by her behavior and attitudes that the distinction is real. Whether she believes that she has enough money depends also upon her social situation, and not alone upon how many dollars she receives weekly. Whether she believes she was better off financially during the marriage than after the marriage is not determined alone by the amount of money she can or could spend.

Nevertheless, these social factors interact *concretely* with the economic. A divorcee who has remarried will be more likely to claim that she "has enough," than a divorcee who has not remarried, *at the same income* level. On the other hand, when the remarried divorcee has much less money than before, this concrete fact will reduce that satisfaction somewhat. If we insist upon the importance of social factors, we cannot concretely ignore the economic. Certainly the divorcee does not ignore them.

Consequently, in this chapter we shall present many of the economic details of the postdivorce period. It is only within this framework that many of the differences caused by social factors can emerge and be interpreted.

Amount of Property. We showed earlier that the average divorced couple had little property to be divided. Most divorces occur in economic strata with little income, and the presence of children in our cases would usually be a further bar to any substantial accumulation. The value of total property to be divided was as follows:

TOTAL VALUE OF PROPERTY AT TIME OF DIVORCE

Value	Percent
No property	40
$ 1.00-$ 249	5
$ 250-$ 999	16
$1000-$1999	14
$2000-$3999	8
$4000 and over	18
Total	101

N = 425

These figures would be higher during an inflationary period. The figures are judgments, and are therefore the resultant of complex factors such as misinformation, ignorance, lying, etc. The wife might not know accurately the market value of the house, but would know the mortgage situation and the value of furniture. She might have been deceived by her husband as to how much money he had taken, or ever possessed. On the other hand, the wives would know how much cash or bonds they *themselves* had received, while perhaps understating slightly their own possessions or money. Certainly, the answers given to these and other economic questions should have been more "reasonable" than the answers given to the court investigators; for the wives had good reason to exaggerate their difficulties to the latter, so as to obtain larger support payments. In general, a longer duration of marriage is associated with a greater accumulation of property.

TOTAL AMOUNT OF PROPERTY, BY DURATION OF MARRIAGE

Duration of Marriage	0	$1-$999	$1000-$3999	$4000 and over	Totals
			Amount of Property		
0- 4 years	65%	14%	18%	3%	100%
5- 9 years	37	25	23	15	100
10-14 years	30	21	25	25	101
15 and over	44	13	13	31	100
Totals	40%	20%	21%	18%	99%

N = 425

In most cases, then, there was no property to divide, except the few odds and ends of a dissolving household.

Division of Property. Of those couples who did have some property, 49% split the property in some fashion. In a moment, we shall look at the nature of these divisions. Forty-four percent of the wives got everything, and in 7% of the cases the husbands got everything.

The amount of total property is associated with the division that was made. The higher the amount, the more likely there was a division. Thus, 15% of the couples who had accumulated less than $500 represented property splits, as against 44% of those with $500-1999, and 69% of those who had more than $2000. By contrast, when there was *less* than $500, 74% of the wives got everything; when there was $500-1999, 45% of the wives got everything; and when there was more than $2000, only 28% of the wives got everything. For the same classes of amounts, the percentages of cases in which the husband got everything were: 11%, 10%, and 3%.

Let us examine these divisions further. We would suppose that toward the middle and upper strata the husband would be more likely to divide the property between them, and this does take place. However, when we control the occupational class of the husband, we find that it is rather the *amount* of property that controls the *type of division,* as between (a) a split, and (b) the wife obtaining everything. A split of the property is nearly twice as likely to occur if there is more than $2000, as when there is less than $2000 (about 63-70% *vs.* 31-41%), for all occupational classes. Correspondingly, the wife is nearly twice as likely to receive everything if there is *less than* $2000, as when there is more than $2000 (50-67% *vs.* 23-37%). Finally, in the upper occupational class there are *no* cases in which the husband got everything; and none in the middle occupational stratum with more than $2000. Nine percent of the husbands in the middle class with less than $2000 got everything; 7% of the husbands in the lower class with more than $2000 got everything. And 13% of the lower class husbands with less than $2000 got everything.

Thus, in general, the total amount of property seems to control the division more than does occupational class, but toward the lower classes there is a greater likelihood that the husband will get everything, or that the wife will.

Middle- and upper-class couples seem more willing to talk over the property division, and to divide the property. There should also be a greater involvement of husband and wife over many years of marriage, and this should make for a property division, as against one or the other taking all of it. Such an association between duration of marriage and a property split, does appear. Again here, as with occupational class, the association is spurious. With increasing duration of marriage, the amount of property increases; and with a greater amount of property the likelihood of a property split increases. But, when we hold *amount of property* constant, there is no significant association between duration and property split. There is also no significant association between number of children and the property division.

Now, we are also interested in which spouse got which type of property. We believe that it is a widespread American custom to give the furniture and/or house to the divorced mother, but that no comparable custom exists for other types of property. Cash and bonds are not tied to sex roles, and the norm is to divide equally. Tools of course go to the husband, but these are "personal" property, and may also be his means of livelihood. We believe that the husband usually gets the automobile, but that this is not a *norm,* as is the rule relating to the house and furniture. That is to say, the latter behavior is "morally expectable." The husband may, by contrast, insist on getting the automobile because he needs it for his job; but he has no moral claim to it.

We do not know whether these statements of American "custom" are correct. In any event, of the 226 divorces in which there was house or furniture, or both, in only eleven cases did the husband get all of it. But in 164 of these 226 cases the mother took all of it. In 26 cases, there was an even split. In 16 cases, she received more than he; and in only 9 cases he got more than she did.

The wife believed, in 82 cases, that there were bonds or cash to be divided. We assume that in some additional instances the husband had cash that she did not know about. In 25 cases, he took all of it; and in 24 cases she took all of it. With reference to the remaining 33 cases, there were 19 cases of equal division, 6 cases in which the wife got more than her husband, and 8 in which the husband got more than she.

In 78 cases there was also still other property. This could include tools, books, businesses, automobiles, etc. Here, the division was more definitely in favor of the husband: in 49 cases, he took all of it, while in 15 cases she took all of it. Of the remainder, there were 4 cases of equal division, 8 cases in which he got more than she did, and 2 cases in which she received more than he.

Thus, even when the ex-wife is reporting, she seems to get more of what little there is, than does the ex-husband. On the other hand, if he is paying for his guilts, he gets a bargain, since in most cases there is little or nothing to divide. And, moreover, the greater the amount available for division, the greater the chance that there will be a split of property (i.e., that he will take a share of it). On the other hand, the symbolic and actual association of children and mother with the home does play a role in the division, for she is particularly likely to obtain the larger share of this type of property.

We may reduce the types of divisions of property to four: (1) both wife and husband got something; (2) husband got something, but wife did not; (3) wife got something, but husband did not; and (4) neither husband nor wife got anything at all. In such a reduction this last category is large. Forty percent of the cases were those in which neither husband nor wife got anything at all other than, we assume, some of the minor trinkets and accumulations of their married life. The reduced table is as seen below:

DIVISION OF PROPERTY (WHEN THERE WAS PROPERTY)

Wife got property	Husband got property		Total
	Yes	No	
Yes	29%	26%	55
No	4	40	44
Totals	33	66	99%

N = 425

As we can see, when there was any property at all to be divided, the wife is more likely than the husband to have received property. The cases in which the husband received property and the wife did not, represent the smallest proportion of all, 4%. On the other hand, the case of the wife's receiving property, while the husband does not, is six times as large, 26%. Finally, we may look at the division by type of property and amount within each type, so as to obtain a fuller picture of how the goods were distributed:

DIVISION OF PROPERTY, BY AMOUNT AND TYPE OF PROPERTY

Value	House and Furniture		Cash and Bonds		Other Property	
	% of wives	% of husbands	% of wives	% of husbands	% of wives	% of husbands
$ 0.00	49	85	87	86	93	85
$ 1-$ 499	13	4	8	6	4	8
$ 500-$ 999	9	4	2	5		
$1000-$1999	11	2	1	2	2	6
$2000-$3999	8	3	1	1		
$4000 and over	9	2	1	—	1	1
Total	99	100	100	100	100	100

N = 425

Approval of Property Division. No matter what form the division took, we would expect some divorcees to object to it. When we asked our respondents whether they thought the division of property represented a fair settlement, the answers fell in a predictable direction:

WHETHER WIFE APPROVED PROPERTY DIVISION, BY WHO RECEIVED THE PROPERTY

Who received property	Percentage saying settlement was fair	Number
Wife received all	79%	(110)
Property split	68	(125)
Husband received all	44	(18)

N = 253

Child Support. Although child support is of great importance, since it represents continuing income, as against the final division of property, it takes on added significance in light of the very limited amount of property to be divided. Yet, since the husband's income was likely to be small, the amount of the support payments is small:

AMOUNT OF SUPPORT PAYMENTS PER CHILD, PAID BY HUSBAND*

Amount per child	Number of Children Receiving this amount	
	Percent	No.
$ 0.01-$ 4.99	5	34
$ 5.00-$ 6.99	20	138
$ 7.00-$ 8.99	34	232
$ 9.00-$10.99	25	175
$11.00 or more	16	108
Subtotal	100	687
No support payments		109
Total		796

*The median amount paid weekly per child is about $8.50.

The approximately 172,000 minor children involved in divorces in Cook County (Chicago) during 1940-1950 received comparably little[1]:

	Percent
No formal court order made	33
Less than $5.00 weekly	3
$ 5.00-$10.00	28
$10.00-$15.00	26
$15.00 and over	10
	100%

However, some divorcees have more than one child. Let us, then, see what the total amount of payments weekly amounted to, as well as what the average total weekly payment was per divorcee.[2]

---

1. *Conference on Divorce, Conference Series,* No. 9, University of Chicago Law School, 1952, remarks of Judge Edwin A. Robson, p. 4.

2. The husband's income is part of the Chancery record, since this is a datum obtained by the Friend of the Court investigator from the employer, if any. When the husband was an independent professional or businessman, the figure was an estimate. However, we obtained our data from the respondent, while also copying income figures from the Chancery records so as to check our sample.

TOTAL AMOUNT OF SUPPORT PAYMENTS PER WEEK

Total Amount	Families Receiving this amount	
	Percent	No.
$ 0.01-$ 5.49	5	18
$ 5.50-$10.49	42	153
$10.50-$15.49	24	87
$15.50-$20.49	16	58
$20.50-$30.49	11	40
$30.50-$75.50	2	9
Subtotal	100	365
No support payments		60
Total		425

The median weekly amount of child support per family of those receiving payments is approximately $12.

Although it was the duty of the Friend of the Court to receive payments from former husbands, and to disburse them to former wives, the system did not achieve its aim in every case. In some instances, the husband made a private arrangement to pay directly to his former wife. When the husband failed to make the payments ordered, there was legal machinery to enforce the court order, and, of course (as is true of all states), the husband could be jailed for nonpayment. However, in general, the court will hold that a husband free to earn money is more useful than a husband jailed. Consequently, the husband need only pay the arrears in order to obtain his freedom. Wives with recalcitrant husbands find that energy and even money are required to set the enforcement in motion again. If she remarries, and is able to pay her bills without the child support, she may decide to drop the matter. In some cases, the ex-spouses may make a joint decision to do so.

The contact between husband and wife decreases over time, so that the husband may feel less obligation to continue the payments. Moreover, the husband himself begins to create a new life in which there are great demands upon his income. Increasingly, he may feel that he simply cannot meet these payments. Thus, in a substantial proportion of cases, the child support payments are not met, as we see in the following table:

CONTINUITY OF CHILD PAYMENTS MADE TO DIVORCED WIFE

Did husband continue to make payments?	Percent
Always	35
Usually	14
Once in a while	11
Rarely or Never	40
	100%

N = 354*

*Excludes cases where wife does not have full custody.

In somewhat less than half of the cases there is apparent continuity of payments. The divorced wife, then, receives relatively little property from the split of joint possessions, is given very little child support, and in two-fifths of the cases does not receive this support regularly.

Since continuity of support furnishes the ex-wife's economic base, and since it relates to other important events in her postdivorce adjustment, let us devote extended attention to it.

Continuity of Child Support Payments. In order to understand the continuity of payments, we must have further knowledge of the husband's situation, and more particularly his definition of that situation. For this knowledge, we must rely upon the wife's report, which will vary in unknown ways from the reality. However, as we shall see, there are important patterns to be uncovered when we accept her opinions as reasonably valid.

Two main characteristics of his situation are most important, (1) his ability to pay, and (2) his relationship to his ex-wife. Now, continuity of support payments requires a continuity of income. No matter what his weekly earnings, if he is frequently out of work it will be difficult for him to avoid missing payments from time to time. The *amount* of earnings seems not to have any relationship to continuity. We do not know what his postdivorce steadiness of employment was, but we do know his employment record during the marriage as the wife reports it. We then find that 51% of the husbands who always or usually had employment during the marriage, *always* made their support payments after the divorce, as against only 17% of the husbands who were frequently unemployed. Thirty-eight percent of the latter rarely made these payments, as against 26% of those who were usually or always employed. We may phrase the matter differently, by noting that 88% of those who always paid were husbands who during the marriage had always or usually been employed.

A parallel comparison with a further dimension may be made by looking at the theme of Nonsupport. We find that 49% of those wives who did not complain of Nonsupport reported that their husbands always made their child support payments later; as against only 24% of those who made this complaint. In this comparison, however, we see the further dimension of his *willingness* to pay, or his *habit* of payment. A hint of this is also contained in the fact that occasional payment was common among those who were frequently unemployed (24% usually); and that among those who usually or always had work, 27% rarely paid.

But the distribution of payment among those charged with Nonsupport contains a high proportion of those who never or rarely made these payments: 46% rarely or never paid, as against 23% of those whose wives did not charge Nonsupport. Those who were occasionally or frequently unemployed could pay now and then, when they had work, and apparently did so. However, those who had refused to support the household *during* the marriage evidently continued to do so *after* the marriage. In a sense, they had adjusted to nonpayment even before the divorce. This comparison, then, probably contains both unwillingness and inability to pay.

We can ask more directly about the husband's attitude toward the payments, as seen by the wife.[3] Of course, he is much less likely to pay regularly if he resents the payments.

---

3. In this question, of course, the wife frequently judged his attitude *only* by his continuity of payment. Consequently, the relationship is at least partially spurious. On the other hand, she often has some independent knowledge of his attitude.

CONTINUITY OF SUPPORT PAYMENTS, BY RESENTMENT OF HUSBAND

Husband resents payments	Always pays	Continuity Occasionally	Rarely	Totals
Yes	24%	36%	40%	100% (172)
No	67	25	8	100 (122)
Totals	42%	32%	26%	100% (294)*

*We are considering only those cases in which support payments were ordered. Through an interviewing failure, 42 respondents were not asked this question. An additional 18 respondents simply replied that the ex-husband never paid.

We also have some indication of his willingness to pay in her report on whether he thought the support payments were too high, although once more *his* judgment of his ability to pay enters.

CONTINUITY OF SUPPORT PAYMENTS, BY HUSBAND'S ATTITUDE TOWARD AMOUNT OF PAYMENT

Husband thinks payments are too much	Always pays	Continuity Occasionally	Rarely	Totals
Yes, way too much	21%	31%	48%	100% (85)
Yes, little too much	37	37	26	100 (57)
No	59	29	12	100 (128)
Totals	42%	32%	26%	100% (270)*

$P < .001$

*Here, also, there was an interviewing failure, so that 41 respondents were not asked the question. 22 respondents answered "Don't know," and 21 stated that he did not ever pay.

Even though these associations contain more than the single dimension of either ability to pay, or of the husband's attitude, we can at least see the high likelihood that both are associated with continuity of payment. Let us further analyze, then, the relations between the two former spouses.

Let us begin with a factor whose importance we have already tested, who first suggested the divorce. As we might predict from our data on the relationship between the first suggestion and trauma, the cases in which there was *mutual* suggestion are least likely to involve husbands who failed to live up to their obligations. Thus, 55% of the "mutuals" always paid, as against 43% of those husbands who suggested first, and 37% of those whose wives first suggested the divorce. However, the differences in the distributions among those who occasionally or rarely paid are less striking, and the relationship is not statistically significant ($.3 > P > .2$).

This relationship hides a further factor. It is true that when there was mutual suggestion there was a greater likelihood of continuity in support: 55% of those who experienced a mutual suggestion had husbands who always paid, as against 39% of those with other types of suggestion patterns. This relationship seems to operate through the postdivorce attitude of the husband towards the payments. Mutual suggestion appears to lead more often to a lack of resentment against the payments (49% of these husbands were resentful of the payments, as against 60% of those with other patterns of first suggestion). And, in turn, *lack* of resentment is associated with *continuity* of payment (24% of the husbands who were resentful of payments always paid, as against 67% of those who were not resentful).

As a consequence, we find that when resentment is held constant, a somewhat different pattern emerges. *If there is resentment of payments after the divorce, then who made the first divorce suggestion makes no difference in continuity* (only 24% always pay). If, on the other hand, there is no resentment of payment, then who first made the suggestion *does* make a difference: (a) When the ex-husband does not resent the payments, *and* there was mutual suggestion, then 94% of the husbands always pay. But (b) when he does not resent the payments, and there was not a mutual suggestion, then 63% always make their child support payments.

This interaction of attitudes and action may also be seen in several minor but interrelated facts which we note here without reproducing the relevant tables: (1) If the wife in general thought that the property settlement was fair, then the husband is slightly *less* likely to think the payments are too high, or to resent them. (2) We had asked her whether her ex-husband had lived up to all, most, some, or none of the agreements. Of those who were said to have lived up to all the agreements, 72% always paid, as against 46% of those who only lived up to "most" of the agreements, and 8% of those who lived up to only "some of them." (3) The husband is somewhat less likely to *resent* the payments, if she reports that he was satisfied with the custody arrangements.

Let us now show the interactional effects of his attitudes toward payments and steady work, upon continuity.

CONTINUITY OF SUPPORT PAYMENTS, BY STEADINESS OF WORK AND
ATTITUDE OF HUSBAND TOWARD PAYMENTS

Did he have steady work during marriage?	Thinks payments are too much?	Always pays	Occasionally or sometimes	Seldom or never	Totals
Yes	No	72%	21%	8%	100% (92)
Yes	Yes	34	28	38	100 (98)
No	No	25	54	23	100 (36)
No	Yes	14	43	43	100 (44)
			No attitude expressed		84
				Sub-total	354
			No payments, etc.		71
					425

A more complex table in which the habit of payment, as indicated by Nonsupport as a theme of complaint, attitude toward payments, and steady work, are shown in interaction, will not be given here, but the same pattern emerges, with intensified differences.

Now, after the divorce the various ties between the spouses slowly give way. The ex-spouses see each other less often, feel less and less commitment to the other's destiny, and build new lives for themselves. If the marriage can be viewed as one type of boundary-maintaining system, so can the attenuating relationship after the divorce. The absence or weakness in the system of various types of factors issues in a divorce, and the lack is even more striking after the divorce. A relationship that is based primarily upon a legally enforced or enforceable financial relationship, and without reciprocal rewards of shared activities, common goals, and so on, is difficult to maintain. Moreover, we believe that the husband increasingly feels morally less obligated; for moral obligations are also dependent for their strength and continuity upon the continuing social interaction with its concomitant sanctions and rewards. Even the role of father contains less social meaning, since he cannot have much interaction with his children.

When, therefore, the ex-wife remarries, these ties and obligations are likely to lose still more of their meaning. This may be partially measured by the lesser continuity of payments: 30% of the wives who have remarried received their payments always, as against 45% of the not remarried. Moreover, although continuity of child support payments actually *appears* to decline over time, this is simply a function of the increasing proportion of ex-wives who have remarried. When we control for remarriage, the relationship between time and failure to pay dwindles to insignificance.

Finally, we can point to one important interactional factor in this decreasing feeling of obligation. There is a slight association between the remarriage of the wife and her report of his resentment. Sixty-eight percent of the women who have remarried report that their ex-husbands resent these payments, as against 55% of the women who have not remarried. This slight association suggests that we ought to hold constant his attitude, to see whether remarriage has any independent effect. We find that her *remarriage has no effect on his payments if there is no resentment*: two-thirds of these ex-husbands always pay. But if there *is* resentment against the payments, then remarriage does have some effect, by accentuating the effect of resentment: (a) twenty-nine percent of the women who have *not* remarried, but whose husbands *are* resentful, always receive their payments; but (b) only 14% of the women who have remarried (and with resentful ex-husbands) get these payments always. Thus, both factors do play a role in continuity.

Many of these attitudes are in part a reflection of one another—we shall document this later in more detail. We might, then, ask whether *his* general attitude toward *her* seems to affect continuity of payments. If we ask her about his attitude toward her, we cannot eliminate entirely the influence of *his payments upon her judgment* about his attitude, but in most cases she will have some observations upon which to base her notion, other than his payments. As we would expect, when she claims that his attitude is "positive" (including "friendly"), he is much more likely to be regular in his support.

CONTINUITY OF SUPPORT PAYMENTS, BY HUSBAND'S ATTITUDE TOWARD EX-WIFE

Wife claims his attitude is	CONTINUITY			
	Always pays	Occasionally	Rarely	Totals
Positive (or friendly)	48%	26%	26%	100%(200)
Negative (or indifferent)	32	32	36	100 (154)
	.01 > P > .001			N = 354

The relationship itself is clear enough, but let us probe one step further. If we hold constant *her* attitude toward *him,* we then find that there is *no relationship* between continuity of support and his attitude toward her. This we interpret to mean that, as their old relationship becomes little more than a financial one mediated through the children, *her* attitude toward him is increasingly a function of his fulfilling his one important role activity, that of making the child support payments. Then, if we control her attitude toward him, his attitude toward her has no *further independent* effect on continuity of payments.

We have no way of measuring (other than through her report) to what extent the husband himself feels unable to make these payments, but it is clear that the wife does not continue to assert fully her legal rights to regularity of payments, and this insistence declines with time. This lack of insistence is also to be seen as an index of her adjustment to a new life. Not only does she no longer depend economically upon the former husband, but she no longer wishes even to assert her rights. At the same time, this frees her morally from any obligation to have contact with him or even to let the children see him. To this extent she can more completely build her new life without taking account of his activities.

Economic Difficulties of Both Spouses. We ought, in any event, to recognize the financial difficulties that ensue for both parties to the divorce. The economic problems involved in child support cannot ordinarily be solved with the resources at the disposal of the two ex-spouses. In most cases they were barely able to get along when the household was intact, and did not accumulate much property. Husband and wife divide the administrative problems of the household, contributing "unpaid" services toward its continuity. When the divorce occurs, the gap cannot be filled. The child support payments must be gauged to fit the wages of the husband; but, if this is true, they cannot cover the contribution which formerly went to feed and clothe the wife also. The expenses of each human unit are greater in the separated or divorced family than in the ongoing family, but the income may not increase to meet the greater demands. If the husband obtains custody of the children, he has no one to take care of the children while he works; and thus once again the previous wages are insufficient. The economic burden is greater for the wife with custody, but the ex-husband's basic income is not usually large enough to permit payments that would bridge the gap that created two households.

We can measure this somewhat more precisely. It is clear that steadiness of employment is important for continuity of payments. Whether or not the divorced husband *wishes* to pay, he *cannot* pay steadily if he does not work regularly. Now, in fixing support payments, the court takes into account the weekly earnings of the husbands, as well as the number of children. For practical purposes, however, steadiness of employment is of equal importance. It is then worth reporting that when there is only one child, the median amount of support which the husband was supposed to pay is no different whether or not the husband had steady work ($9.89 *vs.* $9.57 weekly). This is also true for those with two children ($15.20 *vs.* $14.85). It is only when there are three or more children that we see any difference between the payments ordered for husbands with steady, or with unsteady, employment ($21.39 *vs.* $18.00 weekly).

Moreover, if we compare child support payments with the husband's *reported* income, holding constant the number of children, we find that not even income is always taken into account. If there is only one child, there are no differences in the average payments ordered, as between a weekly income of 0-$45 weekly, $45-60, and $60 and over ($9.74, $9.75, and $10.09). This is not the blindness of the judge, but the simple fact that he cannot feel that lower payments are right whether or not they are more realistic in view of the husband's income. He will not be able to see how the divorced wife can get along on so little, even if it is too much for the husband. Consequently, there are no real differences between these income levels, in the amount of payments ordered for one child, thus denying economic reality on social grounds.

Thus: "Judges and lawyers must try to cut up a piece of cake which is ordinarily too small. Many judges have spoken of the tragedy of sitting every day trying to divide a weekly income of $40, $50, or $60 between a husband and wife and two to five children. It cannot be done satisfactorily."[4]

If there are two children, the only difference that appears is between the first two income levels, and the third ($14.83, $14.78, and $19.57 weekly payments ordered). That is, those who make $60 weekly or more will have to pay more. And, even when there are three children, no large differences appear. The median weekly amount of support payment ordered for those with three children, making 0-$45 weekly, is $20.00. For those making $45-60, it is $20.50, and for those making $60 and over it is $22.50. Thus, not even when there are three children do we find the payments gauged to the income, simply because the judge will ordinarily be unable to see how the wife can survive with so little—or how the husband can pay so much. Naturally, these figures would be higher in the 1950's, but we would suppose that the *relationships* have not changed substantially. The basic economic fact is that costs per human unit in the ongoing household are lower than in the divorced households, but that in the latter there may be no increase in income to cover the greater burden of either ex-wife or ex-husband.

Working Ex-Wife. One consequence of this situation is that the wife may have to work out some sort of arrangement which will permit her to work at least part time. Since a frequent characteristic of the late conflict stage in a divorcing family is the partial or complete withdrawal of economic aid by the husband, the wife may have had to take a job prior to the decree. Of course, as we commented in Chapter VI, during the past decades the working wife has become more common.[5] When we asked our respondents whether they had held jobs during their marriages, their answers were divided as follows:

FREQUENCY OF JOB-HOLDING (FULL AND PART TIME) BY WIVES DURING MARRIAGE

Job held	Percent
All the time	24
Once in a while	35
Seldom	14
Never	28
	101%	N = 425

Of those who had jobs, 71% held full-time jobs, and 29% held part-time jobs.

4. Remarks of William C. Boyden, in *Conference On Divorce, op. cit.,* p. 10.

5. The evidence suggests that these are not career wives, but women who are attempting to supplement the husband's income. A comparable situation has been reported from Germany as early as the twenties: Andres Sternheim, "Materialien zur Wirksamkeit ökonomischer Faktoren in der gegenwärtigen Familie," in *Autorität und Familie* (Paris: Alcan, 1936), pp. 576-577. Sternheim reports that studies in Germany indicated that 80%-90% of working wives offered economic explanations for working.

When the final separation took place, the entire sample was distributed as follows: Full-time jobs, 39%; part-time jobs, 6%; and no job at all, 55%. Unfortunately, we cannot assert that the proportion of job holders increased or decreased, since the entire period of marriage is longer than the period of separation. The chance of a wife's holding a full-time job at some time during the entire marriage (especially prior to having children) might be relatively high. The former group (full-time job holders at any time during the marriage) is 51% of the total, while it forms 39% of the total in the "final separation group." If we compare those who held part-time jobs during the total period of the marriage with those who held similar jobs during the period of final separation, we see that 21% held part-time jobs at some period and 6% such a job during final separation.

We also asked these wives whether they were working at the time of our interview, in order to ascertain what continuing effect the divorce might have had on their financial situation. Thus, we may compare job-holding at any time during the marriage, with job-holding in the separation or early post-divorce period, and with job-holding at the time of the interview, some time after the divorce.

PROPORTION OF WIVES HOLDING JOBS AT DIFFERENT MARITAL PHASES

Job-Holding	During Marriage Percent	Separation Percent	Time of Interview Percent
Never had job	28	55	43
Full Time job	51	39	52
Part Time job	21	6	6
Totals	100	100	101

N = 425

From final separation to time of interview, the proportion of wives holding *full*-time jobs increases from two-fifths to one-half. This would appear to suggest that they are making an adjustment to their new economic problems. Moreover, the financial situation is made up of more than the total amount of money available. If she works she can have a *steady* income. The steadiness of the income is important, as well as who controls it. We shall report in a moment how these women evaluated their financial situation at the time of the interview.

Postdivorce Income. For the present, let us continue with the simple financial details. Earlier, we presented the level of income during the marriage. Now let us see how much pay the working divorcees received, and the total amount of money available from all sources.

TAKE HOME PAY OF WORKING DIVORCEES AT TIME OF INTERVIEW

Weekly Amount	Percent
Less than $20	7
$20.00-$29.99	9
$30.00-$39.99	32
$40.00-$49.99	28
$50.00-$59.99	19
$60 or more	4

N = 244   99

Not working   181

425

As we see, nearly 80% of those working fall into the pay bracket of $30-$60 weekly, with a median figure of about $40.73 for the group as a whole (job-holders only). Of course, we must add support payments and other sources of income to this, so as to see how much these divorcees have for meeting expenses.

TOTAL AMOUNT AVAILABLE PER WEEK (ALL WIVES)

Weekly Amount	Percent
Less than $30.00	17
$30.00 $44.99	24
$45.00-$59.99	25
$60.00-$74.99	14
$75.00-$89.99	7
$90 or more	13
N = 421	100
No answer 4	
425	

Thus, the average amount available weekly to these divorcees was about $51. This amount was less than the weekly income of their husbands during the marriage ($53 weekly), although in some cases the expenses would perhaps be greater, even without the husband's expenses to meet. The household often or usually moves. If the wife works, she may have to pay someone to care for the younger children. Until recently, this expense was not tax deductible, and in any event the tax that is thereby saved at the present time is never as much as the expense itself. New purchases may have to be made in the new household, and there is a smaller network of relatives from whom aid may be expected. Thus, the objective economic position of many divorcees may become difficult after the divorce.

Of course, this last statement lumps together all the divorcees. When we look at them within Time Groups, we see that over time the situation of the divorcees as a group seems to improve. In Time Groups I and II, 26% have less than $30 weekly with which to meet their expenses, but in Groups III and IV (14 and 26 months after the divorce), only 9% and 7% have so little. At the other end of the income scale, 7% and 12% in Time Groups I and II have $75 or more per week, but 27% and 33% in Groups III and IV. We are including all sources of income, from the ex-husband's relatives to governmental help such as Children's Aid. Yet we know that such aid (other than official) is not likely to increase over time. It would rather decrease. Relatives and neighbors may help in a severe crisis, but a continuing crisis does not in an urban society continute to stimulate such help. Let us, then, see where the additional money comes from.

Income and Remarriage. The changes in income over time are almost entirely a function of remarriage. That is, within the remarried segment, there is little change over time. We should expect no important change. Even if the new husbands make an adequate income, it is not likely that, viewed as a group, the divorced women will marry men with a higher economic position than those of the first marriages. Among the semi-skilled and skilled occupations, there are few changes with age, and most of these women will marry within similar circles. The change, then, is not over time for divorcees as a group, but occurs with marriage for each divorcee. Thus, the total divorced group improves economically over time only because an increasingly higher proportion is remarried. Thus, we find that 60% of the remarried in Groups I and II receive $60 or more weekly, 72% in Group III, and 71% in Group IV. There is an apparent increase from Group I to Group II, but it is not significant, since there are only 12 cases in these two groups, within these income cells. Even if we grant some change, as the new household becomes organized, the change is not great. The real change is that an increasing proportion of those in the higher income cells are the remarried: In Group III, 70% of those receiving $60 weekly or more are remarried; and in Group IV, 82% of those receiving so much are remarried.

We cannot precisely compare the income level of those who remarry, with their income level during the previous marriage. There were variations in steadiness of the husband's employment, in the employment of the wife, and in average wages at different times. After the divorce, the divorcee receives child support, and this is added to her new husband's income. However, the child support may be irregular, or may cease. We have attempted rather elaborate calculations in an effort to standardize for these and other complexities, and can only conclude that there *seems* to be no real difference in income between the two marriages, if we consider only the husband's contribution. This conclusion fits expectations, since it would be surprising sociologically if wives married upward in the second marriage. On the other hand, it is possible that they choose steadier workers in the second marriage, and this difference would appear in *annual* incomes.

However, since ex-husbands must continue to pay child support even if the ex-wife remarries (though this event reduces continuity of payments, as we noted), the total amount per week with which to meet expenses is larger for the remarried divorcee than she received during the first marriage.

It is obvious, then, that in economic terms the divorcee who remarries has more money than the one who does not remarry. The difference is large. The average is $80 as against $44 (the first husband averaged $53 weekly).

WEEKLY AMOUNT AVAILABLE FOR EXPENSES, BY REMARRIAGE

Amount per week	Remarried	Not Remarried	Totals
Less than $30	4%	22%	17%
$30-$44	8	30	24
$45-$59	18	28	25
$60-$89	30	17	21
$90 and over	39	3	13
Total	99%	100%	100%

N = 421

There is, then, a Q of association of +.78 between remarriage and having $45 or more weekly with which to meet expenses, or between remarriage and having $60 or more. And +.91 between remarriage and having $75 or more weekly.

When the Divorcee Has Enough Money. After ascertaining how much our divorcees had available each week with which to meet expenses, we asked them whether this was "enough." Forty-three percent said "Yes." In view of the economic differentials between the remarried and the not remarried, the two segments should give different answers to this question. Thus, 69% of the remarried stated that they received enough money, but only 33% of the not remarried. There was a Q of +.65 between remarriage and having enough with which to meet expenses.

"Having enough" is an evaluation of their present postdivorce situation in which both the objective economic facts *and* the meaning of those facts have an independent role, in interaction. Let us begin our analysis with an apparently obvious factor, the number of children in the divorced family.

In general, we have found that the number of children does not affect most postdivorce activities substantially. We have already analyzed the causes for this: there are no childless mothers in our group, so that almost all are committed to motherhood and marriage; for many problems of householding, the problems created by children do not increase arithmetically, as a simple function of *number;* and so on. However, in economic matters it is clear that though one can eke out the morning cereal to feed three rather than two children, one must buy three coats not two. Many necessary purchases must be increased by 50% if there are 50% more children.

Correspondingly, 47% of the women with one or two children said that they had enough, but only 31% of those with three or more children. So far, a simple economic matter appears. However, the difference *between more or fewer children is much smaller, among those who have remarried*. Thus, 71% of those who have remarried, and who have one or two children, say that they have enough, as against 64% of those remarried with three or more children. Finally, by contrast, among those who have *not* remarried, 37% of those with one or two children admit to having enough, but only 13% of those with three or more children. Thus, the objective economic fact of more children does affect their evaluations of their economic situations, but affects that evaluation differently, depending upon remarriage.

On the other hand, since remarriage itself improves the divorcee's economic position, perhaps the above differences prove only that generally the remarried are better off, even if they have more children; and the not remarried are worse off, even if they have fewer children. Let us, then, investigate further these evaluations by the divorcees of their economic situations.

One further ramification of these economic factors is, of course, job-holding. Now, we noted that (1) remarriage and having enough money are associated (Q = +.65). We also showed that (2) remarriage actually increases the amount of money available. The Q between remarriage and having $60 or more weekly was +.8. At the same time, we now report that (3) remarriage is *negatively* associated with job-holding (Q = −.60) on the part of the wife.

From these facts, we can deduce (but did not predict) that (4) holding a job, and having enough with which to meet expenses, are not associated at all. About the same proportion of job-holders claimed they did not have enough, as of women without jobs (56% *vs.* 57%). This is not at all paradoxical, since (5) there is no association at all between holding a job and having $60 or more per week with which to meet expenses (except among the *not* remarried).

There are, then, several factors in interaction. Having more money *is* related to satisfaction with the economic situation. Remarriage is associated with both. Job-holding is negatively associated with remarriage, and is not associated with having enough (evaluation) or having $60 weekly or more (the objective economic situation). So far, the relationships appear simple, if not obvious.

We then raise the question, however, as to whether (1) certain wives work because they feel that they do not have enough money; and whether (2) others feel that they have enough, *because* they hold a job and thus receive an income. Perhaps the remarried divorcees and the not remarried divorcees have different views on these matters. The remarried divorcee is more likely to use as her basis of comparison the situation of other married women. These women will ordinarily not be working, and their income expectations are higher than those of the divorcee prior to remarriage. Concretely, the job-holding, *not* remarried divorcee may have been able to increase her total income to a survival level through the job. But the remarried divorcee has taken a job primarily because her general feeling is that there is not enough.

Our first documentation of this emerging relationship is that (1) *among the remarried,* there is little association between having a job of any kind, and having "enough" ($Q = +.22$). By contrast, (2) among those who have *not* remarried, 78% of those who claim to have enough also hold some job, as against 63% of those who say they do not have enough ($Q = +.34$). Nevertheless, (3) even if we control for remarriage, the association between having $60 weekly or more, and "having enough" remains (among remarried, $+.47$; among those not remarried, $+.51$).

A second item of documentation is not reliable, because the number of cases is too small, but it is suggestive: All of the four cases of the remarried with *part*-time jobs say that they have enough. But three out of four of the 20 *not* remarried divorcees with part-time jobs claim that they do *not* have enough. That is, the part-time job for the remarried raises the income just that amount necessary to feel that there is enough money available. But the not remarried need far more than a part-time job in order to move to a satisfactory income level. Apparently, then, there are different consequences of job-holding among these two segments.

Let us, however, create a larger matrix in which we hold both remarriage and job-holding constant, and relate economic satisfaction to these factors and to the objective level of $60 or more weekly. Then we see further confirmation of our notion that different expectations may shape the meaning of these very different situations.

ECONOMIC ADJUSTMENT: "HAVING ENOUGH," BY MONEY AVAILABLE,
HOLDING CONSTANT REMARRIAGE AND JOB-HOLDING

Remarriage	Job-Holding	Percent having $60 weekly or more	Percent stating they have enough		Totals
Yes	Yes	88%	76%	10%	(42)
Yes	No	61	67	19	(80)
No	Yes	25	38	48	(202)
No	No	9	23	23	(96)
	Totals			100	N = 420

The relationships which emerge from this table are complex and definite, even though the differences are not large.

1. In spite of the close relationship between having $60 weekly or more, and having enough, when the remarried *do* have a job, a *higher* proportion receives $60 weekly or more, than admits they have enough (88% *vs.* 76%).

2. By contrast, when the remarried do *not* have a job, *fewer* receive $60 or more weekly, than *admit* they have enough. That is, the woman's objective economic situation is worse than her apparent satisfaction, when she has no job. She can play her wifely role without interruption if she can manage to get along without working, even with a slightly lesser income; so that she is more likely to express satisfaction with her economic situation.

3. The *not* remarried have lower economic expectations and also expect to work. Thus, they are more likely to admit that they have enough even when they do not receive $60 or more weekly. Consequently, when the *not* remarried do have a job, *fewer* receive $60 weekly or over, than admit they have enough.

4. Similarly, when the *not* remarried do not have a job, a *lower* proportion receive $60 or more weekly than admit they have enough.

Because these relationships appear to fit our previous comments as to the social meaning behind the economic regularities, we are willing to go beyond the data to interpret these facts. In general, the wife prefers to be supported by her husband, and to work only for specific goals that are family-oriented. Working as a breadwinner means that she feels there is not enough for the support of the family. Consequently, if she must hold a job after she has remarried, there is a greater likelihood that she feels there is not enough, even when the total amount available is $60 weekly or over. On the other hand, *not* holding a job means that she relinquishes the role of breadwinner to the new husband. This is in conformity with her role definitions, so that there is a greater likelihood she is satisfied with the amount available even though she might have less than $60.00 weekly for expenses. As we see, in both cases, the objective fact of having such an amount *is* important, and the satisfaction does not vary far from the objective situation. However, the *direction* of the deviation is significantly in harmony with the role rewards of housewife as against those of breadwinner.

On the other hand, the economic expectations of the divorcee who has not remarried are lower. Moreover, other factors are at work. As we have noted before, the steadiness of income and control over it are important, beyond the absolute amount available. When the not remarried do have a job, the percent indicating satisfaction with their financial situation is greater than the percent having $60 weekly or more, simply because some substantial proportion of the money coming in is due to their efforts, and because they can *control* its coming in by continuing to work. Consequently, their feeling of security is greater. One who has not remarried, however, and also has no job, is dependent upon the help of others, including the child support payments from the husband. She has the legitimacy of neither job-holder nor wife. The ambiguity of the social role is that she receives money as mother, but does not discharge the duties of wife. Moreover, there may be conflicts with the former husband, and we have already seen that objectively there is often a failure of payments. Consequently, even when these non-job-holding, not remarried, do have $60 or over weekly with which to meet expenses, they may feel there is no control over the continuity of the money. Nevertheless, not quite half as many of them receive $60 weekly or over, as feel that the amount received is enough, contrary to our theoretical expectations. Possibly the discrepancy is due to their comparing themselves with other women without a breadwinner, or to the lower costs of staying at home.

It is clear, then, that job-holding is connected with "having enough," through the social roles of the divorcee. Correlatively, the objective economic facts are directly related to having enough, the satisfaction being a function of *both* the money available and the social definitions of the divorcee.

Race and Having Enough. The Negro divorcees had less money available to them than did the White divorcees. About 60% of the Whites had jobs at the time of the interview, as against only 40% of the Negroes. Only 41% of the Negro divorcees had as much as $45 available weekly for expenses, as against 64% of the Whites. Once more we note the impact of marriage. Almost all of the difference in money available is found among the *not* remarried, Negro and White. Of those who are remarried, 88% of both Negro and White had $45 weekly or more. By contrast, of those not remarried, only 21% of the Negro divorcees had this much available, as against 54% of the Whites.

There might, then, be substantial differences between the two racial populations in their satisfaction with their economic situations. Actually, it is only the not remarried who differ, and the difference suggests again that differential expectations play a part. In answer to our question, "Is this enough?", 67% of the Negro remarried and 70% of the White remarried said that they had enough. But 25% of the Negro divorcees who were not remarried said they had enough, as against 34% of the Whites. As we see, the difference in satisfaction is much less than the difference in income (having $45 or more is twice as frequent among Whites) and we can suppose that the White divorcees simply have higher expectations as to the necessary minimum level of income.[6]

Comparisons with the Former Marriage. We have emphasized the relationship between the "objective" financial situation, and the social factors which seem to structure the divorcee's *response* to that situation. We can see this in a somewhat sharper way by dividing our cases into those who at the time of interview were economically "worse off," "about the same," and "better off" than during the marriage. In this division, we may do some injustice to their financial situation at either period, since we must compare the income of husband during the marriage, with "amount to meet expenses with" at the time of the interview. As we pointed out earlier, these do not refer to exactly the same item: the amount to meet expenses may not always include such

---

6. A tempting parallel line of analysis is suggested by these factors in interaction with education: The higher the proportion of *remarried* divorcees at a given educational level who report having "enough," the lower the proportion of *not* remarried at that same level who say they have enough. That is, we suppose (but cannot prove) that at each level the not remarried compare their own state with others of their level who are remarried—and the better off the latter are, the worse the former judge their own situation to be. The data are in conformity with this notion, but do not prove it, since we have no information on such images.

things as savings, purchase of durable goods, etc., and might thus lower the total actual income at the time of interview. Consequently, there may be some divorcees whom we classify as "worse off" than were really worse off objectively. (Wife's income during marriage is excluded.)

With this caution (whose degree of effect we cannot ascertain), we find that there are 171 cases who were worse off financially at the time of the interview than during the marriage; 98 who were at the same level, and 137 who were better off financially (19 were not fully ascertainable). As we would expect, the greatest differential factor is remarriage: only 13% of those who remarried were worse off economically, as against 54% of those who had not remarried. This is a further documentation of the financial difficulties that the divorcee falls into before she remarries.

When we look at the divorcee's *judgment* as to whether she had enough to live on, when compared by her objective situation, we see that remarriage is an independent factor just as is the objective difference between the two periods:

ECONOMIC ADJUSTMENT: WHETHER DIVORCEE THINKS SHE HAS "ENOUGH,"
BY REMARRIAGE AND BY WHETHER HER INCOME IS HIGHER
NOW THAN DURING FIRST MARRIAGE

| | Whether amount available now is greater than husband's income during marriage | | | |
	Greater now	Same	Less now	Totals
Remarried				
Has enough	78%	64%	33%	
Does not have enough	22	36	67	
	100(72)	100(28)	100(15)	(115)
Not remarried				
Has enough	53%	33%	24%	
Does not have enough	47	67	76	
	100(64)	100(70)	100(154)	(288)
				R = 22
				N = 425

(1) We note that being remarried and being "worse off" has a negative Q of −.77. (2) We see the obvious connection between the objective financial situation and the judgment as to whether there is enough: "Having enough" is negatively associated with being "worse off," with a Q of −.59. (3) It is clear that a much higher proportion of the remarried who now have a greater total amount of money available *also* say that they have enough, than of the *not* remarried with more money than during the previous marriage: 78% of the remarried who have more also say they have enough, but only 53% of the not remarried with more also report they have enough. The greater security and satisfaction of the wife role should create such a difference. We note (4) that conversely a slightly higher proportion of the *not remarried* say they do not have enough, when their economic situation is worse objectively, than of the remarried. However, the difference is not significant. Finally, and perhaps most significantly, (5) we note that 64% of the remarried who have

actually stayed at about the same income level report that they have enough; but only 33% of the not remarried at the same level make such a report about their situation.

But the divorcee has actually passed through several periods, the marriage itself, the separation and immediate postdivorce period, and perhaps has also entered a new marriage. If our notion is correct that such factors as role ambiguity, control over income, and economic security are important, then the period of "highest" income is not necessarily the "best" period financially. We have, of course, many free comments from our divorcees that now they could plan their own lives, or buy the things they always wanted; or perhaps could know definitely that money would be coming. Let us see, however, whether their economic evaluations lend support to these spontaneous comments.

We asked a series of questions which allowed such evaluations: When was the period of highest income, most savings, most debt; and in which period was the divorcee financially "best off" or "worst off"? Here are the main patterns that emerge.

1. Although 43% of these women admitted that the period of highest income was during the marriage, only 57% in this category reported that the marriage was the best period financially, or 29% of our total sample. Thus, even among those with more money, almost half judge the marriage period not to have been the best financially.

2. The importance of security is seen in a similar comparison for "most savings." Thirty-one percent stated that the marriage had been the period of most savings, and almost the same percentage, 29%, thought it was the best period. Thus, when there is greater financial security, it is more likely to be rated financially better.

3. As we would expect, the changing economic situation of the divorcee changes her judgments. Thirty-eight percent of the divorcees in Group I (two months after the divorce) thought that the marriage had been the best period. However, this proportion drops steadily in each Time Group, and by Time Group IV only 23% thought that the period of the marriage was the best. Correlatively, the proportion saying that "now" is the best rises from 42% to 59% between Time Groups I and IV.

4. Of course, those who have remarried are much more likely to say that "now" is best. Seventy percent of the remarried make this claim, as against 41% of the not remarried. Again, there is little real change among the remarried over time: 65% make this statement in Groups I and II, as against 76% in Group IV. There is also *no improvement* among the not remarried over time. About two-fifths of the not remarried in all four Time Groups say that "now" is the best period. We cannot isolate the important factors here. Those who do not remarry may be different in that they are simply poorer managers. Their situation may *actually* be worsening. We believe that some change may occur among those who had some surplus at separation, and have finally used it up, while no improvement has occurred in any other financial sector. Thus, among the not remarried there is an increase over time of those who think that the period of final separation was the best: from 8% in Time Group I, and 16% in Group II; to 18% and 10% in Groups III and IV.

5. Finally, these are not merely "subjective" evaluations. We have already presented a substantial body of data to show that the objective economic facts do structure these judgments. We are now showing only that other types of factors interact with the mainly economic ones to produce judgments in which the women's new status, and the escape from a bad social situation, make the new economic situation easier for some to bear even when it is objectively the same, or even worse. Nevertheless, their evaluations of "better or worse" are always close to their evaluations of "high or low" savings or income. We noted a moment ago that high savings was correlated closely with a judgment of "better." Now, we merely add that 57% of those who said the marriage was the period of highest income *also* said it was the best period financially; 74% of those who said the separation was the period of highest income also stated it was the best. The factor of social status influences the next comparison, but the objective relationship is also clear: 86% of those who said that "now" was the period of highest income also said it was best. And 59% of those who said there was no difference in income level during these periods also said that they could not judge between them as being worse or better.

We must conclude, then, that especially the remarried judge themselves to be better off financially than during the previous marriage, and that this favorable evaluation is more frequent than an actual improvement in the objective economic situation. Further, among those who do not remarry, there is some tendency to view their situation as even worse than it is objectively. Finally, however, the former marriage becomes steadily less attractive financially to these divorcees; and even among the not remarried there is no increase in those who think the previous marriage was better, but an increase in the proportion believing that the separation was better.

Obtaining Outside Financial Aid. On the other hand, we must not forget that the *expenses* of the divorced period may include crises. Crises continue to occur, whether divorced or married. Where did these women obtain help?

For the most part, they obtained help from their own relatives, and only to a limited degree from the former husband or his family. The help from friends was minimal. We would expect considerable help from friends in small crises, but limited help from them in large and continuing crises, since it is only in the closest of friendships that the moral obligation to help greatly is strong.

MAIN SOURCE OF OUTSIDE FINANCIAL AID WHEN DIVORCEE NEEDED HELP

Source	Totals
Agencies*	26%
Own Family	57
Husband's Family	2
Former Husband	3
Friends	2
Other	9
Subtotal	99
	317 = 75%
Had No Need for Aid	25%
Totals	100% (425)

*Includes Children's Aid, county welfare, and church assistance.

As we see, the important sources of aid are few. Aside from the ex-wife's own family, and the agencies of Children's Aid, churches, and county welfare, no single source makes up more than a small proportion of the total. We have not asked why these other sources were used so little. We would guess that the ex-wife failed to *obtain* aid from her ex-husband's family in part because she did not *seek* it. As we noted earlier, there seems to be an estrangement between the wife and her husband's family during the divorce process (although whether it is a result of mutual ignorance or of genuine conflict, we do not know). The lack of aid from this source is particularly interesting, since the ex-wife usually has in her custody the grandchildren of her ex-husband's family (as well as of her own family, of course). And—if we may be allowed to speculate still further—we would suppose that in general the grandparents are even more emotionally involved with their grandchildren than with the divorce conflict. However, with reference to the aid given by the ex-wife's own family, we do not know whether the aid was based upon the grandchildren's need, or upon the daughter's need. What is clear, on the other hand, is that the need for aid was widespread even though our kinship institutions do not specify the direction and degree of moral obligation that ought to be assumed by the kin.

When we posed the hypothetical question where they *would* go for aid if they needed it at the time of the interview, the distribution is much the same as in the previous table, except that a slightly lower proportion still thought there would be no need for help. In an effort to learn more about their socioeconomic relations with the ex-husband, we asked whether, even as a *second* choice, they would seek aid from their former husbands. Almost two-thirds said that they would not do so, although the context of this series of questions excludes child support, and would suggest the possibility of special or unexpected problems that would require getting help. The Catholic ex-wives were about as willing to seek their ex-husbands' aid (33% *vs.* 28%) as Protestants. Catholics were less likely to have ever considered remarriage to the former husband as a financial solution (7% *vs.* 11%); and only 4% of the Catholics still thought of this as a solution at the time of the interview, as against 8% of the Protestants.

Summary. In the present chapter, we have explored in some detail the economic position of the divorcee in both the separation period and the later divorce period. There is little property to be divided, but in general when there is little property the wife gets most of it. When there is house or furniture, most divorced mothers get it. A property split is more likely, with higher amounts of property, or higher education, but these two factors are interdependent.

Since the child support payments of the former husband form the economic base of the ex-wife's income, we analyzed the factors that appear to affect continuity of payment: ability to pay and willingness to pay, using various items to measure these two fundamental ones. Although these wives had a legal right to force continuity of payments, apparently one-fourth of the ex-husbands rarely or never pay, and about one-third pay only occasionally.

We have also investigated the ex-wife's role as worker and as wife, and her total income available, so as to ascertain the *meaning* of different levels of income for different status situations. In particular, it seems clear that the remarried feel more satisfaction with their economic position than might be expected from the objective income available, but as a group there is also more money available than during the first marriage. For this complex of interacting factors, we analyzed both the divorcees' general feeling of economic satisfaction, and their comparisons with previous phases of their marital lives.

In the succeeding chapters, we begin to explore the divorced mother's social adjustment after divorce.

CHAPTER XVII

SOCIAL ADJUSTMENT: FRIENDSHIPS AND OPPORTUNITIES TO MEET PEOPLE

WHETHER OR NOT the respondent had a traumatic experience during the divorce conflict, in almost all cases she is kept in her old friendship circle, or is drawn into a new friendship circle. Several traditional questions have been raised about this process, and in this chapter we shall raise further questions.

The divorcee begins to carry out those activities that will eventually lead to an integration of her divorce conflict into her life, usually through remarriage. This means an acceptance of the experience by her friendship circle (if she has one) and a movement toward a process that we call courtship. We mean by social adjustment, then, that the individual is going through the phases of once more finding her own identity as a person and being accepted as a person who is eligible to be a spouse. Not all divorcees go through all of these phases, and of course not all remarry. Therefore, in the succeeding sections we shall attempt to show which divorcees seem to find new friends or keep their old friends, find new suitors and move toward remarriage.

Our working definition of "adjustment to divorce," as we stated it in our first chapter, is the integration of the divorce experience into her total life experience, such that the individual lives by the daily and future demands of his or her *new* social position rather than by constant reference to the ties defined by the previous marriage. That is, she has adjusted, even if not remarried, if her usual self-image is no longer "ex-wife of Y——," or "formerly married to Y——"; if her economic position (even if not pleasant) is not the simple result of having lost the family breadwinner; if her problems with her children are no longer to be traced primarily to internal or overt conflicts about or with their father; if her friendship ties whether new or old are threatened only by the ordinary problems between any friends, not by the strains of loyalty decisions for or against one of the spouses.

We do not expect them "to forget the past." We are simply asking whether they are solving the problems of their new position or status, rather than reliving the old.

Yet we are not measuring them as human beings. We do not find them wanting in character or spirit if they have not adjusted after a considerable period of time. Speaking as judge, we might admit that in some instances an early adjustment *ought* not to be expected. The blows of marital misfortune *were* too heavy. We have nevertheless *not* judged them in this way. If we say, Mrs. Y—— has adjusted economically but not in her relation to her former husband, we mean *only* that her emotional life is still bound up with that husband. We do not mean that she *ought* to have adjusted in that area also. If we say, Mrs. R—— has adjusted slowly, we mean that other women who divorced when she did have now rewoven that experience into their total lives more completely than she.

With reference to "social" adjustment, an important question seems to be whether the divorcee kept her old circle of friends. Also, does she have opportunities for getting friends? Even if this statement is technically loose, its negative form is hardly debatable: if the divorcee *still* has no friends at the time of the interview, then her social adjustment is not yet complete. Moreover, friendships and other social opportunities have importance for still another phase of the movement toward a new marriage: dating.

Meaning of "Friendships." The term "friends" in the U. S. does not ordinarily mean great intimacy of relationship. When we speak of our circle of friends we do not necessarily imply that our "closest friend" is in that circle. We ordinarily mean that most of our visiting and our social engagements take place in that group. In some contexts and in some situations, there may be no real "group" of friends. We may have several friends, for example, people with whom we have dinner or lunch somewhat frequently, with whom we gossip and exchange personal opinions; but these people in turn may, because of geographical location or time schedules, have only little to do with one another. This situation is more likely to occur in a metropolitan setting than in small cities or towns. Nevertheless we have to keep in mind the shifting meaning of the term "friends." Here it does not suggest great intimacy of relationship.

On the other hand, if one says that one is *without* friends, this statement has a much more definite meaning. It ordinarily suggests that the individual has no group of acquaintances with which he has much social intercourse.

We wanted to find out not only whether our divorcees had friends during their marriage, but also whether they lost them during the divorce conflict and separation. In the latter event, we also wanted to know whether they had acquired a new circle of friends prior to the interview. We therefore asked them whether during the separation and divorce period their most active friends were those of the marriage. Fifty-two percent of our divorcees stated that during the separation and divorce period their most active friends *were* those of the marriage; 44% had different friends (4% claimed no friends).

Factors Affecting Friendship Changes. Changing one's friends is not necessarily the result of being rejected by them, or even of having decided to reject them and to select a new group of friends. The change may come about merely because a change of residence makes it difficult to continue seeing them. We do not know exactly what proportion of *divorcees* move from their old residence during this adjustmental period. We do know: (a) that *urban Americans* move frequently, and (b) that divorcees move still more frequently. Consequently we would expect a fairly high proportion of *change in friendship groupings* even if there were *no positive or negative attitudes* toward the divorce itself in this society.[1]

Nevertheless, some residue of friendship change might be due at least indirectly to the consequences of the divorce conflict. For example, the decision to get a divorce might be more likely to cause a disruption in friendship circles if those friends were mainly Catholic. It is also possible that when the divorcee is herself guilty in the conflict, or feels that others *believe* her to be, there might be some shifts or even divisions in the circle of friends.

On the other hand, the middle and upper educational and occupational strata should generally experience fewer friendship changes. There may be a slightly stronger disapproval of divorce in these strata, so that these two factors, (a) the tendency to maintain networks of friends and (b) the disapproval of divorce, might act in contrary directions, allowing no clear tendency to emerge.

Against our expectation, there seem to be (1) no differences between religions in the tendency to maintain friends during the separation and divorce period: 52% of the Protestants and 53% each of Catholics and of "other religion" maintained their friends from the marriage period through the separation and divorce period. (2) Almost exactly the same percentage of friendship maintenance (54%-52%) is to be found for both Negroes and Whites. In this study we have found only a few differences between Negro and White in their divorce experience. There seems also to be (3) no consistent relationship between *age of divorcee* at the time of the interview and the tendency to maintain the same friends through the conflict and divorce period. This is somewhat contrary to our expectation, since we had guessed that the younger divorcees with their greater mobility of action and decision, not to mention their measurably greater tendency to engage in dating activities, would be more likely to develop new circles of friends. The differences between age groups are statistically insignificant, small, and without any apparent direction.

On the other hand, our expectations *are* borne out by the data on (4) education of wife, (5) occupational class of husband, and (6) husband's income during marriage. Educational and occupational class show a similar pattern in that *it is only the top category that is differentiated* from the other classes. The remaining groupings are almost exactly the same: 65% of the college group and 65% of the upper occupational group maintain the same circle, against 51% for the other classes. Income of husband shows a very slight but steady increase through each income bracket, from 48% for the lowest (up to $45), to 60% for the highest ($100 and over per week). (7) The effect of chil-

---

1. In a recent study by Peter Rossi, it was found that 47% of all households (Philadelphia) had three *or more* addresses during their first decade of existence (*Why Families Move*, The Free Press, forthcoming). Moreover, since the largest segment of divorcees is lower or lower-middle class, and these segments have in general the highest residential mobility rate, we would expect the mobility of divorcees to be high, even if divorce itself had no effect. Our own data on the residential mobility of our divorcees are not reliable.

dren upon the maintenance of the friendship group seems to be very slight. This slight effect appears to be the result of the wife's being "tied down" by the children: that is, a larger *number of children* appears to have the same effect as having *young* children, so that those with very young children *and* those with a larger number of children seem to maintain their friendships somewhat more firmly. However, the differences are small and statistically not significant.

The divorcee may also have a job during this conflict and separation period, just as she may have had a job during her marriage. (8) These two items seem to have a conflicting direction of effect. (a) Those who had jobs *at separation seem less likely* to have kept their circle of friends during the separation period, but (b) those who "ever" had a job during the marriage seem slightly more likely to have kept their friends in marriage over the separation and conflict period. There are four possibilities here: (a) those who had jobs at some time during the marriage but did not during the separation and immediately postdivorce period; (b) those who had no job at any time; (c) those who had jobs at both phases of their marriage careers; and (d) those who had no job at any time during the marriage but did have a job during the separation and divorce period. These four types, interestingly enough, are listed in order of decreasing tendency to maintain their friends: Sixty-four per cent of Type (a) kept their friends over this period. For Type (b) the figure was 49%, for Type (c) 47%, and for Type (d), 33%. The order of the last three of these four types appears simple to interpret. The first is somewhat more complex.

Let us look at these types: (a) Those who *had* jobs during the marriage but did *not* have a job during the separation period were those mothers who dropped their jobs in order to stay home. Thus, they had increased social time at their disposal, and more time to cultivate and keep their old friends (64% kept them). (b) The apparently "normal" type is that of *not* having a job during the marriage or during the separation. This is the housewife and mother who always stayed at home, and thus kept her friends (49%). (c) Those who had jobs during *both* periods fall slightly below these two previous types, but only very slightly below the norm (47%). That is to say, these are working wives who developed a set of friends on the job and kept them during this adjustment period, as they also kept the job; or, they integrated their circle with the job demands. At least we can say there is no greater change for these people, whether their main friends were to be found on the job or in the neighborhood. (d) The last type, those who had *no* job during the marriage but *did* have a job during the separation, kept their friends least (33%). These appear to be women who had to change their home organization during this period. They had to go to work in order to meet their economic problems. The change in time schedules and in the composition of the groups with which they came most frequently in contact led to a change in their friends.

Whether the *decision* to divorce was *steady* seems not to affect the keeping of the friendship group. Likewise whether the *husband* was in love with another woman seems to have had no great effect. On the other hand, when the *wife herself* was in love with another man, she was less likely to keep her circle of friends: 38% kept their circle of friends, as against 54% for those who were *not* in love with another man. This involvement probably meant a split in the wife's friendship group as well as new allegiances which took her somewhat from her older circle. On the other hand, whether it was the husband or wife who first suggested the divorce makes only a very slight difference: when the husband made the first suggestion, (1) the wife's circle was slightly more likely to be maintained; with (2) mutual suggestion coming next, close to the average; and (3) "wife's suggestion" slightly below this. However, the differences are not statistically significant. Similarly, *when* the separation occurred (before the decision, between decision and filing, or after filing) also seems to make only a very slight difference.

On the other hand, those who took only a very short time to file the suit after coming to the decision were somewhat *more likely* to maintain their friends, than those who took a longer period of time. (0 to one month group, 61%; one to six months, 51%; and seven months and over, 42%). Both these last two items seem to be simple resultants of the length of time for the final conflict. Those who took a longer period of time to file *were* less likely to keep their friends. And those wives who stayed with their husbands to the very last were more likely to maintain their friends. That is to say, when the major decision and action toward divorce occurred a rather *long* time before the actual separation and conflict period, then *sufficient time* elapsed for the ordinary changes of friendship circles which are constantly happening in everyone's life. These tabulations show only small differences, although the relationship between (a) the length of time from the final decision to filing suit and (b) change in friends is statistically significant (.02 > P > .01).

A further element however is involved in this last relationship. When the period from final decision to filing is *very short,* in most cases it was the husband who was pushing for the divorce, and very often this was a triangle situation. When the husband was thus pushing for the divorce, then it is much more likely, we suppose, for her friends to rally around her and to stay with her during the conflict and separation period. Thus, there is less change of friendship circles. Let us look at this further.

We cannot check this very minor hypothesis in all of its dimensions. We can however present some data bearing on the possibility that the divorces in which there is a very *short period* between decision and filing are also those in which the husband is pushing hard for a divorce; and that the wife's friends help her in this crisis where loyalties are not so ambivalent as, for example, in long drawn out conflict where the group sees considerable justice and injustice on both sides.

We may examine Triangle and Desertion as themes of complaint, with reference to the maintenance of the wife's circle of friends. If our notions are correct, we would expect to find that where there is (a) *no* Triangle but there *is* Desertion, the circle of friends ought to change more than the average for our divorced population. The Desertion-only complaint is usually associated with a rather long absence of the husband, so that a considerable period of time elapses. Furthermore, this absence is apparently deliberate on the part of the husband, and the wife must make important changes in her home and even perhaps job organization. Consequently, there would be changes in the friendship circle. At the other extreme is (c) the Triangle complaint without

Desertion. The husband is then presumably in love with another woman, wants very much to get a divorce, and insists upon rather early action. At the same time his behavior is more likely to cause moral disapproval, even by his own friends. The wife's friends (who are almost without exception female) are even more unequivocally disapproving. Consequently, the time lapse is short, and the group support is stronger. Therefore a higher proportion of these wives should maintain their circle of friends from the time of marriage through the conflict and separation period. In between these two extremes should fall (b) Triangle with Desertion. Often this means a Triangle in which the husband abandons his wife and goes off with another woman. Sometimes it is a desertion which ends in a triangle. The time lapse may or may not be long, but the Desertion does require certain kinds of readjustment in home and social organization. Thus we see that (a) in the first type (Desertion without Triangle) only 40% keep the same circle of friends, while (c) in the other extreme type (Triangle without Desertion) 62% keep the same circle of friends. The intermediate type (b) Triangle with Desertion, is one in which 47% keep their friends as against the average for the total population of 52%. When we break down our cases in this fashion, of course, the numbers are small and as a consequence the statistical significance is low ($.2 > P > .1$) even though the data are in the expected direction.

When the divorcee admits that she was in love with another man, she is more likely to change her circle of friends (only 38% maintained their same circle of friends during this period). Further confirmation of the notion that in this case *she* is pushing for a divorce and voluntarily entering a new circle can be gained from our facts on dating period. We asked the divorcee whether she had been dating or had begun to date at the time of separation. When we run this item against the maintenance of friends, we find that those who *had* been dating even before the separation kept their same circle in only 29% of the cases, while those who had *not* been dating before that time kept their friends in 71% of the cases.

"Quality" of Friends. The hypothesis has frequently been offered that at the time of the decree the divorcee is likely to begin associating with people outside her old circle, who are "lower" in their moral standards, or at least are not in all respects equal to the old group. In part, we recognize in this hypothesis our moral bias: the divorcee *ought* to be associating with lower people, because she or he has shown herself or himself to be lower in moral calibre than was expected. In addition this may be felt to be a kind of retribution. It is related to an older set of biases which pictured the "fallen woman" as associating with the dregs of society and slipping lower and lower into the depths.

As we have already seen, however, this hypothesis cannot be true for a large proportion of divorcees, since at least half of them continue to maintain their old circle of friends. At the worst, if these divorcees are associating with persons of low worth, it is simply because they always have done so. Most of us change our circle of friends over a period of years. It is not necessarily the case that they will always be a step downward.

When we asked our respondents whether their circle of friends at separation and divorce seemed to be better, the same, or worse than the friends they had during the marriage, we find that 90% of those with *different* friends believed them to be either better (42%) or the same (48%). Only 10% thought that their new friends were worse than those they had during the marriage. Thus, even when the *circles* of friends changed, the *kinds* of friends are not greatly different.

Thus, almost all of the respondents who had different friends during the separation and conflict period from those during the marriage, claimed that they were to be rated about the same as, or better than, their friends of marriage. Now, it is possible that these respondents are granting to their new friends more than these friends deserve. This we cannot test. We can, on the other hand, ascertain whether there seemed to be some drift of the newly divorced *toward a circle of divorced friends,* by comparing the proportion of respondents having divorced or divorcing friends, among those who kept the same friends, with the proportion among those with a new circle.

Using the categories: (a) two or more friends divorced; (b) one divorced; (c) none divorced, but one or more divorcing; and (d) none divorced or divorcing, we find that those who kept the *same* friends during the separation and conflict period are slightly *less* likely to have (a) two or more divorced friends in their circle and/or to have (b) one divorced friend in their circle. However, the difference is very small (9% *vs.* 13%; 16% *vs.* 19%) and the differences are not statistically significant. Further, those who have kept the *same* friends are slightly *more* likely than those with a different circle to have (c) none divorced but one or more divorcing in their group (9% *vs.* 6%). Again, the difference is not statistically significant, but all three differences are in the predicted direction. The proportion having "none divorced or divorcing" is almost exactly the same in both groups (66% *vs.* 62%), although once more in the expected direction. In short, what has been described by some as a "drifting process" according to which the divorced person moves gradually into those circles where the divorce is most easily accepted, and thus moves into a group of divorcees, does not seem to be the usual experience of the divorcee. This new circle need not be made up mainly or even partially of divorced people. Whether she is drifting to divorced or divorcing friends is less important for her adjustment, we suggest, than whether she stays in or finds a circle of friends whose response to her is made by reference to the present and to the future rather than to the past: that is, whether she is a person in her own right in this circle, and not merely the ex-wife of Mr. So-and-So.

Nevertheless, the respondents who *come from segments or strata* in which the *tendency to divorce* is generally somewhat *higher* would also tend in a higher proportion to have friends in their circle who were also divorced. That is to say, all these respondents would share with one another the greater or lesser tendency to divorce of their own segment, and thus their circle would reflect that tendency. Thus we would expect to find that Negro respondents would be more likely than Whites to have divorced friends in their circle. We would have the same expectation with respect to Protestants as against Catholics. As we see in the succeeding table, this expectation is borne out. The differences are minor for occupational class.

HAVING DIVORCED FRIENDS, BY RACE OR RELIGION

| | | Friends Divorced | | |
	Yes	No, but divorcing	None divorced or divorcing	Totals
Race				
Negro	38%	10%	52%	100% (80)
White	26	7	66	99 (345)
Religion				
Protestant	33	8	59	100 (247)
Catholic	21	7	72	100 (135)

Having a Circle of Friends Now. Some of the respondents who did not maintain their friendships or circle of friends during the conflict also failed to move *immediately* into any new circle of friends. By the time of the interview, some had *already* found a new circle of friends. Still others were still finding friends; or admitted that they did not have such a circle, and were not yet finding such a circle. Since our question about keeping their friends referred mainly to the time of conflict and separation as the base point, we tabulated this aspect of their social adjustment by period of time since separation. We then see a gradually *increasing percentage* of divorcees who claim that they *now* have a circle of friends, and a gradually *decreasing* proportion who state that they neither have such a circle nor are they finding such a circle. The category "finding friends" has such small numbers in it that we cannot use the cell fruitfully. In general, however, the proportion decreases over time, as the proportion "having friends *now*" increases.

SOCIAL ADJUSTMENT: HAVING OR FINDING FRIENDS, BY TIME SINCE SEPARATION

Time since separation	Have friends now	Finding friends	No friends and not finding friends	Total
0-1 year	71%	10%	19%	100% (69)
1-2 years	74	5	21	100 (107)
2-3 years	84	5	11	100 (162)
3 years	86	4	10	100 (84)
Total	80%	5%	15%	100% (422)

Now, it might seem that this association is simply a function of remarriage. An increasing proportion of divorcees has entered a new marriage as the length of time since separation increases, and remarriage might bring new friends. However, when we control for remarriage-nonremarriage, the differentials in finding friends or not finding friends by time since separation remain almost exactly the same. That is to say, the longer the time period since separation, the greater proportion having friends, *whether or not the divorcee gets remarried*.

Moreover, neither race nor religion seems to affect the entrance into a friendship circle. On the other hand, education does affect the distribution. In the collapsed table which follows we see that the higher the amount of education of the respondent, the more likely she is to have a circle of friends now, and the less likely she is to fall into the category, "no friends" (including in this category those who do not have friends but who are finding friends).

SOCIAL ADJUSTMENT: HAVING A CIRCLE OF FRIENDS NOW, BY EDUCATION OF RESPONDENT

Education	Has Circle of Friends	Total No.
Some College, or completed	95%	37
Completed High School	85	128
Some High School	75	199
Grammar School only	72	61

N = 425

$$X^2 = 12.0, .01 > P > .001$$

This finding is parallel to the general fact that those with more education have a wider circle of social contacts, both formal and informal. Since in general in our society most people are not born within the circles of their adulthood, the corollary hypothesis would be that those with more education are also likely, after a status change (or even, we suppose, a geographical change) to enter such new relationships more quickly. They seem to be more likely to keep their friends, also. Moreover, whether or not they kept their friends, education is related to having friends at the time of the interview. However, we cannot test the corollary hypothesis, since our cases are too few.

Later on we want to consider the further possibility, that *maintaining* one's friends during the separation and conflict period is in part due to whether or not the existing *friends actually help* the respondent to meet eligible men. That is to say, her moving from the old friends may in some cases be a function of her passive or active search for dating partners. She would then be more likely to *stay* in her *own* circle if they actually *helped* her to find such men. If this is true, then we would also expect to find that respondents with higher education will also be more likely to have *helpful* friends than the respondents with lesser education. We shall soon test this hypothesis.

Opportunities for Meeting People. As we have already commented, "adjustment" in our report does not refer to something like "achieving happiness" or "adjusting to society's demands."[2] Rather it refers to a change in self-definition: for example, from that of wife to ex-wife; and from ex-wife to "eligible female," or from ex-wife to "new wife." In terms of process or dynamics, we have generally used the term to refer to a change in the wife's orientations, from a continual reference to the past and its problems, toward reference to the problems of the day or the future. We have spoken of it as a "reintegration of the divorce into the total life pattern of the divorcee." We have attempted, as much as possible, to use the expressed attitudes and behavior of the divorcee and of her relevant social groups in judging this adjustment. We could not rely merely on the statement of the divorcee that "everything is fine." As we have seen in our rather lengthy analysis of the structural aspects of this integration—what we have called the institutionalization of divorce adjustment—a most important set of structural factors is that relating to remarriage. Now, remarriage in our society is an act that is preceded by various social activities, usually including the maintenance or formation of a circle of friends, or entrance into a circle of friends. We have just looked at the factors associated with this behavior.

2. On theoretical grounds, however, we would be surprised if all three did not in fact coincide roughly within most societies.

However, (1) forming a circle of friends is not alone sufficient for remarriage, and is not always even necessary. It is a sieve with very wide holes. Parallel to the making of a friendship circle is (2) having opportunities for meeting people. Beyond both is (3) the activity of general dating. This in turn is not entirely necessary for the next step, though in our society it usually precedes that next step: (4) steady dating. Beyond steady dating is usually (5) some form of engagement. (Granted that in our society this engagement for divorcees is shorter, less formal, and associated with fewer traditional activities such as showers, etc., than is the engagement of those who have never married before.)[3] Since all these various activities are in part sequential, let us in this next section consider the unattached divorcee's opportunities for meeting people.

For those who do not have plans for immediate remarriage, the social activities after the separation or divorce are of great importance. One aspect of this adjustment is the maintenance or acquisition of a circle of friends. "Opportunities to meet people" refers, naturally, to both "friends" in the ordinary sense and the possibility of meeting men. For our purposes, the most important segment to be considered here is those who were neither remarried nor going steady at the time of the interview. We are now mainly concerned with the progression from meeting people to dating, and from steady dating to remarriage. In our sample there are 188 divorcees who are neither remarried nor going steady. Let us now look at their opportunities to meet people, and afterwards at the relationship between these opportunities and other aspects of the social adjustment.

OPPORTUNITIES OF DIVORCEES (UNMARRIED AND NOT GOING STEADY) TO MEET PEOPLE
"MOST IMPORTANT OPPORTUNITIES"

"Jobs," "Work," etc.	24%
Church Activities	22
Parties	12
Women's Clubs, P.T.A.	10
Dates	6
Union Meetings	4
Hobbies and Sports	3
Adult Education Classes	2
Other, No Answer	17
	100%

N = 188

Neither race nor religion is associated with having opportunities to meet people. On the other hand, age *is* relevant. The younger have more such opportunities. The variable of age, of course, contains far too many elements for us to be able to tease out all of them. We note that 67% of those aged 20-24 years have "many or some" opportunities as against 49% for those who are 30 years or over ($.05 > P > .02$).

One of the factors that might be concealed in the variable of age is some kind of "optimistic" bias. That is, the young are affected less by the divorce experience, or recover more rapidly, and as a consequence their *attitudes toward* love and marriage are more favorable. Sixty-two percent of those with

3. For this relationship, see A. B. Hollingshead, "Marital Status and Wedding Behavior," *Marriage and Family Living* (November 1952), pp. 308-311.

positive attitudes toward love and marriage claim to have dating opportunities, as against 51% of those with negative attitudes. Thus, when we find that the young seem to have more opportunities, perhaps we are simply measuring their somewhat more favorable responses to the possibilities of love and marriage. Let us test this hypothesis.

When we run age against the opportunities for meeting people, holding motivation constant, we find this interesting relationship: *whether or not the young respondents are positively motivated toward love and marriage, about two-thirds of them have many or some opportunities. However, almost two-thirds of the older respondents who do not want to remarry also fail to report having opportunities to meet people.* Putting the matter in more commonsense terms, the older women who do not particularly care to meet new people manage not to meet them; but the younger women who do not particularly care to meet people are met by them just the same.

We have often noted some of the complexities of economic elements in the adjustmental process. For example, we have several times seen the complex role which job holding seems to play for different segments of the population and at different time phases. With reference to the opportunities for meeting people, we note further interesting facets of this apparently simple economic activity.

First of all, holding a full-time job is associated with having many or some opportunities to meet people. The Q is $+.37$ ($.02 > P > .01$). Of the 188 respondents who were neither remarried nor going steady at the time of the interview, 113 had full time jobs. Of these with full time jobs, 3/5 mentioned "job" or "work" as one type of opportunity to meet people.

However, *not all kinds* of jobs hold equal opportunities for meeting people. Some types of jobs necessarily throw the worker into relationships with other people, while other jobs tend to isolate the individual, not only from his or her neighbors (because of time schedules) but even from coworkers. Consequently, we attempted to ascertain which jobs seem to be most associated with having opportunities to meet people.

OPPORTUNITIES AVAILABLE TO THOSE HOLDING FULL-TIME JOBS, BY JOB TYPE

Type of Job	Those who mention "jobs" as opportunities	Those who have frequent opportunities	Total	
Waitress	80%	70%	100%	(10)
Teacher, Professional	75	50	100	(4)
Sales	73	53	100	(15)
Factory	58	28	100	(36)
Domestic	57	57	100	(7)
Clerical, Secretarial	50	40	100	(40)
Other, No Answer				(1)

N = 113

Thus, we know the proportion who mention jobs *as* an opportunity and who *also* claim to have many or some opportunities to meet people. It is tempting to push our analysis beyond the data at this point. The waitress and the salesgirl do have face to face contact with a clientele, and presumably some proportion of this clientele is male. At the opposite end of this opportunity continuum is factory work, where the physical proximity of many co-workers might lead one to suppose that the opportunities for meeting people are great. However, (1) most of factory work time is spent in a relationship with machines rather than with people. Furthermore, in general, (2) when the woman is a worker, her co-workers are also women. Moreover, we are willing to guess that a further factor plays a role: (3) the female factory worker in most factories has little chance to show her attractiveness; at least we say the tradition is to dress in a practical fashion. Consequently, the available men may not make an active attempt to seek the acquaintance of any but the most obviously pretty female workers. Both salesgirls and waitresses are at the opposite pole of this continuum. It is perhaps also not too much to say that (4) both the salesgirl and the waitress are socially defined as girls with whom the average male is permitted to joke and flirt mildly. Consequently, on the male side it is easier to attempt to make an acquaintanceship with these women.

The numbers of cases are so small, of course, that we cannot take these guesses seriously. However, we shall indulge ourselves a step further. The frequency of opportunities for meeting people is a function not only of (1) the *numbers* of people with whom the worker comes into face to face contact, and (2) their *sex*. It is also a function of (3) the social role of the job. And (4) this is related to the permitted degree of sexual attractiveness of the female worker. Thus, we suggest that the social definition of waitress and salesgirl is that the male is permitted to make friendly overtures to her. Let us note further, however, that in the case of both waitress and salesgirl the social contact with people is *outside* the work force itself. That is, (5) the *kind* of relationship is important. The salesgirl and waitress have a "clientele." The factory worker usually has none; the secretarial and clerical worker only to a limited extent. The female professional worker is likely to be a bureaucrat, a subordinate, and a technician, and thus has a "clientele" only little more than clerical workers. The domestic on the other hand is actually hired by her clientele, and has a different position from either of the other two types.

However, a further factor is involved, besides whether or not the face to face contact is with an *outside* clientele: (6) the *status* of those with whom the female worker comes in contact. In the case of workers in a bureaucracy, whether this is an industrial or a business bureaucracy, the face-to-face contact is usually with female co-workers at the *same status* level as the worker and with *male* co-workers of a *higher* status. There may then be considerable face to face contact with a male superior without any contacts which the workers would describe as "opportunities to meet people." That is, in more commonsense terms, when the boss wants to keep his position clearly defined, the apparent opportunities cannot be defined as real ones.

This barrier is not so strong for the professional worker, since to a considerable extent the working patterns in a professional hierarchy emphasize the characteristic of subordination-superordination much less than in other work hierarchies. One consequence of this is that, in analyzing hierarchies, we distinguish between "staff" and "line" organizations. It is the general experience of such analyses that social relations in the staff group are much less formal, and are shaped more by the possession of knowledge and ideas than of mere hierarchical position. These hypotheses "fit the data" we have, but we emphasize that they go beyond any test we can now make.

While it is true that those who have secretarial or factory jobs are less *likely to mention* that job as an opportunity to meet people, these workers have opportunities *in spite of their jobs,* or at least in spite of the kind of job they have. (1) Having *any* full-time job is associated with having opportunities to meet people and (2) there is also an association between the younger ages and having such opportunities.

It is perhaps worth-while, then, to test whether job-holding and age act as independent factors. In the succeeding table, it is seen that (1) for both age groups the association between job-holding and opportunities to meet people still obtains. Furthermore, (2) for both job groupings (holding a full-time job or not) the association of opportunities to meet people with the lower age group still holds. These factors, then, are independently important.

SOCIAL ADJUSTMENT: OPPORTUNITIES TO MEET PEOPLE, BY JOB-HOLDING AND BY AGE
(UNATTACHED DIVORCEES)

| Has a full-time job | Age | OPPORTUNITIES TO MEET PEOPLE | | |
		Many or some	Few or none	Totals
Yes	20-29	79%	21%	100%(48)
Yes	30 +	55	45	100 (65)
No	20-29	53	47	100 (45)
No	30 +	37	63	100 (30)
Totals		58%	42%	

$$X^2 = 15.0 \quad .01 > P > .001 \quad N = 188$$

Throughout this study, we have emphasized the impossibility of analyzing decisions by any merely rationalistic interpretation. For example, the answer to the question, "Why did you divorce?" does not ever give us the real bases for the decision to divorce. We have suggested implicit or explicit models or schemes for analyzing behavior relative to divorce, and in these schemes we have attempted always to introduce not alone the apparent *attitude* of the divorcee, but also her own *action.* Furthermore, we have tried where possible to bring in the actions and decisions of other people, or even the structural situation when we could describe it properly.

We have been attempting to do this also for the status progression from being an ex-wife to being a new wife. Thus, meeting people is not a simple resultant of the individual's willingness to meet others. It is also structured by the social relationships in which the individual finds himself, and thus is often a function of the divorcee's definition of that position as well. Opportunities are only in part the result of (a) intended efforts. To a considerable extent they are also the by-product of (b) *other actions* of the *same* individual, and of (c) actions of still *other individuals.* Thus, those who are disillusioned and have a low opinion of both love and marriage will be less likely to seek out other people. To this extent, their failure to meet others is a function of their own intention and attitude. However, those who are *young,* even if they are cynical about love and marriage, will have more opportunities than the older respondent, because other people, and in particular men, will seek *them* out. We have seen these general propositions about human behavior illustrated by our discussion of job-holding and opportunities.

Summary. In this chapter, we have dealt with one aspect of the social adjustment after the divorce. In particular, we have asked whether divorcees keep their old friends, and have found that somewhat over half claim to have kept them through the separation and divorce period. For those who changed their friendship circles, we ascertained that religion, race, and age of the divorcee are not related to maintenance of the friendship circle, but that class attributes are: education of the ex-wife, occupational class of her husband, husband's income during the marriage. However, only the top category is distinguished from the others. We also learned that whether job-holding affects the stability of the friendship circle depends on whether the wife had a job during the marriage. When the length of the conflict period was long, change in the friendship circle was more likely.

Contrary to popular assumption, these divorcees felt that their new friends were about the same in "quality" as their old circle, or better. There is a slight and insignificant tendency for these women to have divorced or divorcing friends in the new circle, but the divorcees from strata with a higher divorce rate (e.g., Negroes, Protestants) *are* more likely to be in circles with other divorcees, i.e., similar in this respect to the stratum as a whole.

Finally, we have begun to ascertain whether these divorcees have opportunities for meeting people. These opportunities are related to class, age, job holding, type of job, and the help of friends. Since, however, these factors are of importance for meeting eligible suitors, and for dating, we have presented some of the relevant data in the next chapter.

CHAPTER XVIII

DATING ACTIVITIES:
THE UNATTACHED DIVORCEE

EVEN THOUGH opportunities to meet people do lie somewhat outside the full control of the respondent, they might be supplied or created by friends and family. Social activities, and particularly dating, would then be in part a function of the attitudes of the respondent, but also of opportunities made by her personal characteristics (age, education, etc.), the help given by her social circles, and kinds of social contacts she makes (the precipitating opportunities of churchgoing, other dating, taking care of her children, etc.). In the present chapter, then, we ask what characteristics, behavior, attitudes, or experiences seem to affect her dating behavior.

Meeting Eligible Men. It seems unlikely that the divorcee's family feels a strong obligation to help her establish a new social life or a new marriage. This failure, it must be kept in mind, is not so much a personal decision as it is a failure of the social structure to define just what ought to be the role of the parent family in the formation of a second marriage of that family's children. The ambiguity in social definition is greater when these children *themselves* have children; and of course, still greater, when those grandchildren are no longer infants. Therefore, the keeping and finding of friends is particularly important. Our society is mobile, and the mobility is greater in the urban areas. Our respondents are urban. The parents of many of our respondents were not even to be found in Detroit. On the other hand, we are well aware of how much interest the parents take in the daughter's search for a first husband even when they do not live in the same city.

We would expect friends to be of more day-to-day utility in finding new acquaintances and in meeting eligible suitors, if only for the reason that the divorcee is in day-to-day social interaction with her friends. Of our 188 divorcees who were neither going steady nor remarried at the time of the interview, only 15% were then being helped or had been helped by their families in meeting eligible suitors, as compared with 39% who were then being helped or had been helped by their friends. These answers can be partially checked by reference to opportunities for meeting people. To the extent that this check is suitable, the help of friends *is* more useful than that of family. There is a Q of association of $+.42$ between the giving of help

by the family and many or some opportunities for meeting people
(.05 > P > .02). On the other hand, the Q of association between help given
by friends and having many or some opportunities is +.62, with P < .001.

We should not, however, reason too easily from these facts to the picture
of the urban environment as being a rootless one in which the elder generation disappears. Actually there is a close association between (a) the *family*
helping the respondent to meet eligibles, and (b) *friends* helping the respondent to meet eligibles. The Q of association is +.61, with P < .001. Furthermore, the relationship is cumulative: those who received help from (1) *both*
friends *and* family had the most opportunities and, in turn, those who received
help from (2) *only* one or the other had still more opportunities to meet
people than those who received (3) *no* help from either. This may be seen
in the subsequent collapsed table.

SOCIAL ADJUSTMENT: OPPORTUNITIES TO MEET PEOPLE, BY HELP IN
MEETING ELIGIBLE SUITORS, FROM FRIENDS OR FAMILY

Help from Friends or Family	Opportunities to Meet People			
	Many	Some	Few or None	Totals
Both	47%	32%	21%	100% (19)
Either, but not both	40	36	24	100 (63)
Neither	25	18	57	100 (106)
Totals	32%	26%	42%	

$$X^2 = 21.9 \qquad P < .001 \qquad N = 188$$

We can go a step further in our analysis. At the time of separation and
divorce, some of our respondents remained in their old circle of friends, the
friends of their marriage. Others moved into different circles, and of course,
some lost their friends without obtaining new ones. Now, there is a slight
positive association between (1) having more opportunities to meet people
and (2) having a new set of friends, but this association is statistically insignificant. Much more significant is the association between (1) having opportunities to meet the people, and (2) receiving *help* from one's friends. Also
(3) those whose old friends helped were more likely to have opportunities
than those who got help from new friends.

As we interpret these facts, it seems clear that the network of social relations to be found in the *established* circle of friends is simply more likely
to turn up eligible men than is a new circle of friends, who perhaps feel less
commitment to the divorcees' total life and destiny. Of course, in some cases
those who have a new circle of friends feel that they were to some extent
rejected by their old circle, or perhaps felt that in the conflict of the divorce,
they themselves (the divorcees) were somewhat guilty. As a consequence,
perhaps, they could not in any event have counted upon help from the old
friends.

At all events, keeping the same set of friends is a *condition* under which
the association between opportunities to meet people and obtaining help in
meeting eligibles from one's friends *is maximized*. We present the relevant
table below.

SOCIAL ADJUSTMENT: OPPORTUNITIES FOR MEETING PEOPLE, BY HELP FROM FRIENDS IN MEETING ELIGIBLE SUITORS, HOLDING CONSTANT THE KEEPING OF OLD FRIENDS*

Friends Ever Help?	Same Friends Opportunities			Different Friends Opportunities		
	Many or some	Few or none	Totals	Many or some	Few or none	Totals
Yes	85%	15%	100% (40)	73%	27%	100%(30)
No	39	61	100 (66)	57	43	100 (44)
Totals	57	43	100 (106)	63	37	100 (74)

$Q = + .80$ $x^2 = 21.3$ $P < .001$ $Q = + .35$ $x^2 = 2.1$ $.2 > P > .1$

*8 cases inapplicable.

We shall not carry this point further except to hint at one more complexity: The above table is a collapsed table, in which "many opportunities" and "some opportunities" have been combined. Actually, it is true that of those (a) with *different friends who helped,* a *higher* proportion have *many* opportunities than of (b) those with the *same friends who helped.* Those with the same *and* helping friends have the advantage, however, of having a *higher* proportion falling into "some" opportunities and far *fewer* in the "few or no opportunities" category. That is, the distribution of opportunities for those who have different but helping friends is essentially bi-modal. Most cases fall either into the "many opportunities" category or into the "few or no opportunities" category. These differentials are statistically significant. It then becomes possible to suggest that in this final step we have isolated the two processes that we hinted at earlier: (1) *some* divorcees seek or move into a new set of friends *because* they offer apparently a good opportunity for meeting new people. On the other hand, (2) the *average* set of new friends does not have such a commitment to the divorcee's life and plans as to exploit fully their network of social relationships. As a consequence they do not create for the divorcee as useful a set of opportunities or help. Finally, (3) the divorcee with the *fewest* opportunities was the one who kept the *same* set of friends, but got *no* help from them. The opportunities were fewer even than those of the divorcee who failed to keep the old friends, but got no help from new friends. Presumably these last divorcees had at least some opportunities through the new contacts made, or perhaps the same social activities that made new friends also made new opportunities.

We noted earlier that the young divorcee has a more active social life, even when her attitude toward love and marriage is negative. Additional support for the importance of factors other than simple personal decision is seen in the greater help in *meeting eligibles* that is received from family and friends by the younger divorcee.

SOCIAL ADJUSTMENT: HELP IN MEETING ELIGIBLE MEN, BY AGE

Age	Help from either friends or family		Total
	Received help	Did not receive help	
20-29 years	50%	50%	100%(93)
30 and over	37	63	100 (95)
Total	44	56	100 (188)

$x^2 = 3.6$ $.1 > P > .05$

Dating Frequency: Background Variables. In our society, the path to marriage is typically through dating relationships. The norms and the folklore about dating are oriented toward the assumption that the daters are unmarried boys and girls, and that dating becomes more serious with age, and with length of association. Divorcees are not usually boys or girls, and are not unmarried. On the other hand, the pressures of this society are toward marriage, and there are almost no effective ways to get married except by risking one's time, energy, and emotions in dating. Dating for the divorcee is in part an index of her willingness to start a new life. It is at the same time an introduction and a stimulus to that new life. If she begins to date, we can suppose that she has some minimum willingness to start over. On the other hand, these very activities push her into new relationships, and into a redefinition of her social status as she sees it in others' eyes.

Of our 188 divorcees who were not remarried and were not going steady, 18% had more than one date weekly, 20% had one date each week, 14% had 1-2 dates monthly, and 48% "almost never had a date."

Differences in dating frequency are associated with race, religion, education, and age. All of these except race are significant at about the 1% level or better: (a) Negroes date more frequently than Whites; (b) Protestants more than Catholics; (c) higher levels of education more than lower; and (d) the younger more than the older. To simplify presentation, we give these results in the summarizing tables below.

DATING FREQUENCY AMONG 188 UNATTACHED DIVORCEES

	+1/wk.	1/wk-1/mo.	Almost never	Total	No.
		Frequency			
1. RACE					
Negro	29%	39%	32%	100%	28
White	16	33	51	100	160
	$X^2 = 4.0$ (ever vs. never)		$.05 > P > .02$		
2. RELIGION					
Protestant	26%	37%	37%	100%	102
Catholic	9	27	64	100	63
	$X^2 = 11.8$		$.01 > P > .001$		
2a. RELIGION-RACE* WHITE					
Protestant	25%	34%	40%	99%	79
Catholic	7	29	64	100	58
	$X^2 = 10.3$		$.01 > P > .001$		
3. EDUCATION (WIFE)**					
College	40%	33%	27%	100%	15
Completed High School	16	38	46	100	63
Some High School	16	38	46	100	83
Grammar School	19	11	70	100	27
4. AGE					
20-29	29%	36%	36%	101%	93
30+	7	33	60	100	95
Totals	18%	34%	48%		N = 188
	$X^2 = 18.1$		$P < .001$		

*We exclude the Negroes from the Protestant group here so as to control for race. The Negro Catholics are too few to weigh the religious factor among Negroes.

**A calculation of X^2 is not possible for this table. The theoretical frequencies are too small in some cells. When we collapse our classes to "Ever vs. Never Date," $.02 > P > .01$.

There seem to be few behavioral differences between Catholic and Protestant divorcees. We have understood this fact by reference to the changes in attitude that are necessary within the Catholic woman *before* she obtains a divorce. That is to say, she must somehow adjust to the problem before she can even take seriously the possibility of divorce. Once she has gone through much of this conflict and adjustmental process, her religious doctrine gives her little specific guidance. The prohibition against divorce is absolute, in that doctrinally she remains married to her former husband. However, she has by her legal action already violated that doctrine. Therefore, her behavior should not be greatly different from that of the Protestant divorcee. On the other hand, there will be a lingering feeling among many Catholics that they have no right to enter into new relations with men. Thus, some will not take part in new courtship activity very early. Consequently, as appears in the above table, a lower proportion of Catholic than of Protestant divorcees dates very frequently (9% *vs.* 26%), and a much higher proportion almost never dates (64% *vs.* 37%). The religious differential is about the same when we compare dating frequency of White Protestants with that of White Catholics (Catholic Negroes are too few to allow comparison among Negroes).

Those with more education date more frequently than those with less education. This does not prove that higher education brings a higher "rationality." Rather, we see this effect as having two main dimensions: (a) sets of beliefs, attitudes, or values that are different as between higher and lower educational strata; and (b) the greater definiteness and extent of social networks among these upper strata. The middle and upper strata belong to more formal organizations. They also take more part in more informal friendship and family relationships. We are willing to venture beyond this fact to a further supposition, that the middle and upper class social networks are also (a) larger (i.e., take in a greater number of people), and (b) more definite (i.e., both parties in any given relation are more likely to state that the relationship exists), and thus their members are more likely to respond to each other's pressures and suggestions.

We have several times indicated our right to interpret education as a "social group" variable by showing how influential it is in such contexts as friendship, social approval, and so on. In this context of dating and friendship we can sharpen our notion still further. The association between having friends and dating is clear; and so is the relation between education and having a circle of friends. Now, if our line of reasoning is correct, if we hold constant "having friends," then the relation between education and dating ought to be substantially reduced. It ought not to disappear entirely, since "having friends" is also caused by other social factors than education. As we see in the succeeding pair of tables, this result is actually found.

We shall later show how the factor of age affects dating, under various conditions. Now, we merely note that it is the young who date most frequently. Here, as at several later points in our analysis of age, the data suggest an interpretation we cannot prove: that the group about 30 years of age has lost much of their appeal, but they have not adjusted to this harsh fact. However, the slightly older women, whose appeal is doubtless still less, *have* adjusted. Thus, they accept dates (their dating frequency is slightly higher),

DATING OF UNATTACHED DIVORCEES, BY EDUCATION, HOLDING CONSTANT
THE FACTOR OF "HAVING FRIENDSHIP CIRCLE"

Education of Wife	Friends Now Ever Date Now		
	Yes	No	
College	77%	23%	100% (13)
High School	58	42	100 (111)
Grammar School	28	72	100 (18)

Education of Wife	No Friends Now Ever Date Now		
	Yes	No	
College	50%	50%	100% (2)
High School	43	57	100 (35)
Grammar School	33	67	100 (9)

N = 188

that the slightly younger group would not accept, and therefore are almost as likely to remarry soon as are the slightly younger women.

Dating Frequency: Separation Activities. Now, (1) frequency of dating at the time of the interview for those women who were not yet remarried or even going steady is also associated with (2) dating during the marriage (with husband) and with (3) beginning to date during the separation period. However, when we control for dating during the separation period, we find that the association of frequency of dating now, with ever dating (with the husband) *during* the marriage, almost disappears. That is the pattern of dating after divorce is not a mere carryover from dating during the marriage. On the other hand, the association of (1) dating frequency *now* with (3) dating during the separation is significant at $P < .001$, controlling for (2) dating during the marriage. Further, (4) only 10% of those who dated during the separation "reverted" to nondating by the time of the interview. Putting the matter in more commonsense terms, even if the divorcee begins to date "on the rebound" during separation, as is often claimed, apparently she still continues to date after the separation period. Our data, coupled with the broader remarriage data that have been published indeed suggest that once dating begins, there is little retreat into isolation, and the social interaction usually continues until a new marriage is made.

FREQUENCY OF DATING, BY WHETHER DATED DURING SEPARATION,
FOR THOSE NOT YET REMARRIED OR GOING STEADY

Dating at separation	Dating Frequency at Interview			
	More than once weekly	Once weekly to once monthly	Almost never	Totals
Yes	35%	55%	10%	100% (40)
No	13	29	58	100 (148)

N = 188

We commented earlier on the activities with which the ex-wife filled the social gap when she and her husband stopped living together. Let us see how they relate to frequency of dating.

FREQUENCY OF DATING, BY ACTIVITIES TO FILL GAP AT SEPARATION

	Frequency of Dating				
Activity	More than once weekly	Once weekly to once monthly	Almost Never	Totals	
Did nothing	6%	22%	72%	100%	(18)
Church activities	8	21	71	100	(24)
Movies alone	20	40	40	100	(65)
More attention to children	21	36	43	100	(89)
Girl friends, social club	23	35	42	100	(83)
Dating	35	55	10	100	(40)

Apparently, our respondents were telling us the truth when they said that they "did nothing at all" to fill the gap at separation. These divorcees were less likely than any other group to be dating at the time of our interview. Next are those who took part in church activities. We understand this low frequency of dating to be a function of the divorcee's anomalous position. She is engaged in church activities, in a church whose membership (in this country) is strongly against divorce. Moreover, there are few unmarried persons her age in such church activities. Consequently, even though she may have a *social circle* through these activities, their effectiveness in producing *dates* is low.

We expressed some doubt earlier that the divorcee who goes to movies alone is simply expressing a wish to be alone. Even though it is not a social activity, we suggested that she is thus becoming ready to take part in new relationships with men. Apparently, this is at least partially the case, since her dating frequency is higher than the average. On the other hand, her dating frequency is about the same as that of women who were mainly engaged in social activities with other women when their marriage ended, or of women who claimed to have given more attention to their children at this time. Of course, none of these activities seems to have led to a high frequency of dating by the time of interview as effectively as actually beginning to date at the end of the marriage. Yet, when we later look at remarriage, we shall see that "paying more attention to the children" appears not to be really a turning away from social activities. At least, the fruitfulness of the dates these mothers do have seems to be high.

If our previous analysis of divorce trauma was correct in the main, then those with a higher trauma index should not date as frequently as those with a low trauma index. This is indeed what we find:

DATING FREQUENCY, BY TRAUMA INDEX

	Frequency				
Trauma Index	2 or more times weekly	1 weekly to 1 monthly	Almost never	Totals	
High	14%	39%	47%	100%	(72)
Medium	16	29	55	100	(49)
Low	24	33	43	100	(67)
Totals	18%	34%	48%	100%	(188)

A different dimension of trauma may be found in "lonesomeness." We asked our respondents at which phase of the conflict period they felt most lonely, if ever. We can then ask whether there are any differences in present frequency of dating (among those not remarried or going steady) when there was greater loneliness at one phase, rather than another. We find that (1) when the period of greatest loneliness occurred at the time of final decision, or first filing, the dating frequency at present is highest. (2) When the divorcee claims that there was "never" any period of greatest loneliness, the frequency of dating is exactly that of the group average, although this segment of divorcees makes up less than half of the group. (3) Those who felt most lonely at the time of the decree have the lowest percentage of frequent daters, and those who were feeling most lonely as late as the time of our interview had the highest percentage of infrequent daters. That is, when the feeling of being alone occurred early, before the decree itself, then the divorcee was much more likely to have become able to enter new dating relationships. On the other hand, when the emotional impact of the divorce came much later, or continued much later, then dating was likely to be infrequent.

DATING FREQUENCY, BY PERIOD OF GREATEST LONELINESS

Time of greatest loneliness	Dating Frequency			
	2 or more times weekly	1 weekly to 1 monthly	Almost never	Totals
Final decision	28%	22%	50%	100%(18)
First filing	29	24	48	101 (21)
Final separation	16	41	43	100 (44)
Final decree	10	52	38	100 (21)
Time of interview	13	20	67	100 (15)
Not at any time	17	33	49	99 (69)

From our analysis of who first suggested the divorce, we would expect that when the husband first suggested the divorce, the wife might be more likely to date rarely, but when the wife suggested first, there might be a higher frequency of dating. Indeed, we do find that among the women whose husbands first suggested the divorce those rarely or never dating make up 56%, as against 47% among women who first suggested, and 37% when there was mutual suggestion. Correspondingly, when the wife suggested first, 24% are frequent daters (twice or more weekly)—but here the "mutuals" are *lowest* with 7%, and women whose husbands suggested first are between, with 12%. On the other hand, the mutuals have a very high percentage of medium frequency dating (56% are dating from once weekly to once monthly, as against 33%-29% for husband suggesting or wife suggesting).

Consequently, the pattern that seemed apparent at an earlier stage, according to which the greatest emotional impact on the wife was caused by the husband suggesting first, a medium impact by wife suggesting, and mutual suggesting being the least hurtful to the wife, is modified somewhat here. The most important difference is that *when the wife suggested the divorce, she is more likely to engage in frequent dating before women whose husbands suggested first,* or before those whose divorce suggestion was a mutual one. It seems reasonable to say that whereas mutual suggestion may have led to a lesser *hurt,* the wife suggesting led to greater *activity;* or, better, the emotional independence that permitted her to suggest the divorce also enabled her to move more effectively toward new dating relationships.

On the other hand, although *stability of decision* about the divorce is of some importance early in the adjustment period, it has no association with dating frequency by the time of the interview. Moreover, even themes of conflict have no great effect. Of course, women who made the complaint of Triangle have the lowest dating frequency. Those who battled about Values have perhaps the highest overall frequency, with Desertion, Authority, and Personality following in that order. However, the themes actually refer in time to the marriage itself, rather than to the conflict and trauma of the marital breakup, and seem to have no systematic relation to dating frequency.

Dating Frequency: Other Social Contacts. Although we have tried to understand the processes of conflict and adjustment within the dimension of time, we have not forgotten that time itself is not a true social variable. It often seems to be, since it is *in* time that many social and emotional processes occur. Moreover, we are sometimes unable to abstract the central factors at work, and can only note that "over time" certain effects are observable. We would expect, in general, that (a) dating *frequency* would increase over time, or that (b) the *proportion* of women dating would increase. This is not a simple expectation. From each time group there is a continual flow of divorcees from dating relationships into new marriages. Thus, for any slice of time, we have lost those divorcees who might otherwise be counted as "frequent daters," but who in fact have remarried. Consequently, along the continuum of time, there is likely to be (1) an increase in the proportion of frequent daters, but also (2) a movement of the frequent daters into marriage. On the other hand, (3) there is relatively little change in the *proportion* of those who *never* date. The *absolute* numbers of nondaters decrease, of course, but the numerical base continues to decline as the frequent daters marry. The most apparent changes are to be found (4) in the proportions of women who move from a medium to a higher frequency of dating. Thus, a simplified presentation of the increase in dating frequency by time since separation would center on the *increase* in those who date 2 or more times weekly: 0-1 years since separation, 13% date 2 or more times weekly; 1-2 years, 19%; 2-3 years, 19%; and 3 years and more since separation, 20%. We can also see from these data that after the first time period, the increase is tiny, for those who were once frequent daters are likely to have left the dating group to remarry.

Within any time change, we look for more active elements. We have already discussed various status and background factors. More immediate are the *actions* of the divorcee's social groups, such as (a) giving her help in meeting people, (b) meeting eligible men; or (c) her own attitudes toward love and marriage. Further, these have interesting relationships with such background factors as age, and with behavioral factors such as job-holding.

As we noted earlier, there are important relationships between (1) opportunities for meeting people and (2) getting help from friends or family in meeting eligible men. Both are of course related in turn to (3) frequency of dating. Moreover, *both* of these first two items are *independent* in their effect. When we hold either of them constant, the association between the other and frequency of dating is still maintained (although the effect is smaller). We shall not present here these further partial associations, but instead merely show the effect of these two factors separately.

SOCIAL ADJUSTMENT: FREQUENCY OF DATING BY OPPORTUNITIES TO MEET PEOPLE

Number of Opportunities	Frequency of Dating				
	+ 1/wk.	1/wk.-1/mo.	Almost never	Totals	
Many	26%	46%	28%	100%	(61)
Some	25	33	42	100	(48)
Few or none	8	25	67	100	(79)
Total	18%	34%	48%		(188)

$$X^2 = 23.1 \qquad P < .001$$

Those who received help from (a) *both* friends and family in meeting eligible men had more dates than those who received help from (b) *only one* of these groups, and the divorcees who got help from (c) *neither* had the lowest frequency of dating.

DATING FREQUENCY, BY HELP FROM FAMILY OR FRIENDS
IN MEETING ELIGIBLE MEN*

Help from	Frequency				
	More than one date weekly	Once weekly-once monthly	Almost never	Totals	
Family and friends	37%	32%	32%	101%	(19)
Family or friends, not both	23	44	33	100	(64)
Neither	11	29	60	100	(105)

*A Chi-square calculation is not possible because the theoretical frequency in the first cell is less than 5. If we collapse the three "Help" classes, into two, "Some Help—No Help," P < .001.

Dating Frequency: Her Attitudes. In thus suggesting that her relevant social groups are important in determining the divorcee's dating frequency, we do not forget the influence of her own attitudes. However, we must then ask further, "Attitudes toward what or whom?" Her emotional ties with her ex-husband might have some effect on dating frequency, but it is also possible that her *general* feelings toward love and remarriage would show up in how much she participated in dating (just as they are associated with opportunities for meeting people). As we shall document very shortly, how she feels toward her former spouse and toward love and remarriage affect dating frequency differently under different conditions of dating opportunity, and even age, but let us first see to what extent these attitudes broadly affect dating.

Now, we would take for granted that the woman who is (1) still in love with her former husband would be less willing to date than would the woman who is (2) indifferent to him, or than one who has (3) no more than a generally friendly feeling toward him. On the other hand, we are all sophisticated enough in the complexities of emotion to know that the woman who (4) *hates* her husband may have almost as difficult a problem as the woman who is still in love. She lives and makes her decisions with him in mind as does the woman who loves her ex-husband, but she adds a *general* resentment of men. She is still enmeshed in the complexities of the old relationship. We cannot predict her actions in detail, but we can suppose that many such women are not able to interact easily with new men. Some will not be very willing to date men, or will so displease them by their frequent reference to the old husband, that they will not seem desirable companions. Thus, both types of strong attitudes might lead to less dating.

The two milder attitudes may be distinguished from one another, although their differential effect is not so clear as that between the extremes of strong and weak emotional involvement. We would suppose that when a woman claims to feel (3) no love but some friendliness toward her former husband, she has been able to free herself emotionally from him while nevertheless perceiving why she once found him attractive. That is, she recognizes that he is not really a scoundrel, even though she may no longer wish to live with him. Moreover, if she is now friendly, perhaps the prior marital conflict was not very bitter. On the other hand, the woman who claims that she is (2) indifferent toward him is often speaking defensively rather than with complete accuracy. We believe, then, that her claim of indifference actually contains some resentment against him. It would be difficult for her to be really indifferent to a man by whom she has borne one or more children, with whom she lived for some years, and with whom she was once presumably in love.

If our interpretation of these answers is correct, the pattern of frequency of dating, viewed with reference to the divorcee's feelings toward the ex-husband, becomes more understandable.

FREQUENCY OF DATING, BY AFFECT FOR EX-HUSBAND

Affect toward Ex-Husband	More than 1/week	1/week- 1-2/month	Almost Never	Totals	
In love	18%	36%	46%	100%	(28)
Positive (but not in love)	21	39	39	99	(48)
Indifferent	18	29	53	100	(49)
Negative	16	33	51	100	(63)
				N = 188	

Not all of the postulated relationships hold in fact within this table. Nevertheless, most of them do. We note, for example, that for those dating *most* frequently the rank order from *highest* to *lowest* proportion is: (1) friendly feeling, but not in love with former husband; (2) indifference; (3) in love; (4) negative or antagonistic feeling. For those who date with a medium frequency (once a week to once or twice a month) the four groups become in effect only two: (1) those in love, or with positive feelings toward the husband, with the higher frequency; and (2) those who are indifferent, or have negative feelings toward the husband, with the lower frequency. These women are not leading an active dating life. Apparently, the positive attitude toward the former husband is more conducive to medium dating than is the negative attitude. We follow our previous interpretation of "indifference" as containing tones of resentment, and thus include it with the negatives.

Finally the distribution of those who almost *never* date fits exactly our expectation. A higher proportion of those who have strongly negative feelings toward, or who are in love with, their ex-husbands fall into this dating group. And, because of the distribution of the medium dating segment, the difference between the indifferents and the friendlies shows clearly: those who claim indifference are more likely to be rare daters than are those who claim a friendly but not in love feeling.

It seems reasonable to believe that a strong emotional attachment to the ex-husband affects dating in part by making other men less interesting or attractive. Indeed, those *particular* attitudes should underlie and thus parallel a *general* set of attitudes toward love and remarriage. We can then ask (a) how these general attitudes were distributed among our divorcees, and (b) more specifically how they affected dating frequency. The result is as expected. Even when we include among those who have a positive attitude toward love and marriage those women who are also still in love with their husbands (and thus do not date so frequently as others), it is clear that a positive attitude toward love and remarriage is associated with a higher proportion of frequent daters. In short, those who most want to regain the status of "married mother" are actually engaging in the activities most likely to lead again to that status.

DATING FREQUENCY, BY DIVORCEE'S ATTITUDE TOWARD LOVE AND REMARRIAGE

Att. to Love and Remarriage	Frequency			
	More than 1/wk.	1/wk.-1/mo.	Almost Never	Totals
Positive*	21%	38%	41%	100(130)
Negative	12	24	64	100 (58)

$$X^2 = 8.4 \qquad .02 > P > .01$$

*Includes 15 who are still in love with their ex-husbands.

Final Comments. It is evident from the foregoing analysis of the social adjustment of the unattached divorcee that the variables important for dating have complex empirical interrelationships, and that this complexity is in turn to be expected on theoretical grounds. In this section we shall attempt to suggest how we view these interrelationships, and in so doing we shall reinforce some data already given.

In barest essentials, we are documenting throughout this report the necessity of viewing a "decision" or "action" as not the result of an attitude, predisposition, or belief alone, but as shaped by the objective *social* characteristics of the person, i.e., how she is viewed *by others* (e.g., her age, education, etc.); as shaped by the *actions* of her social group (disapproval, approval, or help from friends, family, etc.); and as shaped by other objective characteristics of her situation (e.g., job, income, number of children, etc.).

Now, dating would appear to be in the first instance a voluntaristic item. That is, those who wish to date will do so, while those who do not, will not. Even the most cautious analyst might concede the second of these propositions. On the other hand, we might suppose that opportunities to meet people —a minimum prerequisite for dating—would be much *less* a function of the divorcee's desires and attitudes (e.g., her motivations toward love and remarriage). These propositions are roughly borne out by our data: (a) The association between wanting to remarry (i.e., her wishes) and opportunities to meet people (i.e., the situation) is relatively *low* (Q = +.23) and is not significant at even the 10% level; but (b) the association between wanting to remarry and frequency of dating (ever vs. never), is higher (Q = +.44), while .01 > P > .001.

Since opportunities seem to be a prerequisite for dating, we have attempted to control opportunities for meeting people, to see what remains of the relationship (Q $= +.44$) between wanting to remarry and the frequency of dating. We find that this association reduces substantially: when opportunities are not present, the relationship between wanting to remarry and frequency of dating drops to $+.19$, and this relationship is not significant ($.5 > P > .3$). Moreover, 74% of those divorcees date who *have* such opportunities *and* who wish to remarry, but only 36% of those date who do *not* have such opportunities but who *do* wish to remarry. Thus, for the positive attitudes toward love and marriage to be expressed in behavior (dating), certain conditions need to be present.

On the other hand, the converse ought to be true if our holistic view of action is correct: Even when the situational variable *is* present, the attitudinal variable is required if the behavioral result (dating) is to be maximized. When the desire to remarry is present, the Q of association between opportunities for meeting people and dating is .67, with $P < .001$. But when the divorcee does *not* wish to remarry, the Q of association between these two drops to $+.36$, and this relationship is not significant even at the 10% level.[1]

There are of course various empirical complexities which might be considered in a more refined analysis. For example, it is apparent that we can deduce the existence of a group of women who seem not to take part in dating as a step toward a new and more permanent attachment, but who seem to be dating rather as an end in itself. They do not wish to remarry, but do wish to continue their relations with men. They are dating, claim *not* to want to remarry, but also state that they do *not have enough dates*. Nevertheless, such complexities do not undermine substantially the line of theory we are here pursuing.

Now, in this empirical context we cannot abstract the various elements that are contained in the variable of age. From our point of view, it is a *social* characteristic, i.e., *a definition made by others*. Crudely put, men are more likely to define young women as attractive, and thus to tempt them with dates. From another point of view, youth is a "biological" characteristic of the individual, and at a most general level it is associated with a high energy output. Again crudely put, young women will move about more than older women, seek men more actively, and be more alert to the chance of meeting men.

Then, the divorcee's *opportunities* to meet people are mainly the resultant of the attitudes and acts of *other* people, and *her* feeling toward love and remarriage is itself her *own* attitude, if not an act of her own will. But the divorcee's *age* does not fall exactly in either category. It is for this reason that we wish to continue our theoretical line with this variable.

Now, youth is associated with opportunities for meeting people, and it is also associated with a positive attitude toward love and marriage. (We continue to refer only to those divorcees who have not yet remarried and are not going steady). It is not then surprising that the young date more frequently, even if the statement were not common information.

1. We can judge roughly from the varying proportions in each cell as we hold each factor constant, that "opportunities" have more weight empirically than attitude, for the specific action of dating. However, this does not change the propositions we are making, which rather emphasize the independent but interactional importance of each factor.

On the other hand, *all three factors are independent.* Furthermore, if we hold opportunities constant, the association between youth and dating persists; and if we hold attitude constant, the association still persists. Moreover, and this is more important theoretically, when each of these two sets is positive, the frequency of dating is maximized. This effect is seen in the following two collapsed tables.

DATING OF UNATTACHED DIVORCEES, BY AGE, CONTROLLING OPPORTUNITIES FOR MEETING PEOPLE (FIRST TABLE); AND CONTROLLING ATTITUDE TOWARD REMARRIAGE (SECOND TABLE)

I.
Dating Now

Many or some opportunities	Under 30 yrs.	Yes	No	Totals	
Yes	Yes	74%	26%	100%	(62)
Yes	No	55	45	100	(47)
No	Yes	45	55	100	(31)
No	No	25	75	100	(48)
	Total				(188)

$$X^2 = 17.0 \qquad P < .001$$

II.
Dating Now

Positive attitudes toward Love and Marriage	Under 30 yrs.	Yes	No	Totals	
Yes	Yes	72%	28%	100%	(67)
Yes	No	46	54	100	(63)
No	Yes	46	54	100	(26)
No	No	28	72	100	(32)
	Total				(188)

$$X^2 = 18.0 \qquad P < .001$$

Space does not permit us to pursue the analysis beyond this point. Suffice it to say that when we hold *both* attitude and opportunities constant, the association between youth and dating persists, and once more we can show that when these independent factors are all positive, the percentage dating is maximized (84%, when the divorcee is under 30 years of age, has many or some opportunities to meet people, and is favorable toward love and remarriage), while the percentage dating is lowest when they are all negative (24%, if the divorcee is 30 years of age or over, has few or no opportunities for meeting people, and has a negative attitude toward remarriage). Moreover, we can even show that when opportunities and attitude are both positive, the percentage dating is higher than for any other two positive factors (61% of even the divorcees 30 years of age or older are then dating). However, the logical and theoretical problems of ordering the eight combinations of these three independent factors in interaction seem to yield only to arbitrary solutions, and these solutions shed little further light on our analysis of social adjustment. We shall, therefore, now turn to what is usually a next phase in the process of moving toward a new marriage: steady dating.

CHAPTER XIX

STEADY DATING, IMMINENT MARRIAGE, AND REMARRIAGE

IN THE VOCABULARY of contemporary American courtship, the stage or status of "steady date" has a different meaning for different social circles and strata, and even for different age groups. These varying meanings need not be discussed here. What is significant is that in our family system we enter marriage typically through courtship, and that therefore a marriage is more likely to grow out of a steady dating relationship than out of an ordinary dating relationship; and much more likely than out of no dating relationship at all. If the normal progression for the unmarried is from dating to steady dating to being engaged, and thus to being married, with each such activity or phase acting as a selective process for the succeeding phase, then we must take steady dating more seriously than general dating, and more seriously than even frequent dating.

On the other hand, precisely because these occur in sequence, grow from the same sets of social relationships, and are affected by the same factors, we need not reproduce for *steady* dating all the tables that merely parallel our findings for dating in general. Although certain factors are associated with general dating that are not associated with steady dating, we have found almost *no* items that run in a *contrary* direction. We shall be able to point to only few factors that facilitate or increase frequency of dating, but hinder or reduce steady dating. Since it is through general dating that people in our society move toward steady dating (and remarriage), factors with a contrary effect at these two consecutive phases should be rare.

For the older or the once married, steady dating is doubtless more closely associated with marriage than for those who are younger or never married. Steady dating in later adolescence is a common pattern, but its social definition points to various types of mutual exploration, with no commitment on either side to an eventual marriage. Two adolescents who are "going steady"[1] are protected from further commitments by this social definition.[2]

---

1. We use the phrases, "going steady," or "dating steady" as acceptable American idiom.
2. Parents of adolescents who are going steady do recognize, however, the statistically greater

By contrast, there is some feeling in most circles that when the couple is older, neither party to a steady dating relationship "has the right" to hold the other in exclusive possession, unless there is some possibility of eventual marriage. The social definitions are, then, that the older or the once married do not have an infinitely wide number of potential marriage partners, or time to find them. Therefore, they should not stay, or hold others, in a steady dating relationship if there is no chance at all of marriage. A basic assumption of our society is, as we have analyzed previously, that almost all *will* get married, and that almost all *should* get married. Thus, relationships are disapproved that hinder adults from entering the statuses, and thereby the role obligations, that are prescribed for them.

For these reasons, we treat both steady dating and remarriage in this chapter, locating some of the factors that appear to be associated with these steps toward resuming the previous status of "married mother." Here, we look at the 303 divorcees who had not yet remarried by the time of the interview.

Let us first state the obvious, that frequency of dating is associated with steady dating: 68% of the frequent daters (more than once weekly at the time of interview) are steady daters, while 38% of the medium daters (once weekly to once a month), and only 5% of the infrequent daters are also steady daters. It is useful to state the obvious, since the obvious is not always correct.

However, the proportion of steady daters might not increase much over time, for over time we also *lose* the steady daters into the remarried group. Thus the proportion of steady daters *can not* increase indefinitely.

Now, the proportion dating steady does increase somewhat with time since separation, from 30% of those separated 0-1 year, to 49% of those separated 3 years and over. However, time since separation does not measure whether they *could* have remarried. Some had separated two or three years before the decree. From such segments, then, we would not lose the remarried, and thus the proportion could increase. By contrast, when we arrange our divorces into Time Groups (since divorce), the proportion of steady daters among all divorcees does not change systematically: they form 27% of Time Group I, and 23% of Group IV.

Those who were not daters become daters. These become frequent and then steady daters, and then remarry. Thus, the *number* of steady daters drops, but so does the numerical base. When we eliminate the remarried, we find that the steady daters form 29% of the not remarried in Group I, and increase to 49% in Group IV. In Time Group IV, there are 51 divorcees who have not remarried; 25 of these are steady daters, 10 are dating without being steady daters, and 16 are not dating. Thus, the ratio of steady daters to ordinary daters rises over these Time Groups. By Group IV, the steady daters are two and one-half times as many as the ordinary daters. With reference to the larger institutional processes, we call attention to the fact that *76% of the divorcees who obtained their decrees 26 months before the interview were either remarried or were going steady by the time of the interview.*

likelihood of still more intimacy, or even marriage, growing out of such a relationship, and consider general dating permissible at an earlier age than steady dating; or forbid steady dating with partners whom the adolescent is allowed to date generally.

Steady Dating and Other Close Relationships. Although Protestants form a slightly higher proportion of steady daters than do Catholics, the difference is small. No apparent relationship seems to exist between (1) the divorcee's education and steady dating, although we saw that there was such a relationship between dating frequency and education. We shall treat this factor once more when we speak of remarriage. (2) Women who had been married to middle-class husbands are less likely to be dating steady at the time of interview than wives of husbands from either upper or lower occupations (33%, vs. 38% and 42%), but this relationship is unimportant. There is no apparent relationship between (3) the length of the marriage and the movement into steady dating: 41% of the women who had been married 15 years or more were going steady at the time of the interview, but 40% of those who had been married less than 5 years were also going steady. Of the themes of conflict, only (4) that of Triangle seems to have a substantial effect, in that a lower percentage of these wives are going steady. (5) Age has a complex relationship with steady dating, as it does with dating frequency. Of course, the younger are more likely to be steady daters than the older ex-wives. But the difference is largely to be found between those who are *less* than 25 years of age and *all others* (48% are steady daters, while of the other age groups 34%-36% are steady daters). The young seem not to move into remarriage swiftly. They date heavily and steadily first. However, we should look at steady dating along with other related patterns. We asked these unmarried divorcees whether there was someone among their close men friends whom they would *consider* marrying, and we also asked whether there was a *fair chance* that this marriage might take place. Let us, then, compare the differences in these answers by reference to their age distribution.

STEADY DATING, EXISTENCE OF ELIGIBLE SPOUSE, AND JUDGMENT THAT THE MARRIAGE MAY TAKE PLACE—BY AGE OF RESPONDENT (NOT REMARRIED)

Age	Dating Steady	Consider Marrying Someone Among Close Men Friends	Fair Chance of This Marriage Taking Place	Base
20-24 yrs.	48%	52%	48%	52
25-29 yrs.	36	42	34	102
30-34 yrs.	36	35	24	84
35 yrs. and over	34	39	25	65
Totals	38%	41%	32%	303

First of all, we see that it is among the youngest age group that the highest frequency of steady dating is to be found, and once more we note that there are few differences among the remaining age groups. With reference to the *existence of potential spouses* among the close friends of the divorcee, however, these relationships change interestingly. For all age brackets except the age bracket 30-34 years, a higher percentage has a potential spouse among the very close friends than has a steady date. Loosely put, more women have their eyes on a potential spouse than have their hands on a steady date. Or, not all have as their steady date the person whom they would consider an eligible spouse.

Whether the age group 30-34 years is really different, we cannot say. The difference is not great and is not statistically significant. We suppose that whether such a potential spouse is to be found among a woman's very close friends depends upon two main factors: (a) the *numbers* of men she is acquainted with, and whom she would consider her "very close men friends," and (b) her standards for a spouse. We have speculated that in the age bracket 30-34 years these women have not yet lowered their standards for a spouse, but their circle of close men friends is smaller than when the women were younger. Consequently the proportion with a potential spouse in mind is smaller than in the other age brackets. By contrast, the age group 35 years and over may have a *smaller* circle of close men friends, but here we believe that their standards for a spouse have lowered to correspond to the objective social situation.

Looking at the table again, we notice that it is in the younger age brackets that the greatest optimism is to be found: as high a percentage believe that there is a *fair chance* of a marriage taking place as are dating steady (48%-48%), and this figure is only slightly lower than the proportion who state that among their close men friends there is someone that they might *consider* marrying. On the other hand, the other age groups seem less optimistic or more realistic. The only difference of significance, however, is found between those who are 30 years and over and those who are under 30 years of age.

There are actually no adequate data for the national population with respect to the effect of children upon the remarriage of divorcees. In this study we cannot, of course, compare the dating and remarriage of divorcees without children as against those with children, since all of our respondents did have one or more children. The slight relationship between number of children and the patterns now under consideration would seem to be the following: (1) There is a slightly higher proportion dating steady among those who have *one* child than among those who have *more* than one child. (2) The proportion dating steady among those who have three children and over is very slightly *higher* than among those who have only two children. This relationship is not significant. (3) Those who have the greatest number of children are slightly more inclined to consider marriage to someone of their close men friends. However, the difference is small and insignificant. (4) Of the proportion of those who say there *is* a fair chance that the marriage might take place, the frequency is *higher* for those with only *one* child, but only *slightly* lower for those who have *two* or more children. Even if these relationships do hold, they are in part spurious, since number of children is also a function of age of spouse; and these relationships have already been outlined in that connection. Perhaps the most important conclusion is simply this: *among divorced mothers the number of children* seems to have almost *no significant effect* on the activities leading to remarriage. This tentative conclusion will *not* be entirely borne out for those who *actually remarry,* as we shall see later.

Indeed, we can summarize our findings by stating that in general the same factors are at work here as in frequency of dating. We cannot locate important factors that move some daters, but not others, into steady dating. This is partly a result of our failure to develop any adequate theory on this point, and to build our theoretical expectations into our interview. On the other hand, we are not certain that there are any *major* differences to be found. That is, (1) almost all daters become steady daters eventually; (2) the factors that lead to steady dating earlier rather than later are the same that lead to frequent dating, but (3) these are fine, cumulative differences rather than major ones. We can distinguish somewhat the factors that lead to early rather than late remarriage, but these items are useful only for major actional differences, while between dating and steady dating the change or difference is not major. Thus, we record what slight differences the apparently relevant factors seem to make, but their combined effect does not seem to be great.

We did find an interesting, puzzling, and complex set of relationships that seem to suggest that the factors of trauma and first suggestion of divorce may have a reversed effect for steady dating, as against dating frequency and remarriage. We shall not present the data or the complexities here, but only the problem. In general, when the husband first suggested the divorce there was higher trauma, and when there was mutual suggestion there was lower trauma. And when there was higher trauma, in general there was a lower dating frequency. But the high trauma respondents are more likely to remarry early, while the effect of trauma upon steady dating is inconsistent when we hold first suggestion constant. Moreover, when we hold trauma constant, there is a consistent relationship between who first suggested the divorce, and both dating and remarriage: mutual suggestion is most positive in its effect, husband suggestion is least, and wife suggestion falls between. But this effect is reversed for steady dating. Factors such as age introduce further complexities. We mention these complexities, without presenting them or interpreting them, only because they suggest at least the possibility that the phase of steady dating deserves more serious study. At the present time, we are inclined to dismiss this notion, and to view the interesting consistencies in some of our tables as no more than statistical accidents. At best, without a true panel study we cannot measure the movement into and out of steady dating.

We have already made some mention of the relationship of steady dating, thinking of someone in the group as a possible spouse, and judging that a marriage with him might take place, when we discussed the influence of age on steady dating. Let us look once more at these judgments.

There are many possibilities of error. The divorcee might not at first take her steady date seriously as a possible spouse, but afterwards be forced by lack of real choice to accept him as a husband. Moreover, any divorcee might be too optimistic or pessimistic regarding the "fair chance" that such a marriage might take place.

Yet it is clear that our respondents differentiated between these two judgments, as we noted in considering age. Considering a man as a possible spouse *is* different from asserting that there is a fair chance that the marriage would occur. Of the total number of unmarried respondents, 38% were dating steady, while 41% said that among their very close men friends there was someone whom they might consider marrying. However, only 32% of these respondents stated that there was a *fair chance* of this marriage taking place.

The attitudes of friends and family toward the divorce are part of the divorcee's background experience by this time, but we suppose that these attitudes would affect remarriage through the help they give the divorcee in meeting people generally and eligible men in particular. The effect of those attitudes upon the patterns now under consideration is very little, after so many intervening experiences, but it is visible and rather consistent. The percentage of (1) steady daters, (2) women who know someone among their close friends whom they might consider marrying, and (3) women who think there is a fair chance that this marriage might occur, is slightly *lower* for (1) divorcees whose family or friends *disapproved* the divorce originally, than for (2) those whose family or friends *approved or felt indifferent* toward the divorce: e.g., 30% of those with family disapproval were steady daters, *vs.* 40% of those whose families were approving or indifferent; 35% *vs.* 37-43% for considering marriage; 23% *vs.* 35% for fair chance the marriage might take place.

Of course, the movement of divorcees from nondating to dating, and thence to steady dating and the consideration of marriage, is a continual sieving and seeping process, so that from each time grouping we are always losing those whose dating relationship becomes a remarriage. Thus, slightly under *one-third* of the divorcees in Time Group I (2 months since divorce) were dating steadily; only slightly more knew someone within their circle of close men friends whom they would consider marrying; and slightly more than one-fourth thought there was a fair chance this marriage would occur. By Time Group IV (26 months after decree) one-half of those not remarried were steady daters, and at least knew someone who could be thought of as a marital candidate; and almost the same proportion thought there was a fair chance this marriage might occur. Moreover, there is a Q of .90 between steady dating and considering someone as a possible spouse, among all Time Groups.

Thus it is that about three-fourths of all our urban, divorced mothers who had divorced 26 months prior to the interview had either remarried, or seemed to be well on the way to a remarriage.

Here, as with dating frequency, it is important to have a circle of friends, and to have opportunities for meeting people. (1) 32% of those who do not have friends and are not finding friends are going steady, as against 40% of those who already have such a circle. About the same difference exists between these two categories with reference to whether there is someone these divorcees would consider marrying. The percentages drop somewhat for the more serious question as to whether there was a fair chance the marriage might occur, and the difference is unimportant (28% *vs.* 32%).

Similarly, when we look at opportunities for meeting people, the main differences are between those who have *no* such opportunities, and those who do have such opportunities. Whether these are few, many, or some is of little significance. About one-fourth of those with no opportunities for meeting people are steady daters and consider someone within their close circle of men friends as a possible spouse (as against two-fifths of those with some such opportunities); and 22% of those with *no* opportunities think that there is a fair chance the marriage might take place, as against 30-34% of those with *some* opportunities.

Help from Friends and Family. We have pointed out that although most divorcees do not receive help from family and friends in meeting eligible mates, this help is fruitful. Of those who obtained help from *both* family and friends, 50% were going steady. Forty-seven percent who got help from the family but *not* from friends, were going steady, as against 38% of those who got help from friends but not from the family. Thirty-four percent of the not remarried who got help from *neither* were going steady.

Now, it is clear that help from both is most fruitful, and there is evidence that help from the family alone is more useful than that from friends alone (47% *vs.* 38%). We would suppose, then, that this documents the thesis that the family has a more continuing commitment to the divorcee's life and happiness, and thus the help they give is more effective because more continuous. The help of friends was more useful for dating frequency.

However, we also asked whether among their close men friends there was someone these divorcees would consider marrying. Then we find that the above ranking is *reversed* (except of course for those who got help from neither friends nor family). That is, 37% of those who obtained help from family *and* friends knew a man they would consider marrying, 41% of those who got help from family but *not* friends, and 52% of those who got help from friends *alone*. (Thirty-six percent of those receiving help from neither knew someone they would consider marrying.)

If we understand these apparent patterns, the help from the family *is* more effective in providing a partner, one who is eligible enough to be a steady date. On the other hand, the peer group is more effective than the family in producing men with whom the *divorcee* would consider marriage, for they know men who are more desirable as potential spouses. To the extent that the peer group does share values, tastes, and activities, an unattached male that is brought in to meet the divorcee will be closer to an acceptable mate. The family, by contrast, will begin from a slightly different set of values, because removed by one generation, and might be more inclined to introduce a "safe" rather than desirable potential mate, an escort rather than a date. Moreover, the same result may occur when both family and friends combine forces, for then they are likely to be in interaction with one another. In this case, their effectiveness is no better than when there is no help from either.

It is almost by definition that those with a high dating frequency are more likely to be steady daters. However, it is worth documenting that it is *also* among the high frequency daters that we find a higher proportion of women actually considering marriage, or judging a hypothetical marriage to have a fair chance of taking place. This relationship is shown in the succeeding table.

STEPS TOWARD REMARRIAGE, BY FREQUENCY OF DATING

Frequency of Dating	Steady Dating	Considering Marriage	Fair Chance of-Marriage	None of These	Base
More than once weekly	68%	64%	53%	24%	105
1/wk. to 2/month	38	44	32	49	103
Almost never	5	13	7	85	95

Emotional Ties with the Ex-Husband. Since we have moved from background factors to items of more immediate importance, let us consider one more such item, the emotional involvement of the ex-wife with the ex-husband. We shall look at this item independently in a later section, but it is useful now to see how similar is its effect upon these steps toward marriage, compared with its effect on dating frequency.

PROPORTION DATING STEADY, CONSIDERING MARRIAGE, OR CLAIMING THAT A MARRIAGE
HAS A FAIR CHANCE OF OCCURRING, BY AFFECT TOWARD EX-HUSBAND

Affect Toward Ex-Husband	Dating Steady	Consider Marrying Someone Among Close Men Friends	Fair-Chance of Marriage Taking Place	Base
Friendly	48%	49%	40%	85
Indifferent	42	45	36	93
In Love	30	35	15	40
Negative	26	31	26	85

There are several points worth bringing out in this table: (1) Again we see that those who express antagonistic *or* loving attitudes toward the former husband show (a) the lowest frequency of steady dating, (b) the lowest frequency of potential spouses among their close men friends, and (c) the lowest frequency of claiming that there is a fair chance the marriage might actually take place. (2) With reference to those who might consider marrying, we note that among those who have antagonistic feelings toward their husbands the proportion who would consider marrying one of their close men friends is *lower* than the corresponding frequency among those who are in love with their former husbands. (3) Once more, however, women who claim a positive but not loving feeling for their former spouses are those most likely to claim that a potential spouse is to be found among their close men friends. On the other hand, (4) the proportions reporting there was a fair chance that such a marriage might occur were almost the same as those going steady, for all groups *except those in love with their former husbands.* Only 15% of this last group stated that there was a fair chance of the marriage taking place, while 30% of them were going steady. In none of the other categories is the difference so great. Thus, these comparisons reflect the readiness for and movement toward remarriage on the part of these divorcees.

Remarriage. Let us continue to follow this movement toward remarriage. We have attempted to outline some of the social activities of the divorced mother after her divorce, and have paid some attention to the dating and courtship patterns which lead to a new marriage. We have sketched in some detail the processes which lead to this reassumption of an old status, that of married mother. We have not, of course, assumed that the marriage ends all problems, and in our chapter on relations with the ex-husband we shall show that not even all of the remarried women have assimilated the divorce experience completely. Nevertheless, as we commented earlier, entering new social activities and new roles may be seen as both an *index* of and a *stimulus* to the social and emotional readjustment of the divorcee. It is an index in that she will ordinarily find these new activities difficult if she is not ready for them in some fashion; and it is a stimulus in that the new roles demand different activities and attitudes from her, and those who associate with her in these new roles come increasingly to ignore the old set of relationships and to emphasize the new ones.

This is particularly true, of course, for the social role of "new wife." With respect to this new status, there are two main sets of facts which we wish to present: (1) We would like to continue to show which divorcees are more likely to remarry within the short 26 months' period of adjustment under our eyes; and in Chapter XXI, (2) we want to ascertain just how these wives feel about their new marriages.

The Chances of Remarriage. Now, the chances of ultimate remarriage are high for the total population of female and male divorcees. We have fairly good knowledge about the proportion in each age and sex category which will *ultimately* remarry—for example, about 94% of all women divorced at age 30 will remarry—but we do not have adequate data on the remarriage of mothers *vs.* nonmothers, Catholics *vs.* Protestants, those with more education *vs.* those with less, etc. That is, we suspect there may be much greater chances of ultimate remarriage for some strata and groups than others, but we have no firm knowledge about these differences. Moreover, and perhaps of greater importance for comparisons of social structures, we do not know much about the differential *rates* of remarriage. That is, even if it is true that Catholics ultimately remarry in as high a *proportion* as Protestants, perhaps they take *longer* to get remarried. Or, even if most divorcees age 38 and under will *eventually* marry, perhaps those 38 and under who were also in love with another person prior to the divorce will get remarried at a faster rate during the first few years after the divorce, than those not in love.

Answers to these two questions—the chances of *ultimate* remarriage for various categories of the divorced, and the *rate* of remarriage year by year, for those categories—can not be obtained from our study. Much larger samples are needed, and the period for recording the information must, of course, extend over many years. Indeed, we shall get these answers, when we finally get them, only from official records. Meanwhile, we shall interpret briefly the suggestive results from our small sample, with its short time span after the divorce.

Differentiating Factors in Remarriage. These data on remarriage point to the following conclusion. Most of the differentiating factors we have already located also have an effect upon remarriage, as they do on dating frequency and steady dating. These factors include such status items as race, religion, education, age (but not rural-urban background), as well as items more immediately from the postdivorce experience, such as trauma, the remarriage of the ex-husband, or activities at separation. However, two qualifications should be added to these statements: (a) Many of these differentiating factors, such as "attitudes of friends toward the divorce," begin to lose much of their effect by Time Group IV. (b) Certain other differentiating factors, such as religion, continue to have an effect through Group IV, but the differential remains about the same. Indeed, we can say that *almost no factor has a cumulatively differentiating effect, and almost all these women seem to be moving toward marriage.*

The structural factors that lead to this consequence have already been discussed. Referring to our comments on accounting models for analyzing decisions, we see that most of our sample would have a strong set of predispositions or values in favor of marriage. If this statement seems paradoxical to some, we must remember that our divorcees did, after all, marry, and they were mothers. It is of course true that some mothers have no great interest in marriage as a life pattern, but it is at least safe to claim that among all women who get married, those who have children are on the average more committed to home and marriage than those who do not have children; and the claim is even safer if we compare them with women who do not even marry once. Aside from these *predisposing factors,* we have analyzed both theoretically and by reference to our field data the pressures which would lead these young, divorced mothers to enter marriage again. Consequently, almost all of them do move in that direction.

As we would expect from our previous data on dating frequency, Negroes appear to move toward remarriage somewhat more rapidly than Whites. By 26 months after the divorce, however, the differences are of no importance, for 59% of the Negroes in Group IV have remarried, as against 53% of the Whites (in Group III, the percentages were 48% *vs.* 37%). Thus, although the one segment starts more rapidly to move back into new marriages, the differences gradually diminish. By contrast, the differential between Protestant and Catholic divorcees remains much the same throughout the time groups, with the percentage of Protestants remarrying always somewhat higher: 17% *vs.* 13% in Group II, 41% *vs.* 35% in Group III (14 months after the divorce) and 59% vs. 49% in Group IV.[3]

We have seen that although those with some college education do seem to find circles of friends, opportunities to meet people, and even dates, more than women with lesser education, there were no educational differences of note between those going steady and those not going steady. Indeed, we would expect that the apparent social advantage enjoyed by the women with more education might be more than wiped out, as we move closer to marriage itself, since it is doubtless still true that women who go to college have less probability of ultimately getting married than those who do not go to college. Just what these probabilities are at present, cannot be easily ascertained. We usually calculate the percentage of college women 45 years old and over who have ever married, but this only gives the probabilities for a generation earlier. In 1940, 6 out of 10 women college graduates of this age had married, compared with 9 out of 10 for the general female population.[4] These 1940 women had, of course, graduated 25 years earlier, while the chances of marriage for women graduates, or women with some college education, have apparently risen substantially.[5] Of course, men college graduates have greater chances of marriage than the general male population.

On the other hand, we do not know what are the chances of *re*marriage for *mothers* who have had some college education. We are here willing to be statistically incautious, by predicting what will be found when we do know: that even though these women have been married, a lower proportion will ultimately remarry than of mothers who have had only some high school or have completed high school education. Through our first two time groups (2 months and 8 months after the divorce), the women with some or a com-

3. To save tedium for those disliking arithmetic, the Catholic proportion in these three groups is the following fraction of the Protestant: .76, .85, .83.

4. F. Lawrence Babcock, *The U. S. College Graduate* (New York: Macmillan, 1941), Table 2, p. 62.

5. See Ernest Haremann and Patricia S. West, *They Went to College* (New York: Harcourt, Brace, 1952), Ch. 5.

pleted college education marry less than other educational strata. This difference is entirely erased by 14 months after the divorce, when 50% of the
college women have remarried, as against 30% of the women with a
completed high school education, 43% of those with some high school,
and 37% of those with only grammar school education. By Time Group IV,
however, the two high-school categories have moved ahead of the college
category slightly, while among the college women there are *still* only 50%
remarried. The grammar-school women remain behind all the rest (39%),
but they continue to enter marriage. All that we see is that they move into
marriage more slowly than the other classes. Since, by contrast, the percentage
married does not change for the *college* women, we are now going beyond
our data to suggest that their chances of ultimate remarriage are not as great
as those of high-school mothers. We believe that this is due mainly to two
structural elements in their mate selection problem: (a) generally, their choice
is narrower than that of other women, since they wish and expect to find a
mate with equal or greater education; and (b) at their age levels there are
proportionately fewer men "between marriages" simply because marriages are
more stable in the higher educational strata. Marital dissolutions from either
death or divorce are lower in rate, while some 60% of the spouses of all these
women will be found among the once married.[6]

Remarriage is affected by age, as were dating frequency and steady dating.
However, once again the greater step that is remarriage affects the changes
over time. Both the youngest (20-24 years) and the oldest (35 years and
over) age groups are slower to re-enter marriage immediately after the divorce
than the middle age brackets. However, by 14 months the youngest class has
moved ahead of all the rest, while the oldest divorcees continue to lag behind.
By 26 months after the divorce, the percentage remarried was as follows:

TIME GROUP IV

Age	Percent remarried	Base
20-24 years	80	10
25-29 years	56	36
30-34 years	50	38
35 years and over	46	26
	N = 110	

We guess that the youngest divorcees simply avoided remarriage for a while,
in order to enjoy themselves a bit, since their dating frequency was so high.
We expect the oldest to remarry more slowly if at all, since the ultimate proportion remarried among those over 35 years old *is* lower than among women
who are younger, for the national population of the divorced.

A parallel but puzzling comparison may be found by looking at the *duration of marriage*. This is to some degree an overlapping comparison, since, in
general, those who have had a short marriage are also more likely to be

---

6. Glick, "Remarriages...," *op. cit.*, p. 728. In contrast with wife's *education* is remarriage
by ex-husband's *occupation*: by Time Group IV, 57% of the *lowers* had remarried, 48% of the
middle occupations, 40% of the upper stratum wives.

younger. However, we have seen before that the effects of these two factors are not always the same. Once again, the rate of remarriage is less in the first period after the divorce for those who have had a short marriage (0-4 years) than for those who have had slightly longer marriage. Similarly, those who have been married 15 years or more also fail to begin marrying during the first two time periods. Important differences between these different lengths of marriage do not begin showing up until 26 months after the divorces, and then the relationship is not a simple one. Those who were married 5-9 years have a *higher* proportion married in the 26-month period (61%), while the women married 10-14 years and 15 years and over show a lower proportion remarrying (47% and 48%); but those married 0-4 years *fall in between* (54%). The failure of those with short marriages to remarry quickly is caused by factors that we do not understand adequately, although various *ad hoc* hypotheses are possible.

The Effect of Children upon Remarriage. We have already hinted that the relationship between the number of children and the movement toward remarriage is complex. In the light of the data already presented, it is interesting to learn that those with *more* children seem to remarry *faster* than do those with fewer children. Let us look at this fact more closely.

It will be remembered that the highest frequency of dating at the time of our interview is to be found among those who dated during the separation period, while the lowest was found among those who "did nothing at all," or took part in church activities to fill the gap caused by the marital breakup. Slightly less than half of the women reported that they gave more attention to their children at that time, and these women were dating *less* frequently at the time of the interview (33% dated more than once weekly) than any other women except those who did nothing or who took part in church activities.

Women who had more children were less likely to date frequently than those who had fewer children (41% of those with one child dated more than once weekly; 34% of those with two children; 19% of those with three or more children). Moreover, to move to steady dating, those who gave more attention to their children during separation are less likely to be dating steady than any other class at the time of interview. Twenty-eight percent of these mothers who paid more attention to their children have steady dates, but 35-38% of those who gave more attention to church activities, went about with their girl friends, went to movies alone, or did nothing, had steady dates. And 50-52% of those who took a part in club activities or dated, were going steady by the time of the interview. Thus, it would appear that the mothers who gave more attention to their children would fail to get married.

Next, those with *more* children were more likely to give *more* attention to their children at the time of the marital breakup. Thirty-three percent of those with one child, 45% of those with two children, and 54% of those with three or more children gave more attention to their offspring. In addition, to make the picture darker still, it is the older mothers of course who have more children: none of those 20-24 years of age had 3 or more children; 13% of those 25-29; 26% of those 30-34; and 30% of those 35 years of age and over. And the older women are less likely to find ultimately a new mate.

These facts seem interrelated, and point to a rather simple set of processes.

That is, the most effective way for a divorcee to remarry, it would appear, is to take part in all those activities which lead away from the home or female associations, and toward men. By dating frequently, she increases the chances of going steady and of remarrying. So far, we seem to be merely documenting the commonsense expectation, that those divorcees who are young and are not burdened by many children, will date frequently and those who date frequently will have a high likelihood of getting remarried promptly. These expectations are indeed borne out.

On the other hand, when we moved to steady dating and the number of children, we found this relationship somewhat ambiguous. Although those with *one* child were more likely to be dating steady than those with more than one child, it was also true that those with three or more children were *more* likely to be dating steady than those with two children. This fact might be a statistical accident, or might suggest there is no relationship between the number of children and remarriage itself. However, we also found that those with *more* children are *more* likely to be remarried soon: By Time Group IV, 45% of those with one child had married; 57% of those with two children had married; and 61% of those with three or more children had married. True enough, those with three or more children had not married at all in the first few months after the divorce, but in the three succeeding time groups those with three or more children ranked either first (II, IV), or were only four percentage points behind first rank in proportion remarried (III).

These facts would suggest that women with many children are more "efficient" in their remarriage activities than those with fewer children. That is, those with more children apparently date less, but get more husbands from those dates, than those with fewer children. Indeed, we are tempted into guessing that there are two main roads toward remarriage, one of which lies through an active participation in dating, and the other through a continued dedication to the home. Or, one way of attracting a new husband is following the model of the never married, in being attractive as a sex and love partner. The other way is not usually open to the never married, that of being an attractive mother and homemaker. For we no longer find the dim picture that was apparent in the dating process. There, it was apparent that the women who went out and met men were destined for early marriage. By contrast, there were women who stayed at home, and dated little, and who therefore seemed headed for a late remarriage, or none. Burdened by many children, they seemed to have little chance of competing with their sisters in divorce.

True enough, those who *had* dated during the separation do marry most rapidly. By Time Group IV, 63% of them have remarried, and they had maintained this lead at each previous time group. However, 60% of the women who had paid more attention to their children at that time have *also* remarried by Time Group IV. No other class of separation activities is as likely as these to be associated with early remarriage. And, as we noted, those with more children were more likely to be remarried by Time Group IV.

In retrospect, it is easy to take these two patterns for granted. It is somewhat more difficult to have predicted them in advance. As we have already noted, divorcees most often select the once-married as partners in a new marriage. The dates of our divorced mothers are older, and most of them have a real interest in home and family life; else they would not be dating mothers. Without denying or lessening the importance of the usual female attributes of graciousness, prettiness, and so on, in attracting husbands, we must keep in mind that men are like women in also weighing a prospective spouse by the standards of homemaking. Also, among the pretty tableaux, or theatrical scenes, that a woman can create is that of the loving mother surrounded by happy children in a pleasant home. Although there is smiling in our day at the old saw, "The way to a man's heart is through his stomach," this proposition when sufficiently broadened is doubtless true (as it is also true for women). Perhaps in our time men find the choice difficult between the gay charm of the popular girl and the quieter charm of the homemaker. Certainly the latter dates less often. However, her commitment to marriage doubtless causes these dates to be more productive. Thus—to take a highly special but pertinent datum—the proportion of women who ultimately marry is almost as high among the college graduates of, say, the Cornell School of Home Economics as it is among the population at large. (As of January, 1955, 85% of all their living graduates had married, and 60% of those graduated less than 5 years previously had married.)[6a] We shall not sketch this kind of courtship process, since it is observable to all. What is striking is that, even among our divorcees, the women who apparently wanted to spend more time with their children, and who were burdened (or blessed) with more children, had less opportunity to date as often as other divorcees, but managed to choose as dates those men who were more inclined to marry. Phrasing it pragmatically, they wasted less time with men who were not serious.

Remarriage and Adjustment to Separation. In general, those who took longer between first serious consideration of the divorce and filing the suit were more likely to remarry early. This we would expect, since this longer period of time allows the divorcee to find a new social role, and thus a new definition of herself. The relationship is fairly consistent in each Time Group, although small. By Group IV (26 months after the divorce), 42% of those who took 0-4 months for these steps had married, and 53% of those who took 5-12 months; while 45% of those who took over one year but less than two had remarried, and 63% of those who took two years and over. Thus, the difference is really between this last class and all others.

We have already presented sufficient evidence that the length of this period is important in readjustment, by showing its relationship to dating and other activities. It might be worth while to indicate once more that the underlying factor is the actual adjustment, rather than a mechanical transition from, say, consideration to filing, or marriage to final divorce. We can, for example, find out whether there are any differences in the remarriage of those who felt most *loneliness* at different periods, since this experience would seem to be connected with understanding that the marriage has ended. We find, in conformity with our previous data, that those in Group IV who said their period of greatest loneliness was at the *time of the interview* had the lowest proportion of the remarried (43%). It might be thought that those who claimed they were never at all lonely might be the most adjusted, and thus might be quickest to move toward remarriage. This is not true. Those (a) who never felt lonely,

6a. Personal letter from Esther H. Stocks, Placement Director, Secretary of the College.

(b) who felt most lonely at the first filing, and (c) who felt most lonely at the final decision were all remarried by Group IV in about the same proportion: 51%, 50%, and 54%. But those who felt most lonely at either of the two *genuine finalities,* (1) the social finality of final separation or (2) the legal finality of the decree, were more likely to remarry soon. Fifty-nine percent of these two groups had remarried by 26 months after the divorce. This is in part a psychodynamic process, of course, in that the loneliness, however painful, seems to be a response to a full recognition that the marriage has really ended. This means that a change in role definition is possible and likely.

We have followed in some detail the continuing influence of first initiation of the divorce on postdivorce activities. We would expect, because this factor has an effect upon entering new social relations, that remarriage might also be affected by it. When the husband suggested the divorce first, remarriage is delayed, and even 26 months after the divorce the difference is still observable. When there was mutual suggestion, remarriage by 14 months is slightly greater than when the wife suggested first; but drops slightly behind by 26 months after divorce.

PERCENTAGE REMARRIED, 14 AND 26 MONTHS AFTER DIVORCE, BY WHO FIRST SUGGESTED THE DIVORCE

	Time Groups	
	III	IV
Who first suggested divorce	14 months after divorce	26 months after divorce
Husband	30%	31%
Mutual	50	58
Wife	41	64

Since we have already discussed this factor, we need not comment further, except to emphasize how long after the divorce these conflict patterns affect the behavior of the divorcee.

With reference to the attitudes of friends toward the divorce, their effect on remarriage is the same as that upon dating behavior. That is, the lowest percentage is found among those whose friends *disapproved* the divorce (46% remarried 26 months after the divorce), and the highest among those whose friends were *indifferent* (56% remarried), with those whose friends approved the divorce falling between (53%). However, the differences are unimportant, as they are for the attitudes of *family* toward the divorce.

Emotional Ties and Remarriage. Of course, if the woman admitted that she was in love with another man prior to the divorce, her movement toward remarriage was much more rapid than if she was not in love with another. The difference begins 2 months after the divorce, and continues to be high.

PERCENTAGE REMARRIED, WITHIN TIME GROUPS, BY WHETHER WOMAN ADMITS SHE WAS IN LOVE WITH ANOTHER MAN BEFORE DIVORCE

Were you in love with another man before the divorce?	I Divorced 2 months	II Divorced 8 months	III Divorced 14 months	IV Divorced 26 months
Yes	12%	44%	71%	81%
No	4	12	34	49

We believe that these women would not, in general, have admitted that they were in love with another prior to the divorce unless the relationship was a fairly serious one. However, it is clear that there was some attrition and disenchantment in this postdivorce period. We suppose that many of these women did not marry the man they were in love with before, since so many failed to marry soon after the divorce became final. On the other hand, having been in love with another man prior to the divorce is an index of her emotional *readiness* to think in terms of future relationships, and of her ability to free herself emotionally from her former husband. Consequently, even 26 months after the divorce, the percentage remarried among those who *had* been in love is much higher than among other ex-wives.

In the following chapter, we shall explore at greater length the various aspects of the wife's continuing emotional involvement with the former husband. By way of anticipation, however, we might see now the relationship between *his* remarrying and *her* remarrying. If, as we have implied at several points in our analysis, their attitudes toward one another are to some degree parallel, then (1) there should be a strong association between the two separate movements toward remarriage. On the other hand, (2) this relationship should *diminish* over time, as each assumes independent social roles within his or her own group.

This is indeed what we do find. In the succeeding table, we present this association, and again note that the women who say that they do not know whether their husbands have remarried seem to be like those who say that he *has* remarried. We have assumed that these men have gone off to assume independent lives (and thus their ex-wives have, too).

RELATIONSHIP BETWEEN HER REMARRYING AND HIS REMARRYING, OVER TIME

Time Groups	She has remarried	He has Remarried			Totals	
		Yes	No	Not known		
I						
Q = .88*	Yes	33%	50%	17%	100%	(6)
	No	4	86	10	100	(108)
II						
Q = .43	Yes	21	43	36	100	(14)
	No	13	65	22	100	(77)
III						
Q = −.13	Yes	28	51	21	100	(43)
	No	36	51	13	100	(67)
IV						
Q = .16	Yes	58	29	14	101	(59)
	No	51	35	14	100	(51)

*Q measures the association between the two "yes" responses.

Thus we see that by 14 months after the divorce (Group III), there is practically no association at all between his remarrying and her remarrying, even though the percentage of the remarried among *both* ex-husbands and ex-wives continues to rise together.

We would expect a similar relationship to hold between (a) dating at the time of separation, and (b) later remarriage. That is, those who began to date at the end of their divorce conflict have already begun to establish new social relationships with other men, and we expect them to move more rapidly than other women toward remarriage. On the other hand, these other women also begin to date, so that the *difference* between these two segments should *decrease* over time. Thus, at 2 months after the divorce, the proportion remarried of those who had dated toward the end of their marriage is six times as large as that of women who had not dated (12% and 2%). By Time Group II (8 months after divorce), this proportion is twice as large (23% and 12%). By 14 months after divorce, the ratio decreases to one and one-half times (53% and 34%), and by 26 months after divorce it is only one and one-third times larger (63% and 48%). By that time those who had not begun to date early have nearly caught up with the average. Thus, the initial advantage of the early daters does decrease over time. We have already discussed the other main differentiating separation activity, devoting more attention to the children. Among the remaining items, there is little differential importance for remarriage. Perhaps the sole fact of significance is that, although those who at the separation filled their social gap with church activities were most likely to date infrequently, they remarry about as rapidly as those who went to movies alone, or who took part in women's clubs, and more rapidly than those who did nothing at all. Thus, their apparent initial disadvantage in the competition for new husbands was lessened considerably when we turn from mere frequency of dating to remarriage itself.

Summary. To a cynic in a mass society such as ours, many of the rewarding activities involving other people seem at times to take on the structural character of a slot machine: the payoff function is very low. All of us attempt many things and fail in many of them. Statistically speaking, far more of us aspire to than achieve the posts, positions, honors, and possibly even pleasures that our society offers. Maintaining this situation, the cynic might claim, are two further circumstances: (a) We have no choice. We must play. (b) If we do not put any coins in any given slot machine, we have no chance at all of getting anything out of that one.

It is true, then, that for both women and men the chance of a love relationship or a marriage growing out of any given date will be low. Those who are bitter about the impersonal patterns of contemporary urban life, who complain of the commercial character of dating, who bewail the lack of a deep relationship between men and women even in the dating process, may have some ethical basis for their objections to the courtship and mating customs of our time.

On the other hand, if one does not date at all in this society, the chances of marriage at all become very low. As against the cynic's disappointment, there is optimism in this: we thus expose ourselves to the chances of good events as well. Those who risk nothing in this process will ordinarily gain nothing. It is true that most of those who try for a given job will fail to receive that job. On the other hand, almost all of those who do not try at all will fail to receive it. Moreover, as we have shown in our lengthy analyses of the interaction of status, situation, motivation, behavior, and the actions of others, the steps from the bitterness of marital conflict to a new marriage do not occur at random. Those who *try* to move again toward marriage appear to *move* most definitely. Those who wish to marry, expose themselves most often to the chance. Moreover, although our society imposes few if any obligations upon friends or family to help the divorcee, many do so nevertheless. Not even the divorcee is alone. Finally, the total effect of the larger institutional pressures as we analyzed them earlier, and of the more immediate temptations and actions of dates, friends, co-workers, and families, appears to lead to the remarriage of almost all divorcees. Few can resist these complex adjustmental factors.

CHAPTER XX

THE DIVORCEE'S TIES WITH HER FORMER HUSBAND

JUST AS THE WIFE and husband usually begin divorcing one another long before the decree, so may this divorcing process continue long afterwards. Either may continue to be in love with the other, and in a few instances they both remain in love with one another. Either may have strong antagonistic feelings against the other, so that each day the ex-spouse is present at least in fantasy. The lost love, the biting comments that unhappily did not come to mind during the marital battles, the imagined acts of retaliation, may color the life of the divorcee. The past life may thus shape the present, until that experience is once more integrated into the present life.

Certainly, the main symbol of that former marriage is the former spouse, and in this chapter we explore the divorcee's emotional ties with her ex-husband. Doubtless the husband or wife is often held to be responsible not only for past acts, but also for the present situation. Thus, we would expect the divorcee who has difficult financial problems to feel more antagonism toward her former husband even if he did not himself cause those problems. When the former husband has ceased being the most important symbol of the former marriage, the ex-wife has succeeded in putting him in a more realistic perspective.

Aside from the *symbolic* importance of the former husband, he is a continuing, living person, whom the wife may see on his visits to the children, whom the wife may even continue to date for a while, and about whom the wife may continue to seek information. What he does seems to affect what she does, and what she believes about his feelings *toward her,* will affect her feelings *toward him.*

Meaning of the Ex-Wife's Answers. At the same time, we cannot be satisfied with the answers our divorcees give us about this matter. A former wife is much readier to accuse her ex-husband of being a scoundrel than to admit that she hates him. It is easier for her to admit that she is lonesome, than to confess that she thinks about him frequently. We are convinced that there is some unmeasurable amount of "bias toward indifference" in the answers they have given.

Of course, we have no way of testing this last claim, and perhaps we do our divorcees an injustice. In our analysis, we have tried to look at their actions as well as their reported attitudes. We do not believe that there is a strong social "norm of indifference," which states that the divorcee "ought" to claim indifference, although there may be some mild pressures in that direction. In general, as we have already suggested, these pressures really take the negative form that both new and old friends simply have no great interest in keeping alive a relationship or role that is not woven into their own daily pattern of life. If she continues to have strong feelings for or against her former husband, her attitude is either boring or a nuisance for her own circle when he is no longer a member of it.

On the other hand, when she admits such strong feelings, she admits *his* importance, and correspondingly makes herself appear abject. This is true, even if she does not love him, but hates him, since this proves his importance equally well.

Consequently, we interpret the answers in this fashion. If the wife claims that she loves or hates her former husband, we believe her. On the other hand, we are certain that some of those who claimed that they felt only indifference toward their former husbands actually had a more definite attitude, certainly for some women a feeling of resentment. Finally, our skepticism toward the apparent indifference of these women does not affect the analysis greatly. The main result is this, that the *differences* between the indifferents and those with admittedly more negative (in a few cases, more positive) feelings, with respect to various actions such as dating, seeing the ex-husband, and so on, may not appear in our tables to be as great as they are in fact. Nevertheless, important differences do appear from the answers as given, and thus the bias toward indifference does not prevent our seeing the main directions of forces playing on the feelings of the divorcee toward her ex-husband.

Punishment and Guilt. Among the dimensions of emotion within which husband and wife are involved is that of punishment and guilt. Most of us think in these terms when we discuss a particular divorce, and we expect a divorcee to have some feeling that the other spouse should be punished. Of course, this feeling does not prevent the same person from also having certain feelings of guilt. We tried to ascertain these emotions by asking the divorcee about her wish to punish the ex-husband:

"Mrs. .... even though a court declares a couple divorced, they still have memories of the times they were together. Now, I'd like to ask a few questions about the way you think of your former husband. First of all. . . . Just before or after the divorce, did you ever feel that he ought to be punished in any way for what he did to you?" a—frequently, b—once in a while, c—rarely, d—never.

Less than half of our respondents admitted that they had ever had such feelings: 28% answered "frequently," and 20% answered "once in a while" or "rarely." Fifty-two percent claimed that they had never wished to punish their former husbands. The question is strongly phrased, but even so the answers seem surprisingly mild. With these answers in hand, however, we could not be surprised that only 28% admitted to a second question that they *still* had such feelings at the time of the interview.

We were not prepared for a further result of our analysis: there is *but little change in these feelings over time,* whether we arrange our respondents by our time groups, or by time since the separation. *When* the separation occurred makes little difference, except that once more there is less affect when the separation took place *after the decree* (16% still wished to punish their husbands, as against 27%-30% of those who separated before the decision, between decision and filing, or between filing and decree).

Let us continue for a moment with our essentially negative findings. When we ranged the various themes of complaint against the wish to punish the former husband, only the two themes of Desertion and Triangle were strongly associated with having such wishes (66% and 67% ever wanted to punish) with conflicts over Consumption coming next (58%). At the other extreme were such themes as Home Life (41%), usually associated with low affect, and Values (35%). The range is not great, and other themes vary little from one another.

Now, a rationalistic explanation of this apparent homogeneity might be that these women actually felt guilty, and thus did not believe that their husbands *should* have been punished. That is, they accepted the burden of guilt as their own. Even if we did not have their rather extended charges against their husbands, their own answers about "fairness" would go against such an explanation. We asked them whether there had been times they felt they had not played fair with their husbands, and we also asked (paralleling our question about punishing the ex-husband) whether they *still* felt that way. About 27% had ever felt "guilty," and 16% still felt guilty at the time of the interview. Again, we failed to expect such a small figure. Moreover, just as was true for our questions on punishment of the husband, there were no important changes over our time groups. Our themes of complaint showed few differences of importance, the percentages of "unfair" being in general somewhat higher for the themes which would in our society be considered inadequate grounds for divorce. (Values theme: 37% had felt either in the past or at the time of the interview that they had been unfair.) When the theme of complaint against the husband was one that is morally somewhat more censured (Triangle, Support) the percentage of wives feeling any unfairness was smaller (21%; 20%). However, these differences are not systematic, and generally are small.

Differences by religion or by church attendance also fail to appear. Protestants and Catholics, and frequent and infrequent churchgoers, are about equally represented among the wives who admitted ever feeling they had been unfair. Finally, *even those who had remarried were not very different* in their reported feelings from those who had not remarried, and no great differences appear when we create combinations of "wife remarried—ex-husband not remarried," and try to find those wives who were more likely to admit they had been unfair to their former husbands.

In-love Patterns: Punishment and Guilt. Now, if there were any differences of importance, or even of statistical significance, they ought to be associated with (1) *occurrences prior to the divorce.* They should also be items associated with (2) the conflict period, rather than background social or economic factors. Moreover, (3) the distribution by themes gives us a hint, even though the themes are not productive as a group. Finally, (4) the kind of item that leads to punitive feelings toward the ex-husband might well be the same type that leads to feelings of guilt. We, therefore, return to the notion suggested by the distributions for Triangle and Support.

Now, these items may have some importance in that they are socially somewhat more censured than other conflict themes, but they are more important along another dimension, the role relationship between husband and wife. In particular, the kinds of behavior that are most likely to be damaging to the spouse's ego and role definitions are also the items most likely to be associated with trauma. We might therefore see whether trauma and punitiveness are associated.

WIFE'S DESIRE TO PUNISH THE HUSBAND AT TIME OF THE DIVORCE, BY WIFE'S TRAUMA

At time of Divorce, wife wanted to punish	Trauma Index			
	High	Medium	Low	Total
Frequently	34%	24%	23%	28%
Occasionally	22	28	13	20
Never	44	48	64	52
Total	100%(180)	100%(89)	100%(156)	100%

N = 425

As we see, the high trauma cases are more likely than the medium or low trauma cases to have wanted to punish their husbands at the time of the divorce conflict. Moreover, when we confine our attention to those who *still* wished to punish at the time of the interview (some of whom, of course, were recent divorcees), one-third of the high trauma cases still wished to punish, while only one-fifth of the low trauma cases continued to feel such a desire.

These few results allow us to guess that one key item for both punitiveness and guilt might be the relation between either spouse and another love interest. We ask, then, whether guilt or punitive feelings are higher if either was in love with another prior to the divorce. Thirty-six percent of the wives claimed that their husbands had been in love with another woman prior to the divorce, as against 13% who admitted they themselves had been in love with another man. An additional 14% claimed that they did not know whether their ex-husbands had been in love with another woman prior to the divorce. As noted earlier, we suspect (from various cross-tabulations) that many of these women, nevertheless, had reason to feel that their husbands actually *were* in love with other women.

Now, we can ask whether the wives who were in love with another man were more likely to feel they had been unfair to their husbands. We can also ask whether those women felt punitive whose husbands' emotions had strayed. Finally, there may be differences when the wives were in love and the husbands were not, as against other possible combinations.

We then find that the factor of emotional involvement toward the end of the marriage does seem to affect these feelings of guilt and punitiveness.

In the succeeding table the relationship between the husband's being in love and the wife's desire to punish him is clear.

WIFE'S DESIRE TO PUNISH HUSBAND, BY WHETHER HUSBAND WAS IN LOVE

	Wish to Punish			
Time of interview	Yes	No	No	
Time of divorce	Yes	Yes	No	
Was husband in love?				**Totals**
Yes	34%	26%	40%	100% (152)
Don't know	29	15	56	100 (59)
No	22	18	60	100 (214)
Totals	28%	20%	52%	

$$X^2 = 14.5 \qquad .01 > P > .001 \qquad N = 425$$

Now, these data also suggest that the punitiveness of the wife might be somewhat reduced if *she herself* had been in love prior to the divorce. When the wife *was* in love and her husband was *not* in love, only 12% of the wives wanted to punish their husbands at the time of the divorce, and still wanted to do so at the time of the interview, while 69% never wished to punish at all $(.01 > P > .001)$.

Our suppositions seem to be borne out, and we feel justified in making a similar test with reference to her feeling that she had not played fair with her husband. Up to this point, we can see a rough parallel between the moral strictures of our society and the reactions of the wife. In general, neither husband nor wife has a right to be involved emotionally with someone else until the divorce has been granted. The woman who does so is more likely, than the woman who does not, to feel that she has not played fair with her husband. On the other hand, she is personally more hurt, and feels more punitive, if he was in love with another.

WHETHER THE WIFE FELT SHE "PLAYED FAIR" WITH HER HUSBAND, BY EMOTIONAL INVOLVEMENT OF HUSBAND AND WIFE

		Did wife ever feel she did not "play fair?"			
	Time of interview	Yes	No	No	
	Time of divorce	Yes	Yes	No	
In Love					
Wife	**Husband**				**Total**
No	No	21%	11%	68%	100% (182)
Yes	Yes				
Yes	Not Known ⎬	13	24	64	101 (55)
Yes	No				
No	Yes ⎫	12	7	81	100 (188)
No	Not Known ⎭				
	Totals	16%	11%	73%	

$$N = 425$$
$$X^2 = 19.9 \qquad P < .001$$

As we see, the wife is least likely to have felt at the time of divorce, that she did not play fair, and still to feel so at the time of interview, if she believes that her husband was perhaps in love with another woman and if she herself *was not* in love with another man. The conformity between moral strictures and her reactions, then, is also confirmed here. In this class, there is a lesser likelihood that she believed she had herself contributed to the conflict leading to the divorce.

Emotional Attachment of Wife to Ex-Husband. The dimensions of guilt and punitiveness do not stand in any simple relationship to that of the wife's attachment to her former husband. This point has already been hinted at in the data on trauma. Those women who were most in love with their husbands were most hurt by his leaving them. Trauma in turn is associated with a desire to punish the husband. But love is not always killed easily: the high trauma cases are also more likely than others to be willing to wipe out the divorce. Twenty percent of the high trauma respondents were willing to wipe out the decree, as against only 5% of the low trauma respondents. It is not, then, a paradox to say that the wives who were most hurt are the ones most likely to be still in love with their former husbands.

However, these are extreme cases, and the question was strongly phrased. Let us broaden our inquiry to include other types of relationship than "still in love." In our discussion of social adjustment, we used four classes: (a) strongly positive; (b) friendly, but not in love; (c) indifferent; and (d) negative. As was then made clear, the negatives and positives are those with stronger affect toward their former husbands, while the indifferents seem to contain an undisclosed proportion of wives with at least low level degrees of resentment. Now, these attitudes should change somewhat over time, so that the distribution of such relationships in Time Group I would be different from that for Time Group IV. It is also possible, of course, that much of this change *begins with the time of separation,* so that time changes by our Time Groups are not so striking as those by time since separation.

Current theory does not allow us to predict in detail the direction of these changes. Presumably, there would be a general change from having a strong affect to having a weak affect or none. That is, the negative and positive groups should diminish. However, we do not understand these processes well enough to predict whether, for example, those who were in love with their former husbands will be more likely to end as "friendly but not in love," or as "indifferent," after a period of several years. On the other hand, we would predict that whatever the specific directions of change, they ought to be associated with certain postdivorce experiences, such as the continuity of child support payments, the attitudes of the ex-husband toward the wife, the intensity of social contact between husband and wife, and possibly the social adjustment of the wife.

Let us begin our analysis with the partial rejection of our initial and basic expectation: In fact, (1) the percentage of women with strong positive affect does decline. However, (2) *the percentage of women with strong negative affect rises.* Further, although (3) the percentage of "indifferents" does rise, (4) the other group with presumably low affect, the friendlies, appears to decline slowly. Moreover, not all these changes seem to occur at the same rate, or regularly: the changes are not, for example, systematic as between our two time bases, (a) time since separation and (b) time since decree. In the following section, we shall attempt to analyze what takes place.

Emotional Ties and Attitudes of the Ex-Husband. There are several important processes that seem to be traceable within the data on emotional involvement of ex-wife and ex-husband. We would expect, for example, that those with high intensity of contact with their ex-husbands, as measured by our "contact index," would be emotionally more involved with these spouses.[1] On the other hand, it is clear that the time dimension contains many elements we have not tapped, and that over time these involvements do take several directions. Moreover, we have already seen how important is the attitude of the ex-husband toward his former wife, so that over time there are several sets of processes to be watched. The new social relations of the wife should also be significant in these changes, and we would include especially the new marriage or steady date. Let us follow out some of these influences.

Now, we cannot adequately interpret the connection of emotional involvement with intensity of contact, since the effect may be created from either side. Wives may have a high intensity of contact because they were attached to their ex-husbands, or the ex-husbands may have facilitated contact because they were attached to their former wives. On the other hand, contact might well help to create or maintain an emotional attachment, or even to develop a mutual antagonism. Let us look first at the relation between contact and attitude toward the ex-husband, among those wives *who had not yet remarried* at the time of the interview.

ATTITUDES OF UNREMARRIED DIVORCEES TOWARD THEIR EX-HUSBANDS, BY CONTACT INDEX

Index of Contact Intensity	In Love	Friendly	Attitude Indifferent	Negative	Total
High	24%	40%	19%	17%	100%(100)
Medium	7	32	32	29	100 (133)
Low	10	14	33	43	100 (70)
	13%	31%	28%	28%	100%
					N = 303

The contact index does not measure frequency, but intensity, of contact, and we see that the percentage of positives decreases with contact intensity, while the proportion of negatives increases as contact decreases, as does also that of the indifferents.

Now, if contact has such importance, then the wife's notion of the ex-husband's attitude toward her would also be significant. The complexities of this relationship are very great, and we shall not attempt to unravel all of

1. These four items formed a fairly good Guttman scale (R=.92): (a) whether the respondent dated her former husband; (b) whether she found out about him; (c) whether she saw him; and (d) whether she would not avoid seeing him. Nevertheless, there were 136 respondents with "error." Thus, the problem of their distribution along the scale was crucial. In order to have a rationale for this distribution, a latent distance model was constructed, with five "latent contact" classes resulting. These five classes are as follows:

Range on Scale	Class	N	%
.853 — 1.000	High	44	10
.651 — .852	Medium High	88	21
.326 — .650	Medium	175	41
.161 — .325	Medium Low	79	19
.001 — .160	Low	39	9
		425	100

The substantive limits to these data are derivative from the time problem. The items refer to different time phases. A simple cross-tabulation by time will not necessarily be productive, since 3 of the 4 items are retrospective, focusing on the period after the separation and divorce. Nevertheless, intensity of contact as measured by the index does diminish over time: e.g., 39% of the wives separated 0-1 year were "high contact," while this percentage drops to 26% of those separated 3 years and over.

them. Certainly her attitude can help to change or maintain his favorable or unfavorable attitude toward her. On the other hand, it is possible that some wives simply project their own attitudes onto the husband. Finally, his attitude may change or maintain her favorable or unfavorable attitude toward him. What is definite, however, is that these two sets of attitudes, as she reports them, are mirror images of one another.

ATTITUDE OF THE EX-WIFE TOWARD THE EX-HUSBAND, BY HIS ATTITUDE
TOWARD HER ATTITUDE

Attitude of Ex-Husband to Respondents	Attitude of Respondents to Ex-Husband			
	Positive	Friendly	Indifferent	Negative
Positive	63%	32%	19%	24%
Friendly	19	42	23	16
Not Known	10	11	21	21
Negative	8	15	37	39
Totals	100%	100%	100%	100%
	(48)	(120)	(126)	(131)
				N = 425

$$X^2 = 73.3 \qquad P < .001$$

Since we must accept her claim that in some cases she does not know *his* attitude, the relationship is not so clear as we should desire. In general, it seems safe to guess that a genuine "don't know" is not frequent, and that it usually means he is "indifferent" or close to "negative." In any event, the closeness of these two sets of attitudes is apparent.

Let us probe this relationship somewhat further by reference to the dimension of time. We can group the positives with the friendlies, and the negatives with the indifferents and "don't know" group, and then ascertain whether the parallel between husband's attachment and wife's attachment remains unchanged *over time,* using time of separation as our base point. (1) We then find that the Q of association is +.85 for our first time group, 0-1 year since separation. However, for succeeding time groups (1-2 years since separation, 2-3 years, and 3 years and over) the Q of association drops to about +.59. (2) For both ex-husband and ex-wife, (a) the percentage of positives (and friendlies) and (b) thus also the proportion both positive decline over time. Correspondingly, the proportion that is "both negative" increases. (3) On the other hand, the Q of association does not change much after the first time segment, because (a) the proportion of cases in which the wife has negative feelings toward her former husband, but believes that *he* has positive feelings toward *her,* remains fairly stable; and (b) the proportion of cases in which the wife has positive feelings toward her husband, but believes that he has negative feelings toward her, is unstable (low-high-low). Thus, the general pattern is fairly clear, but there are individual cells that are somewhat puzzling. We would suppose that a larger sample, with an exact panel design, would clarify these problems if the group were followed over a longer period of time.

At the risk of introducing further complexities into our exposition, let us see whether the factor of contact helps us to understand the patterns better when we also keep in mind the element of time. In our previous table on contact and emotional relationship, we saw that intensity of contact between the *unremarried* divorcee and her former spouse was associated with a positive attitude him. Let us now use a narrower index, and include all our respondents. We ask simply whether the respondents who have recently found out about their husbands are more likely to have strong positive feelings toward him. As we would expect, the answer is affirmative.

ATTITUDE OF EX-WIFE TOWARD EX-HUSBAND, BY WHETHER SHE HAS TRIED
TO FIND OUT WHAT HE IS DOING

Found Out Recently	Ever Did	Attitude Toward Ex-Husband				
		In Love	Friendly	Indifferent	Negative	Total
Yes	Yes	25%	23%	7%	8%	14%
No	Yes	46	24	26	24	27
No	No	29	52	67	67	59
	Total	100%	99%	100%	99%	100%
	Number	48	120	126	131	425

A comparable table, relating this attitude to whether the wife wanted or wants to punish her former husband, shows that, (a) those who *still* want to punish are least positive and most negative; while (b) those who *never* wanted to punish are most positive and least negative. (c) Those who once wanted to punish but no longer wish to do so fall between.

Now, it is possible that some of the apparent complexities in the relationship between the mutual attachment of husband and wife are created by different degrees of *contact* at different times. As we commented before, contact alone may create greater *antagonism* or maintain an *attachment*. It is clearly of importance. In the following simplified table, we have held *constant* the intensity of contact, or contact index, and used only two time categories, to see what happens to the attitude toward the ex-husband. Afterwards, we can revolve our data once more, to see how contact seems to affect *mutuality* of attitude.

ATTITUDE TOWARD EX-HUSBAND, BY CONTACT INDEX AND BY TIME SINCE SEPARATION

Contact Index	Time Since Separation	Positive	Attitude to Ex-Husband		Negative	Totals
			Friendly	Indifferent		
High	0-2 years	19%	44%	23%	14%	100%(57)
	2 or more	22	30	24	24	100 (74)
Medium	0-2 years	10	33	35	22	100 (79)
	2 or more	2	30	31	37	100 (94)
Low	0-2 years	13	22	22	43	100 (40)
	2 or more	5	13	36	46	100 (78)

Several facts emerge from this table to illuminate our problem. We see that although the high-contact-index divorcees are indeed more likely to have positive attitudes toward their former husbands, there are also some high-contact-index divorcees who feel antagonistic toward their former spouses. Further, time has a different effect upon these different categories. Let us summarize these facts. (1) When the contact index is high, time since separation seems to have *no effect* on the proportion of wives who remain strongly positive in their attitudes toward their former husbands (contact is high because of this feeling). But under the same high contact, (2) time since separation does *increase* the proportion of *negatives*. We shall try in a moment to locate factors that might lead to such a difference. It is clear that under some conditions of high contact the divorcee may move toward antagonism and not toward indifference or friendliness.

Moreover, under the situation of low contact, the *reverse* of these propositions is found. (3) Under low contact, time has no effect on the proportion of negatives; but (4) time does seem to decrease the proportion of wives with strong positive feelings (absence makes him less desirable). We leave aside the comparison between the friendlies and the indifferents, although here, too, under low and high contact they are the reverse of one another.

From another point of view, (5) there is no increase throughout these comparisons in either the positives or the friendlies. Also, (6) there is never a large decrease in the negatives or the indifferents. We go beyond our data when we suspect further that (7) under the beginning condition of high contact, the important change of attitude over time is from friendliness to antagonism; and (8) under the beginning condition of low contact, the important change of attitude over time is from positive attachment to indifference. Finally, and again venturing beyond our data, (9) under the beginning condition of medium contact, the main change of attitude over time is from positive attachment to antagonism.[2]

But it has been made clear that the apparent attitudes of the ex-husbands toward the former wives are also important. We have already shown that they parallel each other, but diverge over time. Now, does the intensity of contact make any difference? (10) Thirty-five percent of our respondents thought their former husbands reciprocated their own attitude, whether strong or weak, positive or negative. However, 50% of the *high*-contact wives felt this way, 37% of the medium-high-contact wives, 31% of the medium, 46% of the medium-low spouses, and 33% of the low-contact wives. (11) Roughly, then, half of the high-contact spouses had *similar* attitudes, while about two-thirds of the low-contact spouses had *dissimilar* attitudes. Fifty-five percent of the high-contact spouses with similar attitudes claimed that this attitude was *positive;* 77% of the low-contact spouses with similar attitudes claimed that this attitude was *negative.* Or, the highest proportion of positive-positive cases appears in the two highest contact classes (63% of the positive-positive cases are found in the high- and medium-high-contact classes). The highest proportions of the intermediate and similar attitudes occur in the middle-contact classes (90% of the friendly-friendly cases and 89% of the indifferent-don't know cases in medium, high-medium, medium-low contact). And the highest proportion of the negative-negative cases occurs in the lower-contact classes (80% of them fall in medium, medium-low, or low-contact categories).

Hypotheses about Postdivorce Attachment. It is clear from this series of propositions that we are faced with very complex factors in interaction.

---

2. This series of comparisons is one where the lack of a genuine panel is most painfully felt. For many time comparisons, the pseudo-panel can be useful, and may substitute where the panel losses in a proper panel design might be predicted to be overly high.

Let us examine them. The ex-wife's attitude toward her ex-husband is associated with his apparent attitude toward her. Both are related, in turn, to the intensity of contact in (mainly) the conflict and separation period. High contact is, in turn, associated with relatively strong positive attitudes toward one another, but over time the contact seems to be less, while their attitudes change toward indifference and antagonism. Moreover, during this same period, both ex-husband and ex-wife are finding new mates. Finally, if their contact is less, her attitude over time is less a *reflection of his attitude* or his behavior, and more and more the *result of what she experiences* and does. Perhaps the main exception to this statement is the factor of steadiness of child support payments. It seems reasonable to guess, and we shall test this notion, that if he does continue to pay regularly she is less likely to develop antagonism toward him over time. On the other hand, her most important experience in this connection ought to be her remarriage or going steady. We shall follow out these notions in subsequent sections.

It was clear in our analysis of social adjustment and dating that ex-wives who are intensely emotionally involved with their former husbands seem to have more difficulties than those who claim to feel only friendliness or indifference toward these men. The "involvement," of course, could be antagonism, rather than "love."

Since, in the respondent's judgment, the former husband seemed to share (especially under high contact) her attitude at first, while later these attitudes diverge more (but seem in any event to move toward antagonism and indifference), we are inclined to believe that the observable increase in "antagonism" contains two major dimensions: (a) a direct antagonism toward the former husband because of what he has done to her, or because of the situation in which he has left her; and (b) a derivative and milder negative feeling that begins when she gets a new standard (new husband or new steady date) by which to compare the old relationship. Thus, over time, the proportion of wives with negative feelings grows even without much contact with the former husbands, because these wives enter new relationships in which they come to believe that it was the former husbands who were mainly at fault. Two further commonsense conclusions seem likely. (1) This secondary or derivative antagonism is not a strong affective involvement, and is thus unlike the direct antagonism at an earlier stage of the post-divorce adjustment. (2) Presumably, over a still longer period of time (perhaps four to five years) even this antagonism decreases and ultimately fades away.

Now, if our hypotheses are correct, we ought to find (a) that in the earliest time phase a much higher proportion of the indifferent or friendly wives than of positive or negative wives have entered new relationships, i.e., have a steady date or have remarried; and (b) that the *difference* between the indifferents and friendlies, and the negatives and positives, ought to *decrease* over time. In the succeeding table these two hypotheses are borne out.

As can be seen, (a) beyond three years after the time of separation, the differences among the various attitude groups in the proportions remarried or going steady have dropped. (b) The classes with low emotionality, friendly

PROPORTION OF DIVORCEES REMARRIED OR GOING STEADY, BY TIME AND BY
ATTITUDE TOWARD THE EX-HUSBAND

% Remarried or Going Steady, in each Cell

Time Since Separation	Friendly or Indifferent	Attitude Negative	In love	Totals
0-1 year	46%	7%	22%	35%
Base	(46)	(14)	(9)	(69)
1-2 years	58%	39%	40%	50%
Base	(64)	(28)	(15)	(107)
2-3 years	82%	61%	45%	60%
Base	(68)	(54)	(20)	(162)
3 years and over	74%	66%	50%	70%
Base	(47)	(35)	(2)	(84)

or indifferent, are on the other hand much more likely than the negatives or positives to be remarried or going steady in the early phases of the postdivorce adjustment. (c) Finally, the proportion going steady or remarried in each attitude class rises over time.

A simpler way of showing the relationship between affect toward ex-husband and the new attachment is to bracket the two low-affect classes together, and compare them over time with the two high-affect classes (negative or positive) with reference to new attachments. In the time period 0-1 year since separation, there is a Q of association of +.70 between having a low-affect attitude and being remarried or going steady. However, 1-2 years after separation, this association drops to +.35. The association is still lower 2-3 after separation (+.14), and almost the same (+.22) 3 years and more after the separation. In these last two time periods, the association is negligible.

We may take the distribution of attitudes toward the ex-husband at the time of the divorce as a measure of the wife's emotion toward him because of the marriage relationship. Now, 16% of Group I feel they are still in love with him, in spite of the marital conflict. Thirty percent feel friendly, but are not in love; 30% claim that they are indifferent toward him, and 24% say that they have negative feelings toward him. Presumably, after this point any changes in distribution must occur mainly because of (a) the situation in which she finds herself because of the divorce, and for which she blames him; or because of (b) a new or renewed standard for his behavior and for herself, when she remarries or goes steady, such that by comparison the ex-husband is rated still lower than immediately after the divorce.

This means, then, that although negative feelings increase among *both* the remarried and the not remarried, *different* factors cause the increase. (1) An increasing proportion of ex-wives who are *neither* remarried *nor* going steady feel negatively toward the former husband, because of the position in which they find themselves over time. (2) An increasing proportion of the wives who are remarried or going steady feel negatively, because in comparison with the new attachment the former husband seems even worse than just after the divorce. (3) On the other hand, since almost all the remarried believe their new marriages to be better than the old, we would expect their general sense of well-being to keep this negativism within some limits. (4) Finally, we might expect the bitterness of those not remarried or going steady to be extended to an antagonism against love and marriage generally.

If different factors are at work in this increase in negative feelings, then the increase ought to be different in the two groups: the remarried or going steady, and the rest. Thus, among those separated less than one year, 4% of the remarried or going steady have negative feelings toward the ex-husband, as against 29% of those not remarried or going steady. Of those separated 1-2 years, 20% of those who are remarried or going steady have negative feelings, as against 32% of the rest. By 2-3 years after separation, the percentages are almost exactly the same, 34% as against 33%. But beyond 3 years, a *still higher proportion* of those who are not remarried or going steady have become antagonistic: 48% of the wives who are *not* remarried or going steady have negative feelings, as against 39% of those remarried or going steady.

Now, these figures document the increase, and also suggest that there may be different factors at work in the two groupings. We have gone beyond our data, however, in suggesting that those with new attachments dislike their ex-husbands more because they compare the husband with the new attachment, while women without new attachments come to dislike their former husbands rather because of the unpleasant situation in which they find themselves. Nevertheless, we do have data bearing on this hypothesis. We present the relevant facts in the succeeding paragraphs.

First, it is unlikely that what the husband does *after* the divorce can play an important role in these attitude changes within either grouping of ex-wives (except for the single factor of continuity of child support). The ex-spouses see each other less and less over time, and their lives are increasingly apart. (2) The two classes of ex-wives can not be distinguished much with reference to what the ex-husband did *during* the marriage, and in any event these acts also recede in importance over time. (3) The increasing dislike of the former husband cannot be due, for the *remarried,* to the bad situation in which the remarried find themselves, because in fact their situation is much improved, by their own admission. They cannot dislike their former husbands for having left them in the lurch, since they claim that their lives are now much better. (4) On the other hand, those who have *not* formed new attachments have made no such obvious improvement in their lives. They, too, claim that it would have been bad *not* to have divorced, but their "new" lives have few *positive* advantages. (5) The ex-wife's increasing dislike of her former husband is paralleled by *his* increasingly negative feelings *toward her* over time. However, his dislike of her is greatest when *she herself has married.* We cannot unravel this last complexity. Does she believe that he is less disposed toward her, merely because she sees him less, because he himself is more likely to have remarried, or because she believes he resents her remarriage? Is her attitude toward him an answer to his real increasing dislike, or does she unconsciously project her own dislike onto him? In the latter event, she frees herself from any guilt, since she can therefore claim that he disliked her first. We cannot answer these and other questions now. We can only see that the attitudes of ex-husband and ex-wife continue to parallel one another, and *seem to be most negative when these both remarry.* These facts are at

least in conformity with our notion that the remarried wife's increased negativism toward the former husband is due to her comparing the new love with
the old, and finding the latter wanting.

Now, three further sets of facts need to be added: (6) proof that ex-wives
whose postdivorce situations are unpleasant are *more negative* toward their
former husbands, than those whose situations are less unpleasant; (7) proof
that the remarried are better off, objectively and by self-exaluation, than those
who have not formed new attachments; and (8) proof that for those who
remain *unattached,* the negative feelings toward the former husband are not
focused only on the former husband, but are extended to become negative
feelings toward love and marriage generally. By contrast, those who have
formed new emotional attachments have, of course, highly positive feelings
toward love and marriage, even while their particular, negative feelings toward
the former husband are increasing. We shall now summarize these three sets
of facts.

As to (6) the association between negative feelings toward the ex-husband,
and the unpleasantness of the postdivorce situation of the unattached: (a)
Thirty percent of the unattached who date frequently (1-2 times weekly)
feel antagonistic toward their ex-husbands, as against 36% of those who
date less frequently. (b) Twenty-eight percent of those with many or some
opportunities to meet people have antagonistic feelings toward their ex-husbands, as against 40% of those with only few opportunities, and 41% of
those with no such opportunities. (c) Twenty-five percent of those who
claim that they "have enough" with which to meet expenses feel negatively
toward their ex-husbands, while 38% of those who do *not* feel they have
enough are antagonistic toward their ex-husbands. Moreover, (d) the difference is *greater over time:* 25% of those separated more than 2 years *and*
"having enough" are antagonistic, as against 42% of those who have been
separated more than 2 years and who do not have enough. Finally, (e) 28%
of those with $45 and over per week with which to meet expenses are antago-
nistic, as against 38% of those who have less than $45 per week.

As to (7), the generally better situation of the remarried as against that
of those not remarried, we have discussed this point in some detail in our
chapter on the postdivorce economic situation. And in our chapter on the new
marriage, we shall show further that the remarried are generally better satisfied with their lives than are those who have not yet formed any new emotional
attachment. Suffice it to say that nine-tenths of the remarried assert that they
are better off than during the first marriage. We now want to show, finally, that
(8) for those who remain unattached, the negative feelings toward the former
husband do not remain particularized, but are extended to antagonistic feelings
toward love and marriage generally. We note first that (a) the association
between negative feelings toward the ex-husband and negative attitudes toward
love and marriage is negligible ($Q = +.14$) and is not statistically significant,
for those who have been separated less than 2 years. However, (b) over time
this association *increases,* and among those unattached ex-wives who have been
separated two years and more, the association between particularized negative
feelings and the generally negative attitudes toward love and marriage becomes
$+.45$, and is significant at about the 5% level ($.1 > P > .05$). Moreover, over

time there is actually a *decrease* in generally negative attitudes toward love and marriage among those who *do not* feel antagonistic toward the former husband.

It seems at least highly likely, then, that the increase in negative feelings toward the ex-husband among the remarried and those going steady is due somewhat more to the fact that now these ex-wives have a new or renewed standard of comparison, such that their former husbands appear even less adequate than immediately after the divorce. Put in other terms, they accept the new social definition offered by the new mate or potential mate, according to which they are desirable or worthy, and are thus better able to redefine the old marital relationship in terms of the unworthiness of the ex-husband. On the other hand, as we have seen, the increased antagonism of the unattached seems due somewhat more to the difficulties and problems of the situation in which these ex-wives now live. This interpretation appears to be likely on the basis of the data we have been presenting here, although our design is not adequate for a full demonstration.

If both our theoretical line and our corroborating data are correct, we should be able to test both within a larger matrix, holding Time Groups constant, and relating the attitude of the ex-wife toward ex-husband to the present status of the ex-wife and to such items as opportunities to meet people and continuity of support payments. In such an extended matrix, we run the statistical risk that many of the cells will be too small to be useful. However, we can at least come close to a corroboration of our ideas if they are substantially correct. Without further comment, we present a table which we have collapsed from two larger cross-tabulations.

NEGATIVE ATTITUDES OF THE EX-WIFE TO HER FORMER HUSBAND, BY TIME GROUPS, BY OPPORTUNITIES TO MEET PEOPLE, BY STEPS TOWARD A NEW MARRIAGE, AND BY CONTINUITY OF SUPPORT

(Percent Figures show proportion with *negative* attitudes *within each cell*)

Ex-Husband usually or always pays support	Ex-Wife has many or some opportunities to meet people	Percent with negative attitudes in each cell		Totals
		Remarried or Going Steady	Not going steady or remarried	
Time Groups I and II				
Yes	Yes	18%	26%	58
Yes	No	6	27	48
No	Yes	19	30	58
No	No	29	54	41
Time Groups III and IV				
Yes	Yes	28	24	63
Yes	No	30	39	40
No	Yes	33	35	68
No	No	46	50	49

N = 425

Since many of these propositions have already been treated, we may summarize from the table. We see, first of all, that (1) in the first two Time Groups, the women who are *not* dating steady (whether or not dating frequently) are consistently more negative than are the women who have remarried or found a partner. We learned earlier that women with such negative attitudes do remarry less than others. (2) Moreover, there are no significant differences among the remarried in the first Time Groups, whether or not the child support payments have been continued, or whether the ex-wife has opportunities for meeting people. These are women who have only recently found a new partner. Next, (3) those who have *not* yet found a partner have the same proportion of negative cases in the three first cells , and a really high proportion of negativism is to be found only when the larger situation is bad along *both* dimensions, of social relationships and support payments. (4) In Time Groups III and IV, the proportion of ex-wives who have negative feelings is again larger for the women who have not yet found a new partner; but (5) this proportion *begins lower* (those who have social opportunities *and* continued support payments) and goes *higher* (those who have *neither*) *than for those with new partners*. Finally, (6) there is a steady progression of negativism among *both* those without, and those with, new partners, as we move from the women with social opportunities and continued support, to those with neither.

Since the preceding table was collapsed from larger ones, we may add several minor findings here. (7) When we consider the separate effect of having or not having social opportunities, and of getting or not getting continued support, for all the ex-wives, we find that throughout all Time Groups those who *have such opportunities* are less negative in their attitudes toward the exhusbands than those who do not; and those who receive *continued support* are less negative than those who do not. The proportions are one-fourth to one-half higher for each comparison. (8) The proportional increase of antagonistic ex-wives among all who are with or without *social opportunities,* and for all who receive or who do not receive continued support, is about the same over the Time Groups: from Time Group I to Time Group IV, the proportional increase of negative cases is almost one-half. Thus, the proportion negative in attitude rises steadily from 20% in Time Group I for those who have opportunities, to 32% in Time Group IV for those who have such opportunities. For those who do *not* have such opportunities, the percentage is 27% in Time Group I, while this rises steadily to 41% in Time Group IV. For those who receive continued support, 20% are negative in Time Group I, and 30% in Time Group IV; while 33% of those who do not receive continued support in Time Group I are negative, and this percentage rises steadily to 41% among those who do not receive continued support in Time Group IV.

Finally, and perhaps of significance for future research: (9) although we made clear that even among the remarried there is an increase of negative feelings over time, we suggested that it has an emotionally different tone. It is no longer, we believe, an active dislike of the ex-husband. It is rather a deprecation, a lessened respect, a process of placing the ex-husband in the category of the less worth-while, especially in comparison with the new partner. We also suggested that since these women actually have less contact with their exhusbands as time goes on, the behavior of the latter would not have much to do with this shift in attitude, except for one aspect of his behavior: child support. In our earlier discussion of divorce arrangements, we noted the emotional importance of this factor.

Finally, we have just seen that this increase of negative feeling among the remarried does not apply equally to all the remarried or those going steady. Those who have few social opportunities, or whose ex-husbands do not make the required payments regularly, are more negative in attitude. However, only one of these two factors can rationally be laid at the door of the ex-husband: the continuity of child support. This is not to say that the ex-wife *will* not do so. But particularly the remarried divorcee could be expected, after a time, to put the ex-husband in some perspective, so that whether or not she has opportunities to meet people ought to make no difference in her attitude toward her former spouse. Her present reference is to her *own* actions. We would *not* predict, on the other hand, that those who have *failed* to find a new partner would always, even over the time period we are considering, feel the same toward the ex-husband, whether or not they have opportunities for meeting people. In conformity with this set of notions, we find that *for the remarried,* there is no more negativism toward the ex-husband in Time Group IV among those with little or no opportunities for meeting people, than among those who have such opportunities (38% and 37%), while those who do not receive support payments regularly *are* more negative than those who do receive them (42% negative, as against 32%). This is, by contrast, an action of her ex-spouse. For those who *are not going steady* and who have *not* remarried, the lack of social opportunities still makes a difference in Time Group IV: 41% are antagonistic toward their ex-husbands among those who do have these opportunities, but 55% are negative among those who do not have them.

Willingness to Remarry the Former Husband (Among Divorcees Not Remarried). We have been emphasizing the main direction of changes in attitude toward the former husband. As has already become apparent, there are some wives, who were not only unwilling to be divorced, but who continue to yearn for the old marriage. That this feeling is not simply a postdivorce discovery is seen by reference to trauma. Our data indicated that the high-trauma cases are more likely to be those in which it was the husband who first suggested the divorce, and in which the time for consideration was short. That is, often the wife was attached to her husband, and had not really expected the divorce. It is therefore no paradox that when we asked those not remarried, "Would you be willing to wipe out the divorce?" one out of five high-trauma respondents answered "yes." Fourteen percent of the medium-trauma wives gave this answer, as compared with only 5% of the low-trauma class. The period of postdivorce adjustment under our view extends to 26 months after the divorce, and during this period, the percentage of affirmative replies drops very little, from 14% in Group I (divorced 2 months) to 10% in Group IV. There is, then, considerable persistence in this group.

Thus, some divorcees feel the divorce was a mistake, and seemingly this is not merely because of the many postdivorce problems that beset the divorce. The single most important factor appears to be the emotional attachment of the ex-wife to her former husband, in a society that emphasizes the importance and rightness of romantic love, while socializing most of us to fall in love eventually.

In addition to those who were willing simply to wipe out the divorce, there should be some who believe that changes in the former husband might be probable, which would make them willing to remarry the same man. Correspondingly, within the same context, we wanted to know whether our divorcees thought that changes had occurred *in themselves,* which would make them easier to live with.

One out of five (21%) of those recently divorced (Group I) and not remarried believed that changes in her husband were probable that would make her marry him again. This percentage decreases over time; 12% of those in Group IV (divorced 26 months) believed that such changes were probable. From our previous data on the relation between a short period of consideration and emotional difficulties, we are not surprised that nearly one in four ex-wives (24%) who had seriously considered divorce less than one month before filing suit still believed that some such changes in the former husband were probable. Twenty-three percent of those who gave less than six months to serious consideration had the same belief, but only 13% of those who gave six months or more had such a belief.

We have already seen the parallels between the ex-wife's emotional attachment to her ex-husband, and her belief about his attachment to her. This would lead us to predict a similar pattern for her belief in changes in herself or in him that might make a new marriage possible or successful. We do find, then, that 67% of the not remarried wives who believe that such changes in their husbands are probable, also believe that changes in themselves have occurred that would make them easier to live with. By contrast, 65% of those wives who did not believe that such changes in the former husband were probable, also believed that changes in themselves had not occurred to make them easier to live with. That emotional attachment creates hope is seen in the fact that 46% of the wives with strong positive feelings toward the husband felt that changes in him were probable that would make her willing to remarry him; however, only 27% of the friendlies felt this way, 6% of the indifferents, and 4% of the strongly negative spouses. We have already suggested the complexity of such judgments. Here we only remind the reader that those with strong positive attachments toward the former husband are more likely to believe that he feels similarly about her, and their postdivorce contacts are likely to have been more intimate. These facts are in conformity with our analysis of the strategy of divorce conflict: some of these husbands give their wives good reason to believe that their (the husbands') attitudes are also positive. We do not believe that these feelings herald a remarriage. Rather, we suggest (but have no data on the point) that a high proportion of these husbands are simply trying to soften the emotional hurt of the postdivorce period for the former wife; and that many of the precipitate suggestions to divorce were made because the husband could not work out an adequate divorce strategy.

The relationship between belief in these parallel changes and feelings toward the ex-husband may be seen in the succeeding table. The percentages may be run either way, since the causal direction is not clear, but by either procedure the closeness of association is definite: (1) the highest proportion of positives is to be found among those who think that (a) changes in the ex-husband are probable which would make her willing to marry him and that (b) changes in themselves have also occurred to make them easier to live with; and (2) the highest proportion of wives believing in both kinds of changes is to be found among the positives.

ATTITUDE OF EX-WIFE TOWARD EX-HUSBAND, BY WHETHER SHE BELIEVES THAT CHANGES
IN HIM ARE PROBABLE WHICH WOULD MAKE HER WILLING TO REMARRY HIM,
AND BY WHETHER SHE HAS BECOME EASIER TO LIVE WITH

Changes in him	Changes in you	In love	Attitude to Ex-Husband Friendly	Indifferent	Negative	Totals
Yes	Yes	40%	49%	6%	6%	101% (35)
Yes	No	29	47	18	6	100 (17)
No	Yes	3	37	39	21	100 (87)
No	No	11	22	28	39	100 (164)
	Totals	13%	31%	28%	28%	100%(303)*

*The 122 remarried are excluded.

Remarriage of the Ex-Husband. While these changes are occurring, the former husbands are remarrying, at perhaps a slightly higher rate than the ex-wives: 5% of the husbands in Group I had remarried; 14% of Group II; 33% of Group III; and 55% of Group IV.[3] In addition about one-sixth more in each group may have remarried, although their former wives claimed not to know whether they had indeed remarried. Cross-tabulations suggest, however, that most of these were at least making new lives for themselves.

From the close relationship between her attitude toward him and her belief about his attitude toward her, we would expect a close relationship between his remarrying and her remarrying. On the other hand, we would expect this association to decrease over time. We have already presented these data. The Q of association between the two remarriages is +.88 in Group I (divorced 2 months), while it declines to +.16 in Group IV (divorced 26 months).

Even when the spouse has remarried, or claims to be indifferent toward the other spouse, either spouse may be hurt when the other remarries. In general, we would suppose that the hurt from the husband's remarriage is likely to be less when the ex-wife has already married, than when she has not remarried. We therefore asked these wives whether they had felt unhappy, or would feel unhappy, at the husband's remarriage. As we see in the succeeding table, she is least likely to feel unhappy at the idea of his remarriage if she has already remarried while *he* has *not* remarried. And she is most unhappy if he has remarried while she has not. This pattern reflects the facts that (a) in many cases she has not remarried simply because she is still in love with him, or that (b) she has remarried because she no longer feels concerned about his love life. In addition, there are fairly obvious psychodynamic processes at work.

ATTITUDE OF EX-WIFE TOWARD EX-HUSBAND'S REMARRIAGE

Husband Remarried	Wife Remarried	She would feel, or did feel Unhappy	Happy	Indifferent	Totals
Yes	No	52%	23%	25%	100% (64)
No, or Unknown	No	20	30	50	100 (239)
Yes	Yes	18	29	53	100 (51)
No, or Unknown	Yes	4	30	66	100 (71)
Totals		22%	29%	49%	100% 425

$$X^2 = 50.5 \qquad P < .001$$

3. All studies of remarriage show men are more likely than women to remarry, particularly if the first marriage ended when the person was in his mid-twenties or older. Cf. *Stat. Bull., op. cit.,* 26, No. 5 (1945), pp. 1-3.

It is also worth reporting that the *fact* seems to have more impact than the *idea*: If the husband has *actually remarried,* 37% of our respondents admitted that this fact made them unhappy. However, if the husband had not actually remarried, only 18% of the wives admitted that his getting remarried *would* make them unhappy. The lack of a true panel prevents us from usefully analyzing change over time, since one answer is a retrospective fact, while the other is an attitude. Over time, an increasing proportion of ex-husbands do remarry, so that an increasing proportion of all ex-wives must answer "yes" to the question as to whether they *were* made unhappy by the husbands' remarriage. On the other hand, over time the proportion of divorcees who feel indifferent or negative toward the former husband will also increase, so that if he has not remarried, she is more likely to claim that the *idea* of his remarrying does not make her unhappy. This claim may be partly doubted, since the fact of remarriage might actually hurt her feelings, even though she had really believed it would have no such effect. Of course, if we had *his* date of remarriage, we might analyze these two separately. We must, therefore, content ourselves with noting these facts without speculating further.

Conclusion. In this chapter, we have ventured into some of the complexities of emotion between ex-husband and ex-wife. We have tried with a quasi-panel technique to follow several of the major changes in emotional attachment of the wife to the husband. We have been, we believe, least successful in analyzing conscious guilt and punishment. Even if the main directions of relationship are correct as we have presented them, we are convinced that in fact divorcees feel more guilt and more desire to punish the ex-spouse than our data show. On the other hand, our questions may not be so faulty as they now appear to us, and it may be that by the time the divorce actually occurs, much of the guilt and desire for punishment has been worked out through the marital conflict.

The chief directions of change in affect were not in accord with our expectations, but seem to form a pattern that is internally consistent, and consistent with our larger body of data. Since we were unprepared to find an increase in antagonism even among the remarried ex-wives, we had not included further questions to find out why this is so. We were thus forced to go beyond our data, to the point where we could offer only supporting rather than conclusive facts. It is clear, in any event, that the emotional relationship between husband and wife is not severed merely because the divorce decree has been made final. Not only is there a small proportion of ex-wives who wish to re-establish the old marriage, but the ex-husband's attitude toward her seems to shape her behavior and feelings for long after the decree. Moreover, the ex-husband himself also appears in many cases to be at least involved enough to wish to make her believe that he still cares. Finally, since in fact both ex-wife and ex-husband are finding new mates, we have shown how these two processes affect the ex-wife, both in deed and in contemplation. In the following chapter, we shall turn to the children that were involved in these divorces.

CHAPTER XXI

THE CHILDREN OF DIVORCE

FEW, IF ANY, parents divorce without considering the effect of the divorce upon the children. Almost all American parents agree that when there are children the decision to divorce should be made reluctantly, if at all. Almost all married couples would agree that the divorce experience is damaging to the children in many ways. This supposed effect upon the children is a common theme of deprecation among the friends and relatives of divorcing parents, even when the divorce itself is generally approved. It is, indeed, safe to say that unless there is wide agreement among these circles that one or both of the parents are already harming the child, the divorce is assumed to be damaging to the child. This popular view may be seen as an apparently factual foundation for the disapproval of divorce in general. It is at the same time an expression of that disapproval, which is intensified when children are involved. In this chapter, we ask how, in the view of these mothers, were these children of divorce faring.

Measuring the Effect of Divorce on Children. That these widely accepted judgments of fact are really moral judgments is at least suggested by the general failure to measure in any adequate way the effect of divorce upon children. Neither psychodynamic nor sociological researches have satisfactorily answered the technical problems of this task. It is not an answer, as we commented in Chapter III, to show that there is a simple association between (a) divorce and (b) some characteristic which appears in the child's life later on, such as juvenile delinquency, neurosis, unhappiness in marriage, etc. Often these characteristics, such as juvenile delinquency, may be caused in part by the same set of causes that originally predisposed the couple to the divorce. Indeed, it is safe to say that present-day researchers see juvenile delinquency itself as much more complex and difficult to explain than did students of a generation ago.

The relationship between the child's divorce experience and his other characteristics has not been adequately measured because no one has used an adequate comparison population. Specifically: (1) Are the damaging effects of divorce on the child greater than those of *continued home* conflict? (2) Even if there is a divorce, and we measure some of its effects, which is more important, the divorce itself and its aftermath, or the *conflict* leading to the divorce? (3) What kinds of divorce or marital conflict have *what kinds,* or degrees, of effect on the child? In our first question, we suggest that we must find out whether the effect of home conflict is as great as that of divorce. In our second question, we ask a parallel question within the population of children of divorce. In our third question, we suggest that there are *various* such populations, and that different divorce experiences will have different types and degrees of effect upon the children.

We wish to avoid a debate in which the crucial data are not yet available. In order that our very real caution may not seem to be merely an arrogant rejection of traditional opinion on this subject, let us comment once more with reference to just one of these supposed effects, that of juvenile delinquency. Most of the many studies dealing with the latter subject have shown that a substantially higher proportion of juvenile delinquents come from "broken homes" than come from intact homes. Often, of course, there is not even a distinction made between the *types* of broken homes, such as (a) widowed, (b) widowered, (c) separated, father away, (d) separated, mother away, (e) divorced, father away, etc. Perhaps we would also wish to compare populations of children whose parents were lost by death, separation, or divorce, when *neither* parent remains, and others care for the children.

More important than these distinctions is the known class bias in such aggregations of data on delinquency. Delinquency is *recorded* at a higher rate in the lower social strata, whatever its actual rate of occurrence. Families in higher strata have greater influence and can make financial restitution to avoid prosecution. Moreover, intact families have a similar advantage over broken homes. These biases are, of course, recognized by experts in juvenile delinquency. But divorce also occurs at a greater rate in the lower strata, and this fact is not generally recognized, so that the association between juvenile delinquency and divorce may occur in part because both are linked with lower class life.

The Effect of Other Types of Broken Homes. The criticisms of research in juvenile delinquency have been many, because not even the lay citizen is without an opinion on the subject. Consequently, this research has continued to improve. In one of the more recent studies on a large scale, we do have certain of the distinctions made which we suggested above. This study has a long background of careful planning and data-gathering, and can at least be called a good representative of the best of these studies. The Gluecks relate juvenile delinquency to several types of broken homes, (a) divorced, (b) widowed, and (c) separated.[1] *There is then no doubt that broken homes are related to juvenile delinquency, even within the same economic stratum.* (There is no explicit matching of father's income, but there is matching by neighborhood.) Moreover, 8.7% of the delinquents in their sample come from divorced parents, while only 6.1% of the matching nondelinquent youngsters came from divorced parents. But *the difference is even greater* for the widowed: 18.3% of the delinquents came from widowed parents, *vs.* 13.4% of the nondelinquents; and *still greater* for the separated: 12.4% of the delinquents came from separated parents, *vs.* 4.9% of the nondelinquents. That is to say, the overrepresentation of children of separated parents in the delinquent group is greatest of these three types.

We have cited these facts, rather than reviewed the literature about "di-

1. Sheldon and Eleanor Glueck, *Unraveling Juvenile Delinquency* (Cambridge: Harvard University Press, 1950), Table VIII-19, p. 91.

vorced children," because here (a) the important facts are still missing, and (b) the best facts justify our repeated insistence that the relationship between divorce and other behavioral problems of children is not at all clear. The Gluecks' data indeed furnish additional documentation of our earlier suggestion (Chapter 9) that the *separation* may be more upsetting to the family members than the divorce itself.

In all likelihood, almost every serious researcher in American family behavior has suggested that the effects of continued home conflict might be more serious for the children than the divorce itself. We must go beyond this simple possibility to more precise hypotheses about the effect of the divorce on the over 200,000 children annually whose parents divorce.[2]

There can be little doubt, we believe, that these reported effects *do* occur, even though they are probably somewhat exaggerated in popular opinion. At every developmental phase of childhood, the child needs the father (who is usually the absent parent) as an object of love, security, or identification, or even as a figure against whom to rebel safely. This is the case for both boys and girls. It would be surprising if the absence of the father had no effect on the child. When the absence of the parent is caused by divorce and not death, the psychodynamic structure is further complicated by hostilities and guilts for hostility, by feelings of abandonment, and by guilts from divided loyalties.

On the social level, we would express the same range of behavior by noting that the father and mother have different sets of skills and attitudes to give the child, and the absent parent can not carry out both sets of activity with success. Even in families where the father plays a less continuous and immediate role in socialization, he is used as an ultimate threat of punishment. In still other terms, the child with a missing parent lacks an observational model which he needs in learning the roles of future adulthood, or the complementary sex roles against which to play the adult roles. We would suppose that this lack might leave some gaps in his effective action and understanding in social situations when he is adult. Moreover, the other parent serves the important function of reinforcing most moral injunctions, since in most conflicts in socializing children, the parents will be in agreement with one another. This reinforcement is not to be found in unanimity alone, but also in the further elements of energy-distribution. Parents become physically and psychically weary in their constant attempts to socialize their children, who are their superiors in energy output, speed of energy recovery, and cleverness at finding escapes from pressure. The mother "in the front lines" may from time to time retire and persuade the father to assume direction for a while. Even if we assume that the average husband does this unwillingly, intermittently, and with little skill, his aid is important in socialization.

Even if we have not been able to measure this effect, then, the reasoning from considerable clinical experience and from other bodies of data seems acceptable: Divorce does often damage the child. However, it is obvious that almost all such reasoning applies equally well to the case of children who have lost parents by separation or death. What is different in the case of divorced children?

---

2. Kingsley Davis, "Children of Divorced Parents..." *op. cit.,* p. 713.

We would suppose that on the average (1) the divorced child has experienced as much *home conflict* as (2) the child in the separated home; and that both have experienced more conflict than (3) the child whose home is broken by death. The *social stigma* shows a more definite gradation: most for the divorced child, least for the child who has lost a parent by death. It seems likely that the child's *perception of stigma* (a different matter, and more important) might also be ranked in this same order. Perhaps the *conscious feeling of abandonment* is greatest for the separated child, and least for the child who has lost a parent by death. Whether this is true on the unconscious level is less certain. On the average, too, the divorced child may experience *divided loyalties* most frequently, the child whose parent dies having this experience least frequently. It is not certain which of the three experiences creates on the average more *disruption of his routines and habits,* his expectations and affectional outlets, but we guess it is the child whose parent dies, while the separated child is least disrupted.

All these factors fail to differentiate *sharply* the child in a home broken by divorce from one in a home broken by separation or death. Doubtless, moreover, this *will turn out to be the true situation* when we are in possession of the facts. That is, (1) the child of divorce does have on the average a more difficult experience (though not necessarily a more *painful* experience) than other children, although perhaps little more than the separated child. (2) These differences will show up in a slightly greater tendency toward deviant behavior. (3) Most of this effect is not caused by the divorce itself, but by the divided home and the bitter conflicts that led to the divorce.

The Practical Choice of Parents in Conflict. To make the guess that *on the average* the life problems of the divorced child are slightly greater than those of the child in a separated home or one broken by death does not answer the practical problem many parents must answer: Are the effects of the divorce greater than those of continued conflict in the home? Most couples in a divorce process have only two choices. Until they know the answer to the above central question, most of the classic arguments about the bad effect of divorce on children will miss the point. We *can* make divorce so difficult that none will occur. Spouses *do* have the choice of *not* divorcing even when they are unhappy, and many do make this choice.

However, they do *not usually have the choice of creating a happy home for their children,* even when they are willing to avoid divorce "for the sake of the children." The couple has not, therefore, necessarily made a wise sacrifice in the interests of the child, when they decide to stay together.

Some small corroboration for these notions may be found in a study by Landis of adolescent adjustment among over 4,000 high school seniors in the State of Washington. When these youngsters were asked about their problems in several main areas of life adjustment, it was clear that those from unbroken homes had fewer problems than those from broken homes. However, the data suggest that divorced children may not have on the average a higher number of such problems than children from separated homes, or even from homes broken by death. We have already seen that this conclusion also emerges from the Gluecks' study of juvenile delinquency. Indeed, these data suggest that the separated home perhaps creates slightly more problems for the child than does the home of divorce.[3]

AVERAGE NUMBER OF PROBLEMS 4,394 HIGH SCHOOL SENIORS CHECKED IN
THE MAIN AREAS OF ADJUSTMENT, BY TYPE OF FAMILY

Adjustment Area	No. of Problems in Check List	Average Number of Problems				
		Parents living together	All broken homes	Separated	Divorced	Homes broken by death
Personal Problems	33	4.1	4.5	4.4	4.4	4.5
Family Problems	32	2.0	2.8	2.9	2.8	2.7
Finances—Living Conditions	31	1.7	2.2	2.5	2.1	2.2
Vocational Problems	30	3.0	3.2	3.2	3.0	3.2
Social Problems	30	2.1	2.3	2.3	2.4	2.3
Boy and Girl Problems	34	2.4	2.6	2.4	2.6	2.6
School Problems	30	2.5	2.6	2.4	2.5	2.7
Morals, Ideals, Religion, the Future	30	2.6	2.9	2.8	3.0	2.9
Total	250	20.4	23.1	22.9	22.8	23.1

In the present state of our knowledge, then, we cannot prove that couples in serious conflict can necessarily make the lives of their children easier by simply not divorcing. Our own data on the lives of the children involved in divorce will not answer this central, practical question. Moreover, as we shall point out in a moment, our study design could not answer such a question. We shall rather concentrate upon the divorced mother, and her adjustment with respect the difficulties that the divorce created for her *as a mother*. Within this limited area, there are many complexities that can be clarified somewhat, and we shall point to others which remain to be solved by later research.

Acceptance of Custody Arrangements. In all U. S. jurisdictions, it is customary for the mother to receive custody of the children, unless the father can prove that they would be placed thereby in an environment injurious to their health or morals. Custody followed this rule in our sample, and was distributed as seen below.

HOW CUSTODY OF THE CHILDREN WAS DISTRIBUTED

Who has custody	
Mother	94.8%
Shared	0.2
Father	2.4
Split custody	1.7
Other (grandparents, etc.)	0.9
	100 %

N = 425

---

3. Paul H. Landis, "The Broken Home in Teenage Adjustments," *Rural Sociology Series on the Family*, No. 4 (Pullman, Washington: Institute of Agricultural Sciences, State College of Washington, 1953), p. 10. The data were gathered in 1947. The sample is not random, but includes farm, urban, and metropolitan children. Of course, many children, especially boys, from broken homes have left school before their senior year.

In the cases involving children which went through the divorce courts of Cook County (Chicago) during 1940-1950, about 86% of the women obtained custody. Nine percent of the fathers obtained custody, and in 5% of the cases there was some other arrangement.[4]

This proportion was not greatly different in the Marshall and May studies of divorce in Ohio and Maryland, nearly a generation ago.[5] The wife is, of course, less likely to get custody if the husband is the plaintiff.

Since it is the ex-wife who answers, we would expect that she would maintain that this distribution was agreeable to both parents. Aside from this bias, however, there are many factors to make us believe that the father actually does approve the custody arrangement that gives care of the child to the mother. Most of these factors may be classified under the headings of (a) the social role of the father; (b) male skills; and (c) allocation of time to occupation.

The latter two factors are, of course, derivative from that of social role. The average father is lacking in appropriate "child-care" skills, because his socialization in the male role has (1) led him to deprecate such skills, (2) required him to have little practice in them, and (3) permitted him to hand the appropriate duties over to his wife. The role of husband and father, moreover, is defined particularly as breadwinner, and with few exceptions in our society this activity requires at least eight hours or so daily for at least five days weekly, at the times when children require most care.

In any event, the management of a household with some attempt to meet the usual standards of American cleanliness, order, diet, etc., is difficult if there is only one adult, whether male or female. However they may claim to believe in a "democratic" home with a full sharing of duties traditionally classified as the wife's, few husbands have much ease in the routine household skills such as ironing, cooking, counting and keeping track of clothing, shopping for food and clothing, etc., and only very few can do the job without strain and awkwardness. It is not impossible for a father to care for his children alone, and many widowers are forced to do just that. We have interviewed some male divorcees who accepted the task. However, it is the rare man who will attempt to do so without outside aid, even if he can obtain custody.

Sometimes there is enough money to hire a housekeeper, but the more usual pattern is to call in other female members of the family as surrogate mothers. However, the modern American family is less likely than that of former generations to have an extended network of kin, so that there may be some hesitation in calling upon the relatives. There may be no "family home" to which the divorced child may return with his father. If we are to take Victorian novels seriously, it was the family spinster attached to a large family whose duty it was to become the surrogate mother. However, that figure has all but disappeared. The proportion who finally marry is much greater in our society, and the number of sisters ever available to begin with is smaller now.

---

4. *Conference on Divorce, Conference Series*, No. 9 (Chicago: University of Chicago Law School, 1952), remarks by Judge Edwin A. Robson, p. 4.

5. Leonard C. Marshall and Geoffrey May, *The Divorce Court* (Baltimore: Johns Hopkins University Press, 1932), Vol. 1, *Maryland*, pp. 31, 316; Vol. 2, *Ohio*, p. 346.

These factors operate to make husband custody neither easy nor very desirable (to husbands) in our time. Consequently, we are inclined to believe our respondents when four out of five wives claim that their husbands agreed to the custodial arrangements, which almost always gave custody to the wife. At least it seems safe to believe that in only a few cases did the father attempt to make a strong claim to custody. Both his own patterns of belief and action, and those of his friends and family, reinforce the social acceptance of the mother's claim. This agreement between husband and wife may be seen in the following table.

WERE THE CUSTODY ARRANGEMENTS AGREEABLE TO BOTH HUSBAND AND WIFE?

Yes	84%
Only to wife	14
Only to husband	1
To neither	1
No answer	1
Total	101%

N = 425

As we see, in 14% of the cases the custody arrangements were agreeable only to the wife. In all but one of these cases of husband disagreement, the custody had been given to the wife. The other was a case of split custody. Of the 9 arrangements in which the husband or his mother got custody, 4 were objected to by the wife. On the other hand, 3 wives objected along with their husbands to the fact that the *wife* had received custody. In general, the husbands who objected to their wives being given custody were not different from the husbands who did not object. These were cases in which there was a slightly higher approval of the divorce by the wives' families, a higher percentage of wives suggesting the divorce first, and a higher percentage of couples having frequent or several talks about the divorce arrangements, or ever deciding not to divorce after making their decision to do so.

The Importance of Visits. Whatever the custodial arrangements, these marriages usually continued after the divorce, through the lives of the children. Although this relationship between ex-spouses becomes weaker with time, because of processes we have sketched, the parent without custody may wish to continue his contact with the children, whatever feelings there may be between husband and wife. This relationship is often the only channel through which the other spouse can make legitimate demands upon the other: (a) the wife by support demands; (b) the husband by visitation demands. It may also offer the most convenient means for learning about the activities of the other spouse.

Further, this relationship contains the most important weapons in the conflict of wills between ex-spouses, both during the divorce conflict and afterwards. This exploitation of the parent-child relationship may, of course, be unconscious, since few parents can admit that they use their children as punitive instruments. Our child-centered values are rather strongly against any such open usage. Nevertheless, it is difficult to use the children punitively against the other parent, whether or not done unconsciously, if there are no visits at all. For all these complex techniques mostly fall into two main categories: (a) threatening to withhold visits, or making them difficult; and (b) persuading the children to dislike or to be suspicious of the other parent. Both techniques require some continuing contact (or possibility of it) between children and the parent not awarded custody.

Various agreements are made between husband and wife, or their lawyers, regarding permissible visits. The court will not usually overrule such agreements. This is peculiarly an area in which the divorcee can expiate vague or sharp guilt feelings about previous treatment of the other spouse. By allowing visits, the divorcee can feel that he or she is not holding a grudge. This permission can be mentioned among friends as proof that the post-divorce treatment of the other spouse is just. They may wonder why he or she is willing to be so kind, after hearing a recital of wrongs suffered, but this only accentuates the divorcee's apparent high-mindedness, or his or her willingness to "let bygones be bygones."

We would, then, expect to find that the husband has more rights to see the children than might appear in the simple phrase, "custody awarded to wife." These arrangements were as follows:

FREQUENCY OF PERMITTED VISITS BY PARENT TO CHILDREN

Frequency	Percent	
High frequency		
At any time	32	
Weekly	25	
Sub-Total		57
Low frequency		
Monthly	3	
Summers and/or		
holidays	2	
None arranged	19	
Husband away	18	
No answer	1	
Sub-Total		43
Total	100	

N = 425

There is a moderate association (Q = +.34) between predivorce talks about the children, and "high frequency of permitted visits." The above distribution suggests a rather close interaction between many wives and their former husbands after the divorce, through these visits to their children. However, these are predivorce arrangements, made prior to experience, and we have already analyzed at length the difficulty of making satisfactory arrangements prior to knowing what sort of life will be worked out after divorce. The husband is likely to have exaggerated notions about how much visiting he *can* do, and the wife may have equally unreal notions about how much visiting he *will* do. Most of her complaints were against the man as *husband,* not as *parent,* and she has little grounds for refusing liberal visiting privileges. His insistence on these rights becomes, in turn, an assertion that as *parent* he wants to do his duty. Even when it was his decision that broke the marriage, he is likely to feel that he has been made an outsider when he recognizes that the children and wife will be together. Consequently, he may make promises, to himself and possibly to the children, to visit as often as permitted.

These promises may even take the form of happy anticipations, and case studies of divorce do show examples of the ex-husband or ex-wife attempting to bribe the children by making the visits into gala occasions. Nevertheless, in general these promises are not oriented to the realities of time, energy, and money, and the visits will probably become less frequent with time. The following factors seem to create this result. Even when the husband has strong paternal feelings and maintains them undiminished, he will find that using all his visiting rights would occupy much of his time and money. This may not be the case when visits are only for summers or holidays, but this category is only 2% of our total. The more common patterns are "visits at will" and "weekly," the two together forming about 90% of the cases in which visits were at all *possible*. (1) If the father follows his first inclinations, and attempts to take the children to movies, parks, and playgrounds, buying them presents and sweets, he will find himself spending much of his surplus money (if any exists after support payments) on them, and this is especially so for the lower income groups. (2) *Time* allocation becomes a problem when he and his children are separated by any great distance in the city or between cities. He then has the alternative of frequent and long trips, with a consequent diminution of his own social activities, or of passing up some of his visiting rights.

(3) Even with the best of intentions to "be reasonable about the matter," few former mates are able to hand their children back and forth without tension. (4) Moreover, as we have noted, both spouses come to enter new circles, begin dating, or even marry again. The nonpaternal goals of such visits diminish, as both create new lives. Early in the postdivorce period, the husband may visit in order to find out about his former wife, in addition to seeing the children; later on, he has less desire to be informed about her activities. The visits, then, are not the unalloyed pleasurable experiences that had been anticipated, and they lose their importance as the side-goals of malice, punishment, or even love begin to fade.

In addition, (5) the children themselves contribute to the decreasing frequency of visits. They have little legal choice about the matter, and will not usually even express their wishes openly. However, few children can hide their own reactions, and they are likely to be affected by the tensions of the visits. The promises of a father to visit every weekend sound wonderful to the loyal child, but the child has time and play plans of his own. If the father demands very frequent visits, the child is prevented from having normal contact with his playmates on weekends, or with his mother and her circle. Moreover, (6) when the father does miss one meeting or more, the child begins to develop some insulation against disappointment by withdrawing emotionally, so that there is a less free and easy association. In addition, (7) the daily activities of the child become less and less familiar to the parent, and he may become a less satisfactory companion to the child. We do not suggest a diminution of love, but merely note various processes which make the visits somewhat less pleasurable for both parent and children, than had been anticipated. These processes are obviously of less importance if visits occur only at holidays or vacations.

It must be emphasized that we are not attempting to claim that these are universal processes or factors, and we make no assertions regarding the *attitudes* of either parents or children. We are rather outlining a general set of structural elements in the postdivorce situation, which in turn creates a set of cost-demand processes: the cost of very frequent visits will ordinarily be great, and the visits will decline in frequency unless there are unusual counter-factors at work.

Naturally, a different set of factors enters when either or both parents marry, but their effect is in the same direction: lessening frequency to the point at which the difficulties of visiting are matched by the willingness of the outside parent to pay the cost in time, energy, emotion, and money. We suggest, then, that this level or point will in general be at a lower frequency level than (a) is legally permitted (unless visits are only during vacations); or than (b) is permitted by the informal agreement between the spouses; or than (c) the outside parent (usually the husband) originally believed would be the case. However, for an exact weighting of these factors, we must await further research.

Anticipations of the Mother about the Effect of the Divorce. Whether or not the visits decline in frequency, both ex-wife and children will make new lives for themselves. Their lives are intertwined, but the adjustments of the two may be different. The divorcee makes, or fails to make, some kind of adjustment with respect to the children. And, correlatively, the children have problems of adjustment. We have already discussed how far we are from being able to make definite measurement of the effects of divorce on the children. On the other hand, the *mother's* adjustment in the area of the children *is measured by (1) her belief as to whether there are such untoward effects;* and (2) *her* judgment as to *how well she has been able to carry out her plans while also taking care of the children.* These two areas of adjustment are related, but may be considered separately.

Since we already know how difficult it would be to measure whether the divorce has serious effects on the children, we can not be optimistic about obtaining satisfactory answers from the present research. Moreover, there are obvious factors of bias. (1) We have considerable evidence that our respondents tried to tell the truth, but it is possible that in this area they *could* not do so. (2) In either case, these mothers might have been unable to *perceive* easily the difficulties that the divorce made for the children. The ordinary mother does not have the technical skill necessary to measure these effects. (3) In any event, our interviews occurred at the latest only 26 months after the divorce, and there was usually not enough *time* for these effects to occur. (4) Finally, as we noted earlier, to measure such effects adequately, we need comparison groups of children living in (a) homes under sustained conflict, (b) homes broken by death and (c) homes broken by separation, of various types and under various conditions.

Consequently, we must be cautious in accepting the answers of our respondents, particularly if they claim that the effects do not seem to be serious. On the other hand, such claims do tell us about our *own* focus, *the adjustment of the respondents.*

Without question, these respondents *did* worry about the possible effect of the divorce upon the children, and this theme occurs in free comments here and there through the interview. Even the respondents who thought the divorce would be better for the children came to that conclusion as an *answer to the worry*. Perhaps the only exceptions, and these are doubtful, are those who thought the child was too young to be affected. The range of anticipations may be seen in the succeeding table.

NOW THAT THE DIVORCE IS ALL OVER, WOULD YOU TRY TO TELL ME, IN YOUR OWN WORDS, HOW YOU FELT ABOUT THE DIVORCE AND THE CHILDREN. WHAT WENT THROUGH YOUR MIND WHEN YOU THOUGHT OF THE POSSIBLE EFFECTS OF THE DIVORCE UPON HIM/HER/THEM?

Coded Answers	Percent of respondents giving answer*
Better for them; I was right	31%
Worried about lack of parent; clear ambivalence with no explanation (child needs father, but not this one)	27
No effect, child too young, didn't worry	10
Didn't worry then, but negative items appeared later	3
Worried about possible effects of remarriage on child	2
Worried about social stigma for child	6
Religious difficulties: child in Catholic school; child might be rejected by congregation	1
Finances (other than education): support, clothes, etc.	8
Bad for child (answer not elaborated)	9
Miscellaneous, never thought of it, not sure	6

N = 425

*Some respondents gave more than one answer.

As we see, the two major groups of responses showed that these mothers had given thought to the possible effect of the divorce on their children, but had decided the choice had to be made. Only 19% claimed to have had no initial worry.

When Were the Children Hard to Handle? Whatever their worries, these mothers went through with the divorce. We wanted to know, of course, how these children fared under the divorce. This set of facts would be of more than human interest. The facts are also of theoretical importance for both psychodynamics and sociology. If the structural position of the child is different in the various types of broken homes—and we can say that these positions are certainly differently defined in our culture—then the socialization experience of the child is also likely to be different. These different structural positions, institutional definitions, and socialization experience need to be theoretically examined.

Nevertheless, we have not learned how emotionally taxing the divorce experience was for the child, or how badly the divorce hurt the child. This was no failure. We did not hope to do so, and no survey of this type can gain such knowledge. The reasons are simple, and we have just listed most of them. Besides these, it is likely that major differences in socialization patterns—and thus differential effects on the children—are more properly measured by *differences in the steadiness of warmth and love, in understanding, rather than by the simple structural differences to be found between broken and unbroken homes*. Consequently, an entirely *different type of research* is needed to ascertain the effect of the divorce on the children.

Nevertheless, the divorced mother does know very well whether she is now more or less satisfied or dissatisfied with the child's situation or behavior, as compared with the time of the first marriage. We can also ascertain whether, as is implied in our analysis of the institutionalization of postdivorce adjustment, she is more likely to feel better about the children if she has remarried. In weighing these judgments, we must keep in mind that the divorced mother can not usually compare the lives of the children *now,* with their lives as they *might* have been in an unbroken, happy home. The parents could have kept the home unbroken. By no simple act of will could they have made a happy home. The mother will usually have as her base of comparison, then, the child in a home of considerable conflict.

We should not be surprised, therefore, that in spite of these initial doubts and worries, almost all these mothers thought the children were no worse off after the divorce than before. When we asked our respondents, "When were the children hardest to handle?" 55% claimed that they had always been about the same. Eighteen percent thought that they had been hardest to handle either during the final separation or just after the divorce, while 13% thought that they had been worst during the marriage itself. *Only 14% admitted that at the time of the interview the children were hardest to handle.* If the divorce created worse behavior problems in these children, then, their mothers did not see them, but rather on balance thought about as much had been gained as lost.

The picture is even more favorable among the women who had remarried. Three-fourths of these women thought their children's life was better at the time of the interview, than during the previous marriage; and an additional 15% thought that their life was about the same. *Thus, 92% of these remarried mothers thought that their children's life had either improved or stayed the same.* Only 8% thought that their life had become worse.

Since only 14% of the entire sample of divorced mothers thought that the children were hardest to handle at the time of the interview, and only 8% of the remarried mothers thought that their children's life was worse in the second marriage than in the first marriage, we cannot make any adequate analysis of what factors might have made the postdivorce period worse for this minority. We must conclude that, in general, these mothers did not believe that the divorce had been bad for their children.

Such an overall judgment does not, however, deny the possibility of problems. Most of the unmarried women were dating, and many of even the remarried women were working. At times substitute care for the children was necessary. How was this care?

Substitute Care. If a mother has to work away from home, many arrangements may be made for taking care of the children in her absence. Even in unbroken homes, it is not usually the husband who takes care of them. Both spouses will usually be working at the same time, and husbands are reluctant to take on a steady assignment of child care. Toward the lower strata, a higher proportion of such mothers leave their children with no care or little care beyond the ages 6-8 years, than is true toward the middle and upper strata. When the job is intermittent, it is usually possible to enlist the aid of neighbors or of relatives. This becomes less possible when the job is part-time;

it is very difficult when the job is full-time, unless relatives are living very close by. However, these statements are guesses from our data and other research, rather than fully certified fact.

Most of these mothers who did work away from home relied upon their relatives. Fifty-one percent of the remarried divorcees and 57% of the not remarried put their children in the care of their own relatives when they worked away from home. We attribute this difference to the fact that the remarried usually had more money, and could thus use baby sitters or even housekeepers more than the not remarried. About one in nine put the children in nursery school, or worked mainly while the children were in school. Nine percent of the remarried used the husband's relatives, and only 2% of the not remarried. On the other hand, the not remarried relied somewhat more on the neighbors, since 9% of these women used their friends or neighbors, as against only 3% of the remarried. Various other arrangements were used by the remainder, such as no care at all when at least one child was older, baby sitters, housekeepers, and so on; this is true of 30% of the remarried, as against 20% of the not remarried.

Of course, when the not remarried had dates, it was not possible to place the children in schools, and we would expect a greater reliance on relatives. Thus, 60% of these women got help from their relatives. It is worth noting that even among these women 5% got help from their ex-husband's relatives. Eleven percent were helped by friends or neighbors. The remainder (24%) used baby sitters, or no help at all, or still some other arrangement. In general there are no great differences in these distributions, whether the not remarried are dating or working away from home. Moreover, the attitudes of either the husband's family or the wife's family toward the divorce do not appear to change the degree of reliance on these families when help is needed in caring for the children. This is not surprising, in view of the relationship between grandchildren and grandparents in our culture—grandparents almost invariably feel hurt if they are not allowed to care for the children from time to time—but it does deny, as other data in this study deny, the assumption that in metropolitan life the divorced mother is entirely alone.

Since most of the women who needed help relied upon their relatives, we would suppose that most mothers would feel that this child care is satisfactory. Sixty-five percent of all mothers who used outside help thought that the child care was "excellent," and an additional 24% thought that it was "good." Eight percent considered it "average," while 4% believed that it was poor. These women were simply making the same kinds of adjustments and judgments that working mothers in unbroken homes would make. The working mother living alone with her children has less choice in one direction, since she may have to work, and thus *must* find some child care even if it seems less than adequate. However, most mothers who work but need this kind of help will eventually get help that is adequate. Few will be willing to leave the situation unchanged for long, if they believe it is bad for the children. Since in most elements, the position of the divorced or widowed mother who must work is not greatly different from the non-divorced mother who must work, we do not expect to find that "poor" care is associated with any particular aspects of the divorce experience itself. There appear to be no differences in the percentage of women saying that this care is excellent, whether their education is high or low; whether or not they are dating frequently; whether they are White or Negro. If the woman is dating steady, she is as likely to believe that the substitute child care is excellent, as if she is not dating steady. Moreover, there are no differences that are associated with the length of time after the divorce.

Indeed, the only differences that do appear are very commonsense ones: The mother is more likely to claim that the care is excellent if the children are younger, and if there are fewer children. If the children are young, then the care that most mothers hope for centers on keeping them from being hurt, feeding them regularly, seeing that they take naps, and so on. That is, the mother is most concerned about the safety and health of the child. If the baby sitter meets with no crises, and the young child is in bed most of the evening, then the mother is likely to rate her "excellent." However, with increasing age the child creates fewer but larger problems. The mother is then more concerned with character and morals, with bad companions and study habits, with responsibility for home and outside tasks. The child may, for example, not even come home after school to *be* cared for by the substitute. The surrogate parent is required to have, or needs, authority, the ability to control, or some power of persuasion over children who are increasingly able to evade or fight domination. Consequently, three-fourths of the women with children 0-2 years of age judged this care to be excellent, as against 65% of mothers with children 3-6 years of age. Fifty-eight percent of the mothers with children 7-12 years of age believed that their care was excellent, as against 38% of those with children 13 years of age and over.

With reference to the number of children, the major difference is between the mothers with only one child, and those with two or more children. No further differences appear with successively greater numbers of children. Three out of four mothers with only one child thought that the substitute care was excellent, as against only two out of four mothers with two or more children. This is not alone a function of age, we assume, since it is a fairly widespread parental experience that the problems of handling children multiply considerably between one and two children, and that beyond that point the problems shift rather to the economic and energy areas. Indeed, with three or more children, play groups form among the children, and the children will at times censure and praise one another when needed, so that there may be some easing of the social control problems within the family. In any event, these mothers were less likely to feel that their substitute care for the children was excellent, if there were two or more children in the family.

We found few informants who were willing to admit that the children handicapped them much, whether in work or play. Sixty percent of these mothers claimed that there were no such handicaps at all. Eighteen percent asserted that the children did handicap them in hunting for jobs. An additional 10% thought that the children were a handicap in dating, and 8% saw them as a problem in remarrying. Only 2% of all our respondents expressed the notion that children were generally a handicap. The remaining situations in which children were seen as a problem were club meetings, taking trips (10%), giving parties, and education. (Some respondents mentioned more than one handicap).

Factors Affecting Behavior Problems. Even the most emotionally steady divorcee can not be expected to go through the divorce without communicating some of that tension and unhappiness to the child. It follows, then, that women who experienced the divorce as more traumatic would also find the children hard to handle more often than the women who went through the divorce without great emotional hurt. We find this notion confirmed when we divided our respondents into those who said that their children were "never hard to handle," and those who confessed that at some time (including the time of the interview) the children were hard to handle. We found that the greater the trauma, the higher the proportion of mothers admitting that at some time the children had been harder to handle.

PERCENT OF MOTHERS (WITH CUSTODY) WHOSE CHILDREN WERE "EVER" HARD TO HANDLE

Trauma Index	Percent	Totals
High	54	112
Middle High	52	58
Medium	46	87
Medium Low	38	34
Low	33	112
		N = 403

.01 > P > .001

Now, we learned that only about one out of eight respondents thought that the children had been hardest to handle at the time of the interview, somewhat over half claiming that the children had always been the same. Since, however, there is always some doubt about the validity of a mother's report on her children's behavior, we may ask whether with increasing *time* since the marital breakup these women changed their story, and more of them began to think that there *had never* been any problems with the children. We found no such time change. Nor does such a pattern emerge among the remarried, as against the not remarried.

On the other hand, the divorce trauma of the mother appeared to be reflected in the children's behavior. If this is observable, then the children's relationship to their *father* might also be reflected in behavior problems. Although in almost all cases the wife has custody, the children may continue to see their father, and are very much aware of his existence. We therefore asked how the children felt toward their father. The largest segment of mothers (44%) of course reported that the children felt the same as before the divorce. An additional 20% claimed that the children "never think about him," and 10% claimed that they were too young to know or remember him. Nine percent admitted that the children loved their father more, while 11% asserted that they loved him less. Finally, 5% stated that the children had always disliked their father.

These differences should be reflected to some degree in the mother's assertions as to whether there had ever been times when the children were hard to handle. We find, accordingly, that 73% of the mothers who said that the children were too young to know or remember the father also thought that the children had always been the same, i.e., there had *never* been any period of behavior problems. These children had had little contact with their father, and thus whatever periods of difficulty they went through were mainly the products of the emotional environment the mother had created. The children who had known their father, but had *not changed* their attitudes toward him, were somewhat different; 58% had never gone through any particular periods in which they had been harder to handle. About the same proportion is to be found among those whose mothers believed that they "never thought about him." Fifty-six percent of these children had apparently remained the same through these crises. We believe that this proportion is smaller, because included among these children are some who definitely do think of their fathers, but who do not communicate this fact to their mother; as well as some whose mothers refuse to recognize that their children do think of the father. Next are those who love their fathers *more* than before the divorce, fifty-four percent of whom had at some time been difficult to handle. This slightly higher proportion of "evers" reflects the tensions of allegiance, we believe, that the child feels in his new situation. Loving the mother, but missing the father, the child expressed his difficulties at times in his relations with the mother.

Finally, the lowest proportion of children who *never* showed such behavior is to be found in our two remaining classes, those who *always disliked* the father (38%) and those who loved their father *less* than before the divorce (40%). The former group of children express in their behavior the continuing emotional problems which grew out of an originally unhappy relationship with the father. We can not explore that relationship here, but the connection between that continuing dislike and behavioral problems is clear enough. The second group of children had suffered disappointment and disillusion, or their mothers had succeeded in persuading the children that the father was bad. These had of course experienced a more serious emotional hurt through the divorce than any others. We are only surprised that so low a proportion (60%) showed behavioral difficulties which the mother was willing to recognize.

Effect of the Father's Visits. Half of these women thought that the children were no harder to handle after the father's visits. Such visits are nevertheless often an occasion of considerable tension for children and parents. Either or both spouses have really built new lives, and the exact relationship of *ex*-spouses to one another is not defined by the society. The relationship must then be highly *personalistically* defined, but their social contact with one another is too minimal to make such mutual definitions either constant or easy. The motives and standards of the other seem increasingly unclear or unstable, so that very minor failures or misunderstandings will create emotional disturbances between ex-spouses which are more intense than their friends or group might expect. The relationship between the usually absent parent and the child at such visits is nagged by the fact that the parent and child will separate once again; that the advice and corrections of the absent parent will be overruled; while the assurances of love must carry their own proof during his absence. Since it is a rare young child who sees any reason for his parents to divorce, the haunting suspicion of abandonment gnaws at the enjoyment of the visits.

These elements do not suffice to determine what the child's reaction will be, but they do suggest that the mother might view some of the child's *reactions* as problems; and, indeed, might contribute to this situation by her own emotional reaction. Thus, 25% of these mothers thought that the child was harder to handle after the visits of the father, and only 2% thought that the child or children were easier to handle. An additional 14% said that the father never saw the child at all.

The attitude of most mothers toward such visits is doubtless complex. Most women complain more about their husband's performance in his husbandly role, than in his fatherly role. Gaining custody is one usual victory over the father, but this victory has two directions of guilt: (a) she is thus depriving the father of his rightful association with his children; and (b) she deprives the children of their rightful association with their father. For some period after the divorce, even women who do not like their ex-husbands may look forward to these visits as opportunities to renew a campaign of self-vindication or of accusation. And, of course, women who are still fond of their ex-husbands have a more direct motive for wanting the husband to visit more often. Finally, as we commented earlier, discouraging the visits, or at least wanting them to be less frequent, may also be an expression of her wish to punish him.

There are, then, many motives for wanting the visits to be less or more frequent. Such a desire can not be interpreted as a simple wish for the children to have a less or more intense association with their father, or as a simple desire to punish him or to see him. However, we believe that the most important guiding factors are these: (1) that the divorced mother, like most mothers, views her relationship to the child as more important than the father's relationship to the child. This is a subject of considerable joking among mothers in our society. (2) The divorced mother is likely to feel that her ex-husband has "forfeited" some of his rights as father by his behavior prior to the divorce, and by the divorce. (3) We have already shown that both the ex-wife and the ex-husband gradually come to have less friendly or positive attitudes toward one another as time goes by, and thus each becomes less willing to make concessions to one another. (4) His visits can not ordinarily be fitted into her life or the children's without much coordination of time and expenditure of energy, and they are in any event rarely a pleasure for her.

One consequence of these interacting factors is that, as time goes on, many wives would prefer to have the ex-husband see the child still less than he actually does, or not at all. Indeed, we find that 20% of these divorced mothers would prefer that their former spouses see the children less often; and 14% would like to have *him see them not at all*. Forty-four percent thought that their former husbands should see the children about as frequently as they were seeing them at the time of the interview, while only 21% wanted him to see them more often.

We had supposed that, over time, the proportion wanting the ch to see him more would decrease; and the proportion wanting them him less would increase. Actually, there is such a change, from Tin I to Time Group IV (more often: 25% to 19%; less often: 15%

but the movement is not continuous or clear. Among the remarried there is no definite pattern of change by Time Groups when we divide our respondents into those who want (a) to keep the visits at the same frequency, (b) to increase the frequency, or (c) to decrease the frequency of visits. The proportion of the remarried who want the visits to *decrease* does get larger by time. That is, there are *more* married women who wish to have the visits become *less* frequent, from Time Groups I and II (combined) with 18%, through Time Group III with 34%, and IV with 30%. Moreover, the proportions who want the visits to stay the same, or who want them to increase, both decline over time. On the other hand, among the *not* remarried, there is a shift by time of those who want the visits to be more frequent; this proportion *decreases,* although once again not consistently (Time Group I, 24%; II, 29%; III, 20%; IV, 19%. Indeed, *time as such makes less difference than remarriage,* for 47% of the remarried want the ex-husband to see the children less frequently or not at all, as against 30% of the not remarried. Thirty-seven percent of the remarried want the visits to continue at the same frequency, as against 47% of the not remarried. Only 16% of the remarried want the visits to increase, as against 24% of the not remarried.

We suggested that the relationship of children to mother is more important than their relationship to the father, in determining whether the wife wants more or fewer visits to the children. These factors actually exist in a complex interrelationship. Since the steadiness of his child support payments is associated with her having a favorable attitude toward him, and since by failing to continue these payments he will ordinarily not seem to her to deserve these visits, she should be somewhat more negative toward his visits if he has failed to keep up the payments. Indeed, we do find that although the proportion desiring *more* visits seem not to be affected, the proportions wanting the same or a lesser frequency are affected.

EX-WIFE'S DESIRE TO HAVE THE FATHER VISIT THE CHILDREN MORE OR LESS OFTEN, BY STEADINESS OF HIS CHILD SUPPORT PAYMENTS

Continuity of His Support	Frequency of Visits Desired			
	More Visits	Same Frequency	Fewer Visits or None	Totals
Always or Usually Pays	23%	54%	23%	100%(196)
Occasionally or Seldom	21	39	40	100 (85)
Never	23	33	44	100 (61)
Totals	23%	46%	31%	100 (342)

None ordered, other, or Husband Custody   83

N = 425

We have also suggested that the tensions of such visits might be reflected in the behavior of the children. If, then, the children were actually *easier* to handle after such visits, we would suppose that this means (a) the visits may actually have been *pleasurable for the wife,* and thus she welcomed them; or (b) the fact that the *children* were easier to handle might make her welcome them. As we see in the succeeding table, when the wife admits that the children were easier to handle after these visits, she is more inclined to say that he should visit more frequently. Correspondingly, if they were harder to handle, she is more likely to want them to be less frequent.

EX-WIFE'S DESIRE TO HAVE THE FATHER VISIT THE CHILDREN MORE OR LESS FREQUENTLY, BY WHETHER HIS VISITS MADE THEM HARDER TO HANDLE

After His Visits, Were Children Harder to Handle?	Frequency of Visits Desired			
	More Often	Same Frequency	Less Often	Totals
Easier	50%	40%	10%	100% (10)
Same	25	59	16	100 (178)
Harder	20	37	43	100 (98)
Totals	24%	51%	25%	100%(286)*

*Excludes cases without full custody; where "father never sees child"; and D.A.'s.

On the other hand, as we noted previously, the children's feelings about the father were also related to whether there had ever been periods in which the children were hard to handle. These feelings have, of course, more than a single dimension. For example, some children are reported to love their fathers about the same as always, while other children were said not to remember the father, or never to think of him. We do not really know what kinds of feelings may be hidden in this latter category. Doubtless, it is an accurate statement about some children, but with respect to others it merely suggests that child and mother are not communicating with one another about the father. Even if the child did not know his father, he thinks about him nonetheless. Because of this relationship (1) between their feelings toward the father and their showing some kinds of behavior problems; and (2) between the mother's desire to have the father see the children more or less often, and the children being harder or easier to handle after his visits; we would guess that there may also be a relationship (3) between the children's feelings toward their father, and the mother's wish to have the father visit. Perhaps, at a minimum, if the mother is sensitive enough to see that the children love the father more, she may wish, for their pleasure, to have him visit more often. Let us look at this relationship.

EX-WIFE'S DESIRE TO HAVE THE CHILDREN'S FATHER VISIT MORE OR LESS FREQUENTLY, BY CHILDREN'S FEELINGS TOWARD FATHER

Feelings of Children Toward Father	Frequency Desired				
	More Often	Same as Now	Less Often	Totals	
Love Father more	31%	51%	17%	99%	35
Same as always	22	52	26	100	174
Love him less, or always disliked him	27	34	39	100	64
Do not remember, never think about him	15	40	45	100	105
Totals	22%	46%	32%		N = 378*

*Excludes cases without full custody, "never visits," and D.A.'s.

Our expectations are confirmed, although the multidimensionality of children's feelings about the father (as reported by the mother) mak interpretation of the table complex. Thus, to look at the extreme rig column, we note that the mothers of children who love their fathers *least* likely to say that they want him to visit less often or not at all. This proportion increases for children who love their fathers about the same, and increases still more for those children who always disliked their fathers, or who love him less. The highest proportion of mothers desiring fewer visits (or none) is found for those children who do not remember the father, or who never think of him. This is of course commonsense: the less the children's attachment to the father, the less often the mother wants him to visit.

Looking at the center column, the mothers who want the visits to *remain the same* in frequency, we see that there are only two classes. There are (a) mothers whose children love their father more, or about the same. A higher proportion of these mothers want the visits to remain at the same frequency, than of (b) mothers whose children either dislike the father, or who seem to show no interest in him. Again, the child's attachment appears to help determine the mother's acceptance of his visiting frequency.

With respect to the left-hand column, containing the mothers who want the father to visit *more* frequently, the cells are in conformity with expectation except for one, the children who love their father less, or always disliked him: the mothers whose children love their father *more* after the divorce show the *highest proportion* wanting the father to visit more frequently, followed by the mothers whose children loved him less, or always disliked him. The lowest proportion (15%) is found among those mothers whose children do not remember the father, or never think of him. We had expected that the cell containing the children who *dislike* their fathers would show almost as *low* a proportion of mothers desiring *more* visits, but it is actually about the same (one-fourth) as in the cell above, containing children whose feelings for their father had not changed. We interpret this cell, by supposing that at least some of these mothers thought that the children's dislike of the father was unhealthy, as shown by their being more difficult to handle than other children (60% had been problems); and that the children would therefore be helped by seeing the father more frequently.

We have, of course, no adequate test of this last interpretation. We do have two items of data that bear it out without proving it. First, we have in the above table collapsed two of our classes of children: those who *always* disliked their fathers, and those who *came* to love their fathers less after the divorce. This latter class contains a higher proportion of children who at some time or another were difficult to handle. We have collapsed these two cells because they are alike in one dimension, the dislike of the father, and because the numbers are too small for reliability when divided into three classes of desired frequency of visit. However, we can at least ask whether the mothers whose children had *come* to dislike the father after the divorce are more likely to desire a higher frequency of visits, than those whose children had always disliked the father. This would suggest at least some recognition that the child's relationship to the father is unhealthy, and would thus bear out our interpretation of the above table. And, indeed, we find that 30% of these mothers whose children had come to love their fathers less wanted a higher frequency of visits, as against only 19% of the mothers whose children had always disliked the father. The numbers in each cell are too small for statistical reliability, but the proportions are at least in the predicted direction.

Our second bit of data bearing out our interpretation of the puzzling cell in the previous table deals with the *time when the children were hardest to handle*. Here, then, we see whether the phase of conflict in which the children were hardest to handle affects how frequently she wants the children to see their father.

As we see in the succeeding table, when (a) *the children are hardest to handle at the time of the interview, there is some tendency to want the father to visit more often*. The mother has failed to work out an adequate life for them, or has failed to control them adequately. The situation is, then, not the father's fault except derivatively, but she may feel that he can help. Moreover, many of these children love their father *more* than before the divorce. At the other extreme are (b) the children who were *hardest to handle during the former marriage*. Since the wife has already seen that the father was of no help with the children, or actually made the situation worse, she is *least* willing to have the frequency of his visits increase. Between these two extremes are those cases in which (c) the children were hardest to handle during the separation or immediate postdivorce period, and (d) in which there was never any great difference in their behavior. Moreover, when the children were hardest to handle during the former marriage, we find the highest proportion of mothers wanting the visits to be less frequent. And when the children are most difficult to handle at the time of the interview, the *lowest* proportion of mothers is found among those who want the visits to be less frequent.

DESIRED FREQUENCY OF VISITS TO CHILDREN, BY WHEN THE CHILDREN WERE HARDEST TO HANDLE

When were children hardest to handle?	Frequency of Visits Desired			Totals	
	More Often	Same	Less Often		
Time of Interview	31%	41%	28%	100%	54
Time of Separation or Postdivorce	25	48	28	101	69
Always the same	21	47	32	100	198
During the marriage	9	47	43	99	53

N = 374*

*Excludes "never visits," Other Custody, and D.A.'s.

Thus, we can relate the unexpectedly high proportion of mothers wanting the father to visit more frequently, when their children actually disliked the fathers after the divorce, to other facts which suggest that these women actually desired the help of their ex-husbands in dealing with the children: (a) when the children came to love the father less after the divorce, they were more likely to be at times difficult to handle; (b) when the problems among the children showed up after the marital breakup, the mothers were more willing to have the father visit more often; (c) when the children were easier to handle after these visits, the mother was more willing to have him visit more frequently.

A final reference may be made to the importance of the relationshi͡ ͡tween the ex-spouses for these visits. If some part of the wife's desir͡ higher or lower frequency of visits to the children is derived from he͡ ment toward the ex-husband, then this desire should be related in s͡ systematic fashion to her wish, now or in the past, to punish her former husband for his behavior during the marriage. The following table shows this relationship to be weak but systematic.

HOW FREQUENT THE EX-WIFE WANTS FATHER'S VISITS TO CHILDREN TO BE,
BY WHETHER SHE EVER WANTED HIM TO BE PUNISHED

Wife Ever Wanted Ex-Husband to be Punished		Preferred Frequency of Visits					
Still Does	Once Did	More Frequent	Same	Less Frequent	Not at All	Totals	
Yes	Yes	18%	34%	27%	22%	101%	113
No	Yes	21	42	25	12	100	81
No	No	23	50	15	11	99	209
	Totals	21%	44%	20%	15%	100%	403

(22 Husband or other custody cases excluded)

In thus pointing to this relationship, we do not forget, naturally, that her desire to punish the husband may have remained because he made life difficult for *both* her and the children, and that she is therefore not merely being vindictive in wanting the children to see him less often. She may really believe that he would continue to be an unhealthful influence on the children, as he was before the divorce. It is possible, then, that a desire (now or ever) to punish is associated with a wish to have the father visit the children less frequently, through a prior item that controls both: the ex-wife's judgment that his behavior has proved that he has a bad effect on both wife and children. Whether these cases are many, we do not know.

Other Custody. A small percentage (5%) of our respondents did not have full custody of the children. About 2% of the fathers had custody, and in a few other cases the father's family had custody, or there was split custody. We cannot analyze such small classes systematically, and only wish here to report the judgments of these mothers as to whether the children were in good hands. We remember that three-fourths (77%) of the remarried divorcees thought that their children's life was *better* at the time of the interview than during the former marriage. We may compare this with the 68% of the mothers without full custody who thought that the children not in their care were getting *good* care.

As against the 9% of the mothers with custody who thought that their children loved their father more after the divorce, and the 44% who believed that the children had not changed in their feelings toward the father, we find that 46% *of the mothers without custody claimed that their children missed them very much,* and 9% thought the children missed them "a little," and 32% admitted that their children did not miss them at all. Finally, we wondered whether these mothers without full custody believed that the children might be better off with the mother. It is not surprising, although perhaps a bit inconsistent with the answer that most of the children were getting good care, that exactly half of these mothers claimed that their children would be better off with them. One-third thought that there would be no difference in the care of the children, while 17% of these mothers admitted that the children would actually be worse off with them.

Summary. In this chapter, we have asked about the adjustment of the divorced mother with respect to her children. Although there is general lay agreement that divorce is damaging to children, we have pointed out that research in this area has not been sufficiently precise. When broken marriages are classified into different types (widowed, separated, divorced), there is evidence that the separated home may lead to as many child problems or juvenile delinquency, as divorce itself. Moreover, there is some question as to whether it is the divorce or the marital conflict that does the damage, and whether the different types of parent-child relationships might create the damage, rather than the divorce or the marital conflict.

We found that almost all mothers worried about the effects of the divorce on their children, but that almost all remarried mothers subsequently thought that their children's lives had improved after the divorce. Almost all of them also thought that the substitute care during work or dates was either good or excellent.

We asked, however, to what extent these children had ever been hard to handle, and *when* they were hard to handle. It was learned that if the divorce was traumatic for the wife, then the children were more likely to have at some time shown behavioral problems. The feelings of the children about their father also affected their behavior: the children who "never knew their father" of course showed the least behavior problems, and those who always disliked their father, or loved him less after the divorce, were most likely (three-fifths) to have at some time shown behavioral problems. The wish of the mother to have the father visit more or less often was related to her remarriage (just under half wanted the visits to be less frequent), to his continuity of support, and to her judgment as to whether the children were harder to handle after these visits. We explored this last factor, and learned that she was most willing to have him visit more often if the children loved him more after the divorce, and least willing if she thought they did not remember him or think about him. However, we also explored this relationship further, when we ascertained that she was nearly as willing to let him visit them more often if they actually *disliked* him. We found that this last relationship held mainly for the children who had only come to dislike him *after* the divorce, among whom there were the greatest proportion of behavioral problems. And the *time* when the children were hard to handle was also of importance here: if they were hardest to handle *after* the divorce, the mother was somewhat more willing to let him visit more often (one-third of the wives), while the mother was least willing (9%) if the children were hardest to handle during the former marriage.

Finally, we asked the mothers without custody how their children had fared. Their reports were less favorable than those of mothers with custody, but most of them (68%) at least thought that this care was good—yet nearly half thought that their children missed them very much (23% said, "a little"). One-third thought their children did not miss them at all, and 17% admitted that the children would actually be worse off with them.

Thus, although our research design does not permit any assessing of long-time effects of divorce upon these children, we see that in almost all cases the mothers believed that their children had better lives as d children, than they would have had as children in marital conflict. And, as we noted in the case of economic factors, remarriage seemed to be more important than time itself. Whether these mothers were correct is a matter for future research.

In the next and last chapter, we turn to the new marriages themselves.

CHAPTER XXII

THE NEW MARRIAGE

WE HAVE TRACED the steps of the divorcee as she moves from the marriage to conflict and separation, and then through courtship to remarriage, solving or failing to solve her various problems. At each step, we have tried to locate some of the factors which speed or slow this movement. Soon after the reassumption of their old status, "married mother," we lose her from observation. We wish nevertheless to present some of the important facts about this new marriage. Even if it is granted that remarriage takes care of the major *institutional* problems created by a high divorce rate, we may nevertheless question whether the *divorcee's* problems have been settled.

Unfortunately, we cannot answer the question the reader is likely to have uppermost in his mind: Are second marriages as happy as first marriages? Or, to limit ourselves to our sample, are the second marriages of urban mothers aged 20-38 at the time of divorce as likely to be as happy as first marriages in which there are children? Or, what are the characteristics that seem to lead to unhappiness in second marriages?

We cannot answer these questions, because we lose these wives from view shortly after they remarry. Our Group IV was interviewed 26 months after the divorce, and by that time 53% of this group had remarried. However, some had just remarried, and even those who remarried immediately after the divorce had been remarried only about two years. Although those who do divorce a second time seem to have a shorter second marriage than first marriage, our period of observation is too short for an evaluation of the chances of stable marriages among those who remarry.[1] Doubtless many wives were happy when we interviewed them, who later found that even these second marriages were unhappy.

These warnings are proper because of two contrasting sets of facts which we shall analyze in a moment: (1) 87% of our remarried divorced mothers stated that their *present married life was "much better" than the former,* and 8% claimed that it was a "little better"; (2) yet it is almost certain that for the *whole* population of divorcee remarriages, the chances of a stable marriage are *less* than for the whole population of first marriages. These two sets

---

1. For the comparative durations of first and second marriages, see Wm. M. Kephart, "The Duration of Marriage," *op. cit.,* pp. 290-1; and George P. Hemperly, *Divorce Records S⁻* (Hennepin County, Minnesota, W.P.A. Project, 1941), pp. 134-138. Kephart casts dou' Hemperly's techniques. These are *average* durations, and do not relate the *specific* durat each second marriage with that of each corresponding first marriage.

of facts are not contradictory. We feel sure that later and fuller research will substantially confirm both. Since, however, we would not usually infer the second set of facts from the first, let us examine both separately. Since we wish to examine the new marriage at length, let us first look at the data that are summarized in the second statement, that second marriages are less stable than first marriages.

The Instability of Second Marriages. The greater instability of second marriages has generally been assumed, by both marriage analysts and by common sense. This assumption usually takes the form that those who divorce are by personality simply prone to divorce. They will destroy a second marriage, as they destroyed the first. In this study, we have made two negative comments on this assumption: (a) since divorce has become a statistically more usual phenomenon in our time, perhaps those who divorce now are not so deviant as their counterparts of perhaps fifty years ago; and (b) we can not assume that *both* partners to a divorce are marriage-destroyers. There is some chance that one of them is not, and this partner surely might establish a more stable second marriage. We add to these comments two further possibilities. (c) Even if *basic* personality structures do not change, their *expression in behavior* does, and it might be possible, for example, that a pattern of severely criticizing the first wife might take the form of severe *self*-criticism in a later marriage. It is at least safe to say that the latter behavioral expression of personality is less likely than the former to make the marriage unstable. Moreover, (d) a more adequate accounting scheme for marital instability suggests that *several* types of factors are important; to the extent that these are different as between a first marriage and a second, then the stability of second marriages of even divorcees might be different from that of the first marriages *of the same divorcees.*

The necessary facts for answering these questions have never been gathered, and the questions themselves are rather complex. First, we are only now beginning to include slightly more than half of the states in our national data on divorce.[2] Secondly, *remarriages* are of five different types even if we ignore the sex of the spouse: widowed or widowered X single, widowed or widowered X divorced, widowed or widowered X widowed or widowered, divorced X single, divorced X divorced. The data on second marriages must be sufficiently refined to distinguish the different degree of instability of each of these types. (3) To measure instability properly, we must follow each remarriage of any sample through to its ultimate dissolution by death or divorce. This is a difficult task even for samples of married people, but samples of the divorced are much more difficult to *locate* (because the percentage in the total population is small) and still more difficult to *follow.* (4) The remarried are *older* than the rest of the married population, and thus a different set of *mortality* chances must be used. It is even possible that the mortality of the once-divorced and remarried is greater, *aside* from their age differences. (5) Finally, among the remarried of all types are those who have divorced *more than once.* Doubtless, these have different chances of a stable marriage, and

---

2. See Hugh Carter, "Improving National Marriage and Divorce Statistics," *J. Am. Stat. Assn.*, 48 (1953), 453-61; Samuel C. Newman, "The Development and Status of Vital Statistics on Marriage and Divorce," *Am. Soc. Rev.*, 15 (1950), 426-29.

these chances will be even more difficult to calculate. In short, a definitive answer is not yet in our hands, and rather basic improvements in data collection are necessary before we can get that answer.

On the other hand, we have been approaching an answer for the past fifteen years. Two types of techniques have been used, and they have come to contradictory answers. The first uses instruments for predicting marital adjustment, and they have suggested that the marital adjustment (and presumably the marital stability) of the divorced is not much different from that of the once married. The second is the use of demographic techniques, and they tend to prove that second marriages (mainly of the divorced) are considerably less stable than first marriages. As we stated above, there seems almost no doubt that the second answer is the correct one.

Here, we leave aside such reports from marital clinics as those by Popenoe, who drew upon his experience in the 1930's to judge that the happiness of the divorced who remarry is not greatly different from that of the never divorced.[3] These samples have been even less satisfactory than those of the prediction studies, and the research techniques have been in general much less sophisticated. However, Terman developed an adjustment test, and also found a high proportion (77%) of the divorced-remarried to be happy or very happy. Thus, he was able to report little difference in the happiness of these couples as against that of the never divorced.[4] This study was published in 1938, but by 1949 he had apparently changed his opinion.[5]

Locke has reported on this relationship for two populations, one in Indiana and the other in California.[6] He concludes that the divorced-remarried woman is about as good a risk in the second marriage as never remarried women are in their first; while men in second marriages have somewhat lower chances of married happiness than men in first marriage.

Nevertheless, even the best of these samples, Locke's Indiana group, seems less adequate than those of the U. S. Sample Surveys or of various writers using specific state data. These studies do not solve the technical problems mentioned just previously, but do afford rather definite inferences about the relative chances of the divorced in subsequent remarriages, as against those who marry for the first time. (An additional problem, of course, is that all who divorce and remarry were also once in the first married group, so that there is some overlapping.)

Bossard,[7] Glick,[8] Bowerman[9] and others have shown that those who *remarry* are more likely to select a partner from those who *have been married,* than would occur by chance alone.

3. Paul Popenoe, *Modern Marriage* (New York: Macmillan, 1943), p. 120; "Divorce as a Biologist Views It," *Marriage Hygiene,* 1 (1935), 250. He also collected 200 cases of the divorced who remarried each other again, and reported that 48% of these were happy; 15% were doubtful cases; and 37% were unhappy: "Remarriage of Divorcees to Each Other," *Am. Soc. Rev.,* 3 (1938), 696.

4. Terman, *op cit.,* p. 418.

5. Lewis M. Terman and Paul Wallin, "The Validity of Marriage Prediction and Marital Adjustment Tests," *Am. Soc. Rev.,* 14 (1949), Table I, p. 503. His statement may simply be ambiguous, or refer to a different prediction instrument.

6. Locke, *Predicting Adjustment,* pp. 298-309; Locke and Wm. Klausner, "Prediction of Marital Adjustment of Divorced Persons in Subsequent Marriages," *Proceedings of the Pacific Society, Research Studies of the State College of Washington,* 16 (1948), 30-33.

7. James H. S. Bossard, "Previous Conjugal Condition," *Soc. Forces,* 18 (1939), 243-7, does

Now, most of the remarriages involve divorced persons, and especially so up through about age 40: three-fourths of marriages between single grooms and previously married brides were with divorced women; and divorced men who remarry outnumber widowered men who remarry by about four to one. Monahan gives similar data. Thus, we are able to accept data on remarriages as roughly informing us about the remarriages of divorcees, even though there is considerable error in the assumption.

Monahan has analyzed relatively full data on remarriages for Iowa (1937-1950) and Missouri (1949-1950).[10] When the ratio of divorce percentage to marriage percentage is calculated for various combinations of partners by marital status—e.g., a person never before married, who marries someone who has been married once before; a couple marrying, both of whom have been married twice before, etc.—it is clear that (1) those who have never married before contribute a lesser percentage to total divorces in the state, than they form of the total marriages; while (2) those who have been married before, contribute more to the divorce total than their corresponding percentage of marriages; and (3) this ratio continues to *rise* as the number of previous marriages rises. Thus, when both spouses have been married twice before, they contribute *twice* as high a proportion of divorces as they form of the marriages.[11] His data suggest that Landis' calculations really underestimate the increased instability of second marriages.[12] What seems certain, in any event, is that those who divorce and remarry face a greater likelihood of divorce than those who marry for the first time.

Data of this type include White and Negro, all age groups, and those with or without children. Just how these factors affect stability of different types of remarriages, we do not know. Without further knowledge, however, we have no reason to believe that our optimistic divorcees who have remarried will not, on the average, have a somewhat lower marital stability than those who marry for the first time.

Satisfaction with the Second Marriage. Note, however, that *none* of these studies offers adequate data for a much more central question, which indeed seems never to be raised: Granted, that the divorced who remarry are somewhat more prone to divorce than those who marry for the first time; nevertheless, the only comparison that makes sense to those divorced people is between their second marriage, and *their own first marriage*. Our divorcees

not calculate an index for this overselection, but 6.2% of marriages in New York State (exclusive of New York City) were remarriages for both partners, a much higher figure than would occur by chance alone. Paul C. Glick, "First Marriages and Remarriages," *Am. Soc. Rev.*, 14 (1949), 728, states that there was a pronounced tendency (national sample) for persons who remarry to select a person who had once married. His more refined data show that *of the married once only*, 35 years and over, 7% had spouses who had previously married, but 60% of those who had married before had spouses who had also been married before.

8. Claude E. Bowerman, "Assortative Mating by Previous Marital Status: Seattle, 1939-1946," *Am. Soc. Rev.*, 18 (1953), 170-177, gives still more refined categories. See also August B. Hollingshead, "Age Relationships and Marriage," *Am. Soc. Rev.*, 16 (1951), 493-4.

9. Bowerman, *op. cit.*, p. 173. For Monahan's data, see footnote below.

10. Thomas P. Monahan, "How Stable Are Remarriages?" *Am. J. Soc.*, 58 (1952), 280-288. I assume that Monahan has data for other years for Missouri, but they are not presented in the article.

11. *Ibid.*, p. 288.

12. Paul Landis, "Sequential Marriage," *J. Home Econ.*, 42 (1950), 628.

are not, after all, asserting that their second marriages are better than marriages of *others* who are first married. They are only claiming that their second marriages are "happier" than their *own first* marriages.

Moreover, we rather suspect that they are not far wrong. One hundred percent of these former marriages ended in divorce. Locke's and other data previously cited here would suggest, at the most cautious, that a substantial majority of those who remarry after divorce are and remain relatively happy. Whether this figure is 70% or as high as 80%, we cannot say. We do point out, however: (1) our remarried mothers seemed, on the average, to be committed to marriage as a way of life, as judged by their having children and having reentered married life; (2) it would be surprising, even if we grant a heavy concentration of personality deviation among divorcees, if they did not learn something about getting along in marriage from their previous marriage; (3) they can point out particular ways in which the second marriage was better than the first; and (4) the second marriage of a divorcee has one great advantage: it will usually be compared with a first one that was dissolved in conflict.

This one-sided, pleased response of our remarried divorcees prevents any systematic analysis of the disadvantages of the new marriage. Only 8% thought the second marriage was as good as, or worse than, the first marriage. There are so few negative cases that we cannot find out what might tend to make some second marriages unstable. The young remarried are not more satisfied than the old, and there seems to be no difference by time groups (although the numbers are so few that we cannot be sure). It is possible that the college-educated who remarry are slightly less satisfied than those with high school or less education. Sixty-seven percent of the 11 remarried college women said that their second marriages were "much better," while 81-91% of those with less education rated their second marriages as much better. Nevertheless, the numbers are too small to be reliable. No differences by race appear, or by time since separation. Indeed, only small differences appear when we compare their answers to the question, "How *would* things have been if you hadn't got a divorce?" with their present, actual satisfaction. Of the 15 women who thought that things might have been *better had there been no divorce,* but nevertheless had remarried, only one thought that the second marriage was worse, and 73% thought it was much better (as against 86% for the remarried divorcees as a group). If even those who thought that things might actually have been better without a divorce feel nevertheless that the second marriage is a better one than the old marriage, then we have good reason to believe that these women are not merely reflecting in their favorable judgments some sort of bridal innocence characteristic of the early stages of any marriage or remarriage.

There are also no real differences by religion, although Catholics seem very slightly more inclined to say that the second marriage is much better (92% *vs.* 84%). Of the various themes of conflict, only two seemed to show any deviation from this one-sided satisfaction. Of those women who had complained about Triangle, 74% thought that their second marriages were much better, while 77% of those who complained about Values gave this rating.

Effect of the First Marriage. In addition to the 92% who claimed that their second marriages were better or much better than the first, 2% stated that the second was about the *same* as the first. Since we were interested in comparing the experience of the two marriages, we also asked our respondents whether the experience in the first marriage had made the second one harder or easier. Once again there was a very one-sided response: *84% stated that the first marriage had made the second easier,* while 7% said that there had been no effect; and only 8% thought that the experience in the first had made the second more difficult. Here, however, the experience of having had a husband who deserted, or who left for another woman, did not appear to have made the second marriage harder. Of the themes, only the Complex (helling around, etc.) showed any difference: 75% of these women thought that the first experience had made the second easier (as against 84% for the entire group). Once again, Catholics were slightly more inclined to be optimistic; 92% thought the first marriage had made the second easier, as against 83% of the Protestants. Neither age groups nor time groups showed any differences worth reporting.

There is, then, a general feeling among most of these women that not only is the second marriage a better one, but that the experience in the first marriage had helped them adjust more easily in the second marriage.

As we might expect, the rating given to the *second* marriage affects the judgment as to whether the *first* marriage made things easier in the second. *Eighty-eight* percent of those who rated the second marriage "much better" thought that the *first* experience had made things easier, as against 62% of those who said the second marriage was only "little better," "same," or "worse." Six percent of those rating the second marriage "much better" thought that the first had made things harder; but 25% of the rest thought the first experience had made things harder.

Arguments about the First Husband. Even if the second marriage is felt to be a much better one, and the first marriage a useful learning experience for the second, all who have studied divorce know that the second marriage sometimes has too many people in it.[13] Both widowed and divorced who remarry are living not alone with the second spouse, but to some degree also with the first spouse. This may help or hinder the second marriage, but there is little doubt that the experience is common. The wife calls her second husband by her first husband's name, or prepares a dish for her second husband, which her first husband considered a special treat. The widowered but remarried man may idealize his first wife, and be overly sensitive to the failings of the second. The divorced but remarried woman who fought the domination of her first husband may bristle too quickly at a mild suggestion from the second husband.

All this is common experience, although we do not know how large a part it plays in second marriages. We did, however, ask our divorcees whether they had had frequent arguments with their *second* husband, *about* the first husband. We would expect the answers to be generally negative, even if we had not already learned that these wives rated their second marriages so very high. Indeed, we would suppose that actual *arguments* about the first

13. *Cf.* Jessie Bernard, *Second Marriages* (New York: Dryden Press, 1955).

spouse might be even more frequent in a new marriage of widow and widower. For the divorced spouse has a long list of complaints about the first spouse. In general, the second spouse has no strong motivation to argue against such charges; they only suggest how much more desirable and excellent he or she is. Since even with the best of will the contacts between divorced spouses are likely to be strained and filled with misunderstandings, the second spouse will usually see that first spouse under the least favorable circumstances, and will thus judge that the divorce was justified, and that the charges against the first spouse are substantially true. By contrast, the widow or widower is for various social and psychodynamic reasons more likely to praise the dead spouse; so that in the second marriage of widow or widower there might be more arguments about the first spouse than in the second marriage of a divorcee.

We find that our expectations are borne out, since 74% of these women claimed that they *never* had arguments with the second husband about the first husband. Six percent admitted that such arguments occurred "once in a while" and 8% said that these arguments seldom occurred. One of ten asserted that they "used to have such arguments, but not any more." Only one woman confessed that she frequently had such arguments with the second husband about the first.

The wife's beliefs about her former husband's emotional involvement *with her* should have an effect on such arguments, since we have already shown that (a) the ex-wife's feelings about the ex-husband, and (b) her beliefs about *his* feelings for *her* have a subtle, complex interrelationship. When she believes that he still loves her, she may use him as the theme of an argument with the second husband. She may cite this continued attachment as proof that she is desirable, for example, or use the first husband to make the second jealous. On the other hand, when the ex-husband is so little a part of her new life that she does not even know how he now feels toward her, there would be little occasion for arguments about him with the second husband.

Thus, of the wives who do not know how their ex-husbands feel about them, 84% say that they *never* have arguments about those ex-husbands with the second husbands. By contrast, when the ex-wife believes that her ex-husband is still in love with her, she is more likely to have arguments about him with the second husband: 60% never have such arguments. And, in conformity with one thread of theory we have pursued, when he *dislikes* her, in 64% of the cases there are never arguments. Those ex-wives who report that their former husbands have only friendly feelings, or are "happier not to see her" without disliking her, say in 77% and 78% of the cases that they never have such arguments. To this extent, then, the continuing, varying, postdivorce emotional relationship between ex-husband and ex-wife has some slight effect on the new marriage.

It might be added here, with reference to whether the ex-wife wants her former husband to see the children more or less frequently, that there are no differences in the frequency of arguments with the second husband except for one class: when the ex-husband "never sees the children," not one wife reports any arguments with her second husband about the first husband. This fact has, of course, two facets: (a) the complete absence of the ex-husband from the woman's new life; and (b) the absence of possible arguments and difficulties growing out of the children's relation with their father.

How Did the Divorce Make Things Better? Since we cannot look ahead at what will happen to these women, let us ask further what they think about what *has* happened to them. We have tried throughout to look at their problems as they felt and saw them. We must also continue, as we have done to this point, to look at their adjustment through their own eyes. Although we cannot take their present satisfaction as proof of future marital happiness, we can at least probe this apparent satisfaction to make certain that it is not merely a surface answer.

As one step in such an exploration, we asked *all* our respondents this question: "We seem to have been talking mostly about the problems that you have had to face as a result of the divorce. Now, I'd like you to tell me in what way the divorce has made things a little better for you." Now, we have already seen that only 5% of our respondents reported that the second marriage was about the same as, or worse than, the first marriage. When we extend our question to all these divorced women, including those who were not even dating, only two women out of the entire sample said that the divorce had made things worse without making anything better; and slightly less than 10% thought that things were about the *same* as before, with no improvements to report. All others (90%) reported *some* type of improvement. Of course, for most items the proportion of the remarried reporting any improvement is *higher* than the proportion of the not remarried. However, there are interesting differences which deserve mention; notably, in several areas of improvement there are no differences as between the remarried and the not remarried.

First, as we already know from our discussion of economic readjustment, a higher proportion of the remarried than of the not remarried ought to assert that one area of improvement is the economic. Accordingly, 57% of the remarried spontaneously mentioned this item, as against 34% of those not remarried. We had an earlier discussion of this matter in the form of a series of check questions, asking these women which were the periods of highest income, most debt, most savings, and generally best or worst financially. In that series, of course, we pinpointed the economic factors, and thus expected sharper differences. In the present open-ended question, we did ourselves not bring up these matters. In that series of pinpointing, check questions, we found that 63% of those who had remarried considered the marriage period the worst financially, as against 44% of those not remarried. By contrast, only 6% of the remarried thought that the time of interview was the worst financially, as against 24% of the women who had not remarried. On the other hand, when we asked what was the *best* period financially, only 15% of the remarried thought that the period of the first marriage was best, as against 35% of those not remarried. And, by contrast, 71% of the remarried thought that "now," the time of the interview, was the best of all periods, as against 41% of those not remarried. These data corroborate our earlier, extended analysis of the social aspects of the marriage income, by showing that even in the postdivorce period when income may be lower, a high proportion of women think that economically their situation has improved. A majority of even those not remarried thought that the period of the marriage was not the best.

Equally important, however, is the fact that those who have remarried feel that their situation has improved economically over the first marriage and mention this improvement spontaneously even when economics is not introduced by the interviewer.

Since we are reporting the free answers of our respondents, the failure of a divorcee to mention one area of improvement or another does not mean that there was no such betterment. This means only that these areas were not salient in their minds at the time of questioning. One such area, mentioned by a large proportion of both remarried and the not remarried, was that of "physical and mental improvement"—they expressed this by saying that they "felt better," or more relaxed. Some said that they could now sleep without fear, or had peace of mind. Some reported that their lives had been stabilized. A few stated that now there were no more beatings or arguments. Interestingly enough, in this area it was the *not* remarried who more frequently made a spontaneous comment: 55% as against 44% of the women who had remarried. That is, here is an area of essentially passive betterment, for certain bad things had been removed from their lives. More of the not remarried, therefore, than of the remarried, looked upon the divorce as something which had taken away certain continuing hurts. On the other hand, there were general responses relating to greater freedom ("can do what I please, say what I please"; "more independent now"; "I grew up"; "can do things on my own"), and for this type of comment there are no differences between the remarried and the non-remarried (18% and 19%).

We have discussed the children at length. However, we may point to one inference from our analysis of the institutionalization of postdivorce adjustment, where we suggested that the position of the children is regularized by remarriage; that in most respects the family approaches the norm of the non-divorced family; and that with time the tensions created by the other parent will diminish. We would expect, then, that a higher proportion of the remarried than of the not remarried would spontaneously mention the children as one "area" of improvement. Some mentioned only that the children were physically better off, while others commented on their greater happiness, or emotional health. Twenty-five percent of the remarried mentioned this item, as against 15% of the not remarried.

About the same proportion of the remarried as of the not remarried mentioned that they could now make friends, or see friends more easily (28% and 29%). Of course, almost all were remarried who spontaneously mentioned a relationship with a man as an important area in which the divorce had made things better; and of the remarried, 33% mentioned this item. The remaining items need not be mentioned here, since the differences are small, and very few women mentioned them.

"If You Had Your Own Way...?" Waller reported that some who divorce feel so freed by the notion of escaping from marital bondage, that before the postdivorce adjustment they have rather grandiose visions of what they will be able to do when the marriage has ended. He also expressed some doubt that any such achievements would in fact be made. We did ask our divorcees this question: "Now that the divorce is all over, is there anything you have been able to accomplish by yourself that you have always wanted to do, but

never managed to do before?" It is at least clear that by the time of the interview our divorcees had such grandiose notions no longer if they had ever had them, for just over half had nothing at all to report. Although in general they felt that the divorce had made their lives better, they had not experienced this as a release of some enchained creativity. Of course, Waller's informants were much more likely to speak in such terms, since many moved in literary and intellectual circles. Our question, by contrast, merely elicited the same kinds of answers that came out when we asked how the divorce had made things better, such as getting out of debt, making a better home for the children, and so on. Indeed, only 4% of our respondents mentioned such things as "going to night school," "hearing concerts," or "taking art."

The question did, however, emphasize new accomplishments, and it is therefore interesting to note one difference between the two sets of answers. When we asked about how the divorce had made things better, slightly more than one-fourth of both the remarried and the not remarried mentioned social relationships, friendships, and so on. When we asked, on the other hand, about their postdivorce *accomplishments,* slightly more of the *not* remarried (18%) than of the remarried (11%) mentioned the freedom of choice over *friendships:* "Now I can go out and meet people." "I meet a better class of people." "I can meet and make friends with the people I want to." In this area, at least, they felt some release.

We had supposed that by asking free questions about these divorcees' ideals we would obtain some index to their present adjustment and satisfaction. We therefore asked several questions about work, money, the children, and love and marriage, i.e., various areas of adjustment. These questions took this form: "Try to tell me, in your own words, just how you would like things to be if you could have your own way about the following—How about work, how would that be?"

Only 12% of the remarried said that they *were* working, and *liked work* without any qualification, as against 31% of the not remarried. It might be thought that those who are not remarried are merely rationalizing their situation. They have to work, and claim that they like to do so. However, other answers suggest that there may be real factors at work, whose result is at least in part a selection of those who much prefer married life to work. We have already noted, with respect to the interest in caring for the children and elsewhere, that the motivations of these women toward marriage seem to play an important role in determining who shall be first remarried. Thus, about the same proportion of the married (12%) as of the remarried (14%) claimed that they *would* like to work, but are *not* doing so, without any reference to the possible income earned. But 40% of the remarried, as against 23% of the not remarried, asserted that they simply wanted to remain at home with the children; or even if working claimed that they did not want to do so. Finally, slightly more of the remarried (12%) than of the not remarried (8%) wanted to work, but mentioned that the reason was simply to get more income. Less than one-fourth of either group seemed to express dissatisfaction with this area of their lives.

It should surprise no one, on the other hand, that when we asked about finances just under half of our respondents wanted "more money": 41% of the remarried and 47% of the not remarried mentioned this item. Nevertheless, many claimed that things were fine, that they "got along O.K.," and they wanted "things just the same as they are." The proportion giving this kind of answer was, of course, higher among the remarried (37%) than among the not remarried (17%). In this question, we made no reference to the first marriage, and actually expected to stimulate our respondents to express fantasy wishes. Not only were their desires rather moderate, but a substantial proportion of those who had remarried seemed to feel no great dissatisfaction. We cannot say whether among the *never divorced* there would be a higher proportion saying that they are getting along well, in answer to a question as to how finances *ought* to be. Finally, 9% of the remarried, as against 22% of the not remarried, wished that the income might be steadier, or both larger *and* steadier.

With respect to their wishes for the children, we would expect our divorcees to express the widespread American parental hope that the children will move upward: "I want the kids to meet nicer people. "I'd like to live in a good location for the children." "I hope my son can go to college." Here, there was no difference between the married and the not remarried, and we should expect none: 27% of the married and 25% of the not remarried stated such hopes for their children.

Nearly half of the remarried divorcees claimed that they had no wishes for their children that were not already being satisfied, but these answers took several forms. Some said no more than, "The children aren't any trouble. I don't have any worry about them now." Others simply said the children were fine as they were. Still others put their satisfaction in terms of "watching the kids grow up"; "I want to help them be what they want to be; they're just fine." "They're O.K.; I don't want my ex-husband to interfere with the way they're going." Of those who had remarried, 47% expressed satisfaction in some way with the "way things are," as against 29% of the women who had not remarried. Almost no one expressed any dissatisfaction with the children themselves. Two of the remarried women and nine of the not remarried said that they would prefer to have no children at all. As against these extreme exceptions, 11 of the remarried and 18 of the not remarried expressed a wish to have still more children.

Of course, when we asked our respondents how they would like things to be if they had their way about "love and marriage," almost all (85%) of our remarried divorcees said that they were "satisfied now," or "happily married." None of them, however, showed negative attitudes toward marriage, or scepticism or fear about love and marriage, while 16% of the not remarried did so. Again, these motivations do seem to be associated with action, although we have also noted how important the action itself can be in changing or creating the motivation. Almost all of the not remarried expressed some kind of positive feeling about the possibility of love and marriage, but many did include various qualifications. Thirteen percent, for example, stated that they would like to remarry, "if he would accept the children as well as me"; and another 13% said that they would like to remarry, "if I can find the right person." The largest segment (30%) among the not remarried is, however, those who expressed a simple, unqualified (though often rather general) wish to remarry, or a feeling that love is important. If we were to follow these divorcees further, we would predict that these women would be the first among the not remarried to enter marriage once more.

We have several times brought out the confessions and dissatisfactions of these women, as substantiating our belief that they were trying to tell the truth. Once more, we note that although most of the remarried did seem to feel the second marriage was a good one, in various areas of their adjustment, a few were still unhappy. In this connection, their wishes about love and marriage, we found that two of our divorcees who had already married other men expressed the wish nevertheless that they might remarry their former husband, or simply admitted that they "could not forget him." We do not assume, of course, that there were no more such cases, for the question was designed only to bring out how they would like things to be in the general area of love and marriage. Certainly some of the not remarried who still loved their ex-husbands failed to mention them in this connection, for only 22 did so here as against 40 when we asked the direct question about their emotional attachment to their former husband. Nevertheless, it is clear that even in this area, most divorcees are either fairly satisfied, or have positive attitudes which should lead them eventually to remarriage.

What If There Had Been No Divorce? However, we gave *both* unremarried and remarried divorcees a final chance to reconsider. We phrased our query in this fashion:

Now, you may think this question is pretty hard to answer, but maybe you have thought about it a little before now anyway. Just suppose you hadn't gotten a divorce, and instead simply tried to get along with your marriage the way it was, with all its difficulties. Would you try to tell me how you think your life would be today, in general, if you hadn't got a divorce?

There can be no doubt as to the feelings of most of our divorced mothers about this point. Only 7% thought that without any qualification things would now be better if there had been no divorce. An additional 5% thought that things might be better in certain ways, but worse in others. And 5% gave no answer, or could or would not make a judgment. The remainder, 82%, thought that *without qualification* things would have been worse (56%) or the same (26%) as during the marriage. We have already seen that they considered that marriage to have been bad.

There are no differences by time groups, and almost no differences by remarriage or marriage, except that for most categories the remarried are slightly more inclined to think that things would have been worse without the divorce. The single difference worth reporting is that almost twice as many of the remarried as of the not remarried (37% *vs.* 19%) thought that things would have been worse financially if there had not been a divorce.

We must conclude, then, that in spite of the difficulties through which these divorcees have gone, and the personal tragedies they have experienced, the majority of those divorced 26 months are either remarried or on the way toward remarriage; that the overwhelming majority of the remarried at least believe that their second marriages are better than the first; and over four-fifths of *all* these divorced mothers believe that their present situation would be bad if they had not ended their marriages.

FIELD TECHNIQUES
AND SAMPLING

THIS PROJECT faced several difficult problems in field technique. It goes without saying that not all these were solved to our satisfaction. However, it seems useful to comment on some of these experiences. Thereby, we have the following goals:

1. It is possible to judge more adequately just how far the final conclusions can be trusted.
2. Our experiences may help others who must solve similar problems.
3. Posing the problems and the difficulties may lead some to attempt better techniques for dealing with them.

A Pilot Study. A pilot study of postdivorce adjustment was carried out in Detroit in the spring of 1948. One hundred cases were contacted and 81 interviews were taken. This study has several interesting aspects, but space does not permit dealing with them at any length. One ironic aspect of this earlier phase was the decision to pay relatively little attention to many apparent relationships, because it was clear that the sampling itself was greatly in error. This judgment was based on the failure of the occupational strata to conform to our expectations. These expectations were in turn based upon the usual discussions and assumptions of much published divorce analysis. We expected the divorce rate to be higher in the upper strata. When we found that our data did not correspond, we judged that our sampling was poor, and that as a consequence many of the related data would be erroneous. As a result, an insufficient analysis was given to some of these data. As a consequence of this failure, several questions were not given the revisions which they needed in the interview schedule, which is presented as Appendix II. Actually, as we soon discovered, the divorce rate *is* inversely correlated with occupational rank.

This pilot study also pointed out the almost insoluble problem of *locating* our respondents. No matter how adequate our basic sampling design is, it can be completely destroyed by field operations, if the biases from refusals, nontraceables, etc., are great. Nevertheless, if we wish to locate *particular* persons, rather than categories of persons, we must run the risk of such losses.

The problem is not great if the characteristic which we are trying to investigate is so widely distributed throughout the population that an area sampling design can be used. That is to say, we can draw from the total number of blocks in a given area those blocks or subareas which we wish to sample from, and we can take samples from the residences there, and samples of individuals within those residences, if necessary. It is wasteful to do so in divorce research, for the divorced population constitutes only about 2% of the total population. Furthermore, we were interested in those who had had the experience of divorce at *specified times* prior to the interview. Consequently, we could not use an area sample.

On the other hand, the problem of tracing individuals is extremely great. We do not know at the present time just how much greater it is in the case of divorced people than in the case of others. It is clear from various studies that these losses can be enormous.

In the study reported here, therefore, we drew up elaborate plans to locate every case that we had drawn. We ceased interviewing before we had contacted most of our respondents, but once a case was assigned, it was traced until either located or abandoned as hopeless. Cases were not "put aside for later," once they were assigned. We used eight different tracing techniques, though not in any order (and often the interviewer simply went to our first address and found the respondent there). Since we wished to create "time groups," we could not allow interviewing to extend over many months. Consequently, we had to stop the interviewing phase before all of the cases had been processed. Since any given block of divorcees was traced and interviewed before a next block was begun, this cutoff does not seem to have created any great bias in the resulting sample. We always had a large reservoir of "good" addresses and were always ahead of our interviewers. Our arbitrary time cutoff thus resulted in a large reservoir of "not contacted, not processed" cases. A real "nontraceable" always went through the following tracing processes. (1) We obtained from the original divorce files the first address of the respondent. This address was obtained when the Friend of the Court made its investigation. We also copied the husband's address at the same time. (2) Since the Friend of the Court usually had later contact with the divorced couple, because it is through that agency that most of the child support payments are made, we also checked our addresses by that agency's records. (3) We used the latest cross-indexed telephone directory which lists telephones by street address. We thus attempted to locate the address of the respondent by calling the address in question, or neighboring houses, or even the ex-husband, in an effort to locate the respondent. This saved hundreds of hours of interviewing time. Since we wanted to make a "cold interview," a false explanation of the purpose of the call was given.[1] (4) Since we had both Negro and White respondents, we used the services of the Detroit Interracial Commission in ascertaining beforehand the race of the respondent. (5) We sent postal tracer cards through the Post Office, obtain-

---

1. This procedure raises an obvious ethical problem, to which there seems to be no easy answer. It seemed and seems clear to the writer that to ask the permission of the respondent would have destroyed the validity of the sample. In any event, we are reporting on what was done. Doubtless there are better solutions.

ing a reply from the Post Office as to whether they were delivered at the address given. Again, this saved a substantial amount of interviewer time, for we then had a fair guess that the respondent still lived at the particular address. (6) We checked with the central records of the relief agencies in Detroit, so as to avoid losing the lower-class groups. We attempted to check sampling biases by these records, but found that the data could not be utilized. (7) Interviewers were instructed to track down the respondents at all costs. We wanted to prevent them from interviewing only the easily locatable. This often required canvassing several successive neighborhoods for information. (8) Perhaps the most desperate gamble was taken in the use of our last ditch method, and we are not certain that we would recommend it to any other researcher. We merely insist that we would have lost a substantial number of our respondents had we not used this technique, and we know of no cheaper technique at the present time. We sent several waves of special delivery envelopes, with return address requested. This mailing cost 54 cents for each respondent. The mailing needs to be commented on in detail, since I do not find it reported on elsewhere.

First of all, it must be remembered that a large proportion of the divorced population is in the lower economic stratum. This group is difficult to trace under any circumstances. The lower-class individual has no strong reason to leave a forwarding address, and often does not. He may wish to avoid small bills, on the one hand; and on the other, there are likely to be no monetary or other interests which would make it imperative to him to have his mail forwarded. The few people to whom he would write from time to time would know of his moving, under any circumstances. The problem of tracing, then, is intensified in this stratum. However, it must be kept in mind that we wished to avoid asking our respondents for permission to interview. Indeed, we wished to avoid letting them know that this was even contemplated, since we expected that they would thereupon be more inaccessible than ever. Consequently, in our first mailing, we sent empty envelopes. Since there was no available Post Office box to use as a return address, we were forced to use the street address of the Sociology building at Wayne University. Due to a whim of the assistant who did the actual mailing, the name of F. H. Bradley, the English idealist, was used as the sender of the letter.

We expected that the postman would give considerably greater attention to an envelope bearing 54 cents in stamps, far more than to the correspondent tracer postcard. In addition, the letter was supposed to be given to the particular individual to whom it was addressed, and the address was supposed to be sent to us. Thus we would have the address we wanted and would not have given our respondents any inkling of our plans.

Foolishly, we had not anticipated the reaction of fear on the part of the respondents. Some of these women, as is not infrequent with divorcees, had had trouble with their husbands and were afraid that their husbands were attempting to get in touch with them. Equally common, however, was the feeling that something subversive was in the air. Something was of considerable importance, if so much money was wasted on a single envelope. Since there had to be a return address for the purpose of Post Office accounting, some twenty-five or thirty respondents actually came by the Sociology building, in an attempt to find out what was under way. Some of these respondents were rather upset. After we became aware from the reaction of our first visitor that we would have many visitors, an assistant with a good "meeting and greeting" personality was selected, and appointments were made with these visitors for later interviews. In some cases, the appointments were made for a period later in the week, but we lost almost none of them. All of these respondents were given the same explanation: that the letter was supposed to contain a request for an interview, that by a clerical error (the clerk, F. H. Bradley, had been fired for it) the letter had not been included, but that we were so glad to be able thus to meet them face to face and arrange for an interview. Since they met the research staff at the University in its own environment, they were thus convinced of the authenticity of the research and the deadly seriousness, or pertinacity, with which it was being conducted.

Later waves, however, utilized the same type of mailing, but included a general announcement that the Marital Research Survey planned to contact them within a few days. The announcement was put in general terms of marital research, rather than in terms of a specific inquiry into their own divorce. In response to this very general statement, perhaps eight or ten potential respondents called in to request that they not be called upon. However, in all but two of these cases, we were able to persuade them that they should be interviewed just the same.[2] Consequently, there were no appreciable losses from this general announcement.

Although the reader may feel that the excitement and tension aroused by such a technique is too great for the researcher to undergo, the goal was to obtain our respondents for interviewing. We could not allow the sampling to be ruined by a failure to locate these particular respondents. These cases would probably have been lost otherwise, and the experienced researcher knows how expensive interviewer time can be when it is allocated to tracing respondents in a large metropolitan area. In practical terms, we can make the case very specifically. When we used Post Office tracer cards, the rate of success was approximately 52%, that is to say, we obtained addresses for 52% of the unlocated respondents to whom we sent tracer cards. Naturally, not all of these were good addresses, since for a population of several hundred there would always be some who were in the process of moving, and in other cases a new inhabitant of the dwelling would simply receive the card and throw it away. When we used the registered letter technique, however, we had a location success rate of approximately 95%. That is to say, we received addresses for approximately 95% of the respondents to whom we sent special delivery, return-address-requested envelopes or notices. Again, not all of these were good addresses. In general, they were more reliable than those from the tracer cards.

As we noted earlier, we do not recommend this technique to other researchers, although it is possible that some variation of it may be useful in cases where it is absolutely necessary to locate particular respondents whose mobility may be great. In our study, we believe, we would simply have failed to obtain the interviews if we had not used this technique.

A further problem was that of race. Since we did not previously request

2. The writer himself lost these two cases.

an interview, we could not be absolutely certain of the respondent's race. We nevertheless believed it essential that the interviewer and the respondent be of the same race. It was for this reason that we asked the Detroit Interracial Commission to specify race in each case, with as much accuracy as it could. This effort was successful in the main. Interviewers were given instructions to avoid interviews, if they found that the respondent was of another race. However, it was not always possible to do so, for the best opening question was "Mrs. Jones?" If Mrs. Jones actually answered the door, it would be difficult to back out of that situation with even the most graceful fib. However, since the specification of race was done by address, the cases of error would occur mainly in mixed neighborhoods where there is less racial tension. Consequently, the respondent was not likely to be embarrassed by the situation, and no refusal occurred as a result of such an error. Four interviews were thus obtained by a White interviewer from a Negro respondent, and three cases of the contrary type. These interviews were of course carefully studied, but there seems to be no evidence that there is any bias from this source. We do not have any evidence as to whether it was a correct judgment to insist upon the interviewer being of the same race as the respondent. This was simply a commonsense judgment without much evidence.[3]

The problems of interviewing for field research in highly emotional areas have not been fully analyzed in the literature on research technique, and we cannot devote much space to them here. There has been a double trend in interviewing during the past decade. On the one hand, we have continued to develop *questions* of greater precision, with much less freedom given to the interviewer, so that we can use relatively untrained interviewers. Thus we are able to obtain standardized information for all our respondents. However, when a question is *verbally* exactly the same for all respondents, it may *mean* somewhat different things to respondents of varying educational levels and cultural backgrounds. On the other hand, we have developed the use of *interview guides,* with the interviewer being given some latitude in shaping the question area to fit the knowledge and understanding of the respondent, so that we then rely upon more highly trained interviewers. In this case, we can feel that we have "truly similar" questions asked of each respondent, but the analyst has no control over the interviewer, and cannot really demonstrate what was the question actually asked in the interview situation. Both trends are undoubtedly fruitful for current research and both will be studied further.

In our own situation, we wanted a great deal of standardized information, because the literature does not contain enough descriptive information on the population, "those who get divorced." This information was necessary for the purpose of making sampling checks, and it was also necessary for any preliminary exploration of the factors which might correlate with rapid or slow adjustment. We also wanted many spontaneous or "free" answers, which could be obtained only by allowing the interviewee to shape her own responses. These questions may be seen in Appendix II, containing the schedule actually used. They deal with what the respondent thought was the cause of the divorce, various attitudes toward the husband, adjustment of the children, etc.

---

3. For political attitudes, it is quite clear that when the interviewer is of the same ethnic group as the respondent, a more intense opinion is expressed, even when the opinion is generally the same.

For much of our information then, we could use interviewers with little training, while for certain questions we would prefer to have interviewers with considerable experience. As so often happens in empirical research, our interviewing team did not fall entirely into either category. Some had had experience with the interview schedule used in the pilot study. However, the interview was a long one, and it was essential that *all* the interviewers, whatever their previous experience, be given training in the *particular* schedule. Training sessions were held over a period of three weeks with the interviewing team. Trainees acted alternately as respondent and interviewer, carrying through a portion of the interview, including transitional phases, introduction, etc., with the audience participating by calling attention to failures in reporting, omission of questions, intonation, gesture, etc. Thus, each member of the team took part as participant, both respondent and interviewer, and as audience. Since some of the interviewing teams had had experience in interviews during political campaigns, or in polling research, it was essential that the qualitative differences of this kind of interview be made quite clear. That is to say, a great deal of emphasis was placed upon the necessity of obtaining the particular respondent, and upon the conversational flow of the long interview. It was felt, and experience bore this assumption out, that the intense emotional involvement of the respondent in the subject matter would prevent the interview from being broken off, once it got under way. We found that several members of the interviewing team who would probably not be good choices for polling interviews, were very competent in this kind of interview. One or two interviewers who appeared to be relatively shy or even awkward in approaching strangers, were able to handle the intimate conversation of the postdivorce adjustment interview with considerable skill.

The problem of age was not satisfactorily solved, and we do not as yet have the data which would be necessary for the solution. We used interviewers in the age range of the respondents. The median age of the interviewer was 26.5 years, while one of our interviewers was as old as forty years of age. We are not prepared to say whether an "older," "more mature" group would have done better. It is our general impression that the respondents felt the interviewers to be sympathetic and understanding. It is even possible that our divorcees might have judged a much older group of interviewers to be more conservative in attitude and, therefore, to be somewhat less sympathetic.

Interviewers were evenly divided male and female. Again, we are not clear what the result would have been if all male or all female interviewers had been used. We believe that the factors in this situation are contrary and possibly of equal value. That is to say, the female interviewer is supposed to understand better the problems of the female respondent. On the other hand, other kinds of tensions are conceivable, relating to competition between two females. While the male interviewer might be supposed to symbolize the husband in some way, it is also true that there is a bond of sympathy between the two sexes. It is certain, in any event, that the male interviewer was only rarely refused an interview by the female respondent, if she was alone.

Not all interviewers had had paid interview experience prior to this work. Our judgment was, however, that if the interviewer could succeed in beginning the lengthy interview, the dynamics of the catharsis situation for the divorcee and the persistent inquiry into the details of the respondent's life would ensure an adequate interview response, and would in most cases prevent any substantial bias due to lying. Therefore, we were more concerned with (a) initiating the interview, (b) maintaining interview flow, and (c) adequate recording of what took place, and we emphasized these aspects in interviewer training. Because of our judgment as to the importance of these factors, we were willing to use interviewers without actual interviewing experience, if they had had other experience in meeting strangers, such as house-to-house political canvassing or selling, or even relief and welfare investigation. We considered such experience to be more important than, say, paid work as a polling interviewer. With this broader criterion in mind, all the team had had some experience, and the responses of the interviewees justified the criteria. Of a total of 433 completed interviews, we discarded five interviews as too poorly done. These were cases in which our checks showed that the interviewer allowed an intrusive third party to be present, failed to record adequately, interviewed the wrong respondent, or (one case) faked an interview.[3a]

Nevertheless, to assert that our judgment was correct on this point requires a correlative confession that the lack of much experience with this particular type of interview led to an important failure: not all the interviewers remembered to record fully the answers to our open-ended questions. Caught themselves by the drama they were uncovering, some of them failed at times to write down for later analysis all of those details of wording, gesture, and idiom, which are necessary for good qualitative coding. Almost every researcher has had this experience at some time, but it is always disappointing. Our protocols would have been much richer had we given more emphasis in our training to the recording aspects of the interview.[4]

Sampling. We have supposed that most of our data describe the majority of contemporary American divorces in which there are children, else we would not have bothered to analyze or print them. Most divorces are urban, like ours, and occur while the couple is young; and most divorcees remarry. A high proportion (42% in 1948) does involve children, and this segment is theoretically most interesting and practically most important. Our sample is therefore intended to represent urban divorced American mothers in the most marriageable ages.

Let us see how reasonable this supposition is, by looking at (a) how we drew our sample, and (b) tests of its representativeness.

Of the two acceptable ways of obtaining a random sample, the area sample seemed wasteful because the percentage of (recent) divorcees in the total population is so small. The other procedure is to select a sample from the only available complete list of divorcees, i.e., in the Chancery records of a given county. This was our source. There are two modes of sampling randomly from such a source. (1) We may use a random numbers (or comparable) technique, and obtain a desired fraction of the total cases for any given time interval, e.g., 1940-1950. We did not use this procedure, since we wanted

---

3a. The other three respondents denied the accuracy of the Chancery records.

4. It is possible, of course, that we failed to predict adequately a further possibility, that of interviewer exhaustion. The interviews continued from approximately one hour to two hours, and in some cases actually ran to several hours. It is possible that the factor of exhaustion was of some importance in causing interviewers to fail to record adequately some of this material.

(a) to emphasize the immediate postdivorce experience, and (b) to preserve the homogeneity of our Time Groups. We do not now believe that this was necessary, although it did facilitate analysis. (2) We could instead take a time sample, i.e., a sample of days, weeks, or even months, using again a random numbers or comparable technique for selecting which days' divorcees we would use.

Either procedure is acceptable, but both (we believed) would fail to produce as sharp a time profile among Time Groups as we needed in an exploratory study. Instead, we took a time sample of divorces from only four time periods, about two months, eight months, fourteen months, and twenty-six months prior to interviewing. In terms of strict theory, then, our sample is thus 4, not 425. We thus sacrificed the elegance of a pure random design for what we believed to be the requirements of the problem.

We have checked rather thoroughly, and can find no time bias in the data. There seems to be no reason to expect that divorces granted in, say, June are at all different from those granted in December (marriages *are* different). This is especially the case, since the couple has only a delaying control over the suit, once it enters the court machinery. Moreover, there are no social norms that might make a divorce preferable in one month or season rather than another.

This statement is correct, and empirically relevant, but is, we repeat, irrelevant to pure statistical theory.

We thus selected four time points: September 15, 1948, March 15, 1948, September 15, 1947, and September 15, 1946. Beginning from each time point, we selected the appropriate *Libers* in the Chancery files, and selected *all* the divorces (with the required characteristics) on either side of each time point. These characteristics were: wife aged 20-38 at the time of divorce; wife a resident of metropolitan Detroit; there were children. Selection continued on either side of the time point until we had as many cases as we needed. *No* divorce with these characteristics was omitted. Roughly one month's cases were taken for each Time Group, i.e., about fifteen days on either side of September 15, and so on.

Ideally, we would have created a *panel*. That is, we would have selected a "just divorced" sample, and reinterviewed them at intervals after the divorce. We do not believe that at the present time such a procedure is possible, without such losses of respondents as would destroy the validity of the sample. Even in commercial research, with topics that are less loaded emotionally, the losses over a period of six months to one year are very high, and eventually such panels are discarded because these losses (and the experience of being repeatedly interviewed) change the composition of the panel. We were sure that even letting our divorcees know in advance that we wanted to talk with them about their divorce would have undermined the composition of the sample. We did not, therefore, attempt a true panel, but treated each Time Group as in effect the equivalent of each other Time Group, but at different intervals after the divorce. Thus, we generally assumed that the attitudes of Group II toward their ex-husbands had been, six months before, about those of Group I. And we assumed that the attitudes of Group I would in time be like those of Group IV.

Nevertheless, this is a quasi-panel, or even a pseudo-panel, not a true panel. We have noted at perhaps three points that a true panel would have enabled us to unravel certain complexities which were impossible to understand with our design. For most relationships, no problems are created by this substitution. We used it, we repeat, because we did not believe that we could persuade any random group of divorcees to allow us to return several times for subsequent interviews.

Now, we believe that up to this point our sample was good if not impeccable. But a further, crucial test of any sample must be made *after* the field operations. *All* field studies deviate from a random sampling design to some extent, and the most elegant design can be a failure if these operations destroy its representative character. Every refusal means a departure from strict randomness, and so does every nontraceable respondent. We have already discussed the latter problem. Let us now look at the sample that resulted from our operations after selecting the names.

We drew the names of 892 divorcees. We could not interview all of them, because extending our time of interviewing beyond two months would have destroyed the integrity of the Time Groups. We should not have drawn so large a number. We therefore ceased interviewing after about two months, with 433 respondents. About five were poorly done by one criterion or another. There were three additional cases in which the respondent refused to admit that she was divorced—we noted before that this confusion might occur under the then Michigan law—or that she had children. These eight interviews were discarded, and we were thus left with our 425 respondents.

We actually contacted 537 divorcees. There were therefore 104 refusals, making a refusal rate of 19%. 128 cases could not be traced. 45 were found, but had moved either from the state or outside easy reach in Detroit. The remaining 182 cases, had not gone through our preliminary tracing processes, and had not been contacted at all.

Since we did not ever drop a case, once we had assigned it, until it was (a) nonlocatable, (b) out of reach, (c) interviewed, or (d) a refusal, the unfinished group should not be different from (a) the total list of divorcees in the County records for this general period, or (b) the interviewed. We had actually drawn too many names, and these were simply left uncontacted at the time of our interviewing cutoff. In a moment, we shall test this assertion that they were not different.

By contrast, the refusals and the nonlocatables might well be different from (a) other divorcees, or (b) our interviewees. Perhaps the refusals are those who have a more difficult time of postdivorce adjustment, or are more frightened by the former husband. The nonlocatables might be concentrated in the lower class.

Now, whether there are such differences is an empirical question, not a matter of statistical theory. Let us look at the reasons for refusal.

First, we note that four of these women claimed that the divorce action was never completed, in spite of the fact that a divorce was recorded in the official records. This misunderstanding could arise, and would usually mean that she was not quite ready to cease being her former husband's wife. (These are *not* the cases noted above, in which the interviewer did get some sort of interview in spite of such a claim.) Twenty-five cases were *not refusals by the respondent,* but by members of the family: the mother would not let the interviewer in, the family interrupted the interview, or refused to give the divorcee's address; or some man (ex-husband, fiance, new husband) would not permit the interview. Seven were cases of family illness, and there was sometimes a promise to allow an interview in the future.

The remainder, 65% of our refusals, were genuine refusals: (a) twenty respondents said that the matter was "too personal" or they skipped appointments; (b) forty-five were "general refusals"—they would give no reason, or said that they were "not interested," or claimed they had previously been interviewed (in the pilot study).

Unfortunately, such a listing does not really tell us enough about their postdivorce experiences. Perhaps these women *were* really "not interested"; or simply preferred not to talk over their problems with a stranger, whether or not they had had great personal difficulties. We cannot assume that refusals are deviant merely because they will not answer the questions we are interested in.

Nevertheless, even if our refusals are *not* different from those we interview, this situation gives us no reassurance if (a) the refusal rate is overly high, or (b) we cannot demonstrate that those we interview are not different from those we fail to interview.

If we consider only what we call "genuine" refusals, our refusal rate is 15-17%. The gross refusal rate is 19%, and this was our prior estimate before field operations. This estimate was based on Cantril's summary data (*Gauging Public Opinion,* Ch. IX) for refusal rates for various populations (population, 500,000 and over, 21%; income if 60% poor, 21%; women, 15%; etc.). Of course, those populations were being interviewed about less personal matters, their opinions on public issues, but the estimate proved to be at least roughly correct. Locke's study had a refusal rate of 15% (*Am. Soc. Rev.,* 12 [1947], 188.). Refusal rates have varied from 1.3% to 45% in public opinion studies.[5]

Although a modal figure for refusals in public opinion polling might fall between 10-14%, even established polling organizations have at times suffered losses as high as 17-18%.

We must conclude, then, that our losses were not overly high, even though any researcher is troubled by losses beyond 8-10%.

Whether the losses are high or low, the crucial empirical question is whether they make any difference. Even if we ignore the large reservoir of divorcees whom we did not contact simply because their turn to be interviewed did not come up before we ceased interviewing, we have both refusals and nontraceables to consider. It is an obligation of the researcher to show not only (a) *how* he departs from strict randomness in his field operations, but also (b) what consequences flow from that departure.

---

5. See, for example: E. E. Maccoby and R. E. Holt, "Interviewing Problems in Financial Surveys," *Int. J. Op. Att. Res.,* 1 (1947), 31-39; Paul B. Sheatsley, "The Public Relations of the Polls," *Ibid.,* 2 (1948-49), 453-458. Only one study has reported rates as low as the first given: Herbert G. Heneman and Donald G. Paterson, "Refusal Rates and Interviewer Quality," *Ibid.,* 3 (1949), 392-398. This was a labor force survey. See also E. Schoenberg and M. Parten, "Methods and Problems of Sampling Presented by the Urban Study of Consumer Purchases," *J. Am. Stat. Assn.,* 32 (1937), 311-322.

It is not always possible to make these checks. Although various techniques of "double sampling" have been used to make such checks in questionnaire and field interviewing, they add to research costs and are not always simple to carry out.[6] And, of course, we never obtain more than a few items for such checks; if we had all the data we need about those we do not interview, then there would be no need of the research.

Happily, we can make various *external* checks of the representativeness of our sample, and we can moreover measure those we did interview against those we did not interview. There are two kinds of data for the first, external type of check: (1) data for divorcees from other samples approximating randomness, including Sample Surveys of the Bureau of the Census; and (2) national Census data. Throughout this study, we have pointed out the correspondence of our basic descriptive data, and of basic relationships, with these broader data. They include such items as occupational distributions, Negro-White distributions, number of children, length of engagement, income patterns, homogamy, and so on. We have also explained those few instances in which there appeared to be some discrepancy between our data and other surveys.

The second type of check must be an internal check, and must compare the interviewed with the following: (1) all noninterviewed; (2) refusals; (3) nontraceables; (4) those locatable but out of reach; and (5) those we did not completely process and did not interview or even contact. If these groups are not greatly different from our interviewed, then we have still further assurance (beyond the above external checks) that our resulting sample is representative.

Our data were obtained from the divorce records in Chancery, and were originally obtained by social workers of the Michigan Friend of the Court. In all cases involving children, this agency must make an investigation of the couple and the home, so as to ascertain whether the home is adequate for the children. It also attempts to ascertain how much property the couple possesses, how much the husband earns (if he has not disappeared), and something about the divorce conflict. The data are not standardized, so that we cannot obtain a broad range of data for all cases.

However, we are able to compare these items of information: (1) age of husband; (2) age of wife; (3) age difference between wife and husband; (4) number of children; (5) religion of wife; (6) religion of husband; and (7) income of husband. We made tabulations of these characteristics, and then calculated Chi-squares for each of the comparisons in the succeeding table. We have presented in this table the chances that whatever differences do appear between (a) the interviewed and (b) the noninterviewed are not reliable, i.e., not repeatable in successively drawn samples from the same populations. When our Chi-square computations indicate that these differences *are* reliable, we shall then present the relevant tabulations, so that the reader may see *how* different the reliable difference is. Although the characteristics used are not ideal, we have already shown (except for age difference between husband and wife) that they are important in the relationships analyzed in this study.

6. See William J. Goode and Paul K. Hatt, *Methods in Social Research* (New York: McGraw-Hill, 1952), pp. 223-225.

Consequently, if no difference is reliable, or if a reliable difference is very small, then we have still further empirical grounds for believing that the conclusions of this study may be applied to a wider divorced population than our particular sample. We now present these comparisons.

SIGNIFICANCE OF DIFFERENCES BETWEEN INTERVIEWED AND VARIOUS NONINTERVIEWED
SEGMENTS OF TOTAL DIVORCEE SAMPLE
(BASED ON CHI-SQUARE COMPUTATIONS)

Item Compared	Refused (104)	Unfinished, Not contacted (182)	Nonlocatable (128)	Out of Reach (45)	All Non-interviewed (459)
No. Children (1-2, vs. 3 and over)	.7>P>.5	.9>P>.8	.95>P>.90	.5>P>.3	.98>P>.95
Age of Husband (27 or younger, 28 and over)	.5>P>.3	.7>P>.5	.98>P>.95	.8>P>.7	.9>P>.8
Age of Wife (27 or younger, 28 and over)	.95>P>.90	.8>P>.7	.5>P>.3	.5>P>.3	.7>P>.5
Age Difference (Husband 3 or more years older, husband younger to 2 years older)	.2>P>.1	.1>P>.05	.5>P>.3	.9>P>.8	.3>P>.2
Religion of Wife (Catholic, non-Catholic)	.01>P>.001	.8>P>.7	.01>P>.001	.8>P>.7	.9>P>.8
Religion of Husband (Catholic, non-Catholic)	.01>P>.001	.8>P>.7	.05>P>.02	.5>P>.3	.9>P>.8
Income of Husband ($0-$29, $30-$59, $60 and over)	.1>P>.05	.5>P>.3	.5>P>.3	.3>P>.2	.1>P>.05

Our comparisons are both reassuring and disappointing. It is clear that the *refusals* and the *nonlocatables* vary reliably from the interviewed with respect to religion of *both* husband and wife. Also, though the difference is not quite significant at the 5% level, it seems that income differences for the refused might be looked at more closely. On the other hand, no other differences are reliable at this level, so that we have some further assurance that our divorcees are not greatly different from those we drew, but did not interview. This fact allows us to hope that our data can be applied more widely than to our particular sample.

Let us first look at the item of religion. First, we must keep in mind that all these comparisons are taken from the Friend of the Court data that are included with the official documents in the Chancery record. In most cases, the investigator spoke with the husband, but in an unknown proportion of cases the husband was not available. Second, we point out that although both refusals and nonlocatables are reliably different from the interviewed, the *total noninterviewed* are not significantly different from the interviewed with respect to religion. This suggests that within the two categories that were different, the differences are in opposed directions.

This is indeed what we find. Within the Friend of the Court records, 33% of those we interviewed were Catholic, the remainder Protestant, Jewish, Greek Orthodox, or "no preference." However, the refusals contained 48% Catholic. This 15% difference is, we suppose, due to the lesser willingness of some Catholics to discuss this violation of doctrine; or it may be that these are more devout Catholics. Although we have pointed out the importance of religious differences in several of our analyses, we suppose that certain of these differences might have been greater, had we succeeded in interviewing these refusals. On the other hand, it is equally possible that most of the difference is accounted for by the divorcee's Catholic *family*, who did not wish to let her be interviewed. The same order of difference is to be found for the religion of the husband. Here, there was a 12% difference, since 28% of the interviewed (according to these records) were Catholic, as against 40% of the refusals.

With regard to the nonlocatables, the difference is in the *opposite* direction. In these records, 33% of the interviewed women were Catholic, but among the nonlocatable only 19% were Catholic, a difference of 14%. For the husbands, the difference is 11%, since 28% of the interviewed were Catholic, but only 17% of the nonlocatables. We cannot be certain of the cause of these two differences. From an inspection of the addresses, we have some reason to believe that many of these are Negroes, who are particularly difficult to trace.

Both segments are different from any known data for larger divorced segments: the refusals have too many Catholics, the nonlocatables too few. Therefore, our interviewed group *should* be different from them in important respects.

Although the differences are somewhat disappointing to us, we are at least pleased that no reliable differences appear for either (a) the segment that we did not interview because we did not finish processing them, or (b) the noninterviewed as a whole. This documents further our belief that those we did interview are not significantly different from the larger population of the urban divorced with children. We thus venture to predict that later and more extensive investigations will substantiate most of our conclusions.

Finally, however, we noted that the refusals were not (at the 5% level) reliably different from the interviewed with respect to income, but that the reliability is close enough to warrant further investigation. It is possible, for example, that the slightly lower income level of Catholics has created a slightly lower level of income for the refusals. In the following comparison, we present the income distribution of the interviewed, the refusals, the nonlocatables, the "unfinished, not processed, not contacted" segments, and of the noninterviewed as a whole.

INCOME OF HUSBAND (TIME OF DIVORCE) IN VARIOUS NONINTERVIEWED SEGMENTS
(all data from Friend of Court Records)

Weekly Income	Interviewed	Refusals	Non-locatables	Not Processed	All Non-interviewed
$ 0-$14	2%	5%	4%	6%	5%
$15-$29	13	2	6	6	5
$30-$59	60	58	64	57	58
$60-$100	23	29	25	29	29
$100 and over	2	6	1	2	3
	100	100	100	100	100
	(392)	(88)	(91)	(140)	(351)

From these distributions, we ascertain two facts. (1) Although one of the comparisons showed that the difference between (a) refusals and (b) interviewed approached this arbitrary level of significance, the distribution indicates that the difference is not large. (2) The direction of difference suggests that the *interviewed* are very slightly lower in income than the refusals, or than the large segment that was not processed or contacted. (This is also true for the Out of Reach.) The interviewed have 8% more in the "below $30 weekly" classes, and 10% less in the "$60 and over weekly" class, than the refusals. The difference is not large, but does suggest that in many cases we have a lower segment of a given occupational stratum in our sample, than was in the refusal group. Consequently, some cross-tabulations by occupation might be less sharp than would have occurred with these refusals in the sample. On the other hand, the difference between the total noninterviewed and the interviewed is still smaller. Finally, it is possible that even these differences would disappear if we had complete data, since for all these categories the proportion of husbands' incomes that were *not* recorded by the Friend of the Court investigator was higher than for the interviewed. That is, we would expect many of these husbands who were "unavailable" to these official investigators to have somewhat lower incomes, so that the resulting distribution would be even closer to that for the interviewed.

In any event, we cannot be disappointed with these comparisons as a whole. They corroborate the many checks of representativeness which we have included throughout this monograph, when we compared our results with parallel data drawn from previous national or other samples of the divorced. Those comparisons showed that our data can be relied upon, and the comparisons just presented, drawn from internal analyses of segments of the total sample drawn, lead to the same conclusion: We have good reason to hope that successive samples drawn from other divorced populations will not be significantly different from our own, and that consequently most of our broad conclusions will be corroborated by later research.

SCHEDULE USED IN THE STUDY

MARITAL RESEARCH SURVEY

(Suppose we begin with some general questions about yourself; would you mind telling me . . .)

1. How long have you lived in Detroit (Closest number of years)?
2. How long have you lived at this address (years and months)?
3. Did you grow up in a a—rural area. b—small town. c—city.
4. What was the last grade you completed in school? a—completed college. b—some college. c—completed high. d—some high. e—completed grammar. f—5-7 years grammar. g—1-4 years grammar. h—no formal schooling.
5. What was the main kind of work your father did? *(Probe: Don't be satisfied with general answer. Large or small shop? Journeyman, apprentice, or master craftsman?* EXACT OCCUPATION)
6. What was the last grade your father completed in school? a—completed college. b—some college. c—completed high. d—some high. e—completed grammar. f—5-7 years grammar. g—1-4 years grammar. h—no formal schooling.
7. What would you guess his weekly income was, when you were in your teens? *(Probe: Ask again, to be certain of an answer: Well, what would your* GUESS *be? Etc., etc.)*
8. Do you have a job at the present? a—full time. b—part time. c—none.
9. What kind of work are you now doing? (or, if not working, what do you usually do)? *Be specific)*

(By now, respondent should be at her ease. Shift the discussion to the marriage)

10. What was your age, to the nearest birthday, when you married?
11. What is your age *now,* to the nearest birthday?
12. What are the ages of your children?
13. Do you remember the exact date of your final divorce decree?
13a. *(Well let's see, that means you were married about .... years doesn't it)?*
14. How long did you know your former husband before marriage? (in years and months)
15. How long were you engaged? (in months)
16. Did your former husband grow up in a a—rural area. b—small town. c—city.
17. What was the last grade he completed in school? a—completed college. b—some college. c—completed high. d—some high. e—completed grammar. f—5-7 years grammar. g—1-4 years grammar. h—no formal schooling.
18. What is his usual occupation? *(Specify: Be exact. Insist on definite answer, not a general one).*
19. About what was his average weekly income while you were married?
20. Was he a steady worker or not? a—always had work. b—steady except for unavoidable layoffs. c—frequent layoffs. d—never worked for long periods.

21. (*Now, would you try to tell me*) How many months before the *filing of the suit* did YOU YOURSELF first seriously *consider* divorce?

22. (*Now, that was when you first considered divorce.... Then tell me*) How many months before the *filing of the suit* did you definitely *decide* on a divorce?

23. Which of you first suggested the idea of a divorce? a—respondent. b—husband. c—mutual.

24. Later on, which of you *continued* to insist most on a divorce? a—respondent. b—husband. c—mutual.

25. Did either of you consult any marriage counsellor or marriage clinic before acting? a—yes. b—no.

If yes, then ask 25a and 25b.

    25a. What kind was it? a—Friend of Court. b—priest or pastor. c—social work agency. d—private marriage clinic. e—other (*specify*)

    25b. What was their advice? a—patch it up. b—wait a while before acting. c—separate for a while. d—get a divorce. e—other (*specify*)

26. When was the final separation actually made? a—before decision. b—between decision and filing. c—between filing and decree. d—after decree. e—never.

If a, b, or c, then ask 26a.

    26a. How long before the court decree did you make the final separation? (in *months*)

27. How long was it between the *filing of the suit* and the *final court decree?* (in months)

28. After finally deciding on the divorce, did you and your former husband have many talks about the details of the divorce? a—many. b—some. c—very few. d—none.

If a, b, or c, then ask 28a, 28b.

    28a. What did you discuss mostly? a—division of property. b—effect on child/ children. c—alimony or support. d—remarriage to other persons. e—seeing each other, after divorce. f—other (*specify*)

    28b. Were you able to come to a general agreement about any of these matters? a—yes. b—no.

    28c. Which ones? (a, b, c, d, f. *Repeat each!*)

If yes, then ask 28b1 and 28b2.

        28b1. Did he live up to these agreements? a—all. b—most. c—some. d—none.

        28b2. Were you yourself able to live up to these agreements? a—all. b—most. c—some. d—none.

29. After you first *seriously considered* divorce, how often did periods occur when you or your former husband decided not to carry it out? a—frequently. b—several times. c—rarely. d—never.

(*When people get a divorce, Mrs............, they often wonder what their friends and relatives think about it. Would you try to tell me* IN GENERAL *what the following people thought about your divorce:*) (*Use the following scale and read each separately*). a—strong approval. b—mild approval. c—indifferent. d—mild disapproval. e—strong disapproval.

30a. His family.

30b. Your family.

30c. His close friends.

30d. Your close friends.

30e. Mutual friends.

30f. Priest or pastor.

30g. Co-workers.

30h. Others (*Specify. Probe: Others?*)

On the other hand, Mrs. ...., most of these people also had some sort of opinion about your marriage in the first place. Would you try to tell me, IN GENERAL, *what these people thought about your marriage several years ago, when you were beginning this marriage? Did they think you should get married to him to begin with? (Use the following scale. Repeat for each item!)* a—strong approval. b—mild approval. c—indifferent. d—mild disapproval. e—strong disapproval.

31a. His family.
31b. Your family.
31c. His close friends.
31d. Your close friends.
31e. Mutual friends.
31f. Priest or pastor.
31g. Co-workers.
31h. Others (*Specify. Probe*)

32. Would you state, in your own words, what was the main cause of your divorce? (*Try to get an accurate statement. Probe: Anything else? Is this about what* HE *would say? Then read it back to her*)

33. During the course of your marriage, was your former husband a member of the armed forces? a—yes. b—no.

34. (*Now, Mrs. ...., sometimes a husband's work or military service takes him away from home for a long while, or even a temporary misunderstanding may result in a temporary separation. Would you try to remember and tell me whether you and your former husband were separated,* FOR ANY REASON WHATSOEVER, *for—(if never separated write 0 for 34*)

34a. One month (*write number of times*)
34b. Three months (*write number of times*)
34c. Six months (*write number of times*)
34d. One year (*write number of times*)
34e. Longer than a year (*write number of times*)

(*Well, Mrs. ...., when the divorce was finally granted, certain decisions had to be made about the children, such as, support, etc. Suppose I ask a few questions about these matters.*)

35. Who received custody of the children? a—respondent. b—husband. c—other (*specify*)

(*Now, Mrs. ...., I know it's always hard for a parent to give up a child, but . . .*)

36. *In general*, was this arrangement agreeable to both parties? a—yes. b—only to wife. c—only to husband. d—to neither.

37. What arrangements were made for visits with the other parent? a—weekly. b—monthly. c—summers. d—holidays. e—no visits. f—other (*specify*) *include combinations.*

(*If husband does* NOT *have custody, then ask* 38 *and* 39)

38. Of course, no matter who has the (child/children) there are bills to be paid. About how much is your former husband supposed to contribute weekly for each child?
    Amount per week per child: a—0 to $2.99. b—3 to $4.99. c—5 to $6.99. d—7 to $8.99. e—9 to $10.99. f—11 to $12.99. g—13 to $14.99. h—15 to $16.99. i—17 and over.
    38a. *Total weekly payment.*

39. Has he continued to pay this amount? a—always. b—usually. c—once in a while. d—seldom. e—never.

40. How was the property divided? (*Write* APPROXIMATE *value in proper box*).
    (If no property write 0 for 40)
40a. House and furniture (in dollars)
40b. Cash (in dollars)
40c. Bonds (in dollars)
40d. Other (*specify*) (in dollars)
41. Do you, in general, consider this a fair settlement? a—yes. b—no.
(*Well, Mrs. ...., you have had to face many problems during the past several
    years. One problem that most people have to face is that of money. Would
    you mind telling me if ...*)
42. During the marriage itself, did you have a job? a—all the time. b—once in a
    while. c—seldom. d—never.
If a, b, or c, *then ask* 42a.
    42a. Was this job: a—part time. b—full time.
43. At the time of final separation did you have a job? a—full time. b—part time.
    c—no job.
If respondent has a job now ask 44.
44. About what is your average take home pay each week? (that is, on the average,
    how much is your weekly check after all deductions).
45. *If respondent has* NOT *remarried ... ask ...* now would you tell me about how
    much *on the average* you have each week to meet your expenses with (*from
    the job, former husband, and so on*)?
    45a. Do you feel that this is enough? a—yes. b—no.
46. *If respondents* HAS *remarried, ask ...* Now would you try to tell me about how
    much *on the average* you have each week to meet your expenses with (*from
    the job, former husband, present husband, and so on*)?
    46a. Do you feel that this is enough? a—yes. b—no.
47. (*Now Mrs. ...., this question may be a little hard. We'd like to compare
    your financial situation at different periods; namely*—a—during the marriage.
    b—final separation. c—now. *(d—no difference) Repeat for each item.
    47a. Which period showed the highest income? (a, b, c, or d.)
    47b. Which period showed most savings? (a, b, c, or d.)
    47c. Which period showed the most debt? (a, b, c, or d.)
    47d. Which period was the worst financially? (a, b, c, or d.)
    47e. Which period was the best financially? (a, b, c, or d.)
(*Of course, we can't always plan things completely, Mrs. ...., and sometimes
    bills pile up until we simply don't know where to turn. Tell me ...*)
48. If you had to get outside *financial* help since the divorce, to whom did you
    turn? a—Children's Aid. b—own family. c—husband's family. d—church help.
    e—county welfare. f—husband (former) g—friends. h—other (*specify who
    this was*). i—no need for help.
(*If not remarried. Ask* 49 and 50)
49. If you needed financial help right now, where would you turn first? (*Same as*
    48: *Repeat each item*)
If answer to 49 *is not* f (husband), *ask* 49a.
            49a. Would you ask for financial aid from your former husband, even as a
                second choice? a—yes. b—no.
50. How frequently have you thought of marriage as a *possible* solution to your
    financial problems? a—often. b—once in a while. c—seldom. d—in the past
    but not now. e—never.
If answer to 50 *is* a, b, or c, *ask* 50a.
            50a. Did you ever think of remarriage to your *former husband* as a financial
                solution? a—yes. b—no. c—formerly, but not now.

II

(*Mrs. ....,* *even without financial problems, one kind of problem usually faces most divorced women—the problem of social activities. Suppose we talk about these for a few moments. For instance . . .*)

1. While you were married, how frequently did you and your husband go out together? a—almost never. b—once a month. c—twice a month. d—once a week. e—twice a week or more.

2. What kinds of activities did you two share together? a—going to movies. b—watching sports. c—taking part in sports. d—concerts. e—work around the house. f—reading. g—travel. h—dancing. i—social drinking in bars. j—other (*specify*) (*indicate three highest*)

3. When the separation happened, what did you do to fill the gap in your social life? a—club activities. b—church activities. c—went alone to movies. d—began dating other men. e—had already been dating other men. f—greater attention to children. g—went around with girl friends. h—did nothing to fill it. i—other. (*Specify*)

   3a. Which two of these were the *most* important? (*Read each again*)

4. During the final separation and divorce period, were your most active friends the ones you had with your husband during the marriage? a—yes. b—no.

   4a. (*Now I know it's very difficult to* RATE *friends but would you mind trying to tell me . . .*) How would you *rate* these friends you had during the final separation or after the divorce? a—better than previous friends. b—not quite as worth while as previous friends. *(c—about the same).

   4b. About how many of them were divorced? a—three or more. b—two. c—one. d—none divorced but some getting divorces. e—none divorced or divorcing.

If answer to 4a *is* b, *then ask "Did you ever stop to wonder why you might have gone with a crowd not quite up to your own level?"—Take down answer in detail; encourage her to talk.*

5. *Well, what about your friends* NOW? Would you tell me whether you *now* have a small circle of close friends whom you see regularly? a—yes. b—no.

If answer to 5 *is no, then ask* 5a.

   5a. Then are you gradually *finding* such a group? a—yes. b—no.

6. In general, do you have many opportunities for meeting people? a—great many. b—some. c—few. d—none.

If any opportunities exist, ask . . .

   6a. What are some of these opportunities? a—women's clubs. b—PTA. e—church activities. d—union meetings. e—parties. f—dates. g—hobbies or sports. h—adult education classes. i—other (*specify*)

   6b. Which of these is most important?

If respondent has NOT *remarried, ask questions* 7 *through* 13.

If remarried, go to question 14.

7. Would you guess the number of dates you have weekly as: a—three or more. b—two. c—one. d—twice a month. e—once a month. f—almost never.

8. Do you go steady with anyone? a—yes. b—no.

9. *It's hard to guess the future, I know, but could you tell me. . . .* Among your very close men friends, is there someone whom you would even *consider* marrying? a—yes. b—no.

If answer to 9 *is yes, then ask* 9a.

   9a. Is there a *fair chance* of this marriage taking place? a—yes. b—no.

If answer to 9a is yes, ask 9a1.

> 9a1. Do you think that you and he have worked out together the problems that were *not* worked out with your former husband? a—all. b—all *important* ones. c—a few. d—no important ones.

10. Do your parents or any relatives ever try to help you meet any eligible men at the present time? a—yes. b—no.

11. Did they ever do this, after the final separation and divorce? a—yes. b—no.

12. Do your friends try to see to it that you meet eligible men now? a—yes. b—no.

> 12a. Did they used to do this, after the final separation and divorce? a—yes. b—no.

13. *Now, Mrs. ...., you have mentioned the number of dates you have. . . .* Would you say, *in general,* that you have: a—not enough dates. b—too many dates *(c—about the right number of dates.)

14. Outside of your job or housework, what are your main recreational activities? a—taking part in sports. b—watching sports. c—dancing. d—card parties with girls. e—dates. f—movies alone. g—concerts. h—social drinking. i—church activities. j—no recreational activities. k—other (*specify*)

15. Which of these is the most important to you?

16. Have you ever been in a social situation in which you felt that someone thought less of you when he or she found out that you were divorced? a—yes. b—no.

If yes, ask 16a.

> 16a. Tell me about it?

17. *We seem to have been talking mostly about the problems that you have had to face as a result of the divorce. Now I'd like you to tell me in what ways the divorce has made things a little better for you. (Encourage her to talk. Probe: Ask "What about jobs, friends, money, freedom, and so on?)*

III

Mrs. ...., some women are very unhappy while going through a divorce. We need to know whether this affects their actions in any way. Would you try to remember . . .

1. Just after the separation, did you find it more difficult to fall asleep at night? a—yes. b—no.

2. Do you think that your health was poorer just after the separation? a—yes. b—no.

3. Did you begin to smoke more at that time? a—yes. b—no.

Well, Mrs. ...., perhaps some of these things did happen to you, but they may have started before the separation. Will you try to remember . . .

4. If there was some increase in your smoking, was it most apparent during the period of: a—final decision. b—final separation. c—first filing for divorce. d—final divorce decree. e—at the present time. *(f—never any increase.)

5. During which periods do you think your health was generally poorer? (a, b, c, d, e, or f)? (*Repeat each choice!*)

6. When did you have the greatest difficulty in sleeping? (a, b, c, d, e, or f)? (*Repeat each choice!*)

7. If there was an increase in your drinking, when was it at its highest? (a, b, c, d, e, f)? (*Repeat each choice!*)

8. If you had any difficulty in remembering things, when did it bother you most? (a, b, c, d, e, f)? (*Repeat each choice!*)

9. During which period did a feeling of loneliness or of being without friends become the greatest? (a, b, c, d, e, f)? (*Repeat each choice!*)

10. When did you have the most difficulty in doing your work efficiently? (a, b, c, d, e, f)? (*Repeat each choice!*)

11. Would you mind telling me, in your own words, about your feelings during all this period: how you felt about the idea of the divorce, how you felt about the court process, and so on. (*Encourage her to talk. Take down as much of her statement as possible*).

12. Now, you may think this question is pretty hard to answer, but maybe you have thought about it a little before now anyway. Just suppose you hadn't gotten a divorce, and instead, simply tried to get along with your marriage the way it was, with all its difficulties. Would you try to tell me how you think your life would be today, in general, if you hadn't gotten a divorce. (*Try to get an expression of opinion about finances, former husband, children, happiness, etc. Try to see whether there is any bitterness against the husband*).

IV

Mrs. ...., even though a court declares a couple divorced, they still have memories of the times they were together. Now I'd like to ask a few questions about the way you think of your former husband. First of all . . .

1. Just before or after the divorce, did you ever feel that he ought to be punished in any way for what he did to you? a—frequently. b—once in a while. c—rarely. d—never.

If answer to 1 is affirmative, ask 1a.

    1a. Do you still feel that he should be punished? a—yes. b—no.

2. At the time of the first visits to the child, did you and your former husband see each other? a—yes. b—no.

If answer to 2 is yes, ask 2a and 2b.

    2a. How frequently did you and he date during this period? a—once a week or more. b—once a month. c—almost never. d—never.

If answer to 2a is affirmative, ask 2a1.

    2a1. Was it easier to get along with him on these dates than when you were married? a—yes. b—no.

    2b. Were there occasions after the divorce when you had sex relations with him? a—yes. b—no.

3. Whether you actually saw him or not, you may have been curious to know how he was and what he was doing. How did you satisfy this curiosity? For example, some make it a point to see their former spouses at "accidental" meetings. Or you may have tried to contact mutual friends. What did *you* do? a—contacted mutual friends. b—wrote or telephoned. c—arranged a meeting. *(d—did absolutely nothing.) e—other (specify).

If answer to 3 is negative, then ask 3a.

    3a. Have you done any of these things within the last month? a—yes. b—no.

4. If you knew you might meet your former husband accidentally, would you try to avoid meeting him? a—yes. b—no.

5. Why do you feel this way? (*Write it all down!*)

6. Have there ever been times when you felt that you did not play fair with your former husband? a—yes. b—no.

If answer to 6 is yes, then ask 6a.

    6a. Do you ever feel that way at the present time? a—yes. b—no.

7. *Sometimes, Mrs. ...., troubles happen unexpectedly, and we need help.* In case of a sudden illness, or a financial emergency, would you turn first to your former husband for help? a—yes. b—no.

If answer to 7 is negative, ask 7a.

    7a. Would you seek his aid as a second choice? a—yes. b—no.

8. *I know this may be a hard question to answer, but just suppose you could wipe out the divorce.* Would you be willing to do this, that is, be still married to your former husband just as he is? a—yes. b—no.

9. Do you think any changes in him are probable which would make you willing to marry him? a—yes. b—no.

10. Do you believe that you *yourself* have changed in ways which would make living with you easier than before? a—yes. b—no.

11. Would you mind giving me your opinion about this: Do you think your former husband was in love with another woman before the divorce? a—yes or I think so. b—no. c—have no idea.

If answer to 11 is yes ask 11a.

    11a. Do you think that knowing this made you try to adjust better to the problems of divorce? a—yes. b—no.

12. Were you *yourself* in love with another man before the divorce? a—yes. b—no.

13. How would you describe your former husband's feelings towards you now? a—still in love. b—not in love but misses you very much. c—friendly but does not miss you very much. d—just as happy if he does not see you. e—actually dislikes you. *(f—have no idea).

14. Now, how about your feelings toward him? Would you try to describe them as accurately as possible? (*Take down a full statement. Do not allow her to choose lazily one of the above six possibilities. Probe*)

15. Has your former husband remarried? a—yes. b—no. *(c—don't know.)

If answer to 15 is yes, ask 15a. If no, ask 15b.

    15a. *Now, I know it's hard to be perfectly frank about these things, but. . . .* How did you *really* feel about his remarriage when you heard of it? a—a little upset. b—very unhappy. c—very happy. d—mildly pleased. *(e—no feeling at all.)

    15b. *Now, I know it's hard to be perfectly frank about these things, but. . . .* How would you *really* feel if he remarried? a—a little upset. b—very unhappy. c—very happy. d—mildly pleased. *(e—no feeling at all.)

V

Well, Mrs. ...., every marriage breakup must affect the (child/children) in some way. Suppose we discuss that situation a bit. . . .

(*If respondent has custody, start with question 1. If not, skip to question 7*)

1. If you have to work away from home, how (is/are) the (child/children) cared for? a—your relatives. b—husband's relatives. c—neighbors. d—friends. e—nursery school. f—regular public school. g—don't have to work away. h—other (*specify which of wife's relatives*)

If not g, ask 1a.

    1a. How would you rate this temporary care? a—excellent. b—good. c—average. d—poor.

2. When you have dates, who cares for them? (*Repeat choices in question 1*)

3. What activities of yours are most handicapped by having the (children/child) with you? a—trips. b—job possibilities. c—dates. d—club meetings. e—giving parties. f—education. g—remarriage. h—other (*specify*)

4. Would you like to have your former husband see the (child/children) a—less often. b—more often. *(c—about the same as at present).

5. (Is/are) the (child/children) harder to handle after these visits? a—harder. b—easier. c—about same.

6. Would you say, in general, that the (child/children) (was/were) harder to handle at the time of: a—final separation. b—just after the divorce. c—now. d—during the marriage. *(e—about the same always).

7. *Now this may be difficult, to be sure, but would you try to tell me....* (Does/do) the (child/children) feel the same toward the father now as when you were still married? a—loves father more. b—loves father less. c—always disliked father. d—never thinks about him. *(e—feels same now as before.)

If respondent does not have custody, ask 8, 9, and 10.

8. *Mrs. .... , even though you do not have custody of the (child/children), you are certainly interested in (his/her/their) welfare.* Do you feel in general that the (child/children) is getting satisfactory care? a—yes. b—no.

9. (Does/do) the (child/children) seem to miss you a great deal? a—very much. b—a little. c—not at all.

10. Do you feel that the (child/children) would be better off with you? a—better off. b—worse. *(c—about the same.)

11. Does your former husband consider the support payments to be: a—far too much. b—a little too much. c—too little. *(d—about right.)

12. Do you ever feel that he resents these payments? a—yes. b—no.

VI

What about church activities, Mrs. .... ? You know, some people go to church often, others never go at all. Would you say . . .

1. You attend church services: a—once or more a week. b—twice a month. c—once a month. d—only for important religious days. e—never.

If answer to 1 is affirmative, then ask 1a.

    1a. What church do you prefer? a—Protestant. b—Jewish. c—Catholic. d—Eastern orthodox. e—other. (*Specify*)

2. During which period would you say you attended church services most frequently? a—during marriage. b—final separation. c—divorce itself. d—now. *(e—always about the same).

3. Do you feel that going to church has helped you in any way during this period? a—yes. b—no.

If yes, ask 3a.

    3a. In what ways (*Probe: Ask in what other ways? etc.*)

4. Have you ever talked with a religious advisor about the divorce? a—yes. b—no.

5. Do you feel that talking with him helped you at all? a—yes. b—no.

6. What would you say is the main reason for going to church now? a—your friends. b—to meet new friends. c—find consolation in religion. d—so that (child/children) will go. *(e—never think about the reason).

VII

(*If respondent has* NOT *remarried, skip to part VIII.*)
Now, Mrs. .... , I know it may be difficult to answer these questions, but it would be very helpful if you could tell us . . .

1. In general, how does your present married life compare to your former married life? a—much better. b—a little better. c—about the same. d—a little worse. e—much worse.

2. Do you feel that the experiences you had in your former marriage make it harder or easier to get along in this one? a—harder. b—easier. *(c—no effect).

3. How often would you say you and your present husband argue about your former marriage or your former husband? a—frequently. b—once in a while. c—we used to do so, but not now. d—seldom. e—never.

If respondent has custody, ask:

How would you rate the child's/children's life at present as compared with the period—

4a. During your former marriage? Is it now: a—better. b—worse. *(c—about the same).

4b. During final separation? Is it now: a—better. b—worse. *(c—about the same).

4c. Just after the divorce? Is it now: a—better. b—worse. *(c—about the same).

VIII

Well, Mrs. ...., just a few questions now, and we can wind this up.

1. Now that the divorce is all over, would you try to tell me in your own words how you felt about the divorce and the child/children. What went through your mind when you thought of the possible effects of the divorce on (him/her/them)? (*Take down all details*)

2. Did these things happen as you believed they would? a—yes. b—no.

3. Did you ever make a decision never to remarry? a—yes. b—no.

If yes and if not now remarried, ask 3a.

3a. Do you still feel this way? a—yes. b—no.

4. Now that the divorce is all over, is there anything you have been able to accomplish by yourself that you have always wanted to do, but never managed to do it before? a—yes. b—no.

If yes, then ask 4a.

4a. What are these things?

5. One final question, Mrs. .... Try to tell me in your own words just how you would like things to be, if you could have your own way about the following:

a. How about work? How should that be? (not working, type of work, etc.)

b. And the children? *(grown up, away, no children, etc.?)

c. And finances? *(steadier, larger, the same, etc.?)

d. How about love and marriage *(forget about it, remarry, etc.?)

e. How about other things? (*Probe: What else? Get a further expression*)

Well, Mrs. ...., I must say you have given very helpful answers. I have enjoyed talking with you very much, and I hope you have also. Thank you very much.
(*Don't rush away. Put away the interview. Then say . . .*)
You know, I sometimes wonder about something. In answering all these questions, do you feel that the interviewer can get a true picture of your problems and how you have met them, from your answers to these questions?
Probe: Go back to any given question, and repeat it as an example. AFTER LEAVING, write down these remarks. CHECK EVERY QUESTION BEFORE LEAVING TO BE CERTAIN YOU HAVE AN ANSWER TO IT!!)

INDEX

ABILITY to pay, 227
Absences, 181
Accomplishments, 340
Accounting scheme for divorce rate differentials, 64-68
Accumulation of property, 74-75
Acknowledgment of failure, 187
Acquaintance, Ch. VII
Action framework and adjustment, 253-54
Adequacy of substitute care, 318-321
Adjustmental conflict, 151
Adjustment, definition of, 18, 241-242, 249
Adjustment prior to divorce, 200
Adjustment to second marriage, Ch. XXII
Adjustment to separation, 282-3
Adolescence and steady dating, 269-70
Adult nonmarried, 214
    see Institutionalization
Adult socialization, 205
Adult world and child, 207
Affect, 295 ff.
    see In love
Affect toward husband, 264, 265
    see Ex-husband
Age, 11, 28, 40-1, 96, 152, 189, 258-9, 273, 280, 353
Age and children, 280
Age and dating, 258-9, 266 ff.
Age and dating in marriage, 96
Age and divorce, 40, 41, 141, 163
Age and duration of marriage, 97, 103-4
Age and help in meeting men, 257
Age and meeting eligibles, 257
Age and opportunities, 250 ff.
Age and optimism, 250
Age and remarriage, 29, 207, 278-9
Age and second marriage, 336
    see Remarriage
Age and social life, 257 ff.
Age and steady dating, 269-70, 271, 272, 273
Age and suggestion, 148

Age and time for divorce action, 154
Age and trauma, 192, 193
Age at divorce, 40
Age of children, 181
Age of children and care, 320
Age of children and friendships, 243, 244
Age of interviewers, 347
Aggression, unilinear, 9
Agreement in talks, 161 ff.
Agreement on custody, 313 ff.
Agreements, keeping of, 155, 164 ff.
Aid from husband, 239
Aid from husband's family, 238-9
Aid from relatives, 238-9
Alimony, 13, 158-162
    see Support
Allardt, Erik, 61
Allegiance, family, 150
Allegiance to father, 321 ff.
Allocation of energy, 213
Alternative spouse, 212
Alternatives to divorce, 196
Alternatives to marriage, 140 ff., 190, 194
Ambiguity of parental status, 208
Ambiguity of roles, 14, 206, 209, 210, 255
Ambiguity of separation, 174
Ambivalence toward court process, 183
Ambivalence toward divorce, and trauma, 195
Amount of property, 161
    see Property
Anderson, C. A., 98
Anonymity, 17, 183, 210
Another woman, 117
    see Triangle
Antagonism, 293 ff., 297 ff., 302, 303
Anticipated effects of divorce on children, 316-7
Anticipatory socialization, 6
Anti-divorce sentiment, 183
    see Values
Anxiety-reducing activities, 6

FREE PRESS PAPERBACKS

A Series of Paperbound Books in the Social and Natural Sciences, Philosophy, and the Humanities

These books, chosen for their intellectual importance and editorial excellence, are printed on good quality book paper, in large and readable type, and are Smyth-sewn for enduring use. Free Press Paperbacks conform in every significant way to the high editorial and production standards maintained in the higher-priced, case-bound books published by The Free Press.

Andrews, Wayne	*Architecture, Ambition, and Americans*	90067
Aron, Raymond	*German Sociology*	90105
Beard, Charles A.	*An Economic Interpretation of the Constitution of the United States*	90203
Bettelheim, Bruno	*Truants From Life*	90345
Chapman, Charles E.	*History of Spain*	90533
Cohen, Morris Raphael	*Reason and Nature*	90609
Coser, Lewis	*The Functions of Social Conflict*	90681
Durkheim, Emile	*The Division of Labor in Society*	90785
Durkheim, Emile	*The Rules of Sociological Method*	90850
Edel, Abraham	*Ethical Judgment*	90890
Edwards, Paul	*The Logic of Moral Discourse*	90914
Eisenstadt, S. N.	*From Generation to Generation*	90938
Evans-Pritchard, E. E.	*Social Anthropology and Other Essays*	90987
Frazier, E. Franklin	*Black Bourgeoisie*	91058
Friedmann, Georges	*The Anatomy of Work*	91082
Friedmann, Georges	*Industrial Society*	91090
Geertz, Clifford	*The Religion of Java*	91146
Goode, William J.	*Women After Divorce*	91234
Goode, William J.	*Religion Among the Primitives*	91242
Gouldner, Alvin W.	*Patterns of Industrial Bureaucracy*	91274
Hayek, F. A.	*The Counter-Revolution of Science*	91436
Henry, Andrew F., and James F. Short, Jr.	*Suicide and Homicide*	91442
Heschel, Abraham J.	*Between God and Man:* EDITED BY FRITZ A. ROTHSCHILD	91451
Hoselitz, Bert F., et al.	*Theories of Economic Growth*	91522
Janowitz, Morris	*The Professional Soldier*	91618
Katz, Elihu, and Paul F. Lazarsfeld	*Personal Influence*	91715
Kluckhohn, Clyde	*Culture and Behavior*	91745
Lane, Robert E.	*Political Life*	91787
Lerner, David, with Lucille W. Pevsner	*The Passing of Traditional Society*	91859
Madariaga, Salvador de	*The Rise of the Spanish American Empire*	90717
Maximoff, G. P.	*The Political Philosophy of Bakunin*	90121
Meyerson, Martin, and Edward C. Banfield	*Politics, Planning and the Public Interest*	92123
Munitz, Milton K.	*Theories of the Universe*	92227
Murdock, George P.	*Social Structure*	92229
MacIver, Robert M.	*The Web of Government*	91960
Neumann, Franz	*The Democratic and the Authoritarian State*	92291
Park, Robert Ezra	*Race and Culture*	92379
Parsons, Talcott and Neil J. Smelser	*Economy and Society*	92395
Parsons, Talcott	*Essays in Sociological Theory*	92403
Parsons, Talcott	*The Social System*	92419
Redl, Fritz and David Wineman	*Controls From Within*	92604
Reiss, Ira L.	*Premarital Sexual Standards in America*	92620
Riesman, David	*Individualism Reconsidered:* UNABRIDGED EDITION	92650
Robinson, James Harvey	*The New History:* EDITED BY HARVEY WISH	92661
Skinner, B. F.	*Science and Human Behavior*	92904
Simmel, Georg	*Conflict* AND *The Web of Group Affiliations*	92884
Simmel, Georg	*The Sociology of Georg Simmel*	92892
Sorokin, Pitirim A.	*Social and Cultural Mobility*	93028
Spitz, David	*Patterns of Anti-Democratic Thought:* REVISED EDITION	93054
Wagner, Philip	*The Human Use of the Earth*	93357
Weber, Max	*The Theory of Social and Economic Organization*	93493
White, Andrew Dixon	*A History of the Warfare of Science with Theology in Christendom:* ABRIDGED AND REVISED BY BRUCE MAZLISH	93507

Many of these books are available in their original cloth bindings. A complete catalogue of all Free Press titles will be sent on request